THATCHER'S GOLD

Previous books by the Authors

Paul Halloran:

A Bit on the Side. Politicians, Who Pays Them? (with Mark Hollingsworth) (Simon & Schuster, 1994)

Mark Hollingsworth:

The Press and Political Dissent (Pluto Press, 1986)
Blacklist. The Inside Story of Political Vetting (with Richard Norton Taylor) (Hogarth Press, 1988)
The Economic League: A Silent McCarthyism (with Charles Tremayne) (Liberty Publications, 1989)
MPs For Hire. The Secret World of Political Lobbying (Bloomsbury, 1991)
A Bit on the Side. Politicians, Who Pays Them? (with Paul Halloran) (Simon & Schuster, 1994)

THATCHER'S GOLD

The Life and Times of Mark Thatcher

Paul Halloran and Mark Hollingsworth

POCKET
BOOKS

LONDON · SYDNEY · NEW YORK · TOKYO · SINGAPORE · TORONTO

First published in Great Britain by Simon & Schuster, 1995
First published by Pocket Books,
an imprint of Simon & Schuster, 1997
A Viacom Company

Simon & Schuster Ltd
West Garden Place
Kendal Street
London W2 2AQ

Simon & Schuster Australia
Sydney

A CIP catalogue record for this book is available from the
British Library

ISBN 0-671-85112-8

3 5 7 9 10 8 6 4 2

Typeset in Times 10.5/12pt by
Palimpsest Book Production Limited, Polmont, Stirlingshire
Printed and bound in Great Britain by
Caledonian International Book Manufacturing, Glasgow

*This book is dedicated to the late
Commander E. K. Somerville-Jones
who started it all.*

'Mark Thatcher is a twit. In my opinion he has nothing to offer the world.'

Sir Tim Bell at a private dinner party in 1983.

Contents

Preface

In April 1993, Mark Thatcher attended a secret meeting at the City offices of Peter Carter-Ruck & Partners, the expensive and controversial law firm specializing in libel, not always successfully. Around the table with Lady Thatcher's son were Alasdair Pepper, a senior partner who deals with many of the firm's politically sensitive cases, and Alex Wade, an articled clerk. Mark asked for the meeting because he had a problem. His problem was us.

Six months earlier we had been commissioned to write his biography and one of the first people we approached was Mark Thatcher. Despite several requests for an interview, he did not respond – unlike all the other members of his family. The only contact had been when he sent an impatient faxed letter to one of the authors on 8 November 1991, while the writer was working for Granada TV's *World In Action* programme. He wrote: 'Dear Mr Hollingsworth, As you have previously been informed, I do not wish to speak to you nor do I have anything to say to you. Good Bye. Mark Thatcher.'

And so, as he discussed our investigation with one of Carter-Ruck's deputies, it was clear he did not want to co-operate. But going to Carter-Ruck showed he was concerned. He asked them how he should deal with us. Pepper advised caution and counselled him to wait until nearer the time of publication. Mark Thatcher accepted this but asked the law firm to keep a running brief on our book's progress and paid them a monthly retainer.

That was not the end of Thatcher's connection with Carter-Ruck. For Britain's most famous libel law firm was used by Mark Thatcher to pass on payments for one of his business deals. A month after his meeting, in May 1993 he commissioned a company called Saladin Holdings Ltd, a security and arms-dealing firm,[1] to do some work on a commercial project in the Middle East and the USA.

The funds were paid to Saladin Holdings by Carter-Ruck & Partners. For one deal £10,000 was paid to two security consultants. This sum included £5,000 for one to travel to the Middle East between 13 and 17 May 1993, and the other to visit the USA. Their fees were £600 per day plus £250 subsistence and VAT.

Mark Thatcher hired Saladin on the recommendation of David Hart, the controversial right-wing business-man. Hart, an adviser to Margaret Thatcher while she was prime minister, is best known for helping bankroll the working miners during the 1984–5 strike. He knew Saladin through his friendship with Major David Walker, the company's chairman.[2] It was Hart who telephoned Alasdair Pepper to say that Mark Thatcher needed the client account number and bank details for payment purposes.

When asked about his relationship with his heroine's son, Hart replied, 'He's a friend of mine. Decent chap. I see him occasionally when he's in town. We've shot a couple of times together.' But when questioned about introducing Saladin to Thatcher, he denied it: 'It's untrue. It never happened.'

*

This book's origins lie in 1981 when Paul Halloran was working for *Private Eye*. One day he was visited in his office in Greek Street, Soho, by a retired naval commander and pilot. His name was E. K. Somerville-Jones and he had a story to tell. Somerville-Jones had retired from the navy and wanted to continue to work. He was first employed by International Military Services, the government-owned arms-export agency, selling guided missiles. He was not very successful, so ended up as a pilot for one of Britain's major defence contractors. But Somerville-Jones was unhappy. He had been flying on the company's private jet to Holland, Switzerland and the USA, delivering what he called 'bribe money' on behalf of his employer. Paying off 'foreigners' was one thing, he said, but what he objected to was that some of the bribe cash was being kicked back to his own senior executives, with suitcases full of the money being ferried by him from Switzerland to London. Somerville-Jones always maintained that a good proportion of it was on its way to Whitehall. But when he complained to the chairman's office, the former naval commander was told 'to stop noseying around and causing trouble'.

Encouraged by Somerville-Jones, Halloran began investigating this aspect of the arms trade. However, it was only after Margaret Thatcher left 10 Downing Street in November 1990 that he was in a position to propose a book project. While she was in power, key sources were too nervous to talk. From 1991 onwards people who had held the Thatchers in awe or owed something to them were prepared to open up. In general these people were exasperated with Mark's rudeness and arrogance. In their view, he had shamelessly exploited his mother's name to promote his own business interests or to ingratiate himself with them through her.

In October 1992, after Paul Halloran linked up with Mark Hollingsworth, then working on similar investigations for Granada TV's *World In Action*, the synopsis for this book was written. It was at a time when every journalist in town was trying to solve the Mark Thatcher mystery. Not a lot has changed since then. How did a young man who opted out of accountancy, after failing his exams, and former jewellery salesman with no higher educational or professional qualifications become a multimillionaire? What did the former prime minister's son actually do and how did he accumulate his vast wealth? He declared no stated profession, apart from the meaningless 'consultant'. From 1984 onwards, he was not a director or shareholder of any companies, apart from Emergency Networks Inc. He did not have an office, apart from two small rooms and a name-plate in Dallas, Texas. His 'firm', Grantham, was not registered as a company. Everything was shrouded in remarkable secrecy. Business deals were conducted through intermediaries, bank accounts were offshore and shareholdings were held by nominees. Virtually no part of his commercial affairs was accountable to the public or the regulatory authorities and so there was no paper trail.

Piecing together the puzzle of how Thatcher acquired his millions has been a challenging if often frustrating experience. Lines of enquiry have led to blind alleys, trails have run cold and information from several potential sources has proved unreliable. There is a Mark Thatcher industry in the British media, which has produced as many myths and hoaxes as genuine disclosures. Consequently, this biography could not have been written without the co-operation of a small but key group of sources. They know who they are but nobody else will. The truth is that the people who helped us the most are the ones we cannot thank publicly.

To borrow Tennessee Williams's phrase from *A Streetcar Named Desire*, used since by the biographer Michael Sheldon, we have been dependent on the kindness of strangers.

In the UK we are particularly grateful to Wolfgang Michel for his generous support and insights into the defence world. Michel is a remarkable and laconic man. He merits a book on his own. For their assistance and friendship, we would like to thank Charles Johnston and the staff of J and P Security Services Ltd. They watched those who were watching us. We are also grateful to Jon Lewis and Mary Kalmus (for their invaluable research into Mark Thatcher's time at Harrow).

Very special thanks are due to Gary Smith, the international oil trader. He was one of our primary sources who dealt directly with Mark Thatcher, and who was particularly helpful.

The following deserve our appreciation either for their help in supplying information or for agreeing to be interviewed: the delightful Misbah Baki, Simon Berthon, Steve Brownson, Michael Cockerell from the BBC, Charlie Crichton-Stuart, Alan Curtis, Sir Edward du Cann, Ed Harriman, Nigel Hart, Gerald James, Peter Jansen, Don Jordan from Granada TV, David Leigh and Paul Lashmar, Ivor Lucas, the former UK ambassador in Oman, Norman Luck of the *Daily Express*, the financial journalist Patrick Masters, James Montagu, Barrie Penrose of the *Sunday Express*, the defence consultant John Reed, Tiny Rowland, Kate

Roy, Olga Sheppard, Tony Shepherd, Andy Stewart, Paul Vickers and Dorothy Wyndham-Lewis.

Our search for Thatcher's gold has taken us to many countries. In the United States we would like to thank Al and Jane Ross (for their hospitality in New York City), Nathan Adams of *Reader's Digest*, Juval Aviv of Interfor Inc, Frank Greve of the *Philadelphia Inquirer*, Margaret Hall in Washington, Christopher Ogden of *Time* magazine and author of *Maggie*, Maureen Orth of *Vanity Fair* and the investigative writer Gerald Posner. At the National Security Archive we are particularly grateful to Will Ferroggiaro for his diligent and selfless research on our behalf. In Texas Gary Howard, his family and many influential friends have been a constant source of friendship and support. We also appreciate the co-operation of Jay Laughlin, former president of Ameristar Fuels Inc. Further south, in Latin America we received assistance from Maria Laura Avignolo, Patrick Buckley and Leonardis Walger. In Hong Kong we owe a huge debt to Amanda and George Rosenberg for their generous help and hospitality. Also to Dean Nelson of the *Observer*, Neville De Silva of the *Hong Kong Standard* and Nancy Ng and Raymonde Sacklynne of *Target* magazine for their help in introducing us to sources of information.

To others such as Matthew Evans, chairman of Faber and Faber, and Ian Hislop, Francis Wheen and Christopher Silvester of *Private Eye* we also owe a debt. They collectively opined at one of *Private Eye*'s more indigestible lunches that this book would never be finished or published. They and people like them have been a great incentive to us.

So too has Sir Tim Bell, Mark Thatcher's public relations adviser. He has been entertaining visitors with his views on this book and why it would not come out, couldn't work, and so on. Sir Tim, you would be surprised how many of your visitors were on the phone regaling us with your latest opinions as soon as you uttered them. Your cheerful indiscretions helped us a great deal. We owe you at least another lunch.

We would like to also thank our lawyer, Barry Shaw, of Wright Webb and Syrett, and our accountant, James Mackie. Oscar Beuselinck, the former senior partner of Wright Webb and Syrett, was always eager to help and offered advice when asked. We could not have had a better legal team.

For their patience and perseverance, we are grateful to our agent, Vivienne Schuster, and editor, Nick Webb. We were more than lucky in finding Nick Webb as a publisher. His support and insight helped us immeasurably. We were also fortunate to have as our copy-editor Helen Simpson, who was highly competent and meticulous.

The burden on families and loved ones during a book project is enormous. Monique, Toby and Anna Halloran have tolerated much. They have been very patient and a source of great comfort and understanding.

Mark Hollingsworth and Paul Halloran
London, September 1996

Chapter One

The Search for Eldorado

'In Margaret Thatcher's eyes, there is nothing for which Mark requires forgiveness.'

Andrew Thomson, constituency agent
to Margaret Thatcher, 1982–7[1]

The search for Thatcher's gold has been long and challenging. It has taken us to Washington, DC, Dallas, Houston, New York City, Hong Kong, Malaysia, Israel, Switzerland and Liechtenstein. We have met some strange people in some strange places. But the treasure hunt began and ended in Jersey, the largest of the five Channel Islands, just 250 km south-west of London and 300 km north-west of Paris. The island is a haven for wealthy international businessmen with its generous taxation benefits. Income tax has remained at 20 per cent since 1940 and corporation tax is a mere £300 a year. Jersey also serves as a base for overseas funds and by the end of 1993 the island's banks had received about $75 billion in foreign deposits.

Living quietly there in a large two-storeyed house in St Helier, the capital of Jersey, is an unassuming sixty-four-year-old banker and economist called Dr Ian Hugh Thurston. Since the late 1970s Thurston

has been the banker and chief financial adviser to
Margaret Thatcher and her son, Mark. He has set up
many tax shelters for the family and travels on their
behalf. It is Thurston who knows the secret details of
the Mark Thatcher fortune. For he has devised a secret
pattern of offshore trusts and companies in Jersey and
in Switzerland to hide Thatcher the Younger's vast
wealth. That pattern is so intricate that if Mark died
in an air crash only Thurston could unravel it. It also
means he would inherit much of the loot. 'God forbid
anything should happen to Mark,' he once remarked
jokingly with a wry smile.

Working alongside Thurston as the keeper of
Thatcher's treasure is a Jersey accountant called
Leonard Henry Day, who works from his well-
protected Spanish-style home in St Clement and is
treasurer of the island's Variety Club. Together they
manage Mark's funds through three Jersey companies
– Zariba Management Ltd, Eastcoast Investments Ltd
and Diversified Capital Ltd. Zariba is used to pay
domestic and personal bills, while Eastcoast owns
his house at 1 Tregunter Road, Kensington, west
London. Diversified is a vehicle for moving funds
for investments, notably for channelling money to the
United States. Leonard Day is a shareholder of all three,
while Thurston controls Eastcoast and Diversified.

It is in taxation that Thurston's secret services are
most valuable, because that is where Margaret's son
is most vulnerable. The banker–client relationship is
not a warm one. 'Hugh does not like Mark because
he sees him as a loose cannon and detrimental to his
mother, whom he hero-worships,' said a source who
has had business dealings with Thurston. 'He would
help Mrs Thatcher with her tax affairs and then find
that Mark had talked to her and changed her mind,' said

a different source. 'This made Hugh very angry, which is unusual because he is a very mild-mannered man.'

The treasurer of Thatcher's gold has a conventional background. Born in Balham, south London, in 1931, Thurston was educated at Wellington School in Somerset and Rotterdam Economics High School in Holland. He was seriously ill for much of his childhood. 'I have never been very tough, as a result of it,' he later reflected. 'I would have been interested in entering the political field in England but I think the life would have been too strenuous for me.'[2] Instead Thurston turned to economics and accountancy. He worked for British and Commonwealth Shipping from 1956 until 1961, when he joined Bridor, Hamlyn and Fry, a firm of business consultants. As their economic adviser, Thurston set up their overseas network, including their branch office in Switzerland. 'Yes, I did know some of the Gnomes of Zurich,' he said.[3]

In May 1967, Thurston moved to Jersey and became an adviser to the government on the economic consequences for the island if the UK entered the Common Market. For the next six years he was the States of Jersey's economic adviser, helping to set up a special office to regulate locally registered companies, business licences and the vetting of licences of prospective wealthy residents.[4] In the mid-1970s he returned to the private sector and became a director of Cope Allman International. More intriguingly, he joined the board of Jersey General Investment Trust Ltd, whose nominal share capital was £20 million. This company – whose aim was to 'deal with any stock, bonds, debentures, shares or securities' – changed its name to Pandale Holdings Ltd in July 1989. Three weeks later it was dissolved.

Thurston's main commercial job in the 1980s was

as director of Citibank, the American-owned bank, well-known for offering its clients offshore services. He was head of its Jersey office but ran into controversy during the Gulf war in 1991. The *Jersey Evening Post* wanted to publish an article about the transfer of staff from Citibank's offices in the Gulf to Jersey. This appeared to contravene the island's strict rules on hiring extra foreign employees and so would have caused some embarrassment for the bank. So it applied, unsuccessfully, for an injunction against the newspaper and Thurston represented Citibank in court. He is no longer on the board of Citibank but in 1993 became a director of the merchant bank Lazard Brothers and Co (Jersey) Ltd.

Thurston knows all the answers to the questions about Mark's millions and the true wealth of the son of Lady Thatcher. But when we approached him at his expensive, antiques-filled home at Claremont Court, Jersey, he refused even to come to the door. His loyalty to the Thatchers remains resolute, despite severe misgivings about Mark. The other treasurer of Thatcher's gold, accountant Leonard Day, was also unforthcoming. When we arrived at his office to ask for information about Zariba Management Ltd, he was very nervous. 'You've been digging, you've been digging,' he said repeatedly, his hands shaking. When questioned about Zariba, he replied, 'It's a personal private company owned by myself.'

'Then why have you issued cheques on behalf of Diane Thatcher?' we asked.

'So what? What's wrong with that? Look, I have better things to do with my time.'

So how much is Mark Thatcher really worth? Mark himself has always publicly denied being in the Big Rich league. 'It would be significantly wrong to conclude that I am worth more than £5 million,' he told the *Financial Times* in October, 1994. 'There is just nothing to support it apart from innuendo. This whole idea that I have had tremendous success is just a myth. If I had tremendous success, I would not be running around trying to do the things that I am doing. I would be sitting on my own private island in the South Pacific, but I am not.'[5] However, Thatcher's own banker had a different view. In 1991, one of Hugh Thurston's clients asked him: 'How much is Mark worth?' The Jersey banker paused for thought. 'About £40 million, at least,' he replied. Since then, it is true, his net value has fallen rapidly, down to less than £10 million. This is due to ill-judged investments and Mark's habitually extravagant life-style.

How Mark Thatcher accumulated a multimillion-pound fortune is one of the unsolved mysteries during his mother's eleven-year tenure of 10 Downing Street. For, although he is the son of the longest-serving prime minister of the twentieth century, Mark's business activities have not come under any public scrutiny. In the United States the commercial affairs of the president's relatives are closely monitored. In stark contrast, Mark Thatcher has been allowed to keep the source of his vast wealth secret. He has not been a director of any companies since 1984, apart from Emergency Networks Inc, and hides his money offshore through an intricate series of bank accounts and companies and the skilful use of intermediaries and nominees.

This book is about how Mark Thatcher amassed that wealth while his mother was prime minister. It is an attempt to untangle some of the confusion surrounding his commercial activities and the myths that have grown up around them. But it is not just the story of how a young man became fabulously rich comparatively quickly and without visible financial means of support. It is also an account of how the son of the most controversial and politically successful premier this century used his access to the very highest echelons of government. And, most significantly, of how Lady Thatcher herself had knowledge of, and in some cases assisted in promoting, business that Mark benefited from financially.

A Family Affair – Margaret

The Mark Thatcher story really begins on 13 October 1925, the day Margaret Hilda Roberts was born in Grantham, a quiet market town in Lincolnshire. Grantham was the epitome of Middle England, priding itself on its ordinariness and old-fashioned values. Margaret's father, Alfred Roberts, personified that life-style. A tall, imposing figure, he had a profound and lasting effect on the future prime minister. 'I owe almost everything to my father,' she later reflected.[6]

Alfred Roberts ran his own grocer's shop and was a pillar of the community. A Methodist lay preacher, Rotarian and local alderman, he took life very seriously. He did not drink alcohol and believed in hard work, the Church and civic duty. There was not much fun or emotion in the Roberts household, and that was where the Victorian values that later guided Margaret's political life were first nurtured. 'My father's view was that life was a serious matter,' said Margaret soon after becoming leader of the Tory Party. 'His maxim was that you did not sit idle.'[7]

Another favourite family saying was: 'Never be in

anyone's debt.' Money was for saving not spending. Hence Margaret was brought up with few possessions or home comforts. There was no garden to play in or bicycle to ride. Holidays were rare. Yet this was due to her father's meanness with money rather than to genuine poverty. For the family business prospered as Margaret grew up. It was an austere and ascetic upbringing for the grocer's young daughter. But working in her father's shop had a lasting influence on Margaret. While prime minister she used to say that 10 Downing Street was like 'living above the shop'.[8]

Her mother, Beatrice, a local seamstress, was, in contrast to Alfred, a mouse-like figure who appeared chained to the family shop and house and was hardly seen in the town. A gentle, unassuming woman, she was not prone to displays of emotion towards her children and appeared intimidated by her husband.[9] Margaret clearly did not regard her with much affection. She barely mentioned her mother's name in later life and it was highly significant that Beatrice Roberts's name was omitted by Margaret from her *Who's Who* entries. This was seen by some as proof of her anti-female, pro-male bias which manifested itself in her attitude towards Mark's behaviour and activities.

From the age of ten, Margaret Roberts went to Kesteven and Grantham Grammar School. She worked ferociously hard and became a star pupil, excelling at almost everything, including games and drama. The only exception was art, largely because it was the one subject not dependent on hard graft and swotting. 'Her contemporaries remember her as a model pupil of demure habits and tediously impeccable behaviour,' wrote Hugo Young, her most authoritative biographer. 'She never put a foot wrong, in the classroom or on the hockey field.'[10] She had few close friends at school, mainly because she took life so seriously and rarely joined in the fun and frolics of her peers. Even her adoring, ultra-earnest father said of her: 'Margaret is 99.5 per cent perfect. The half per cent is that she could be a little bit warmer.'[11]

Margaret's major outside interest was public speaking. She took private elocution lessons outside school hours. 'One simply must talk properly,' she told her father when she asked him to pay for them. He agreed, but once her classmates noticed her new contrived accent they began calling her 'Snobby Roberts'.[12] Unperturbed, she was an active member of the school debating club, where she showed unusual self-confidence for one so young. Her style was more that of a steamroller than a Rolls-Royce, a ponderous, relentless delivery which wore down rather than inspired her young audience.

But politics was in her blood, actively encouraged by her father. Alfred Roberts sat as an Independent on Grantham Borough Council and so Margaret soon learnt the art of electioneering. Even at the tender age of ten, she was helping the local Conservative candidate as a runner during the 1935 election campaign.[13]

She was a Conservative from her first day at Somerville College, Oxford, in 1943. This blue allegiance stood out in a sea of Labour red. 'She was to me extremely interesting because she was a Conservative,' recalled Janet Vaughan, Margaret's Principal at Somerville. 'The young at that time, especially at Somerville, were all pretty left-wing. . . . If I had interesting, amusing people staying with me, I would never have thought of asking Margaret Roberts – except as a Conservative.'[14]

Margaret was painfully homesick at Oxford, particularly when she was teased about the shrill Lincolnshire accent she had not quite suppressed. One biographer, Chris Ogden, London bureau chief of *Time* magazine during her premiership, summed up her personality at the time. His description is an uncannily accurate portrayal of her son, Mark, in later life: 'She knew almost no-one [at Oxford] and kept to herself. Socially inept, awkward and totally lost with men, she was badgered by the other girls. Her references to "Daddy, the Mayor" didn't help. Nor did her frank admissions about aiming for big things. Her ambition was boundless, her candour guileless.'[15]

Despite her youth, Margaret Roberts was set in her ways. Political discussion for her tended to monologue rather than dialogue. She was not popular among fellow students, mainly because of an inability to smile and relax – another characteristic she shares with Mark. Her only friends were Methodists, Conservatives or those who shared her political views and undisguised ambitions. Despite her preference for the company of men, she had no romantic relationship at Oxford – her strict religious upbringing saw to that.

By the 1945 general election, Margaret was consumed by politics. She canvassed for Quintin Hogg (later Lord Hailsham) in his campaign for the Oxford City seat against Labour's Frank Pakenham (now Lord Longford). But the family's financial circumstances meant she could not seriously contemplate politics as a career until 1946, when the government increased MPs' pay from £600 to £1,000.

The following year Margaret graduated from Oxford with only a second-class BSc degree, mainly because she devoted most of her time to politics and the Oxford University Conservative Association. She regretted studying chemistry. 'I should have read law,' she said. 'That's what I need for politics. I shall just have to go and read law now.'[16] But she could not afford to continue her studies, so in 1947 she went to work as a research chemist with British Xylonite Plastics in Colchester.

According to Penny Junor, whose biography is the best account of her early life, the grocer's daughter again did not fit in: 'Margaret found it agonizing. She was quite incapable of communicating with the men on the factory floor in any way at all. Where her fellow females might ask, "Hey, Charlie, what about trying this, I think it might work," and play along with the odd nudge and wink, Margaret would stand rather awkwardly over the man, and in her well-modulated, and now perfected true blue accent, would say "Mr So-and-So, would you mind trying it this way?" This method, as often as not, elicited the two finger response, and earned Margaret the nickname "Duchess".'[17]

Socially, Margaret Roberts was out of her depth, largely because she concealed her lower-middle-class background and her conversation was humourless and dogmatic. But when it came to politics she was supremely confident, and spoke fluently and convincingly. Her big break came at the 1948 Tory Party conference in Llandudno, north Wales. Among the delegates was John Grant, director of Blackwell's, the Oxford bookshop, who knew the young chemistry graduate well. There he met John Miller, chairman of Dartford Conservative Association, who was looking for a new candidate. Grant recommended the eager Margaret Roberts.

She was delighted, despite Dartford's being a safe Labour seat. She also felt at home with the middle-class folk of north Kent rather than in metropolitan London. At her interview she dazzled the selection committee with a well-informed presentation, delivered without a note. In a political setting she glittered and glowed; and on 28 February 1949 she was selected as the party's parliamentary candidate.

That evening a dinner was held to mark Margaret's adoption. One of the guests was a prosperous thirty-four-year-old Kent businessman called Denis Thatcher. He was only attending the dinner to make up the numbers. But he was immediately impressed by the young candidate. 'She was beautiful, gay, very kind and thoughtful,' he later reflected. 'Who could meet Margaret without being completely slain by her personality and intellectual brilliance?'[18] After the dinner Denis drove Margaret back to London, where she took a train back to her flat in Colchester. Denis owned a sandy-coloured Jaguar and liked to drive fast, which did not impress the serious-minded parliamentary candidate. But they had enough in common to chat away. Their next encounter was at a Rotary Club meeting and, despite the ten-year age gap, their courtship blossomed.

Denis

Denis Thatcher's origins lie in the unlikely setting of Wanganui, a coastal town in New Zealand. The Kiwi Thatchers were a more upper-middle-class family than the Robertses: 'the last of the Edwardian snobs', as Denis later described them.[19] But, like the Robertses, they were active in the local community and there is even a street in Wanganui named after them. Their money came from sheep-farming and brewing, but also from devising a special weed-killer which could be used on railway tracks. This was marketed abroad and firms were set up in America and Europe.

In 1908, Denis's father, Tom Thatcher, aged twenty-eight, settled in London to manage the British parent company, Atlas Preservatives Ltd. Tom was an extrovert and likeable character. A typical member of the Edwardian middle class, he became a Freemason and a devotee of rugby football and the Kipling Society. He married Lillian Bird, herself an astute businesswoman, whose father was a south London horse dealer.

On 10 May 1915, Lillian Thatcher gave birth to Denis at their house in Southbrook Road, Lewisham, south London. Eight years later Denis was dispatched to prep school in Bognor Regis and then, at the age of thirteen, to Mill Hill School, north London. It was an institution, more interested in games and social control than in academic excellence. According to the school's 'Plan', each resident master was to 'watch over the morals of the boys, as with parental solicitude, and to take every opportunity of inculcating sound principles and good dispositions'.[20]

Growing up during the pioneering days of the British Empire influenced Denis profoundly. His world view was shaped by the heroic tales and patriotic poetry of Macauley and Kipling, which glamorized the annexation of 'lesser nations'. For Denis's class and generation, that was the bedrock of their way of life. It resulted in an imperialist right-wing brand of Conservatism which he has always retained.

Denis was not a success academically. He was more interested in sport (he was a dogged cricketer and rugby player) and attending the annual Duke of York's camp, a curious neo-military event whose one rule was: 'Play the Game.'[21] Denis was in his element. Clubbable by nature, he loved the comradeship and the patriotic atmosphere of the camp with its emphasis on outdoor pursuits.

In 1933, aged seventeen, he left school and joined Atlas Preservatives Ltd, the family firm, which had by then incorporated paint and other chemicals. Denis's basic character was quite different from Margaret's. Unlike his future wife, he was self-effacing and diffident, and he retained a self-deprecatory sense of humour. Even later in life, he would describe himself as 'a not unsuccessful businessman' rather than a 'successful' one.[22] He was essentially a cautious conformist who respected his elders and authority, almost unquestioningly. But, like Margaret, Denis was not afraid of speaking his mind in sharp and colourful language.[23] He must have found it excruciating and frustrating to hold his tongue during his time at 10 Downing Street.

As it did on most of his generation, the Second World War had a huge impact on Denis Thatcher's life. Already a Territorial Army officer, he joined the 34th Searchlight Regiment of the Royal Artillery. However, because of poor eyesight he was a junior staff officer rather than an active soldier in the field. He served in France and Italy and then became a staff captain in the 9th Anti-Aircraft Division.

It was during the most tense period of the war, in 1941, that Denis fell in love with Margaret Kempson, a beautiful high-spirited woman he had met at an officers' tea-dance. According to Diana Farr, author of the most authoritative account of Denis's early life, Kempson 'bore an uncanny resemblance to the second Margaret Thatcher'.[24] Margaret Kempson was also very exuberant, 'working terribly hard driving lorries, tearing about delivering Mosquito parts from the factory to dispersal points around the country'.[25]

It was a classic wartime whirlwind romance and within weeks they were married, on 28 March 1942, in Monken Hadley Church, Hertfordshire. Although they were initially very happy, the war prevented them from living together permanently. The marriage was a series of snatched moments of intimacy, governed by their service requirements.

In July 1943, two days before Denis was dispatched abroad for Operation Husky – the invasion of Sicily – his father died. It was a devastating blow but he went on the mission, and was later mentioned in dispatches for 'gallant and distinguished service'.

By early 1945 Denis's exceptional organizational talents were being put to good use and he was promoted to major. His great triumph was Operation Goldflake – the movement of thousands of Canadian and British troops from Italy to Belgium. Because they were scattered far and wide, Marseilles was used as a transit camp. It was a perilously exposed location, and the troops' presence could easily have been detected by the enemy. Denis was based at the British HQ in Marseilles and he worked day and night to help co-ordinate the successful operation, which involved both the utmost secrecy and diversionary tactics.

Denis Thatcher was subsequently awarded the MBE (military). In her book *Five At Ten*, Diana Farr quoted from the citation: 'Major Thatcher set an outstanding example of energy, initiative and drive. He deserved most of the credit for the very fine message of appreciation which has been conveyed to me from Field Marshal Montgomery as to the excellence of the work done.'[26]

Denis enjoyed the camaraderie of military life and did not want to leave the army.[27] But when he returned home he was unexpectedly summoned to run the family business, Atlas Preservatives, and soon became managing director. His marriage was not such a success. The couple had drifted apart and they found they now had little in common. In 1948 an amicable divorce was agreed. 'It was one of those war-time marriages which never really got off the ground,' the first Mrs Thatcher (now Lady Hickman) said years later.[28]

For twenty-five years Denis and Margaret Thatcher never mentioned his first marriage. Margaret found the subject acutely embarrassing and did not even tell her children until 1976, when they were twenty-three years old, after journalists began asking questions. Mark and Carol were shocked by the news but Margaret was almost Edwardian in her attitude. 'One didn't keep it a secret he'd been married before,' she said. 'One wasn't asked. One just didn't talk about a thing like that.'[29]

Unlike Margaret Thatcher, Denis was gregarious and at ease with people. He was popular with the workforce at his office in Erith, Kent, and was, and remains, genuinely interested in the welfare of others. While Margaret aspired to the aristocracy, Denis disliked the pomposity and pretensions of the upper classes. He also developed a saloon-bar sense of humour which made him an entertaining drinking companion. 'When I'm not absolutely paralytic, I play a little golf'[30] and 'He's about as much use as a one-legged man at an arse-kicking party'[31] are typical Denis remarks. As Diana Farr put it: 'By now he had slipped into the use of sporting and business terms to explain everyday reactions or more solemn matters, an eccentricity which remains with him today. He will speak, sometimes, for example, of unattractive propositions that present a "large downside risk" and "no upside gain", even when talking to women who cannot be expected to understand such jargon.'[32]

Denis's political views and world outlook were heavily influenced by the war. He had always been an old-fashioned Conservative. But the war accentuated the class system in his eyes. For Denis the world was divided into Officers and Men. He was an Officer and socially he was only really interested in mixing with other Officers. 'Loyalty, to me, is the one quality all men must have,' Denis said later. 'I learnt this in the Army – loyalty to the organisation and loyalty to the man you work for. That's the indispensable quality in life.'[33]

According to James Montagu, who was a neighbour of the Thatchers in Kent in the mid-1960s, the standard topic of conversation when Denis and his friends congregated was their wartime experiences. 'Denis has never really cared what other people think of him,' said Montagu. 'Like a lot of other former officers, he took the view of "I confronted death and got through the war. Everything else pales by comparison. Who cares what other people think?"'[34] It was that independent spirit that later endeared him to so many people.

By 1949 Denis was firmly established in the north Kent community. He was an active member of the Dartford Conservative Association and was building up a successful family firm. Outside business, his chief interest was sport, particularly rugby union (he was to become a highly respected referee), golf and sailing. He was friendly and good company, so it is not hard to see why the young Margaret Roberts found Denis an attractive suitor.

The Marriage

The Thatcher courtship was far from a whirlwind
romance. Margaret was later asked if meeting Denis
was a case of love at first sight. 'Certainly not!' she
exclaimed.[35] Their relationship developed slowly but
steadily. 'We dined out from time to time,' recalled
Margaret, 'and went to the occasional cinema or theatre. But they were still rather dark days in 1949 and
1950. There wasn't a lot of gay life about.'[36] Denis was
more set on a long-term relationship, particularly after
taking her to a dinner-dance at his trade association.
Towards the end of the evening, his company chairman
leaned over to him and whispered: 'That's it, Denis –
that's the one.'[37]

One common interest was money. Margaret admired
Denis for his business experience and for running his
own company. She liked his direct style of talking
and they spent hours discussing politics and finance.
She felt comfortable in his company and he was a
Methodist, which helped. Denis also had a physical
resemblance to Margaret's father – tall and striking,
with thick-lensed spectacles. But her exhaustive life-
style, combining a job with food manufacturer J. Lyons
and political activity in the evening, precluded any
impetuous romance.

Most of her evenings were taken up by canvassing
in Dartford for the forthcoming general election. The
campaign in February 1950 was bitterly fought and
even then Margaret Roberts's slogans were apocalyptic
in tone. The election was a choice between two ways
of life. 'One leads inevitably to slavery, the other
to freedom,' declared the intense young candidate.

Another favourite was borrowed from her father. 'A caged bird has social security. It has food and warmth. But what good is all that if it has not the freedom to fly out and live its own life?'[38]

Despite her defeat, the Dartford Conservatives were pleased with her energetic performance and she was readopted for the second election in October 1951. But this was a more low-key campaign. Margaret Roberts faced a 13,000 Labour majority and was not able to rekindle her enthusiasm. Besides she was distracted. Denis had been courting her. He had always been more keen on her than she on him. But they had enough in common for Margaret to treat him seriously, if not passionately.

In September 1951, he returned from a trip to France and proposed marriage. Margaret's only doubt was that he had been married before. Divorce was strongly frowned on by the Methodist Church but, in a rare act of social rebellion, she overlooked this inconvenient fact. She accepted, but was in the midst of the election campaign. When the result was declared in Dartford town hall, Margaret Roberts had lost but had cut Labour's majority by 1,000. She thanked her party workers, who were celebrating a national Conservative victory, and said she had some other good news. Then Denis took over the podium and announced their impending marriage.

Margaret Roberts became Margaret Thatcher six weeks later, on 13 December 1951, at Wesley's Chapel, a Methodist church in London's City Road. For their honeymoon the couple went to Portugal, then Madeira, and finally spent a few days in Paris, where Denis indulged in a little business activity.[39] They then moved into Denis's rented flat at 112 Swan Court in Flood Street, Chelsea. Margaret began her law studies at the Council of Legal Education while Denis continued his job with Atlas Preservatives, the family firm in Erith, Kent.

For Margaret, it was far from a love match. 'He was in the paint and chemicals business,' she later remarked. 'He was on the financial side, I was interested in economics. We were both interested in politics and we had a lot in common.'[40] Denis's financial support was crucial in enabling the twenty-six-year-old Margaret to pursue her political career without distractions. 'Denis's money got me on my way,' she later reflected.[41]

From the beginning it was a marriage of two busy professional people. 'This is a deal that we have always done,' Margaret said later. 'Work is the most important thing, and it comes first, and therefore you do it.'[42] Indeed, it was a very modern relationship for such a Conservative couple. Despite her reliance on Denis's salary, Margaret achieved independence through her work and political ambitions. In many ways she was a pioneering feminist, arguing that women could and should have careers. 'In this way, gifts and talents that would otherwise be wasted are developed to the benefit of the community,' she wrote at the time. 'The idea that the family suffers is, I believe, quite mistaken.'[43]

The Twins

It was in this context that the Thatchers planned to have children, one of each sex. Their dream came true on Saturday, 15 August 1953, when Margaret gave birth to twins, a boy and a girl, seven weeks ahead of schedule, at Princess Beatrice Hospital, in Chelsea, west London.

It was a long, arduous labour until her doctors decided on a caesarian delivery. The boy was born first at 2.50pm, weighing four pounds, and two minutes later his sister appeared. Margaret was surprised but ecstatic with her double offspring, but had yet to choose names. Mark and Carol were selected. 'We just wanted simple names that couldn't be shortened,' their mother said. 'We didn't like nicknames.'[44]

Denis was not present for the birth. As the twins were not due until October, he went to the Oval for the test match between England and Australia. England won the game and the Ashes, so Denis and his friends went off to the pub to celebrate. Naturally, he could not be contacted, so Margaret travelled to the hospital alone. '*Do* I remember,' she later told *Time* magazine's Chris Ogden in mock anger [her emphasis]. 'We couldn't find my husband anywhere. He had mooched off.'[45]

Despite his absence Denis was delighted with the twins. 'Typical of Margaret,' he remarked. 'She produced twins and avoided the necessity of a second pregnancy.'[46] He marked their arrival by buying their mother a double string of pearls, which she often wears to this day.[47]

As Margaret lay exhausted in her hospital bed for two weeks, she was already thinking about her future career. 'I was concerned, particularly with two [children], that I might be tempted to spend all my time on the household and looking after them and not continue to read or use my mind or experience,' she recalled. 'I felt I must really use the rest of me as well.'[48]

She told another biographer: 'I remember lying there and thinking: "If I don't, now that I'm in hospital, actually fill in the entrance form for the final of the law, I may never go back to it. But if I fill in the entrance form now, pride will not let me fail." And so I did. That was really an effort of will.'[49]

Four months later Margaret passed her final Bar exams and the more routine hours of a tax lawyer enabled her to spend more time looking after her young children. But she still needed outside assistance. So the couple rented the adjoining flat in Swan Court, knocked down the wall and installed a live-in nanny and housekeeper with Mark and Carol. 'You tend to need some sort of help with twins, who wake for feeding at different hours of the day and night,' she said.[50] Margaret found motherhood nerve-racking and exhausting: 'I worried all the time. Of course, 90 per cent of the time, you worry about things that don't happen, but still you worry.'[51]

For a brief period politics took a back seat as Margaret concentrated on the twins. She was a very attentive mother. Although the nanny tended to comfort the children if they cried during the night, Margaret always devoted time to them. She always dressed them immaculately, and she read to them before they went to sleep. On their fourth or fifth birthday she spent two days making and icing cakes – one was in the shape of a fort for Mark, the other a car for Carol.[52]

There is no doubt that in their early formative years her children were her priority. But it was also quite a formal Victorian upbringing. There were no nicknames and neither Margaret nor Denis romped around or played with the kids for the sheer hell of it.[53] In some ways she resembled an affectionate, benevolent teacher rather than a mother. 'She never shouted at them,' said Margaret's sister, Muriel, 'it was all sweet reason. I could have screamed at her sometimes for being so reasonable. Her attitude all the time was to *teach* the twins interesting things. Everything she did with them was teaching, but always in such a kind way. They arrived at our farm once when we were in the middle of lifting potatoes and straight away she said, "Oh good, we can teach the twins how the machine works." Again, one holiday I can remember us all going out in a boat. To me it was just a trip in a boat, but Margaret immediately said to the twins, "Now you'll be able to *learn* how to crew" [her emphasis]. She was always so imaginative with them, so stimulating.'[54]

Denis also tended to have a formal relationship with the twins. According to Penny Junor's biography of Margaret Thatcher: 'He insisted on manners and correct behaviour, would never allow the children to keep pets, wouldn't tolerate slippers and insisted on everything being neat and tidy in the house. The only games he played were ball games in the back garden, where he had set up a cricket net, bowling Mark balls to hit.'[55]

Like Margaret, Denis was guilty of regular absences from home – either on trips abroad or not arriving from work until well after the children were put to bed. Denis raised his hand to the twins only once during their childhood.[56] But he could be assertive when the occasion required it. During a cocktail party in the mid-1980s at 10 Downing Street the conversation turned to the rearing of children. 'Never had any trouble with my two,' said the prime minister's consort proudly. 'They always got on so well together. I can think of only one occasion when we had a problem.' He paused for a refill of his drink. 'On the road to Portsmouth, it was. Carol and Mark started bickering in the back. So I put my foot down. I stopped the car and I said: "Right, you three – get out." So they got out of the car. And I said: "Right, Margaret! Deal with them." '[57]

Margaret doted on her children but her thoughts were

never far away from the challenging male worlds of the law and politics. 'The children were going to need a lot of looking after,' she said later. 'And, of course, they do become the centre of your life and you live for them as you've never lived for anyone else. . . . And yet, I knew that I had something else to give.'[58] At first her assiduous search for a parliamentary seat was frustrated by prejudiced Tory selection committees, who claimed she should be at home looking after her young children.

Life changed abruptly for the Thatchers in early 1959, when Margaret was chosen as the parliamentary candidate for Finchley, north London. The family had just moved into 'Dormers', a four-bedroomed detached house in a residential cul-de-sac near Farnborough, Kent. It was a typical middle-class Conservative area, inhabited by the 'gin and Jag set', where the talk in the golf club bar was of money, sport, the war and how the country was 'going to the dogs'. The men commuted to London and their wives stayed at home to look after the children. Margaret Thatcher was very much an anomaly as she took the train every day to Lincoln's Inn to work as a tax barrister.

Their mother's absences meant Mark and Carol depended on nannies for maternal affection. It also meant they spent more time outside the house on their own, playing with local children, and would make short excursions on their bicycles. As the 1959 general election approached the twins' unintentional isolation from their parents increased. Mrs Thatcher completely absorbed herself in the campaign, utilizing her legendary energy, and on 8 October 1959 she was elected the Conservative member of parliament for Finchley.

Even at the age of six, her son was basking in his

mother's glory. 'My Mummy's a member of parliament,' he boasted the next day as he was surrounded by a group of small boys in the school playground in Farnborough, Kent.[59] Mark has given varying accounts of how his mother's initial success affected him. 'I knew my mother was something special the very first day she became a Member of Parliament,' he said in 1974.[60] But in a later interview he said: 'It didn't really affect my life at all. In fact, I very well remember the day she was elected walking into the garage and seeing the car covered in blue ribbon and confetti. I couldn't quite work it out because the car never looked like that before, but even though I was only six, I can remember thinking, "She's really going places."'[61]

According to her biographers, Margaret Thatcher then began to distance herself from her home town of Grantham. She rarely visited her birthplace, now viewing it as tedious and small-minded. Instead her life was in London and the House of Commons was effectively her new home. She did her best to devote time to the twins, always driving them to school in the mornings. But the truth was that during the week she rarely saw her children, mainly because of late-night parliamentary sittings. She did make their breakfast early in the morning and telephoned them at 6pm to say goodnight. But in their infant years they were brought up by their nanny and housekeeper, a devoted and extrovert older woman called Abby, who became virtually their surrogate mother. 'Ssshhh,' she would whisper to the twins in the evening. 'Your mother's working.'[62]

One topic concerning their children to which Margaret and Denis did devote considerable time and thought was their education. They decided on private boarding schools, partly because it was Denis's preference but also to separate Mark and Carol, who were not getting on. Their mother even used to say they were 'mortal enemies'.[63] Carol herself does not look back on their relationship with any fondness: 'The two of us used to bicker about small things.'[64] Mark's habit of saying things like 'I have to open all my birthday presents two minutes earlier than you, because I am two minutes older' did not exactly endear him to his twin sister.

So in September 1961, aged eight, Mark was sent to Belmont, the preparatory school for Mill Hill where Denis had spent many happy years, near his mother's north London constituency.

It was not an auspicious period for the local MP's son. 'He was a very quiet boy,' recalled David Gee, his housemaster and form-master. 'He was not clever, to put it mildly, and was overshadowed by his sister, Carol, who was much brighter. He was not that good at games and it seemed to me he had an inferiority complex a lot of the time. I would say he was happy enough but his school record was very average.'[65]

A month after Mark's arrival at Belmont, on 9 October 1961 his mother was appointed a junior social security minister in charge of pensions in Harold Macmillan's Conservative government. That evening the twins were given two new books and sat in bed planning what they would like for Christmas.[66] Their lives were going through another sea change. 'I then realised she had a very wonderful career ahead of her as a politician,' said Mark later. 'She was so busy one could only assume she was very successful. . . . I'd always known that she was in the fast track.'[67]

Despite the long separations from her children, Margaret was a very diligent mother and would always make up for lost time. When Mark was ill at Belmont boarding school, his mother made regular trips to his bedside. 'Mum just kept popping up,' said Mark later. 'I was amazed how much she managed to be there. And she was a Minister by then. She has always been a really devoted mother and she still is.'[68]

However, Denis believed she over-compensated for her absence by excessive fussing and worrying about the twins. It also became clear that she favoured Mark over Carol. According to Penny Junor, she 'pampered him as a child, fetched and carried for him when she was at home' and, most significantly, 'seldom corrected him'. Mark's upbringing was a curious combination of a formal, cold and detached boarding-school education and sudden brief but extravagantly intense binges of maternal affection.[69]

As a young boy Mark was much more like his father. Some childhood friends say he almost hero-worshipped Denis, to the extent of imitating his voice. Unsuspecting telephone callers were often bemused, and not a little irritated, when Mark answered the phone by barking 'Thatcher' loudly into the receiver, trying to copy his father.[70] Mark was soon banned from answering the phone in this way. But he retained his adoration of Denis. 'Mark worshipped his father,' said James Montagu, a neighbour of the family. 'He wanted to be just like him and was always saying "My Dad says this" or "My Dad does that".'[71]

Despite her own strict, temperate upbringing and disciplined approach to life, Margaret was curiously conciliatory towards her son. This was despite Mark's being an often mischievous and disruptive child. A mother who knew the family well noticed this anomaly: 'When Margaret first got elected, the papers were full of headlines like "New woman MP calls for the return of the lash", yet she never raised a finger to the twins. Instead she used that low hypnotic voice of hers at

times when I would have belted my kids. I vividly
remember her saying, "Now Mark, you mustn't poke
that sharp stick into your sister's eye, otherwise she
won't grow up into a pretty little girl." I'd have
walloped him.'[72]

This was later confirmed by the twins. 'We weren't
brought up very strictly,' said Mark. 'It was a sort
of back-scratching operation. If I did the things she
expected of me as far as work was concerned and
behaved in a reasonably civilized fashion, it was
fairly easy-going. If I misbehaved or did something
idiotic, then it was trouble, just as it would be with
any Mum.'[73] 'I don't remember her being a tough
disciplinarian – definitely not a shrieker,' said Carol.
'If she ever smacked me I don't recall it. She had such
a strict upbringing herself that she was conscious that
ours would be different. But nor did I grow up in one
of those homes where people climb into bed with their
parents on Sunday morning.'[74]

Although by all accounts Mark was emotionally
spoilt as a child, his mother did not bestow on him lavish gifts and unlimited pocket-money. He did receive
dancing and riding lessons and the house was full of
toys. But she never indulged him in a materialistic
way. This was due, say family friends, to her ascetic
and serious nature, encouraged by her own parents.

In 1963 the Thatchers sold 'Dormers' and bought
a flat in Westminster Gardens, just off Artillery Row
in Victoria. As Denis hated London at weekends, the
family also rented a cottage in Horsmonden, near
Tunbridge Wells, while they looked around for a new
country house. The rented house was on Shere Farm,
part of the estate of Commander Christopher Powell,
a powerful and influential parliamentary lobbyist who
was a close friend and adviser of the Thatchers.

Two years later, in 1965, Denis became a wealthy man when he sold his family company to Castrol, earning himself £560,000. This enabled him to purchase 'The Mount', a reconstructed eight-bedroomed mock-Tudor mansion in Lamberhurst, Kent, five miles from Shere Farm. The house was complete with three acres of garden, a tennis court and an outdoor swimming pool.[75] Next door to the Thatchers lived William Montagu, a retired naval officer who owned a pharmaceutical company, who had told Denis about the availability of 'The Mount'. His son James, a year younger than Mark, was a regular visitor to the Thatcher household as he liked to use the swimming pool. James spent a lot of time with Mark but has no fond recollections. 'He was a horrible and unpleasant person,' said James Montagu. 'He was very bumptious and boastful and behaved as if he knew better than anyone else. He had a knack of putting people's backs up. I'll never forget how forward he was to other parents. On one occasion he sat in the back of our car and began advising my mother how to drive.'[76]

From an early age, pomposity was a feature of Mark's character, according to Penny Junor, a biographer of Margaret Thatcher and the daughter of a close friend of the prime minister, former *Sunday Express* editor Sir John Junor. In her book, Junor recounts what happened when Margaret took the twins to visit an old friend who had children much the same age as the Thatchers': 'While the mothers talked indoors, the children all played together in the sandpit outside. When the time came to leave Mark, dressed as he invariably was like Little Lord Fauntleroy, didn't volunteer any farewells to his host in the sandpit. When instructed to do so by his mother, he regarded scathingly this child who looked appropriately grubby for the end of a day in the garden, and said, "Oh no, Mummy, I couldn't possibly say goodbye to someone so scruffy." '77

However, a childhood neighbour from the mid-1960s, Eric 'Ricki' Laws, now a doctor in Southampton, has a slightly different recollection. 'I actually got on with Mark and liked him because he was so thick-skinned,' said Laws 'I was always amused at his inability to understand the least subtle of hints. It is true he was bumptious and lacked social grace but I enjoyed his company.'78

By the time Mark entered his teenage years Margaret was emerging as the dominant figure in the Thatcher family. 'She was definitely in charge,' said James Montagu. It was not for nothing that both Denis and Mark referred to her as 'The Boss' – a nickname they use to this day.79 An indication of this status was the choice of Mark's senior school. It was always Denis's hope that his son, like himself, would go to Mill Hill. But, according to David Gee, Mark's housemaster at preparatory school, Margaret Thatcher vetoed the idea because Mill Hill had an unofficial Jewish 'quota' of boys. The Finchley MP believed that, if Mark was admitted, then it would have been perceived that she had used her influence with her Jewish constituents. Instead he was sent to Harrow.

A Reluctant Harrovian

Mark Thatcher went up to Harrow (motto: 'May the Fortune of the House be Steered by the Faithful Stewardship of the Gifts of God') in January 1967, aged thirteen. Founded in 1572, it was originally a free grammar school for the study of classics by local boys, and only became fee-paying and private with an influx of pupils with wealthy parents from outside the parish. More significantly, it became the training school for the Establishment, rivalled only by Eton, whose headmaster, Lord Charteris, once explained its appeal: 'The boys discover very early that they've got to get round people to get their way. It's the ideal training ground for statesmen, politicians, entrepreneurs. And pirates.'[80]

Grooming the boys for greatness is the school's underlying philosophy – the future generation who are to sustain and preserve basic Establishment institutions. Hence Harrow has created eight prime ministers, notably Winston Churchill, and between 1900 and 1985 eighty-three government ministers. Its current school governors include Sir Robin Butler, cabinet secretary and head of the civil service, Sir Evelyn de Rothschild and the Duke of Westminster.

Over the years the Harrow culture became immensely status-conscious and class-ridden, according to one of its distinguished former pupils. Lord Deedes, Old Harrovian, former Conservative cabinet minister, former editor of the *Daily Telegraph* and close friend of Denis Thatcher, recalls how he was taught to look up to authority, almost literally tugging his forelock. 'We were taught that to respect authority was the most important thing in life,' said Lord Deedes, 'and there were whole obligations to privilege.'[81] When Mark was a pupil in the late 1960s, Harrow retained those snobbish characteristics. It was one of those curious ironies that Margaret Thatcher should send her son to an élitist school run by an Establishment class that she later opposed so bitterly and would dismiss as 'those grandees'.[82]

However, Harrow was going through a mildly transitional stage when Mark joined. The 'fag' system, whereby first-year pupils act as personal servants to sixth-form members, was being reformed. This meant that by the time Mark was in the sixth form a new rule – 'boy calls' – was in place. If a sixth-former wanted an errand run, he would shout, 'Boy, boy, boy,' and all the fags in the House would have to come running. 'The aim of the "fag" system,' one Old Harrovian told us, 'was that it taught boys a fair use of power, in that you experienced the position of the servant before becoming a master.'

In fact, it accentuated class divisions, so that anyone arriving at Harrow with even the slightest hint of an 'inferior' social background would become very insecure. This is exactly what happened to Mark Thatcher, who was essentially from a petty bourgeois or *nouveau riche* family. 'When he arrived at school he was not comfortable with himself,' said John Pearson, a contemporary. 'He never let himself get walked over, though, as he stuck up for himself. But people formed the impression that he was a bit of an oddball.'[83]

Mark's misfortune was his native London–Kent accent which was deemed 'common' and 'below-stairs'. He was teased and mimicked mercilessly, as it contrasted sharply with the plummy aristocratic tones of his peers. The boys found it particularly amusing because it clashed with the refined, if affected, accent of his mother on television when she was shadow minister for transport. Consequently, he was nicknamed 'Mawk Fatcher' or 'Mork Scratcher' (because of his acne problems). Margaret's son responded, unconvincingly, that he had picked up the accent from workers on a building site near the family home in London. He also tried to deflate his embarrassment and divert attention by performing his Harrow party piece. This involved jumping in the air, clicking his heels and shouting "'Allo, sunshine' at anyone he regarded as socially inferior.[84] But this served only to focus attention on himself and his own insecurities, rather than to amuse his fellow pupils.

Instead of laughing off the jibes at his accent and blending in, Mark adopted a pompous and bumptious stance towards his fellow pupils. This attitude coincided with the election of the Conservative government in June 1970 and the elevation of his mother as secretary of state for education. 'When she got a place in the Cabinet,' he said later, 'it really started to affect me. I was beginning to grow up and understand what it was all about.'[85]

However, some of the masters were not so quick to recognize his mother's status. One day she arrived at Harrow to talk to Mark's housemaster, Mark Tindall. On that particular day, Tindall was interviewing for new domestic staff, so she waited patiently outside his rooms. Suddenly, he opened his study door and noticed her sitting in the corridor. 'Ah,' he said, 'you must have come about the new under-matron vacancy.' Margaret Thatcher was not amused.[86]

Margaret wanted her son to adapt, adjust and behave like the other boys. But Mark had a tendency to conduct himself as though his mother were already prime minister.[87] This did not endear him to his fellow pupils. 'He had the reputation for being fairly conceited,' recalled Clive Staveley, who was in the same house (Bradbys) as Mark. 'He was awarded colours early on, which meant you were allowed to wear a coloured scarf on half-days. He went right out and bought his but wasn't allowed to wear it, as people took a dim view of youngsters wearing them. He was only allowed to wear it three years later, by which time I think it had moth holes in it.'[88]

His fellow teenagers took a delight in belittling the son of 'Thatcher the Milk-snatcher' (her nickname as the minister who abolished free milk for schoolchildren). 'I remember with some glee playing in a rugby match against Mark's house,' said a contemporary. 'Mark was going for a try and I smashed him into touch. I really enjoyed it because he was the son of the Milk-snatcher.' Mark dutifully defended his mother: 'I think she did the right thing because it gave her the opportunity to reallocate the £22 million to other educational programmes.'[89]

Having a famous parent was not Mark's problem at Harrow (the place was, after all, full of them). The truth was that he just could not, or would not, acclimatize. 'He was a bit of a loner, who didn't fit into the British public-school environment,' said Andrew Blamey, now an executive head-hunter, who was in the same house. 'He couldn't hack it in an institutional atmosphere, and Harrow was a very institutionalized place because its purpose was to equip people to become part of the established institutions.'[90] Robin Ward, now at Lloyd's, who had the room opposite Mark's in Bradbys House, agreed: 'He was a little different from the other boys in that he didn't fit into Harrow as smoothly as some. . . . To be honest, Mark wasn't everybody's cup of tea. He had a very sort of confident and cocky manner, which was sometimes misplaced. He was not necessarily the sort of boy you'd expect to go to public school and he was never really gregarious with the other boys. . . . A lot of boys there were a lot richer than he was. His background meant that maybe he felt that he had more to prove because of his humble origins. He did have a slightly unfortunate air about him in that he tended to upset people by his mannerisms. He did have a fairly quick wit, though.'[91]

Essentially, public schools are run on a collegiate, club-like basis, whereby loyalty to each other and abiding by the rules are more important than individual achievement. Mark was never 'clubbable'. He was an outsider and his arrogant manner, social background and insecurities prevented him from being accepted. That is why he was never able to adapt, blend in and be truly happy at Harrow.

However, Mark was not an outcast and did have some friends. He was particularly close to Jonathan Prenn, now head of Lacoste Sportswear, and James Lepp, now a jeweller, but they refused to talk to the authors. One Old Harrovian contemporary, Philip Oppenheim, son of former Conservative minister Sally Oppenheim and now a Tory MP, is one of the few to have spoken well of him. Mark, he said, was 'a thoroughly nice chap'.[92] Others who knew him at school say he was pleasant enough on his own but his manner changed dramatically in a group of boys – a characteristic he retained in later life.

In Mark's defence, it is argued that his parents underestimated and misjudged the impact of their achievements on their children. 'It has been said to me that having two successful parents might put them [the twins] under a bit of pressure,' said Denis Thatcher while Mark was at Harrow. 'Their schoolmasters and schoolmistresses think so, but I don't myself know that it's affected them, bless their little golden hearts. They certainly know what hard work means, there's no doubt about *that*' [his emphasis].[93]

In fact, the desire and underlying pressure to live up to his parents' expectations unquestionably did affect

Mark. Although he developed a thick skin against mockery, Mark was never at ease and often on edge. 'He had a very hard time,' said Blamey, 'because he doesn't mix very well and is convinced that everyone is trying to rip him off. I'm sure that if I called him now – even if it was just to ask him to come to a school dinner – he would run a mile.'[94] 'He was very closed up as a personality,' recalls another old schoolmate. 'I would say he was almost neurotic. My abiding memory of him was that he used to run everywhere. "There goes Thatcher, running again," we used to say. He *always* ran everywhere, books under arm, head back, from lesson to lesson. Quite extraordinary.'

The one redeeming feature of Mark's time at Harrow was that he was a brilliant sportsman – an important quality at any public school. Encouraged by Denis, his prowess at games also made him more popular in his house. Mark excelled at racquets – a fast, dangerous game similar to squash, but using a hard ball like a golf ball and special racquets. It is played mainly by wealthy people because the racquets break regularly and so new ones are frequently needed. 'Few people could afford to play,' said Robin Ward, 'and he seemed to be fairly well off because he once told me that he broke five racquets in one game.'[95]

Racquets is a game requiring skill, courage and fast reflexes. Mark was Harrow and national public schools champion with his friend Jonathan Prenn in his last year, 1970–71. His prowess was regularly chronicled in the school magazine, the *Old Harrovian*. One report also provided a hint of Mark's personality: 'Thatcher, who, as captain of racquets, has been outstandingly alert and capable, is as confident off the court as he is unpredictable on it. His game bears all the marks of an impromptu performance – shots beaten above, below and on to the board; last-second calls to his partner; expressions of disgust with himself or indignant queries to the referee. All this means that the result of a single rally, let alone that of the whole competition, is beyond the range of rational prediction.'[96]

Mark was also a very fine all-round cricketer. He was a member of Harrow's First XI two years running – no mean feat. In his last year he was the team's fourth best batsman, amassing a total of 172 runs at an average of 15.63, with a top score of 51 not out. He was also a very useful spin bowler. His high point was playing against Eton at Lord's. Unfortunately, Mark would later spoil things by overstating the significance of his sporting record. 'I won something at the racquets championship,' he said. 'That gave me a discipline to set targets on an annual basis.'[97]

His sporting success pleased his father but his mother was not so impressed by Mark's academic record. He was more interested in cars than in books. 'He was considered by us to be a bit of a dunce, poor in classes and generally not very bright,' recalled Jan Kruse, now living in Spain.[98] Mark was not lazy, worked hard and wanted to please his mother, who was ambitious for him. But he just did not have an aptitude for the work and was nicknamed 'Thickie Mork'. In July 1969, he gained only three 'O' levels – he had to retake them in November – and he later obtained only mediocre 'A' levels. This was in contrast to his sister, Carol, who acquired seven 'O' levels at the first attempt at St Paul's School for Girls. Mark's scholastic failure was a source of great disappointment to his mother, although she was careful to conceal it. 'Mark doesn't seem as academically ambitious as Carol,' she said at the time.[99]

Despite his sub-standard academic performance,

Mark stayed on an extra term to study for Oxbridge. To the astonishment of his fellow pupils, he was offered a place at Keble College, Oxford. To this day, Old Harrovians are amazed that he qualified and achieved the required results. Neither Harrow nor Keble would provide any information about Mark Thatcher's academic performances. 'The Governors of Harrow have long had a policy of not releasing information about Old Harrovians and their achievements whilst at the school,' said the current headmaster, N. R. Bomford.[100]

Mark decided not to take up his place at Keble. 'I think that Mummy and Daddy, in their heart of hearts, were terribly upset that one member of their family had chosen not to go to Oxford,' he said years later. 'But I thought I could use the time I would have spent at Oxford better. Four years is a long time when you are 18. My parents do not force things through. Nor do they stride up to their children and say: "I told you so. Now you are in a mess, now you've got trouble." They simply told me: "You've thought about it and you've put forward a very good argument. If that is what you want to do, that is fine by us."'[101]

Towards the end of his time at Harrow Mark talked about being a professional sportsman. By then he had developed his interest in motor racing. 'I know that he wanted to become a racing driver or sportsman,' said John Pearson, who was in Mark's house and left school at the same time, 'but I'm certain his father and mother felt that he should get a professional qualification before getting into sport.'[102]

Mark does not have fond memories of his school years (although he is considering sending his son, Michael, to Harrow). He has not been an active member of the Harrow Association and his response to a circular letter sent out in 1986, two years after he moved to Texas, did not endear him to Old Harrovians. The questionnaire asked for details of his school record and an up-to-date address. After a brief reference to his sporting achievements, Mrs Thatcher's son inserted as his address: '10 Downing Street, London SW1.'

Chapter Two

Setting up Shop

'But don't you know who I am? I am the Prime Minister's son.'

Mark Thatcher[1]

Mark left Harrow in July 1971, with a moderate academic record, a growing passion for motor sport and a keen desire to emulate his father as a businessman. He talked to Denis about his career prospects and how to make money. 'I told Mark,' said Denis, 'if you want to run two houses and two motor cars, the only way you can do it is work.'[2]

Through his father's business connections, Mark went to Hong Kong. He worked as a trainee at the giant trading group Jardine Matheson there and then briefly at the company's South African subsidiary, Rennies. In October 1972, aged nineteen, he joined the stockbrokers Davis, Borkum and Hare, where he spent four months researching reports on the motor industry.

This eighteen-month period was clearly work experience as, in January 1973, Mark returned to England to train as a chartered accountant with Touche Ross. The move was very much part of his desire to follow in his father's footsteps. 'He was very keen to emulate his father in business,' said James Montagu, who knew Mark during his teens. 'That's why he tried to be an accountant, because Denis was a financial executive, knew all about balance sheets and had written a book on accountancy [*Accounting and Costing in the Paint Industry*], which he gave to my father [William Montagu].'[3]

Mark joined Touche Ross as a trainee in September 1973, at their head office at 3 London Wall, near Moorgate in the City of London. His fellow trainees were surprised to see the education secretary's son, as the three-year course was strictly for graduates and Mark had not been to university. They argued he could have gained entry only through the political or business influence of his parents. Mark saw his time at Touche Ross as a lay-by on the highway to wealth and fame, according to his fellow trainees. 'His general attitude was that the job didn't matter to him,' said Steve Brownson, a former Conservative councillor, who worked with him. 'He gave the impression that he was destined for greater things.'[4]

In the office Mark was very aloof. He would drift in at 10am and often spend up to an hour on the phone, speaking to girlfriends or fixing up badminton games for that evening. After a leisurely lunch he would wander back and check some audit figures. Former graduates can recall barely any conversations with him, apart from 'Pass that file'. He did not mix socially and would often sit alone in the common room in a corner reading a Frederick Forsyth novel.

Despite being paid only £1,500 a year, Mark seemed to have plenty of money. 'He used to carry a wad of £10 notes with him which he would peel off for taxi fares and expenses,' recalled one trainee. This was a curious observation as Mark later claimed, 'I haven't had a cent from them [his parents] since I was twenty-one.'[5] This presumably meant his allowance was cut off midway through his course.

The overriding impression of Margaret Thatcher's son at Touche Ross was that he was 'a law unto himself', said Steve Brownson. This was reflected in his attitude towards the work. As part of the course, Mark worked on the audits of specific companies under the supervision of a group manager. One task was to calculate how much tax a firm was due to pay. He was told by his tax supervisor that he would need to present his results by 4.30pm on the Friday. 'I can't be here on Friday afternoon,' replied Mark. 'I'm flying off to South Africa for an important business trip.' The manager and his colleagues were stunned into silence by the offhand way in which he spoke. But this became a regular occurrence, as Mark would often leave early on a Friday afternoon, saying he needed to catch a 4pm flight from Heathrow. He said it was for 'business' but by 1975 it was more likely to be racing practice. On 21 July 1975 Mark told his manager he was ill and needed the day off. His boss was not amused to open the newspaper the next day and see a photograph of Mrs Thatcher's son taking a brilliant diving catch in the Commons *v* the MCC cricket match at Hurlingham Club in Fulham.

While Mark's accountancy career was declining and in some jeopardy, his mother's political career was rocketing. On Tuesday, 11 February 1975, Margaret Thatcher was dramatically elected leader of the Conservative Party. It was a historic victory and a celebration party was held that night at the flat of Airey

Neave, her campaign manager, off Chelsea Embankment. Mark attended and struck up a conversation with his mother's key adviser.

'You realise that overnight you have been elevated to the superhuman league,' said Neave.

'Oh, I don't think so,' replied Mark.

'Overnight, everybody has far higher expectations of you,' Neave insisted.[6]

It was a prophetic comment but rather lost in the joviality of the occasion as the champagne flowed. Outside Neave's flat reporters were waiting eagerly for a comment from Margaret Thatcher as she left for the evening. One of them was Norman Luck, the award-winning *Daily Express* journalist. Luck had brought his precious white Fiat 850 car, which he had recently repaired and renovated with great care and affection. He parked across the street, behind an Audi belonging to Denis Thatcher, and joined the shivering reporters.

When Margaret, Denis, Carol and Mark finally emerged late that night, they refused to say anything to the assembled media. Much to the reporters' frustration, the family bundled into the Audi. But instead of driving away Denis, who had been celebrating with some vigour, reversed straight into the back of Norman Luck's beloved Fiat. Luck was beside himself. 'Look what you've done to my car,' he shouted at Denis. Suddenly Mark leapt out of the rear seat and approached him. 'I'm sorry, but I'm sure we can sort this out,' he said. 'Dad's had a few and we don't want to get the police involved, do we?' But Luck was fuming and wanted to call the police. Eventually, Mark persuaded him to change his mind. 'Look, I'll have a quick chat with Mum and she'll give you a quote,' he said. 'Here's my card. Let's get together.'

The next day Luck telephoned Mark Thatcher at his Touche Ross office and they met for lunch. The journalist found the son of the new Tory Party leader an agitated, intense young man, lacking in confidence and unable to relax. He told Luck he was keen to secure a favourable public profile for himself. The conversation was hardly profound, as Mark talked mainly about his girlfriends. 'I suppose people will start trying to marry me off,' he said. 'It makes no difference whether I live in Chelsea or if we move into 10 Downing Street. I know the type of girl I am looking for.' That afternoon Luck wrote a story which was published the next day: 'Overnight Mark Thatcher has become one of Britain's eligible bachelors.'[7]

The Tory leader's son was a good contact for Luck so they met regularly. They set up a secret arrangement whereby Mark would telephone Luck the day before he was taking out a girl so he could be waiting there with a *Daily Express* photographer. Then when Mark and his girlfriend arrived or came out of the nightspot, often Annabel's, she would be shocked to find her picture being taken. This started barely ten days after Margaret Thatcher's accession to the leadership, when Mark took Maryon Gill, a twenty-year-old student nurse, to Mirabelle's for dinner. As they arrived at the restaurant there were Norman Luck and photographer Tom Smith waiting. The next day, 'Only in the *Express*', the story began: 'Handsome Mark Thatcher, snowed under with fan mail since his mother became Tory leader, last night revealed his "Cinderella" romance with a student nurse.'[8]

Two days later Mark telephoned Luck when he took out Caroline Lepp, the seventeen-year-old sister of James, whom he had known at Harrow. 'Mark wanted me to smooth his image,' recalled Luck. 'He loved being in the papers and lapped up the attention. He liked being in with journalists and would call me the day after the story appeared and say thank you. He loved the publicity. It was only when things got tough later on that he started hating journalists.'[9]

The delicious irony of Mark Thatcher consorting with tabloid newshounds was not lost on Peter Tory, then the *Daily Express* diarist. 'He used to lounge around the old William Hickey office and supply rather weak gossip about other politicians,' said Tory.[10] He also continued to supply the paper with a running account of his own love life – 'Mark's Coalition with a New Girl.'[11]

While Mark merrily continued secretly to feed and co-operate with the *Daily Express*, publicly he complained about invasions of privacy. 'When she was elected, it was a source of very great pride to me – God, I can't tell you how proud I was,' he said in 1978. 'The press, however, had found a new toy for a couple of months and I soon learnt that I had to be very careful. One evening I went to a restaurant with some friends and took along a girl I'd known for some time. Afterwards, we went on somewhere else for coffee and I picked up the first editions of the newspapers. Wham! I was horror-struck, there on the front page was a large picture of myself and this girl walking into the restaurant. Of course she did her nut and I can't blame her.'[12]

During the aftermath of his mother's triumph Mark began contemplating its implications. 'For the first six or seven months after it happened,' he later reflected, 'I used to think, "What makes me so special to be the son of the Leader of the Opposition? I've done nothing to deserve it, nothing at all." I realised that suddenly I was in a different league where I was expected to behave in a certain way otherwise I'd get crucified by the world outside. So I try and fulfil other people's expectations of me.'[13]

At first he even talked about a political career. In May 1975, he delivered a speech to the Hendon Rotary Club and Chamber of Commerce on 'Freedom of Choice and the Common Market', as it was just before the referendum on whether Britain should remain in the EEC. 'Mother will probably see my speech,' he said. 'She has given me a lot of encouragement but it really is all my own work.'[14] Later on he speculated about applying to be on the official list of prospective Tory candidates at Central Office, but nothing came of it.[15]

When asked about a political career, Mark never ruled it out but said, 'I had other priorities.'[16] But he used to boast about knowing what was happening inside government. 'He told me he was involved in helping draft his mother's speeches and advising her on her campaigns,' said Nick Faure, who knew Mark during his motor-racing career. 'It sounded like bravura and bluster and I didn't believe him.'[17] Mark's political ambitions were 'pure fantasy', according to one of his closest friends. 'He knew nothing about politics and it was the one area where she would not have taken him seriously. It was the kind of thing he said to impress girlfriends.' This seemed to be confirmed by Mark himself when he said in 1991, 'It was never suggested that I should go into politics.'[18]

In April 1976, after failing his Intermediate and Part One accountancy examinations, Mark went to Manchester for a six-week crash course to prepare for his retakes. He was happy that the course was in Lancashire because he genuinely believed that people north of Watford were more stupid and hence he would have a better chance of passing. 'The grades and marks are always lower outside of London,' he said soon after his arrival at the London School of Accountancy, a firm of private tutors. This did not endear him to his new colleagues, who found him haughty and pompous. 'He thought he was royalty,' recalled a fellow trainee who sat behind him in class. 'The first time I saw him he was on the telephone. He turned to me and said, "Be a good chap, get me a coffee," as if I was some kind of servant. . . . He was a terrible name-dropper and always bragging about going through the VIP lounge at the airport on his way to some motor-racing event in Paris or Frankfurt.'

Mark's colleagues remember him as always being on the telephone and asking inept questions in a loud voice – a far cry from his surly, taciturn presence at Touche Ross two years earlier. 'There are two kinds of people that sit in the front of the class – the bright ones and the gobby ones. He was a gobby one,' recalled the trainee who sat next to him throughout the six weeks. 'He behaved as if he knew better than anyone else. He used to turn round and lecture the class. If the lecturer was making a point, Thatcher would turn round and explain it loudly. The problem was that he was thick, quite frankly, and so he would often get it wrong.'

The lecturers were also irritated by this habit. During one seminar a tutor was discussing one of the questions in the previous examination. 'Yeah, it was *simple*,' interrupted Mark (his emphasis). 'Why did you fail, then?' responded the lecturer, quick as a flash, who clearly enjoyed humiliating him.

Mark's behaviour reflected an arrogance beyond his twenty-two years. It was based more on his perceived newly inherited 'status' as the son of the Leader of the Opposition than on any mature self-confidence. 'He just thought he was better than us and was destined for higher things,' said a fellow trainee who is now a successful accountant. 'That was quite ironic really, because there were six of us in the front row of the class. Five of us passed and he didn't.' The reason for his failure was self-evident – he did not work, but spent most of his time planning his racing excursions. After an initial flurry of enthusiasm, his lack of diligence became apparent when he walked out of tests half-way through, unable to answer all the questions.

Despite this disappointment, Mark Thatcher soldiered on and eventually passed his Intermediate and Part One examinations at the third attempt.

The next year he sat Part Two of his finals but was unsuccessful as he passed three but failed two of the exams. For his retakes he was sent to the Financial Training Company, a firm of accountancy lecturers whose deputy chairman was the convivial Jeremy Hanley, now Tory MP for Richmond and Barnes and former chairman of the Conservative Party. 'I taught Mark Thatcher and I found him extremely hard-working, pleasant and energetic,' said Hanley, then the adopted parliamentary candidate for Lambeth Central.[19] Despite passing the exam taught by Hanley, Mark again failed his finals.

Shortly after he received his results, Mark invited Hanley over to Flood Street to discuss his future with his mother. The budding Conservative candidate advised that her son should continue his accountancy studies and try again in six months' time. Margaret Thatcher agreed. 'She wanted him to continue because she was very keen for him to have a professional qualification,' recalled Hanley. Mark disagreed and felt he did not need to pass his finals to make his way in the business world.

His professional prospects were left unresolved at the end of the meeting. But privately Mark had already decided to quit accountancy because by early 1977 he was already receiving potential business offers and was keen to launch his motor-racing career. A month later he called it a day and left Touche Ross.

Margaret was not pleased with the outcome, but hardly condemnatory. 'You know, the trouble with Mark is he just can't pass exams,' she said at the time.[20] 'Margaret was disappointed that he did not qualify and regretted it,' said a former cabinet minister. 'She would have liked him to pass but just thought that whatever he did was right.' Denis was much more dejected. 'Failing to complete his accountancy studies was the thing that disappointed him most,' said a former Tory minister and a close friend of Mark's father. 'He was unhappy that Mark did not have a serious professional career or occupation.'

Mark's unhappy period as a trainee accountant later returned to haunt him. Five weeks after his mother became prime minister, in June 1979, a press statement was released, announcing Mark's participation in a charity motor race at Brands Hatch. It stated that he 'returned to this country in 1973 to commence his chartered accountancy studies, qualifying in 1977'.[21] After the press hand-out was delivered, the radio news bulletins described him as 'a chartered accountant', a term which newspapers had used for some years. This, of course, was misleading but remained uncorrected, much to the fury of his Touche Ross colleagues who had passed their exams. Even the prime minister's office was economical with the actualité. 'Yes, he is an accountant, but he is not fully qualified,' said a spokesperson in 1979. 'He works as an accountant, but it is not

technically correct to call him a chartered accountant.'[22]

While he was still at Touche Ross, Mark devoted
a considerable amount of time to his first love,
motor racing. For many years he had set his heart
on racing as his career, and he drove in several
races in South Africa. 'My mother is a little appre-
hensive about my ambitions to be a top-class racing
driver, but she respects my judgement and would
not stand in my way,' he said at the time.[23] In fact,
Margaret Thatcher was never keen on his chosen
career. She had never been interested in cars and
always saw them as a means of transport rather
than recreation. However, it was during his early
attempts to establish his driving credentials that
he met Stephen Tipping – later his most important
business partner and confidant during the Downing
Street years.

Stephen William Tipping was born in Deal on the
Kent coast, on 27 October 1951. His father, Geoffrey
Tipping, was a sergeant in the Royal Marines. After
leaving the Marines Geoffrey had an assortment of
jobs, from taxi driver to antiques dealer. He also
stood unsuccessfully as a Conservative candidate in
local elections. Steve spent most of his early years in
Dover, Kent. The Tippings are a close family of dealers
and traders, and Steve was no exception. He started
out working in the family garage and filling-station
business, Monteagle Motors Ltd, in Yateley, near
Camberley, Surrey.

Steve's passion was motor racing and that is how he
met Mark Thatcher. A racing driver from the age of
nineteen, Tipping competed in the Super Vee Class,
the European equivalent of Formula Three. In 1973 he
came third in the championship, collecting £1,000 in

prize money. But he was always handicapped by lack of funds and back-up staff.

The following year Tipping was competing in Zolder, Holland, when he was forced to change the tyres by himself during the race. So he advertised in *Motor Sport* for a mechanic, and within a few days Mark Thatcher telephoned to apply for the job. Mark was not qualified and pretended he knew more than he did. Tipping soon realized this, but was won over by his boyish enthusiasm; it also helped that Formula Three engines are not complicated. And so Mark became Tipping's mechanic. More importantly, the two became firm friends. Tipping admired Mark's middle-class, public-school self-confidence, while Thatcher liked Steve's street-wise business savvy and sense of humour. It was the beginning of a close friendship and a happy business partnership, which later led to Thatcher being godfather to Tipping's son, named, appropriately, Mark. They also shared a fanatical enthusiasm for motor sport.

In March 1975 Tipping and Thatcher decided to step up their racing careers. They launched Mark Thatcher Racing, originally to compete in Formula Three but ultimately intended to propel them into the big time. However, they soon realized they needed £20,000 sponsorship cash for the season. So they placed an advertisement with a box number in *Autosport* asking for fund-raisers. They recruited Nigel Hart, a twenty-year-old biochemistry student and racing enthusiast, who met Tipping in his flat in Yateley, Surrey. 'They wanted me to find sponsorship and raise money,' recalled Hart. 'I worked for them on the basis that if I got the sponsorship I would receive a percentage. I then wrote a number of letters to companies on specially headed note-paper which used his mother's name by implication rather than directly.'[24] The basic idea was to offer companies guaranteed press coverage by ensuring their name would be blazoned across Mark Thatcher's car. 'The deal was that we would offer certain newspapers special inside information about Mark Thatcher Racing with photographs on an exclusive basis,' Hart told us. 'This would give an incentive for companies to sponsor us because they knew they were getting press coverage out of it. We were acting like a public relations agency for ourselves, but it didn't work out because I don't think the companies were convinced about it.'[25]

One company Mark approached was London Rubber, manufacturers of the contraceptive Durex. He wrote to them asking for sponsorship but the marketing director, Mike Broadbridge, was not impressed by his application. 'Our venture into Formula One racing was very successful,' said Broadbridge, 'so we decided the next step should be to sponsor young drivers with winning potential. We decided, however, that Mark Thatcher did not really fit into that category. . . . Durex is such an emotional product. We didn't want to get in a political hassle with the Leader of the Opposition or future Prime Minister.'[26]

The firm Mark used to promote his sponsorship drive was CSS Promotions Ltd, a sports marketing and PR agency that specialized in motor racing. A successful and effective company, their activities included promoting Marlboro cigarettes in grand prix racing and representing the late James Hunt, then world champion, and Mario Andretti.

For Mark motor sport was almost like a release from the tensions of his life. 'I found a thrill in driving a racing car that I had not experienced before,' he said later. 'I felt completely comfortable in it and driving it.

It is something you have either got – or you haven't. A racing car is where I feel at home. When I am racing there is a sort of metronome in my brain. As it goes faster and faster, my brain says, "Be careful, you need to watch this" and "Look out for that." . . . I find motor racing a form of relaxation. I take three or four days off every few weeks and do something totally different from my normal business life. Racing flushes all those other problems out of your mind.'[27]

As regards his career prospects, Mark saw racing as 'a very serious hobby. . . . I approach it very seriously and it's something I enjoy doing very much, but that's as far as it goes.'[28] He considered himself 'a gifted amateur',[29] but believed he was capable of being a high-calibre driver. 'I have a well-developed competitive sense,' he said. 'I am hungry, ambitious and competitive.'[30] All he needed was financial backing and this could be obtained by high-powered media promotion for himself and potential sponsors. That was why CSS Promotions were hired, on an *ad hoc* basis. 'It was fairly obvious that he wanted publicity and to get known because he could not get sponsorship,' recalled a former senior CSS director.[31]

Mark Thatcher Racing lasted just over two years. It failed because Mark and Steve Tipping were unable to persuade sponsors to provide enough cash. 'They wouldn't sponsor him because he just wasn't good enough,' said the former CSS director. And so in the summer of 1977 Tipping and Thatcher temporarily went their separate ways. Tipping decided to become 'an entrepreneur' and set up his own trading company, SW Tipping (UK) Ltd. Based at the back of his house in Yateley, it was essentially an import–export business. His chief interest was the printing and selling of T-shirts through a chain of companies – Wizard

Design Ltd, Go-Gear (London) Ltd and Biscotin Ltd. Within two years he was importing 250,000 T-shirts a year from Europe and Hong Kong, as well as buying from British wholesalers.

Tipping also became a director of Hudson Armoured Car Security Services Ltd (intended as a UK base for an American company, but never incorporated), Caterland Ltd (selling gas-fired barbecues from Dallas into the UK), and Daco Office Equipment Ltd (a furniture, equipment and stationery company). These were all potentially highly profitable enterprises but they eventually collapsed.

In the meantime Mark was struggling. He was unemployed and his racing career was in neutral. Then, in the autumn of 1977, he secured a job in a Manchester jewellery shop owned by L. J. Jewellery Import Ltd, part of the Lepp chain of companies based in Altrincham, Cheshire. Mark was hired because he was friendly with John Lepp, who had introduced him to motor racing, and his nephew Jamie Lepp, who had been at Harrow with him in the mid-1960s.[32]

The Lepp family became fabulously wealthy as manufacturers and wholesalers of up-market luxury jewellery. L. J. Jewellery Import Ltd was owned by Sessna Holdings Ltd, incorporated in the Isle of Man, and their offshore connections were strengthened when Jim Lepp, Jamie's father, moved to Guernsey in 1977. Now retired and still living on the Channel Island, Jim Lepp would talk to the authors only if he received remuneration. 'How much are you going to pay me?' he said. We refused.

John Lepp, a life-long friend of the Thatchers, declined to talk to the authors without Mark's permission. His reluctance is perhaps not surprising, given the uneven progress of his company. In 1986 John Lepp

sold his Altrincham shop to J. T. Cottrill and Sons Ltd,
another successful Cheshire jeweller at the time.

Mark, then twenty-four, was a sales manager of one
of their wholesale jewellery shops and did some on-the-
road selling. He was an enthusiastic worker. 'He was
a very good salesman,' said his former boss, Anthony
Kliger, who visited Aspreys and Garrard with young
Thatcher in tow. 'If he had kept at it he could have
made his mark. I think it might have been beneficial
for him if he had stayed in the business. However, his
eyes were on higher things.'[33]

Another businessman who knew him at the time was
Clive Kandell, who had a shop on the King's Road,
Chelsea. One day the Opposition leader's son walked
in and introduced himself. 'I'm selling jewellery,' he
said. 'I live round the corner so I can always come in
and see you. The name's Thatcher.' 'You mean you're
related to her?' asked Kandell. 'Yes,' replied Mark.
The Chelsea businessman eventually bought jewellery
from the keen young rep.

However, the jewellery job was a side-show. Mark
Thatcher's mind was always on motor racing and he
left in the summer of 1978, barely nine months into
the job. Those late summer and early autumn months
saw him at his lowest ebb. He had no career prospects.
He was often seen engrossed in *Motoring Weekly* but
his racing prospects were bleak. Even his decision not
to go to university was under question. 'There were
times, say two years ago, when I thought I had made
the wrong decision,' he said in 1980.[34]

Despite his anxiety, he remained full of bravado
with people. Sarah Standing, who twice went out
to dinner with him during this period, recorded her
impressions in her diary: 'Mark means well and seems
a nice enough man, but alas, it's all "me, me, me" and

his dialogue is riddled with brash boasts. On being top dog. On naming prices and then on securing a "money-no-object" image. He is what used to be considered a playboy but at the same time he says he deplores the term. Uses words like "honking" a lot and calls his mother "mummy" all the time.'[35]

Carol Thatcher, in the meantime, was prospering. In January 1978, she left England for Melbourne, Australia, after completing her legal training, and worked for Peter Jansen, a flamboyant and wealthy New Zealand businessman and socialite with interests ranging from gold-mining to motor racing and horses. 'Carol was wonderful,' recalled Jansen. 'She was highly intelligent and the hardest worker I ever employed. I have the highest respect for her.'[36] She also later worked on a cattle ranch, as a journalist on the *Sydney Morning Herald* and for a television current affairs programme. 'I loved Australia,' she said later. 'I was my own person – rather than my mother's daughter.'[37] But her hostility towards her twin brother remained. Whenever his name cropped up in conversation, she would say, 'Oh, yes,' and change the subject abruptly.

It was Carol who inadvertently rescued Mark from his latest crisis. At a dinner party in Sydney hosted by Peter Jansen she had met Gordon Barton, chairman of the International Parcel Express Corporation (IPEC), a highly successful Australian conglomerate with interests in transport, property, insurance, publishing and hotels. Barton was impressed by Carol and he became a friend of the Thatcher family.

In the summer of 1978, Gordon Barton was invited by Margaret Thatcher for Sunday lunch at their Kent retreat near Lamberhurst. Just before lunch Denis

Thatcher approached Gordon Barton when Margaret was out of earshot. 'I don't know what I'm going to do about the boy,' he said, almost exasperated. 'Well, if I can help you I will,' replied Barton. 'If there is anything you can do, I would be most grateful,' said Denis. According to one of the other guests present, 'Denis made it crystal clear, without actually using the precise words, that Mark was a problem and needed a job to settle him down.'

Barton did not have a vacancy at the time, but an opportunity arose three months later when he commissioned a feasibility study into launching IPEC in Europe. The IPEC chairman needed freight depots in European ports, so he thought this was the moment to give Mark a job, as he planned to set up a British base.

At the time the Barton family happened to be on holiday driving around Europe in their luxury Mercedes Sedan. When they reached Rome, Gordon Barton saw an ideal opportunity for Mark to learn the business from Ron Devonish, a rough, tough Australian brought over to do the feasibility study. The Mercedes needed to be returned to London while the Bartons flew on to Greece and then back to Australia. So Gordon suggested that Mark Thatcher and Ron Devonish drive the car back to London together and discuss their forthcoming business project during the journey.

Within barely fifty miles it was clear the two travellers did not get on. In fact, they hated each other. Known as 'the Rock Spider' to his colleagues back in Australia, Devonish was a no-nonsense, take-no-prisoners Aussie, who bristled when Mark wittered on endlessly about the saintly qualities of 'Mummy'. Also, Mark drove as if he were competing at Brands Hatch. By the time they reached Switzerland Devonish could stand it no longer. He baled out of the car and told Margaret Thatcher's son he could drive the rest of the way alone while he, Devonish, flew back to London. However, the trip went from bad to worse when Mark crashed the Mercedes in Amsterdam and the car was wrecked.

Despite this inauspicious start, Devonish and Thatcher set up an office in the Bartons' London apartment in Three Kings Yard, just behind Claridge's Hotel in Mayfair. It was a curious setting for a feasibility study into a new transport company. The flat was emerald-green, with green walls and carpets, and had previously been used by Lord Lambton, the infamous Conservative defence minister, to entertain prostitutes in the early 1970s.

Mark was basically a gofer and office boy for Devonish. But the Tory leader's son saw his job in a rather grander light. 'I am to be the London representative of a Far East firm with a very large annual turnover,' he announced to the *Daily Express* in October 1978.[38] 'I'm working for a Far East conglomerate whose head comes over here five or six times a year,' he told the *Daily Mail*. 'Getting the job had absolutely nothing to do with who my mother is.'[39]

However, according to former senior IPEC managers, his duties were far less glamorous. 'He was employed as a runner, which basically meant doing research when we were planning to acquire a new company,' a former IPEC executive told us. 'My impression was that he thought the job was beneath him and he should have been higher up in the company. He also seemed more interested in what new car he was racing than working for us.'

Mark was a competent employee but he was constantly trying to use his mother's position as Leader of the Opposition. On several occasions, when IPEC executives discussed the problems of moving freight quickly and dealing with government agencies like Customs, Mark said, 'Don't worry, Mummy can plug us in there.' According to an IPEC manager who was present, the company saw this as naive and ham-fisted as well as wrong.

It was not long before Ron 'the Rock Spider' Devonish, his immediate boss, had the boy's measure. One day an IPEC executive walked into the office to witness a sight which is forever imprinted on his memory. Devonish was sprawled across the sofa with a can of Fosters in his hand, barking out orders in his best Aussie drawl. Mark was standing by a blackboard and writing out what 'the Rock Spider' called 'Thatcher's Ten Commandments'. Among the most prominent was 'Thou Shall Not Mention or Use My Mother's Name In Vain!!'

In early 1979, IPEC was looking for a European services branch and bought Sayer Transport Ltd, a highly successful trucking firm, for £3.5 million. Mark became personal assistant to Ian Sayer, the twenty-six-year-old founder of the company, and continued his job as a 'runner', driving around the country inspecting IPEC haulage depots.

Sayer, who was known to be an avid collector of Nazi memorabilia, was impressed by his assistant's connections and the two men became friends. But he later became a sharp critic. 'If Mark's mother wasn't Prime Minister, he wouldn't be anything,' he said many years later. 'In a way you could describe him as a second-rate Arthur Daley.'[40] Sayer now says he cannot recall anything about Mark's work for him until the 1979 general election. 'Everything changed after Mrs Thatcher became prime minister,' he told us.

Marketing Mark

Margaret Thatcher's victory at the 1979 general election was the pivotal moment in Mark's life. At the time he was walking a treadmill at IPEC-Sayer, expending a lot of energy but not going anywhere. During the campaign itself he accompanied his mother occasionally, trailing after her almost like an appendage to her retinue. He dutifully appeared at set-piece rallies but did not make much impression. 'Nobody took much notice of him,' a senior former Tory Central Office official told us. 'He just did not have the personality. All I can remember is that he would make excessive demands like always wanting to be in the lead group of cars.'

Unlike Carol, who had returned from Australia to work on her mother's campaign, Mark was only sporadically involved. 'I shall go out with her at strategic times,' he said.[41] 'I'm canvassing about two nights a week and at weekends, but I won't be speaking.'[42] Instead, he continued to work at IPEC-Sayer, although there was an embarrassing incident on the evening of 23 April 1979, when he was noticed at a Mayfair casino. 'I really shouldn't be here,' Margaret's son said, nervously looking around. 'I came with a business associate who is a member.'[43]

On election night, Thursday, 4 May 1979, Mark appeared briefly in his mother's constituency at Finchley town hall for the count and then drove home to 19 Flood Street, Chelsea, to watch the results on television. At the moment when Alastair Burnet announced on ITN that the Tories had secured an absolute majority in the Commons, Mark recalled Airey Neave's remark four years earlier when Margaret Thatcher became Tory Party leader: 'You realise that overnight you have been elevated to the superhuman league.'[44] And as the news that his mother was to be prime minister sank in, Mark became more emotional. 'I sat there inwardly crying for joy for her,' he said. 'I remember going up to her, almost bursting into tears, and saying . . . well, *how* do you say what you feel when a member of your family is elected to the highest position in the land? You are speechless, it is unbelievable' [his emphasis].[45]

At noon the next day, Friday, 5 May, Mark, Carol and Denis accompanied the new premier to Conservative Central Office to celebrate the victory with champagne and slices of a huge chocolate cake made in the shape of the 10 Downing Street door. After lunch the Thatcher family retired to Margaret's office to await the summons from Buckingham Palace. Denis was dozing quietly when the telephone call came through from Sir Philip Moore, the Queen's private secretary. Margaret took the call in another room and then reappeared. 'Right, we're off,' she said briskly. Denis straightened his tie. Mark put his arms around his mother and said, 'Prime minister.' 'Not yet, dear,' replied Margaret. 'The car may break down,' suggested Denis helpfully.[46]

As they walked downstairs, Mark strode ahead and opened the door of the car which drove Mrs Thatcher to Buckingham Palace to be 'invited' by the Queen to form a government. 'Opening that door was the proudest moment of my life,' he said later. 'I have a photograph of it. It's my greatest treasure.'[47]

The implications of being the son of the prime minister were not lost on young Thatcher. Three days after the election, on 7 May 1979, some letters arrived at his office with the address scratched out and marked, 'Redirect to Penthouse Flat, 10 Downing Street.' He also began receiving dozens of telephone calls from 'friends' and people he barely knew.[48] But his mind was on other matters.

Mark's master plan, once his mother was ensconced in 10 Downing Street, was graphically spelt out to a Thatcherite minister at a drinks reception soon after the election. The minister, one of the original eight disciples who orchestrated Mrs Thatcher's Tory Party leadership triumph in 1975, was standing next to Denis and Margaret when their son commented, 'I have set myself a target. I want to make a million by the time I am thirty.' The expressions on the faces of the premier and her consort barely flickered. But the minister, who would serve in the government for six years, was stunned. 'When he [Mark] said that I thought to myself, "To do that you need to remove a few fingers from people's hands,"' he told the authors.

Amputation of businessmen's fingers was not quite what Mark had in mind. But he was keen to set up his version of Mark Thatcher Enterprises. 'I had always known what I wanted,' he said later. 'Success in business, to be as successful as both Mummy and Daddy had been. They helped – we have always been a close, helping, caring family – but I haven't had a cent off them since I was twenty-one.'[49]

His commercial outlet was launched six weeks after the election, when Mark Thatcher set up a business partnership with his best friend, Stephen Tipping. On 19 June 1979, Monteagle Marketing (London) Ltd was incorporated as a 'marketing consultancy company'. It acted as 'marketing consultants and agents for and on behalf of any person, firm or company in respect of any goods or services whether in the UK or abroad'.[50] Within a week international businessmen were expressing interest. On 30 June, Mark flew by Concorde from Switzerland to New York and then by private jet to Greenville, South Carolina, for a lunch reception with local businessmen. They believed his presence was a 'business booster'.[51]

Mark formally became a director of Monteagle Marketing on 9 August 1979, describing himself as a 'company director'. Tipping was chairman and joined the board on 8 October 1979, as 'a managing executive'.[52] The next day, the first day of that year's Tory Party conference, the company commenced trading. Mark owned 99 per cent of the shares with Tipping retaining 1 per cent. The company's closeness to Margaret Thatcher herself was illustrated by the fact that they shared the same accountant: Philip J. Gee of Lithgow and Nelson, a relatively small firm based at 127 Clerkenwell Road, London EC1. Gee is also a trustee of the Margaret Thatcher Charitable Trust.

Monteagle Marketing was a very low-key, secretive operation. At first the premier's son refused to disclose even basic details about the company – its name, his business partner, its location, how many people he employed (one) or even its general nature. It even had an ex-directory telephone number. Based at Forge Court, Yateley, Surrey, the office was in a converted seventeenth-century coaching house, and consisted of a tiny reception area and one first-floor office used by Mark, Steve and Brenda Sanger, the company secretary.

During the company's infant months the atmosphere inside the office was one of frenetic activity. Mark and Steve conducted business as if every day were their last. 'They were always rushing around,' a business associate told us. 'Steve in particular was very manic and intense. They have both calmed down now but I would guess that's because they have made all their money.' There was also a feeling that they had a limited amount of time, because in the early years it was unclear for how long Margaret Thatcher was going to be prime minister. 'I remember Steve telling me that we've only got about five years before she goes,' said a former director of one of Tipping's companies.

Some – but not much – money flowed in initially, as Tipping and Thatcher paid themselves an annual salary of only £10,000 each, although that was far from derisory by 1979 standards. 'Mark opened the doors on the deals,' said a source who worked in the office at the time. 'It was always known that he did not have the business acumen and so Steve sorted out the detail and the nuts and bolts.' This was, in effect, confirmed by Mark: 'He [Tipping] watches the shop while I am away and I trust him implicitly. I consider that I have many weaknesses so he stands right behind me and tells me when he thinks I'm going wrong.'[53]

The company had various functions. Essentially, it was a conduit for Mark Thatcher and Tipping to be marketing agents, middlemen and consultants for corporations. Or, as one wit later quipped, 'an up-market sandwich board'.[54]

This description was, inadvertently, confirmed by Brenda Sanger, Thatcher's personal assistant and the company secretary. She said Monteagle's work was commercial 'catering'. 'By catering, we mean knowing the right people. Somebody who knows somebody can put them in touch with somebody else,' she said.[55] It also exported British luxury cars, and there was an associate firm, Monteagle International, which consulted on property deals, notably a shop and office

complex in Southampton. 'The services are not desperately sophisticated,' a spokesperson for one of
their future clients, Cementation International Ltd,
commented.[56]

Mark saw the company in a more grandiose light.
He said Monteagle specialized in 'turnkey' operations:
'Turnkey means that, for example, if a prospective
buyer needs a cement plant, I will go along with my
clients, persuade them that we are the people they need,
then design, finance, build, train their staff and run it
until an agreed take-over date. Then, all they have to
do is turn the key and walk into a ready-made concern.
It's the sort of thing I had always wanted to do. I had to
wait for the right opportunity and when it came along,
I grabbed it. I own the company, pay the wages and
generate the income.'[57]

However, former business associates who spent time
in the Monteagle office, though not employed there,
cannot recall any clients that fit this description.
Instead, they say, Mark and Tipping were spending
most of their time abroad. Mark confirmed this. 'I
don't have to stay in this country to earn my living.
All my marketing consultancy business is overseas,'
he said in February 1980. 'I can do it from the South
of France, Central Europe, the Middle East or Hong
Kong.'[58]

As a company, Monteagle was never the enterprise
Mark hoped it would be. It was consistently late in
filing annual accounts and financial returns, once only
just avoiding prosecution after repeated warnings from
Companies House. The accounts showed either small
pre-tax profits or that losses and liabilities exceeded
assets. It was a long, long way from being the respected
family firm that his father, Denis, had nurtured.

Chapter Three

Racing Days

*'The episode [Mark getting lost in the desert]
did have one benefit. We could relax a little, for
Mark had hung an occupied sign on the family's
"embarrassing relative" slot.'*

Carol Thatcher, p.187, *Below the Parapet – The
Biography of Denis Thatcher* (HarperCollins, 1996)

His mother's ascendancy to the premiership not only
transformed Mark's business interests, but also revived
his flagging racing career. Margaret Thatcher never
shared her son's fascination with fast cars and privately
was horrified by his racing ambitions. But, as with almost
everything he did, she could never bring herself to ask
him to stop. 'Mum's a bit worried about me,' said Mark,
'but that's a mother's natural protective instinct. When I
told her I was going to race she said: "Are you sure you
know what you're doing?" But she didn't try to talk me
out of it. She trusts my judgement and ability.'[1]

Two weeks after the 1979 general election Mark
Thatcher Racing was revived, and he began training
at Brands Hatch racing school. He made his début on
10 June, racing a ShellSport Sunbeam Ti to victory in
the annual Commons *v* Lords race. Under the tutelage
of John Webb, head of motor-circuit developments at

Brands Hatch and Oulton Park, Mark's career suddenly took off. He acquired two important sponsors,
Marlboro cigarettes and Playboy Toiletries For Men,
whose maroon and gold livery he displayed on his
racing overalls and car.

Mark's first major international race was in September 1979, when he competed in the seven-hour Hardie
Ferodo 1,000-km road race around the 6-km Mount
Panorama circuit in New South Wales, Australia. It
was also his first major spot of controversy. The trouble
started on 17 September at Heathrow, when he boarded
a JAL flight to Tokyo *en route* to Australia. 'Get the
Japan Airlines bag in the picture. They've given me
a good deal,' Thatcher snapped at photographers at
the airport. 'No airline bag, no pictures!' He travelled
first-class, paid for by Toyota cars, for whom Mark
was driving alongside Kiyoshi Misaki, the Japanese
national champion.[2]

However, it was the fact that the prime minister's son
was driving a Japanese car at a time when the British
motor industry was in crisis that caused a mini-furore.
'I was asked to drive for them by the chap who runs
the Toyota team because he thought I could drive, *not*
because of who I was – even though that gave them
a bonus,' responded Mark [his emphasis]. 'Let's face
it, if I hadn't been any good and I'd injured or killed
myself, that would not have been any good to them
at all.'[3] Unfortunately, it was not a successful début.
After twelve laps, despite leading their class, Mark
and his co-driver had to retire when the distributor
drive-gear broke.[4]

The Australian trip marked a turning point in the
way Mark dealt with people in business and social
situations. It was almost as if he had just discovered
the true potential of being the prime minister's only

son. One businessman who met him in Sydney and on other occasions said, 'He is the biggest user of people I have ever come across. When you met him at parties he would stop at nothing to hustle for money, mainly for his racing career. If you talked to him, he would never look at you. It was always at starboard or port to see who was more important. I remember being at a party once with him and I noticed he was looking across the room. He then said, "I say, she's rather nice. Why don't you ask her what she's doing later and see if she will have dinner with me later?" I told him to do his own chatting up. I wasn't his bloody pimp.'[5]

The relaunch of Mark Thatcher Racing coincided with a closer relationship with CSS Promotions Ltd, his PR and marketing agency. This was crucial, as Mark desperately needed sponsorship funding and that would be forthcoming only if he could guarantee media exposure for the sponsors via himself. The CSS arrangement was on an *ad hoc* basis. When Mark was offered a race he telephoned the agency's office and asked for promotional work to finance it. The plan was to plug Thatcher's name everywhere, with press packs and photo opportunities widely distributed. But in those days he was often short of money and he never paid CSS. When asked to settle invoices, he would reply, 'Oh, I'll deal with it when I get back from my trip.' But he never delivered and Steve Tipping had to pick up the bill.

CSS's strategy worked as the sponsorship offers flowed in, but Mark's chequered racing career was still impeded by funding problems. As a result he often seemed indiscriminate in his choice of benefactors. On 12 February 1980, he signed an agreement to promote the multinational Japanese textile company, Kanebo

Ltd. This included modelling the company's clothes,
except in Britain. In Europe and the Far East he was to
appear in press and billboard advertisements wearing
Kanebo products, mainly synthetic-suede garments.
One publicity photograph, taken in the south of France,
showed him wearing an imitation-antelope-skin coat
sold in Harrods. Another showed him posing alongside
Isabella Rossellini, daughter of the actress Ingrid
Bergman, in an artificial-leather racing suit.[6]

Mark also agreed to wear Kanebo's name and
symbol, embroidered in gold, on his racing overalls
and jacket. The company then used photographs of him
decked out in his racing gear in their advertisements,
which were released to the media. However, the British
people were deprived of seeing Mark's modelling work
unless it was directly related to his racing activities.

In return Kanebo provided 'personal sponsorship'
by paying him £10,000 to cover his living and travel
expenses while racing a Formula Three car at Japan's
Suzuka circuit and in Formula Atlantic at the Macao
grand prix.[7] The money was paid in a curious way,
according to Nigel Hart, then working for Mark and
Stephen Tipping. Hart recalls being with Tipping at
a Heathrow airport hotel waiting for Mark, who was
flying in from the south of France after posing for some
publicity photos. 'I remember Stephen picking up Mark
from the airport,' said Hart. 'He then came back to the
hotel with a travelling bag full of cash. We then drove
off to a Lloyds Bank branch in Blackwater, Surrey, and
converted the money into a banker's draft.'[8]

The Japanese sponsorship deal resulted in brief
but intense controversy. Gerald French, director of
the British Clothing Manufacturers' Federation, con-
demned it as 'shameful and shameless' and issued a
furious statement: 'Any kudos accruing to the family

because of Mrs Thatcher's position as Prime Minister
should surely be used to boost Britain and not Japan.
We are particularly upset because at this moment the
British clothing industry is struggling desperately just
to keep alive and could do with any helping hand held
out to us.' The National Union of Tailors and Garment
Workers, which had lost 13,000 jobs in the previous
five months, partly because of Japanese imports, took
a similar line. 'People in the public eye have a major
responsibility to Britain and this displays a distinct
lack of concern and even shortage of patriotism,'
said Neil Kearney, the union's head of research and
information.[9]

Thatcher responded by saying he had spent £1,000
over two months trying, in vain, to persuade British
companies to sponsor his driving. He had lobbied
Unipart, a subsidiary of British Leyland, then a publicly
owned corporation. 'I was swiftly shown the door,'
he said. So he turned to Kanebo. 'The Japanese
clothing industry got off their backsides and asked
me and put a very good package to me to do it,' he
added.[10] 'It is no good British industry bleating about
foreign sponsorship deals. They should get off their fat
backsides and do something about marketing their own
products. British companies are very bad at supporting
sport, particularly motor racing.'[11]

Mark did not consult the prime minister about
the Kanebo deal and she was not amused. On the
afternoon of the agreement's announcement, Monday,
12 February, Mark said confidently, 'I don't know what
my mother's attitude will be but she is not aggressive
about this sort of thing and will doubtless see my point
of view.'[12]

But when interviewed the next morning at the family
home in Flood Street, he had a different view: 'She

must be particularly upset about this and I wouldn't blame her. I'm sure she'll go up the wall. . . . She'll think I've made a big mistake and blame it all on me. She might tell me either to give up motor racing or leave Britain. I wouldn't be at all surprised if she said that. In that case, I'd leave Britain like a shot. I expected there might be a little fuss but I never expected people would be so vindictive. If the row doesn't blow over soon I'll leave this country for good. . . . My work as a management consultant is all abroad so it would be easy to move. It would also be advantageous for tax purposes. But I'd only leave because I've been hounded out of this country.'[13]

Within a few hours of his comments appearing in the press, Mark finally discussed the Kanebo deal with his mother. She told him the situation was not serious enough for him either to leave the country or to give up motor racing. But she suggested he should be more cautious in his remarks to journalists and not pose for photographs.[14] 'There has been no acrimony,' said Mark defensively. 'There were no big scenes and we agreed what is done is done. It is not her or my way of doing things to sit down and have big post-mortems. Family life with us is the bedrock of our existence.'[15]

Kanebo's motives were made crystal clear by their London representative. 'Our head office are delighted to have signed Mr Thatcher and are ready to bask in the reflected glory from the Prime Minister's son,' he said. 'He has no personal charisma so far as I am concerned. I wouldn't recognise him if I saw him.'[16]

In Japan the company seemed pleased to have hired him cheaply. 'Thatcher has more news value than a drunken singer or a playboy type image and since he's not a professional model we don't have to pay him as much,' said a Kanebo representative.[17]

Eventually Mark said '*sayonara*' to Kanebo, claiming that the use of his family name by the firm was 'in breach' of his agreement. He issued a curt two-sentence statement from 10 Downing Street: 'I will not now be driving in Japan as previously planned. I have now signed to drive for an all-British team based at Brands Hatch.'[18] 'I had to buy out the contract,' he said a year later. 'It cost me a very large amount of money – much more than the deal was worth in the first place. Looking back on it, it is possible I made an error of judgement. Certainly there could be no question of my driving for a Japanese car company as long as my mother is prime minister. That would be as out of place as a pork pie at a bar mitzvah.'[19]

At first glance the Kanebo episode was a disaster for Mark. He lost £20,000-worth of British sponsorship money immediately and the bad publicity hardly endeared him to the racing fraternity. It did not help matters that in almost every interview he said he would 'emigrate' if his critics did not 'lay off'.[20] However, publicity is vital in attracting sponsors, and ironically the Kanebo saga resulted in interest from new benefactors.

One offer that was taken seriously came from Paul Raymond, the millionaire strip-club-owner and publisher of soft-porn girlie magazines. On 14 February 1980, three days after his deal with Kanebo was announced, Raymond sent a telegram to Mark Thatcher's Chelsea home offering him £25,000 a year to join his new *Men Only* Racing for Britain team. 'I was amazed to hear that no English company would sponsor him,' said the Soho businessman and owner of Raymond's Revue Bar. 'I thought it was appalling that a young man of his education should have to go abroad for sponsorship rather than stay in Britain.' He added that Mark would not have to pose with naked women but his car would be required to advertise *Men Only* magazine on its side.[21]

The next day Mark Thatcher and Paul Raymond met for an hour at the Windmill Theatre, Soho, to discuss the deal. It was a bizarre venue for the prime minister's son to attend a business meeting. There were entertaining side-shows for the photographers and reporters waiting outside. As they gazed at the posters for the theatre's latest production – *Rip Off, The Erotic Experience* – they were kept busy by the locals, usually women in high-heeled brown leather boots, asking them if they would 'like some action'.[22]

Eventually Mark emerged from the theatre, smiling sheepishly, but he refused to say whether he had accepted the offer. 'I have nothing to say,' he declared. When asked what he thought his mother's reaction would be to his latest sponsorship solicitation, he replied, 'She's on tour at the moment.' Raymond was more forthcoming: 'As far as we are concerned, he is well worth sponsoring and we sincerely hope he will be a new James Hunt. I would like to boost Britain. . . . I think that all young guys should be given every opportunity to stay here.' Before driving Mark away in his chocolate-brown Rolls-Royce, Raymond added that the £25,000 'might well be worth more than that in the long run'.[23]

Another meeting was scheduled for the weekend and Raymond expected a contract to be signed on the Monday. But then the proposed *Men Only* deal was abruptly cancelled. Mark had spoken to John Webb and other officials at Brands Hatch, who did not approve. 'I was told that he has various contractual obligations with Brands Hatch and they are not in favour of the deal with me,' said Raymond. 'It looks as if they want to

keep in control of Mark themselves.'[24] Certainly, Mark
seemed happy dealing with the soft-porn king. 'I think
his [Raymond's] publicity machine handled the event
in a way that was in my best interests,' he said.[25]

Despite Mark's talk of a 'media witch-hunt' against
him,[26] the publicity did not harm his financial prospects. In the midst of the Kanebo row, John Cronony,
managing director of the clothes firm John Peter, said,
'We will pay him the money to further his racing career
if he will advertise our products. We would certainly
not get £10,000-worth of business through signing him
up. But it would be far better than the British textile
industry getting another kick in the teeth from foreign
competition.'[27]

Within a week Thatcher secured £40,000-worth of
sponsorship. His main benefactors were Kelly Girl
Service, the temp employment agency whose slogan
was 'If you're good – you're Kelly!', roller-skate
manufacturers Morris Vulcan Group, Shell Oil, Talbot
Motor Company, Wendy Wools and the Truck Development Company. This package was cleared with 10
Downing Street. Previously, the prime minister's office
would merely comment: 'It's nothing to do with us.
Mark Thatcher is a private individual not a member of
the Government.'[28] But now they were taking a close
interest, according to Brands Hatch officials.[29]

On 28 February 1980, Mark was able to call a press
conference at Brands Hatch to announce details of his
race schedule for the year. The invitation stated that
his 'all-British car racing programme was supported
entirely by British-based companies and incorporating
feminine interest'. But the media call was not without
tension. Mark was nervous and edgy on the public
platform. Journalists were told they could not ask
questions about the Japanese Kanebo deal. When a

BBC reporter did so, Mark refused to answer and
passed the microphone to John Webb, head of Brands
Hatch, who gave a bland response about nearly all
drivers seeking sponsorship. Mark did later talk about
his mother's attitude, but it was clear that mention of
foreign sponsorship of his racing career touched a raw
nerve.[30]

Nevertheless, it was an impressive seven-month
programme and Mark did seem to have resolved his
sponsorship problems. His colleagues at Brands Hatch
were also building up his chances. 'He's going to be
very good, if people will leave him alone to get on
with it,' said fellow driver Jackie Epstein. 'He's very
courageous, although tending a little bit at the moment
perhaps to try too hard.'[31] John Webb agreed: 'He's a
very aggressive driver with a great future ahead of him.
But he is not a potential world champion and nobody
here is trying to pretend he will be. We see him as a
very good long-distance driver who could eventually
win the Le Mans 24-hour race one day.'[32]

The prestigious Brands Hatch programme was a
real morale boost for Mark. But this served only to
make him even more self-conscious about his unique
proximity to the heart of government. His friends
were quick to notice the change in manner. One of
his marketing agents at the time, who liked Mark,
recalled telling him about a sponsorship proposition.
'That seems a good idea,' replied Mark. 'I shall have
to refer that to the Prime Minister.' 'No, you'll have
to refer that to your mother,' said his agent caustically,
who thought he needed bringing down to earth. This
exploitation of his new-found status was confirmed by
Mark himself. 'When we are alone together she's just
Mum, of course,' he said. 'But if I introduce anybody
to her, then I call her Prime Minister.'[33]

Others who knew him at the time were less charitable. 'The point about Mark,' said Nick Faure, a fellow racing driver who spent a lot of time with him in the early months of 1980, 'was that the only thing he could do was cash in on the fact that he was the prime minister's son, and he's been very successful because he had this ability to project himself in that way.'[34]

Faure would go for dinner at the Thatchers' house in Flood Street, Chelsea, and invite Mark down to his home in Aldershot. 'He admitted to me that he was going to make as much money out of being the prime minister's son as he possibly could,' recalled Faure. 'He used the words "cash in" and that is exactly what he has done.' His fellow racing driver claimed Mark was motivated almost entirely by money. 'The guy's got profit stamped all over his brain,' said Faure, 'but I have to say it was mainly his insecurity. He had a lonely upbringing and I actually have some sympathy for him because his mother was nearly always away and he must have had a difficult time growing up.'

Despite the successful relaunch at Brands Hatch, Mark Thatcher continued to seek sponsorship for his racing career. One method he used was to promise companies media coverage. 'He only got on the racing track because he could almost guarantee sponsors press and television coverage,' said Faure. 'He was a 100 per cent publicity-seeker. He thrived on the media and loved every minute of it.'

This obsession with the media was crystallized when Mark invited Faure over for dinner in March 1980 at the Thatcher family home in Flood Street, Chelsea. Faure was stunned when Mark proudly played him a home video compilation of every single television bulletin and newspaper clipping about himself, including those that merely mentioned his name in passing. 'He wanted to show me what a big publicity vehicle he was for sponsors,' said Faure, looking back on an incident rich in irony.

Like everyone else, Faure saw the advantage of using the prime minister's son to acquire sponsors. In April 1980, Mark agreed to be one of his drivers for that year's 24-hour Le Mans race and brought in Diagrit Diamond as one of the sponsors. 'The managing director was very excited about it,' recalled Faure. Mark, number 2 driver to the Italian Lella Lombardi, was confident about driving the Lola T380 with a Formula One engine. 'It is a very tough race and I have not entered into it lightly,' he said. 'I have taken advice from experienced drivers who have told me that I am up to it.'[35]

As it turned out Mark did not race for Faure and Le Mans was not a success. On Sunday, 15 June 1980, Mark lost control on the approach to a corner and the car spun into a crash barrier. Although his car was only slightly damaged, it could not be restarted and Mark had to retire from the race. The crash occurred despite fresh tyres being fitted to the car. 'I feel very tired, but I enjoyed the race enormously and hope to be back next year,' said Mark afterwards.[36]

There is some dispute among fellow drivers about Mark's racing ability. Nick Faure is dismissive. 'I would never have considered employing him if he wasn't the prime minister's son,' he said. 'He just wasn't good enough.' Others argue he was a capable and promising club racer, though never up to international standard. Brands Hatch's then chief press officer, Juliette Brindlay, was more benevolent. 'He was quick, courageous and didn't get into too much trouble,' she told the authors at Wentworth Golf Club, where she now works. 'The other drivers gave him some stick but he stood his ground. But he needed more track experience to make it big-time. He only raced one full season (1979–80) and I got on well with him and went to Chequers a couple of times. He always did what we asked of him on the PR front.'

According to Barrie Williams, who raced with him and was a friend on the circuit, Mark had a lot of potential but never devoted enough time to practice. 'He was always so busy doing other things with his business deals and travelling about.'[37] Even Mark acknowledged this. 'The trick is to think ahead,' he said in 1980. 'But my weakness has always been my concentration.'[38] A trait which held back Mark's racing career was his impatience. 'I got on very well with Mark and liked him,' said Barrie Williams, 'but he was very bad at taking advice, and acted as though he always knew best. To his credit, he was always in control when driving and he did listen when he was in trouble with the car. But he could also be very pompous and aloof, which didn't help because racing is all about team-work and getting on with people. He had this habit of looking down at people – quite literally. He would stand right in front of you and stretch himself up on to his toes so he was peering down at you.'[39]

Another respected veteran of the racing circuit who knew Mark well was Peter Jopp, secretary of the British Racing Drivers' Club. 'My feeling about Mark is that he was a good driver, a bit better than club standard but not international. But he was a user of people. He used his name to get sponsorship and would only be friendly with people when it suited him.' Jopp said that, once Mark's racing career picked up, suddenly he was too busy. 'Sorry, Peter, I haven't got time to talk,' he once said when approached by the driver. Then, when Jopp was commentating on the Macao grand prix, Mark literally followed him around because he was deemed important again.[40]

Despite qualified votes of confidence from some fellow drivers, Mark became prone to accidents. Soon after his mother entered 10 Downing Street he crashed at Mallory Park in Leicestershire and was pulled from the blazing wreckage of his car. During one meeting at Brands Hatch, he crashed twice in the same race and had to retire.[41] On another occasion he lost control on an S-bend and collided with the barriers. Then, at Hockenheim in West Germany, he had a lucky escape, receiving only minor scratches when his 140-mph Formula Super Vee car was wrecked during a practice run. But he was criticized by other competitors for driving too slowly on the racing line during the race.[42]

Mark always maintained his mother was happy about his racing. 'As long as I am not doing something incredibly stupid she is happy for me to pursue my motor racing interests,' he said.[43] But Margaret and Denis were not happy. She alluded to this: 'I am always a bit nervous when I know he is racing and quite honestly he often won't tell me about it for that reason. I have never been to see him race because I feel that he would be doubly anxious to win and might do something . . . You can't stop your children doing these things if they want to do them and you mustn't.'[44]

The truth was that Margaret secretly urged Mark's friends and associates to discourage his racing career. 'It was made abundantly clear to me that Mrs Thatcher was keen for Mark to be kept away from racing,' said a marketing agent who represented Mark in the early 1980s. 'She was frightened out of her wits about his racing, so Denis very discreetly asked his business friends not to sponsor him. Think about it. If it had been made known by Mrs Thatcher that she was supportive of his racing, the sponsorship money would have poured in.'[45]

This was borne out by the way Mark was plagued by sponsorship problems throughout his career. But he often saw fund-raising as a business challenge. In September 1980, he said that although he raced largely for fun he was also 'a commercial son of a bitch. I make it pay.'[46] So while he was a client of CSS, that was for media promotion and representation. When it came to the intricate world of persuading companies to sponsor him, Mark assumed he could do it himself because he believed he was a good businessman. 'I'm a good salesman, I have the gift of the gab,' he boasted. 'When I landed one particular account, even Mum couldn't believe it.'[47]

One of the businessmen Mark pursued for money was David Thieme, a flamboyant millionaire American oil trader who had access to the oil sheikhs in the Gulf and Brunei. Thieme also sponsored Team Lotus racing cars, Mark's favourite automobiles, and the two met regularly. The oil trader paid him for 'one-off projects' but they used each other for their respective contacts.

Thieme's main commercial vehicle was his company Essex Petroleum and he talked to Mark Thatcher about organizing a special event which would promote Essex and also Lotus. Mark agreed to help and offered to ensure the prime minister would appear. So, on Friday, 13 February 1981, Thieme hired the Royal Albert Hall for an extravagant promotional evening. The hall was transformed into a night-club, resplendent with silver palm-trees, and an extra gallery was installed in front of the theatre boxes as a cocktail area. The orchestra pit was turned into a stage with two grand prix racing cars

displayed on hydraulic lifts. Shirley Bassey provided
the musical entertainment, and even the food was
specially arranged. Top chef Roger Verger in Cannes
created the first course, which was flown to London,
British culinary wizard, Anton Mosimann, cooked the
main course and the Roux Brothers did the dessert. The
total cost, met by Thieme, was about £1 million.

The event was ostensibly to launch the new Lotus
Essex Elan sports car which was to compete against
Ferrari. But for Mark it was a perfect opportunity to
introduce potentially useful businessmen to the prime
minister. He had arranged for her to attend and was in
a very excited mood that evening as 400 businessmen,
mostly oil traders, packed into the Royal Albert Hall.
Mark strode around the hall in his white tuxedo with
a police hand-set intercom, barking orders to his three
police bodyguards ('Right, I'm coming over to the
car now'). This irritated the Special Branch officers
on duty and one of them removed the hand-set from
him, only to be even more frustrated when Mark later
retrieved it.

As the evening wore on Mark became more excited
about the arrival of the special guest, the prime
minister. 'Mummy is coming, Mummy is coming,'
he boasted to the guests. When she arrived towards
the end of the evening, her son ushered her upstairs
to meet David Thieme and Colin Chapman, chairman
of Lotus Cars (who was later accused of fraud over the
collapsed DeLorean sports car company).

Mark then introduced her to two oil spot businessmen, one from Tamoil, who had specifically asked
him to arrange the meeting. After chatting to Thieme
and Chapman, Margaret Thatcher and the two oilmen
retired to an outside room for a private talk. She
was also introduced to senior executives of Shell

and BP and Marc Rich, the Swiss oil trader (now wanted by the US government on massive tax fraud charges). The other businessman keen to talk to her was Mansour Ojjeh, the Saudi Arabian son of the owner of TAG, the French aviation and construction group that sponsored Frank Williams Racing. This meeting was also arranged by Mark. Margaret Thatcher stayed for an hour and a half and then returned to Downing Street before dinner, with just her bodyguard as no officials accompanied her – Downing Street said she was 'acting in a purely private capacity with her son'.

Mark's pay-off for his promotional work was to cut a deal with Lotus. In return for publicizing and promoting the luxury car, he was given a free Lotus plus expenses. The car was a blue turbo-charged Lotus Esprit sports car with red and silver markings. Then valued at £21,000, it was, Lotus at first claimed, 'a loan in return for promotional projects' on a month's trial basis. 'After that,' said Chapman, 'we'll see if we can come to some more permanent arrangement.'[48] In fact, Mark was allowed to keep the car and later bought it for only £11,000 – at least £10,000 less than the list price.

Six months later Mrs Thatcher again helped promote Lotus, courtesy of Mark. On 5 August 1981, accompanied by reporters and TV crews, she flew to Norwich airport in a private Cessna jet chartered by Colin Chapman. On the tarmac waiting for her was a silver and red Lotus Turbo Esprit, resplendent with black and gold John Player Special cigarette logos. She looked over the car while Chapman explained its refinements.[49] She took the wheel and drove along a deserted runway, accompanied by Chapman, and then returned to where her husband, Denis, was standing. 'This is the car that Mark drives,' she said. 'It's lively,

it's British and it's good for our exports.'[50] It was also
a wonderful free advertisement for Lotus, who were
indirectly paying her son.

Mark loved dashing around town in his Lotus, which
he considered 'the perfect car for London'.[51] But he
was still obsessed with motor racing and decided that
one way of keeping on the inside track was to ingratiate
himself with the Frank Williams team. Mark was used
as a fixer and facilitator, particularly on resolving
sponsorship problems for the prestigious team. He was
never paid a fee but in 1981 Frank Williams gave him
a Formula One racing car, a 170-mph FWO7C model,
similar to the one driven by the 1980 world champion,
Alan Jones. Then worth £100,000, at 1996 prices the
car would be valued at about £510,000. 'It was a gift
to curry favour,' said one of Frank Williams's closest
advisers. The car was later donated to Lord Montagu
of Beaulieu, for his motor museum.

Mark certainly responded to this inducement. He
was keen to help because he wanted to race at the top
level and saw Williams as his entrée. On one occasion
a government minister was astonished to be told by one
of his officials that 'a Mr Mark Thatcher is downstairs
and wants to deliver a letter'. The minister was furious
and refused to see him. 'I thought it was outrageous
that he was even in the building,' he recalled.

Like most Formula One racing teams, Williams was
afflicted by sponsorship troubles at that time. Since
1978 the team had been sponsored by the Saudi royal
family and a TAG subsidiary owned by the Ojjeh
family, who were close to the Saudis. The Ojjehs were
racing enthusiasts, attended all the grand prix meetings
and contributed some £6 million to Williams, while the
Saudi royals paid another £4 million.

But by the early 1980s the Ojjehs believed their

funding had achieved its purpose – the Williams team winning 50 per cent of all grands prix – so they moved to McLaren. This caused a mini-crisis in the Williams team and consultants were asked to find new sponsors. One of those targeted was Gallaher Ltd, the company that made Silk Cut cigarettes and sponsored Jaguar cars. It was decided to use the Thatcher family to solicit the funding, so Mark was approached. 'Yeah, sure, I'll do it,' he said. Two weeks later a meeting took place in the green reception room at 10 Downing Street, where Stuart Cameron, chief executive and chairman of Gallaher Ltd, met Mark and Denis Thatcher. The Thatchers asked whether Gallaher would sponsor Williams Racing, but Cameron explained this was not possible because of long-term financial commitments to Jaguar. Mark and Denis tried to persuade him but it was to no avail. Cameron, now a director of Saatchi & Saatchi, was uncomfortable about the meeting but refused to talk to the authors, except through Gallaher's public affairs office. He confirmed that the meeting took place, but would not comment on what benefits were offered to the company if they agreed to sponsor Williams Racing.

An experienced adviser to Williams on procuring sponsorship said that Cameron was more hard-headed than most. He told us Mark Thatcher was used by racing teams purely because people were susceptible to his name and influence: 'You have to remember that businessmen on the racing circuit – and I'm talking about chief executives and chairmen of major companies – are easily impressed by politicians and people close to power, and you could not get much closer than the son of the prime minister. So we used Mark to soften them up, but the problem for us was Mark's lack of sensitivity, and so when I introduced

him to businessmen I would never leave him alone
because he was about as subtle as a Chieftain tank.'

By the spring of 1981, Mark was marketing himself in
a broader way. He was still besotted with motor racing.
But he now believed he had a multi-faceted career.
When asked by the *Sunday Telegraph* what he actually
did [their emphasis], he replied: 'Basically speaking,
there are what I call three parts to Mark Thatcher.
There is Mark Thatcher the businessman. That takes
up 75 per cent of my time. . . . There is then what I
call Mark Thatcher the personality, which is split into
two parts. [The first] is my motor racing activities
and the things that come from that. The second part
of Mark Thatcher the personality, if you want, is the
promotional side whereby someone will come up to
me and say, "We would like you to do this. Come and
open a supermarket in Bury or something." '[52]

He was still on the books of CSS Promotions. But
that was always a loose arrangement and he now
seemed prepared to do almost any form of promotional
work. On the day of Prince Charles's wedding to
Lady Diana Spencer, Mark even gave an address on
'The Workings of the Parliamentary System' during a
special luncheon at the Café Royal. 'He will be giving
a speech on politics and parliamentary procedure in
this country and an insight into it,' said Philip Hughes,
director of VIP Entertainment, the organizers who had
signed him up.

Hughes refused to say how much Thatcher was paid
but said his contribution was part of a week-long series
of events, including an optional visit to a gaming club,
to celebrate the royal wedding. As tickets cost £1,995
each for the week (up to £3,500 for Americans), Mark's
fee would have been not inconsiderable.[53]

Thatcher was also keen on breaking into the American 'celebrity' marketing business. In March 1981, he signed a long-term £50,000-a-year contract with Prosurv Incorporated, a management promotional company based in Washington, DC. Run by Donald Dell, the former US Davis Cup team captain, Prosurv represents the commercial interests of sports stars. 'Our function is to help them earn as much as possible,' said Francis Craighill, one of their partners, 'and to conserve as much as possible. We put them on an allowance, develop a budget, pay their bills, analyse their investments, advise them on endorsements and offer assistance from A to Z.'[54]

The company was not reticent about why they were keen to represent Mark. 'He's promotable in the sense that he's a motor racer and he is the son of Mrs Thatcher,' said Stephen Disson, the vice-president responsible for marketing and special events. 'He's a rather bright and aggressive person and we like that.'[55] Another Prosurv executive was more explicit: 'Our job is to find him work. Because of his background he is a highly marketable commodity. There is no doubt that his name and the position his mother holds make people want him to promote their products.'[56]

Mark's first assignment was to promote and find outlets in Britain for American sportswear, mainly tennis outfits. He also appeared on television in the USA talking about how he wanted to break into motor racing and was paid £5,000 by NBC TV to commentate on the Las Vegas grand prix.[57]

Although it was a short-lived contract, Prosurv Inc did obtain one lucrative commission for Thatcher. This involved appearing in television commercials in Japan promoting Cutty Sark 12, a brand of Scotch whisky. As part of the advertising campaign, he also posed for photographs which appeared in Japanese newspapers and on posters, endorsing the whisky. The fee was estimated to be in the region of £40,000 but Mark denied it was that much. 'No, I'm not being paid anything like that,' he said. 'I mean, that is just light years away from the truth. But it is important to remember that it is a British product.'[58] A difference between this and his previous Japanese sponsorship deal – with the clothing firm Kanebo – was that this time the prime minister was consulted beforehand and gave her approval of the whisky promotion.[59]

Despite his mother's endorsement of selling Scotch to the Far East, Mark remained a source of anxiety within the family. It was his tendency to take money indiscriminately or consider commercial propositions from virtually anyone that caused most concern. Denis, with his sharp business antennae, was acutely aware of it from day one but kept quiet. His twin sister Carol also identified the problem, but was more prepared to refer to it publicly, if only obliquely. 'We get on quite well but we aren't particularly close,' she said. 'I don't do many "Child of the Prime Minister" things like he does. . . . Mark has done some things which were *bound* to land him in the papers [her emphasis], and I do think, "You silly boy, you're giving them the perfect ammunition." But what can I do? He's not keen on sisterly advice. If I ring up and tell him to pipe down, it's unlikely to be well received.'[60]

Lost in the Desert

For a brief but emotionally fraught period Denis and

Carol Thatcher's apprehensiveness about Mark's business activities was forgotten. Instead their anxiety was focused on an event which put him firmly in the public eye but also encapsulated the intensity of Margaret's relationship with her son – the six days when he was missing in the Sahara desert.

On New Year's Day 1982, Mark and his highly experienced co-driver, thirty-eight-year-old Anne-Charlotte Verney, set off in their white Peugeot 504 to take part in the Paris-to-Dakar motor rally. Competing against 392 other drivers, they aimed to complete the gruelling 6,200-mile journey in about twenty days. However, by the time Mark and his crew reached the Sahara desert a week later they had run into serious trouble. Their car's back axle snapped during the sixth leg of the race and they failed to turn up for a checkpoint at Timeiaouine, at the southern tip of Algeria. Then the organizers lost radio contact with the car and Mark, Charlotte and their mechanic, Jean Garnier, were stranded in the African wilderness, forty-three miles north of Timeiaouine.[61]

At first it was claimed they had been spotted by reconnaissance planes and directed by nomadic tribesmen to safety. But these were false reports and Mark and Charlotte remained missing. By the end of the fourth day, Monday, 11 January, the prime minister was 'very concerned' as there was 'no trace' of her son or his crew and desert conditions could be very harsh. But then an Algerian news agency report that evening stated Mark had been rescued by helicopter. She even received a telegram saying he was 'safe'.[62] Relief turned to despair later that evening, though, when a two-line telex arrived, informing her that Mark was 'officially still missing' and the 'rescue' information applied to a different competitor. The prime minister

later said her 'heart stopped' when she read that
telex.[63] She immediately telephoned Algeria to ask
for an official search.[64]

The rescue operation was hampered by two natural
factors – heavy sandstorms and the barren and mountainous location, with no telephone lines for hundreds
of square miles. It was also slow and dominated by
confusing and conflicting media stories. Margaret
Thatcher became even more worried on the fifth day,
Tuesday, 12 January, when Derek Howe, her political
secretary, came up to the Downing Street flat and told
Denis and Carol: 'There's very bad news. Mark is
still missing.'[65] Troops and aircraft then joined the
operation. But her state of mind was not helped by
French reports about political abductions and Mark
being kidnapped by a guerrilla gang, with 'possible
Libyan links'.[66]

However, Mark was in 'no serious or immediate danger', according to Thierry Sabine, the rally organizer.
'The desert is more inhabited than generally thought,'
he said, 'and this time of year the climate is reasonable.
Their car carries enough provisions and water to allow
them to survive for a long time.'[67] The crew had
also made a makeshift tent, in which they sheltered.
'Luckily, they did not try to go off into the desert,'
said Ben Strachan, British ambassador in Algeria.[68]
Mark later remarked that he passed the time by reading
the same book twice – *The Fifth Horseman*, a thriller
about a plot by Colonel Gaddafi to blow up New York
City with an atomic bomb – and playing solitaire with
pebbles.[69]

Still, Margaret was increasingly distraught at the
absence of positive action and news. On the sixth day
it arrived. Early that morning she received a telephone
call from Sir Hector (now Lord) Laing, then chairman

of United Biscuits and former joint treasurer of the Tory Party. Sir Hector was concerned and offered to lend his private jet so that Denis could fly out to the Sahara. Margaret was delighted and within hours the twin-engine eight-seater Beechcraft KingAir 200 aircraft was ready. Her husband was in the bath at the time and was astounded to hear his wife banging on the bathroom door shouting, 'Get out of the bath, Denis. The plane's there – you must go now.' Denis wearily bundled himself out of the 10 Downing Street flat, still dripping wet, and made his way to the airport at Denham, Buckinghamshire.[70]

While Denis was flying out to Algiers and then on to the oasis town of Tamanrasset with Ben Strachan, the British ambassador, Margaret was, understandably, extremely distressed. She had desperately wanted to accompany her husband to Algeria but was persuaded to stay in London. At midday she arrived at the Imperial Hotel, Russell Square, for a meeting of the Federation of Small Businesses, accompanied by Ian Gow, her parliamentary private secretary.

Waiting reporters noticed how drawn her face was, and her red eyes indicated she had been crying. 'I am afraid there is no news,' she said. 'I am naturally very concerned.' She walked into the foyer but broke down and sobbed for thirty seconds, her head low. Tears were streaming down her face as she leaned on the shoulder of one of her personal detectives. After recovering her composure she walked towards the reception room. She broke down again, stumbling slightly, but then quickly composed herself and delivered her speech. It was the first time Margaret Thatcher had shown such emotion in public and indicated the extent of her anxiety.[71]

Meanwhile, Denis had arrived in the Algerian desert. He had flown out there, according to Barrie Gill,

Mark's marketing and PR agent, to help and 'to stir things up' among the search organizers.[72] But when Denis telephoned his wife from the search HQ that evening to report back, there was not much news. He told her the French and Algerian air forces had called a temporary halt to the search as darkness set in, but would reconvene at first light. Denis also said the operation was plagued by false unofficial reports of sightings. The British embassy was reliant on the rally organizers for accurate information but they had drawn a blank – as had the Algerian authorities.

In London the next morning Margaret Thatcher was waiting by the telephone in 10 Downing Street with her daughter Carol. 'It's all I *can* do,' said Mark's twin sister [her emphasis].[73] Margaret continued to work on her ministerial red boxes but would suddenly look up and say: 'I wonder if there is any news.'[74] But they did not have to wait long. At 11.30 the next morning, Thursday, 14 January 1982, Mark and his crew were found by a Hercules aircraft in Taoumdert, 50 km off the rally route. They were safe and well, standing by their Peugeot waving a shirt to attract attention.

That afternoon Mark and Charlotte were flown to Tamanrasset to be reunited with a delighted Denis.[75] He then announced the discovery on the lunch-time television news, watched by a much-relieved wife and daughter. 'When he was found I just felt on top of the world,' Margaret said later.[76] When Mark met journalists he looked relatively fit and well, if scruffy and tired. He shrugged off the six-day ordeal with 'Why the fuss?' and claimed to be 'simply staggered' by the media interest in his plight.

Back home, officials in 10 Downing Street braced themselves for a vintage Mark Thatcher performance.

It was a mixture of bravado, condescension and insensitivity. 'We were not lost,' he announced at the Tahat Hotel. 'We knew where we were, although we weren't where we were supposed to be. I wasn't frightened at all. I would have liked a couple of ham sandwiches now and again, but we were all right for water. . . . We could have gone on for another 12 days. We had enough water, food and no problems at all. I planned on an eight-day stay. Then, when the rally plane didn't see us, I changed to a fortnight plan.'[77] As he spoke Charlotte Verney, his co-driver, was being led shakily into a local hospital. 'All she's suffering from,' said Mark as she passed by, 'is air sickness and I think she drank too much water.'[78]

Foreign Office and 10 Downing Street officials winced at Mark Thatcher's absence of tact and gratitude to those who had rescued him. So the next day a member of the prime minister's staff telephoned Barrie Gill, Mark's PR agent and joint head of CSS Promotions, at his Strand office. Gill was asked to get down to Heathrow airport and oversee Mark's press conference. There was some concern, he said, about his client's injudicious remarks and Gill was asked to advise Mark to be more diplomatic in his public comments.

The PR agent immediately drove down to Heathrow, just in time to meet his client as he arrived on the president of Algeria's personal jet. Gill accompanied Mark off the aircraft and minutes later flanked Mark during his press conference. The tone and content of his remarks were amazingly transformed. Gone was the arrogance. Suddenly there was conciliation, almost humility. 'I am delighted to be back,' said Mark, 'and very sorry that a lot of trouble has been caused. I am only now becoming aware of the amount of concern that has actually been pointed towards me. I am simply amazed and embarrassed.'[79]

As for Anne-Charlotte Verney, she naturally got to know Mark quite well during the six days they were stranded in the desert. 'He likes being the son of the Prime Minister,' she reflected. 'He knows it helps him to do things he could never do otherwise. Mark has given in to the temptation of doing too much too soon – because it's easy for him as Margaret Thatcher's son.'[80]

She was also amazed at Mark's relaxed disposition. 'He was very nervous when the car first broke down,' she said, 'but when he realised we could do nothing about it he accepted the situation and made the best of it. He was always very calm and collected and organised everything. We slept 15 hours a day to conserve energy, then we would read. After two days I began to get worried inside. I began to think we might not make it but Mark made me feel safe. He was so confident.'[81]

It was this curiously laid-back attitude that increased speculation among racing experts and promoters that Mark exploited the 'lost-in-desert' saga as a publicity stunt. One senior executive of CSS Promotions, Thatcher's PR agency, believes his client may have taken advantage of the situation to create publicity for his beleaguered racing career. Certainly, it is hard to escape the irony of increased sponsorship interest after the incident.

There are also indications that Mark was not completely stranded. For example, there was a curious incident when he was actually located on the fourth day of the search by Michael Bosi, a Swiss driver, but would not move. 'I got the impression young Thatcher was panicking,' said Bosi. 'He ignored my advice that they should get into my van and insisted on staying behind with his broken-down car.'[82] But it was Mark's remarkably composed attitude that led some to claim that he was far from lost and knew exactly the publicity implications of what he was doing.

Mark was eventually reunited with his mother at Chequers on the evening of his arrival. Margaret asked him not to continue his motor-rallying exploits. However, despite the enormous anxiety and emotional stress inflicted on her, Mark appeared reluctant to give up cross-country motor rallying. When asked about his future, he replied, 'I am contracted to drive cars next year and that is what I shall do.'[83] He later repeated his intention to continue rallying, much to Denis's irritation. 'I expect he'll get on with whatever he wants,' said Denis, 'but I hope it won't be rallying.'[84] Carol Thatcher agreed: 'I must say I hope this is the last of Mark's motor racing. Having seen the strain Mum has suffered this week, she can do without the additional hassle.'[85] Her twin brother was annoyed by this and told her to 'stick to her own business and he would keep to his'.[86]

As for Margaret, she was characteristically reluctant to lay down the law. 'I am not that kind of mother,' she said. 'My son is grown up and in charge of his own life. You can't have grown men and women on their mothers' apron strings.'[87] She was also happy to pay part of the costs of the rescue operation, which involved five Algerian aircraft, two helicopters, three French aircraft and over twenty cars. Margaret's contribution was to pay the hotel bills of her son, her husband and the British ambassador in Tamanrasset.[88]

Sponsor Me

After the Sahara desert débâcle, and much to the consternation of his family, Mark Thatcher was keen to resume his racing career. Within a week of returning to London, he announced plans to drive for the Goodwin Racing Team in the British Formula One championships at Brands Hatch. This was one of the most dangerous and difficult circuits because of the high speeds reached, often more than 200 mph. Experts also expressed surprise at the news because of Mark's inexperience at that level (he had not even driven a Formula One car before). Also access to Formula One racing is very restricted and usually a driver needs to qualify through the junior ranks.[89]

However, Mark had been given a free car by Frank Williams and so felt confident about making the grade. He made this clear when he sent out a detailed file about his ambitious plans to 600 companies who might be interested in sponsoring him: 'I think it's reasonable to say my future motor sport activities will take place on circuits rather than the rough stuff'.[90]

The Thatcher family were again not pleased. Margaret let it be known, non-attributably, to political correspondents that she was 'not happy but accepts she could not dissuade him.'[91] Carol went on the record: 'Everyone knows her feelings about the dangers of motor racing.'[92] Unperturbed, Mark set off in pursuit of corporations who would collectively or individually sponsor him for the £250,000 needed for his Formula One campaign.

One of the people he approached was a wealthy

Swiss businessman with a string of computer companies. In early 1982, the businessman was surprised to receive a dispatch postmarked 10 Downing Street, London SW1. It was a letter from Mark asking for an introduction to the Swiss commercial community. At first the businessman was reluctant to co-operate but as the request came from the son of the British prime minister, he agreed to host a lunch of bankers at his home in Zurich.

As the lunch progressed this Swiss executive became increasingly uneasy at what he saw as Thatcher's commercial opportunism. Mark came straight to the point. 'I need £30,000 for sponsorship,' he blurted out. The bankers looked at each other, embarrassed and said nothing. 'Does your mother know you're seeking sponsorship money?' one asked. 'Of course, she knows,' Mark replied briskly. 'I've got six years to make my fortune and I'm bloody well going to do it.'[93]

The businessman politely declined to fund his racing activities. 'Oh, it doesn't matter,' Thatcher responded. 'One of the others I'm seeing here in Switzerland will give me the money.' He then handed his Swiss host a list of people he was meeting in Zurich. This enraged the businessman because he felt he had been tricked into meeting Mark Thatcher. Bristling with anger, he telephoned all those on the list and advised them not to give the young entrepreneur any financial backing. Consequently, the prime minister's son left Switzerland empty-handed.

Two weeks later the financier invited a British friend to stay at his Zurich home. Almost as soon as the visitor arrived, he was greeted with: 'I recently had lunch with the most objectionable young man I have ever met.'

'Who was it?'

'Mark Thatcher, the son of your prime minister.'[94]

Such an approach hardly endeared Mark to potential financial backers and so his corporate canvassing rapidly ran off course. He was scheduled to drive his Williams car for the Goodwin team on 9 April 1982 at Oulton Park, and on 12 April at Brands Hatch. But this arrangement was cancelled just two days before the first race because the sponsorship money never materialized. Some cash was acquired but not nearly enough to cover their costs.

Ivor Goodwin, who hoped to manage Mark's Formula One career, was mystified as to the reason. 'The recession has something to do with it,' he said. 'But I get the feeling the companies who were canvassed were very nervous as to what the public were going to say about it. We have had one or two bitter blows. One or two companies we thought were going to join in the sponsorship have left us high and dry. I just can't comprehend it at all. We had got so much television coverage lined up – I can't believe there are companies who could let so much publicity slip through their fingers.'[95]

Perhaps one reason was Mark's public comments on the performance of British companies. In March 1982, at the height of the economic recession and two days after the budget, he declared: 'If you sit back on your big arse and say "It's no good, we've been hit by the recession," then it's a self-fulfilling prophecy. I would actually decry the notion that there is a recession. I mean, the people we do business with are only interested in work-rate and results. If you put in the necessary work-rate and have the commitment to succeed, then you will succeed, no matter what the business environment is. It's not difficult to sell British products overseas – it just comes down to work-rate.

All the people who work for me are doers. They're very well paid and they perform. It's as simple as that. If they don't, then we have a look at it.'[96]

British industry was not amused at being lectured by the twenty-eight-year-old 'marketing consultant'. Unfazed, Mark continued his search for financial benefactors. But by late 1982, it was clear that the quest was fruitless. So he tried a different approach. As well as lobbying for cash, he attempted to persuade companies who were already sponsors of motor sport to allow him to join their racing team.

One businessman he set his sights on was Jerry D. Dominelli, whose investment advisory company, J. David, sponsored the Porsche racing team of British driver John Fitzpatrick. Mark had heard about the Californian financier from Fitzpatrick and was eager to meet him. So in January 1983, he invited Dominelli, based in La Jolla, near San Diego, to London. Over dinner they discussed the possibility of Mark's driving for the Fitzpatrick team. They could not agree terms but the investment adviser clearly enjoyed the meeting, during which they talked about Margaret Thatcher. 'Mark has a very strong fondness for his mother,' said Dominelli. 'We discussed his relationship [with her] and the pressure she was under during the Falklands crisis.'[97]

Dominelli, also known as 'Captain Money', was a typical example of the kind of businessman with whom Mark was associating in the early 1980s. At the time of his meeting with Thatcher, Captain Money was being investigated for embezzlement and theft. Since 1981 he had been running an investment racket called a Ponzi scheme. 'In a Ponzi scheme, investors' money is not invested in anything,' said Donald Bauder, author of a book on Dominelli. 'The early investors are paid off with money coming in from later investors. Thus the survival of the scam depends on the continuing recruitment of new investors. But with each new investor, the scheme goes further into the hole long-term. The roof has to cave in at some point.'98

Dominelli told potential customers that he could earn them a steady 40 to 50 per cent annual return on their investment on the foreign currency market. But the roof collapsed and the scam went horrendously wrong. Captain Money had spent much of the investors' funds on furs, fast foreign cars, jewellery and high living. The money disappeared.

In February 1984, a month after meeting Mark Thatcher, the robbed investors sued Dominelli to place his company in bankruptcy. Two months later Captain Money fled to the Caribbean island of Montserrat, claiming he would pay back the money from there. Instead, things got worse. In late April 1984, he was arrested for illegal possession of firearms and sent back to San Diego for prosecution. He was convicted of fraud and sentenced to twenty years in prison. Two years later his crimes were compounded when he was found guilty of illegally channelling company money to fund a political campaign.99 Jerry Dominelli now languishes in a southern California jail.

For Mark Thatcher, lobbying Dominelli was almost a last-gasp attempt to break into the big-time racing scene. Much to the annoyance of his family, he even returned to rally driving. He competed in one of the world's most dangerous cross-country motor races, the Baja 1000, an arduous 935-mile trip across the cactus-dotted Mexican desert.

A police helicopter, spotter plane and high-speed car were put on alert just for Mark and he did not disappoint them. As darkness fell early in the race,

Thatcher and his co-driver went missing. An all-night 'priority alert' was ordered by the rally organizer, Ric Miller. 'We felt it was necessary because this is the most horrendous part of the course,' said Miller. 'It enables other drivers and checkers to be watchful for someone lost or in trouble. We have no idea why Thatcher and his co-driver got out of touch.'[100] After eight hours Mark was discovered arriving at a designated check-point in his two-ton Dodge pick-up truck. He eventually completed the course, but later said it was his last rally.

The Baja 1000 was effectively the end of his racing career. Its death knell was due to his mother's increasing anxiety about safety and also to insufficient sponsorship. But he did make a successful, if brief, comeback in March 1988 when he came fourth in the European Touring Car championships. Driving a 150-mph BMW M3, he was praised by the professional drivers in the race. 'I'm very pleased, although I didn't drive as well as I can but then that's to be expected,' said Mark. 'I will be celebrating with a shower. I don't drink much. I will also be phoning my mother. I phone her every Sunday night without fail from wherever I am in the world.'[101]

Despite an accomplished fourteen-race series with BMW, Mark retired from competitive racing six months later. He finally came to realize that he could not step up a grade from touring cars. But the real reason was the amount of time racing consumed. As the Thatcher decade wore on and Mark's business interests blossomed, he simply could not devote the time to his favourite hobby. The premier's son had other things on his mind.

Chapter Four

Batting for Thatcher

'Unlike my brother, I have never made swags of cash.'

Carol Thatcher, *The Lady*, September 1996

In February 1981, Sayid Ahmad Halifah Suwaydi, a senior United Arab Emirates diplomat and former foreign minister, was asked by Mark Thatcher to Sunday lunch at the prime minister's weekend retreat at Chequers. Mark told him not to inform the Foreign Office or his embassy about the visit or to use his official car. 'This lunch must be kept strictly confidential,' he said. This was most unusual and troubled Suwaydi. When he arrived at Chequers, he was greeted by Margaret Thatcher and was surprised to find only three places set at the lunch-table – for himself, the prime minister and Mark Thatcher.

Over lunch Mrs Thatcher was keen to discuss business, not politics. Among various commercial projects she pressed him about was an order British Aerospace was seeking, to sell Hawk aircraft to Abu Dhabi, one of the member states of the United Arab Emirates (UAE). After the meal she withdrew and left him alone with her son. Mark immediately began talking about an oil deal he was involved in brokering between British Petroleum (BP) and the Abu Dhabi National Oil Company (ADNOC). BP had an agreement to supply crude oil to ADNOC and wanted to renew the contract and also to increase the supply by 5,000 barrels a day. Mark was representing BP's interests, without their official knowledge, on behalf of a third party – an oil trader based in the Bahamas. As they sat in the prime minister's official residence, Thatcher insisted he wanted prompt action on the contract, as he was working under commission – a potential $2 million spread over one year.

Suwaydi responded that he would need instructions from his government before such decisions could be implemented, as they were beyond his authority and competence. When he returned to his hotel, the Churchill Intercontinental in Portman Square, the diplomat was uncomfortable about Thatcher's approach. He was a politician not a businessman and felt he was being used. But he reported back to Sheikh Zayed bin Sultan al-Nahayan, Ruler of Abu Dhabi and president of the UAE. A source in the UAE presidential court said Sheikh Zayed was surprised by Mark's request. But he was keen to help Margaret Thatcher and recommended that ADNOC back the BP course of action. Zayed then delegated Sheikh Sorour, president of his royal court, to inform ADNOC that they should sign BP's new agreement because 'Mark Thatcher was behind it'.

A few weeks later Mark flew to Abu Dhabi, capital of the UAE, with Jamil Amyuni, a Lebanese businessman who was working with Mark on the deal despite also representing Cementation International in the Middle East. They booked into the Sheraton Hotel and prepared to continue negotiations. The next day Mark arrived for meetings with ADNOC officials with a present, a portrait of his mother in a silver frame.

The UAE delegation were keen to please, as they saw it, the British prime minister, and agreed to BP's renewal application for the extra oil supply. But the deal went sour when the BP executive arrived in Abu Dhabi to sign the contract and discovered Thatcher's involvement. The BP representative had flown in at almost the same time and even stayed on the same floor at the Sheraton Hotel. But he was unaware of Thatcher's presence.

At a meeting to finalize the details, a senior ADNOC director asked, 'Where is Mark Thatcher?' 'What's he got to do with it?' replied the shocked BP executive. 'I was told this deal was for Mark Thatcher,' said the director. 'I am sorry, we will have to adjourn this meeting until tomorrow because I know nothing about this,' said the BP executive. He then returned to the Sheraton and telephoned BP's head office, who instructed him to cancel the contract and return to London.

The aborted oil deal was the beginning of a long and prosperous relationship between Mark Thatcher and the Gulf states. It is an area of the Middle East where business is conducted on the basis of trust and connections, through personal and family introductions rather than through orthodox Western commercial practices; where the ruling Gulf families prefer to deal with brokers, middlemen and heads of state rather than being lobbied directly by grey-suited corporation executives; and where commission fees, based on a percentage of the contract's value, are paid through locally owned subsidiary companies.

It is a commercial culture that is ideally suited to the way Mark Thatcher likes to do business – secretly, using intermediaries and relying on political dynasties rather than being employed on a permanent basis by a company seeking a contract. The United Arab Emirates (incorporating Abu Dhabi, Ajman, Dubai, Sharjah and Umm al-Qaiwain), Oman, Kuwait and Qatar are also geared to the business sectors that thrive and rely on the use of agents – oil, construction and arms. It was an environment in which the prime minister's son could thrive.

Mark Thatcher's original entrée to the Gulf was an informal meeting just after the 1979 general election with Victor Matthews, then chief executive of the conglomerate Trafalgar House plc. Matthews, a former property speculator, was a close friend and fervent supporter of Margaret Thatcher. As chairman of Fleet Publishing International, the Trafalgar House subsidiary which owned Express Group newspapers, he was in a key position to cheer-lead her to victory. His papers, the *Daily Express*, London *Evening Standard*, *Daily Star* and *Sunday Express*, led the vociferous campaign to elect Margaret Thatcher. What's more, Trafalgar House paid £40,000 into Tory Party coffers in 1979 and organized a celebration lunch for the new prime minister at the Ritz Hotel on the morning of her triumph. The following year Victor Matthews became Baron Matthews of Southgate.

So when the Trafalgar House boss arrived at 19 Flood Street, Chelsea, to see Margaret Thatcher, he was well-disposed to help her. After he had chatted to the new premier, her son told Matthews about his work on two construction deals. 'I am looking for contractors,' he said. 'Do you know any companies that might be interested in two contracts I am involved in?' Matthews said he would arrange a meeting with William (now Sir William) Francis, chairman of Cementation International Ltd, Trafalgar's overseas construction subsidiary. Francis was told that Mark Thatcher 'needed some business experience' and 'wanted to get into the export side of industry'.[2]

On the basis of Lord Matthews's introduction, Mark was hired as a consultant to Cementation International Ltd. In early 1980, a contract was drawn up with Thatcher's company, Monteagle Marketing (London) Ltd, and Mark was placed on the payroll with a fixed retainer plus commission. He was immediately assigned to two highly influential Cementation executives – Jamil Amyuni and Ghassan Shaker – who were to play a vital role in helping to accumulate the first major instalment of Thatcher's gold.

Jamil Chafic Amyuni, the company's marketing director in the Middle East since 1967, was responsible for securing new contracts. Amyuni, who has a Lebanese passport and British citizenship, took Mark under his wing and educated him in the ways and means of doing business in the Arab world. He arranged for the keen consultant to accompany him on overseas trips and introduced him to key operators in the region.

But it was soon apparent that Mark was being used as an introductory agent and influence-peddler rather than for his commercial acumen, according to former Cementation executives. Jamil Amyuni dealt with the middle managers and ministers, but Mark was able to get them to see the heads of state, according to a former senior director. 'He was helpful to us as a door-opener and gave us an extra lever to win contracts, but I would not have hired him as a corporate manager. He just did not have the business ability.'

The two worked very closely together and Amyuni met the prime minister on more than one occasion.

He was introduced to her by Mark during a constituency dinner in the London Inter-Continental Hotel in October 1980, held to celebrate Margaret Thatcher's twenty-one years as the MP for Finchley. He was also a dinner guest at Chequers and 10 Downing Street, accompanied by Mark. Mrs Thatcher later admitted encountering Amyuni but only privately. 'I have not met him in any official capacity,' she said.[3] A 10 Downing Street statement confirmed the meetings but added that 'no business was discussed'.

Amyuni, who now runs a string of property companies and retains a UK base, refused to speak to the authors. 'I have nothing to say,' he remarked. 'I'm not going to talk about it. There's no point.'

Mark Thatcher's other mentor at Cementation, Ghassan Ibrahim Shaker, was a Saudi national with a Turkish father. He was educated at Victoria College, Alexandria, Egypt, at the same time as King Hussein of Jordan and the two became good friends. Of the middlemen who broker arms and construction contracts in the Gulf, Shaker is the most civilized. 'At least you can talk to Ghassan,' Sayyid Tarik, the Sultan's uncle, remarked to a security adviser to the sultan. 'He's a gentleman. The others are shits.'

Shaker is impeccably connected. His brother, Ghazi, has represented King Hussein on major defence contracts, notably the abortive attempt to buy Tornados. Ghassan Shaker is also close to Kamal Adham, former head of Saudi Arabia's intelligence services. On the commercial front, he has a controlling stake in the Oman subsidiary of Joannou and Paraskevaides (Overseas) Ltd, owned by George Paraskevaides, a Greek businessman whose J and P Group is the largest construction company in the Middle East and was a major sub-contractor to British Aerospace on the Al Yamamah arms deal with Saudi Arabia.

Shaker played a vital supporting role in the acquisition of Thatcher's gold as the 51 per cent shareholder of Cementation (Saudi Arabia) Ltd, a joint-venture company with Cementation International. It was as Cementation's agent in Saudi, that he was asked by a Trafalgar House executive to get Mark Thatcher 'on board' for major contracts. Shaker agreed and so in early 1980 Mark went to see him at his apartment at 17 Grosvenor Square, Mayfair, to discuss potential deals in the Middle East.

The focus of their attention was the oil-rich state of Oman, which lies in a key strategic position on the Gulf, close to the Straits of Hormuz. By 1980 its oil revenue was 44.4 million Omani rials a year. But little of this wealth trickled down to its one million people. Instead, much of the money – at least 50 per cent – was spent on military equipment for its armed forces. This was largely due to the country's strategic importance. Oman has the ports, airfields and radar to make it a very useful base for any British or American force keen to protect the lucrative oilfields.[4] For many years Oman was also faced with an aggressive southern neighbour in communist South Yemen.

As any instability in the country could have serious repercussions for the West, the British have always retained a strong presence. Since 1798 they have been patrons of the sultans, intervening whenever required to prop up the regime. In the 1960s SAS officers were used to crush a rebellion in the southern province of Dhofar. British military intelligence officers, or 'advisers' as they were officially described, were omnipresent in the sultan's inner circle. In 1970 they were instrumental in the *coup d'état* in which the current sultan overthrew his despotic father. At that time there were at least 600 British soldiers in the Omani armed forces, most under contract but some on secondment.[5]

The Sultan of Oman, Qaboos bin Said, is heavily dependent on the United Kingdom and HMG for his throne and wealth. Hence, any approach by the Thatchers would be given a friendly reception. Ghassan Shaker, who had known Sultan Qaboos since the early 1970s, realized this and argued Oman was a good business prospect but short of cash. So they decided to consult Sheikh Zayed, president of the United Arab Emirates and the most influential figure in the Gulf.

Zayed was a very close ally of Margaret Thatcher and it was during this period that she helped her son in the Gulf in a way which could benefit his business career. On 8 November 1980, she provided a hand-written and signed letter of introduction, underneath her photograph, for Mark to Sheikh Zayed: 'I have asked my son to convey to you my personal message of warm regards and good wishes.' The note, which we have in our possession, is evidence of how the prime minister effectively assisted her son's commercial interests.

Armed with this letter, Mark flew to Lausanne, Switzerland, to meet the sheikh. 'Go to Qaboos,' said Zayed, 'and ask him what he wants, and I will finance it from my purse.' When Mark approached the Sultan of Oman on behalf of Sheikh Zayed and Cementation he was given a cordial welcome. But the cordiality was tinged with caution and scepticism. Qaboos distrusted Zayed and did not believe the funds would be forthcoming. Mark was conciliatory and asked him at least to consider the proposal. 'Well, we have designs for a new sports stadium,' said the

sultan, 'so that is something that would interest us.'
Thatcher returned to Abu Dhabi to report back. Sheikh
Zayed disapproved of the choice and said he preferred
a project that would benefit the Omani population. The
discussion ended with the sheikh telling Mark, 'They
[the Omanis] don't need a sports stadium. They need
a university.'

At first Sultan Qaboos was resistant to the idea of
a university because he resented Zayed's inferences
about his regime. But Cementation International Ltd,
through Mark Thatcher and Ghassan Shaker, managed
to change Qaboos's mind by lobbying his advisers. The
sultan was won over because it was a prestige project
and had the extra attraction of deterring young Omanis
from a Western education, in which they would be
subject to non-Islamic and democratic philosophies.
So he discussed the proposed university with Sheikh
Amer, his education minister, who was enthusiastic.
Amer, an Oxford-educated Anglophile, was then twice
dispatched to England for discussions with eminent
academics.

The obstacle was that Oman was short of cash and
the university would soak up scarce resources. The
government had spent so much of its oil revenue on
arms that it had no budget for such a scheme. This
was resolved when the UK Export Credit Guarantee
Department (ECGD) guaranteed a £150 million loan,
made available by a syndicate of banks led by Morgan
Grenfell, to finance the contract.

Mark Thatcher was used to help secure this financial
backing. It was such a delicate, secret operation that
whenever he discussed it on the telephone he used code
words and names – for example, the prime minister was
referred to as 'Big John'.

In November 1980, on Oman's national day, the

sultan publicly announced the university scheme, to be built over five years. Enter Sadiq Ismail, a Zanzibari expatriate and an influential figure in Omani education policy. In February 1981, he travelled to England, under British Council auspices, to conduct a fresh canvas of academics. The British Council in Oman arranged a meeting with Margaret Thatcher but it was cancelled because, according to Council sources, 'she had some political crisis at the time'.[6]

By now the multimillion-pound contract was there for the bidding and the taking. Mark was to be closely involved because of his prior knowledge, and his immediate boss, Jamil Amyuni, was head of Cementation's negotiating team.

In March 1981, after Sadiq Ismail's visit to England, the Omani government released the official requirements that contractors were expected to fulfil. 'A reputable establishment renowned for its experience in building universities will be selected,' said the plan. The document spelt out that the contract would be awarded on the basis of competitive tendering, with sealed bids by rival firms: 'All government contracts are awarded through the Tender Board.' This system was based on a law passed in 1975 after Omani government advisers were found to have been securing secret business deals for foreign corporations.[7] 'The whole purpose of a tender board is to eliminate a behind-closed-doors system,' said Jeremy Cripps, a chartered accountant who scrutinized many contracts in Oman.[8]

And yet Cementation International Ltd, a subsidiary of Trafalgar House plc, was awarded the £300 million university design and construction contract by direct private negotiations. When the decision was made known, rival bidders like Costain, Wimpey and Taylor

Woodrow were outraged, and two executives went
to see Ivor Lucas, then the British ambassador in
Oman, after the contract was awarded. They were
furious because the business had never been put out
to competitive tender.

The contractors were especially resentful because
Cementation had only just returned to Oman after a
three-year absence, while they had maintained a permanent base in the country (Taylor Woodrow had built
the sultan's Salalah Palace). Apart from that, the firm
had never built a university before. Even worse was
that Cementation had withdrawn its plant equipment.
As it had its own plants in Oman, Taylor Woodrow in
particular could have easily underbid Cementation.

The construction executives also told Lucas that no
independent architects had been hired to design the
university. This was despite the fact that two fully
qualified and experienced firms of architects – Robert
Matthew-Johnson, Marshall & Partner (RMJM) and
James Cubitt and Partners – actively sought to bid
for the design contracts. After receiving a circular
on the project from the British Overseas Trade Board
(BOTB), both companies submitted written proposals
to the Omani Education Ministry. They had high hopes
after receiving a second BOTB circular on 11 May
1981, which stated: 'An architects' brief is being
prepared . . . in preparation for design tenders being
called in 1982.'[9]

However, in September 1981, the Omani government suddenly not only awarded the civil engineering
contract to Cementation International Ltd but also
allowed them to appoint their own architects. This
design contract was given to another Trafalgar House
subsidiary. The negotiations had clearly taken place
without the knowledge of the interested bidders.

'The whole deal was a stitch-up for Cementation,' an angry rival contractor later complained to Ivor Lucas, sitting in the British embassy in Muscat, the capital of Oman.

Lucas found it impossible to disagree and reported their grievances to the Foreign Office and the Department of Trade. The ambassador's dispatch was noted but nothing was done. Three months later Lucas left Oman and became the British ambassador in Syria.

The story of how Cementation secured the £300 million university contract by secret, private lobbying lies at the heart of the way Thatcher's gold was acquired. For the deal was done largely through a coterie of well-placed middlemen and the use of political and family influence and patronage at the very highest level.

It started in early April 1981, two weeks before an overseas tour by Margaret Thatcher. As part of her preparation, she received a briefing from the British Council on the academic and design aspects of the proposed university in Oman.[10] The prime minister was already aware of the project. 'I knew of the announcement of the Omani government in 1980 that it had decided to establish a university,' she said, 'and of the opportunities for British industry which this might represent.'[11]

The Oman trip was just one leg of an extensive trade mission by Margaret Thatcher. On 14 April 1981 she flew to India, where she spent five days in often fraught negotiations with Prime Minister Indira Gandhi over quotas on textile imports. But major defence contracts were soon occupying her attention. Accompanied by Sir Ronald Ellis, her chief of defence sales, Thatcher then flew to Riyadh, Saudi Arabia.

For the next three days she was locked in discussions

with King Khalid, the head of state, and Crown Prince
Fahd, the prime minister, over future arms deals. She
told the Saudis that Britain had neglected the region but
she 'intended to put that right in the future'.[12] During
her stay she also made a speech to British businessmen
in Riyadh. 'Gradually one has come to see,' she said,
that there are times when the battle is not necessarily
between company and company but between country
and country.'[13]

The next afternoon, Tuesday, 21 April 1981, Margaret
Thatcher flew into Abu Dhabi and attended a party at
the British embassy to celebrate the Queen's birthday.
During the evening her private staff were surprised to
see her son arrive. There was an embarrassing moment
when Mark failed to withdraw discreetly when UAE
diplomats wanted to talk politics with his mother. Journalists were prevented from attending the reception, but
Mark was noticed by Herbie Knott, a freelance press
photographer, who asked him whether he was part of
the official party. 'No,' was the characteristically curt
response.[14]

Mark had just flown in by Gulf Air with Jamil
Amyuni, Cementation International's marketing director. The company was seeking a contract to build a
giant irrigation scheme in the desert oasis of al-Ain
in Abu Dhabi. After meeting his mother, he stayed
overnight at the Sheraton Hotel.

The next day Mark and Amyuni were engaged in
negotiations with UAE officials. These were only
partially successful. A Trafalgar House specialist subsidiary, Cementation Frankipile Overseas, did later
obtain work in the area. But the al-Ain contract
faltered because test borings showed there was not
enough water available.[15]

That same morning, 22 April 1981, the prime

minister had a meeting with Sheikh Zayed. They
spoke mainly about arms sales, but there was also
clearly a bond between them. 'Sheikh Zayed spoke for
all the world like an Arab poet and was a man of great
charm,' Margaret Thatcher recalled in her memoirs.[16]
She then called on Crown Prince Khalifa, his son and
deputy commander of the UAE armed forces. Those
discussions laid the foundation for the sale of eighteen
British Aerospace Hawk aircraft worth £60 million.
Despite the welcome export order, British Aerospace
would not have made much profit from the deal as at
least 9 per cent commissions were paid out to agents
in the Gulf and London.[17]

After a lunch hosted by the Abu Dhabi government,
Margaret Thatcher and her entourage went to Dubai
for the afternoon before returning to Abu Dhabi. That
evening she flew to Muscat, the capital of Oman, with
her party, which included Douglas Hurd, the Foreign
Office minister of state, Sir Ronald Ellis, head of
defence sales, Bernard Ingham, her press secretary,
and Denis and Carol Thatcher. The prime minister
stayed at the royal palace.

The following morning, 23 April, Margaret Thatcher
visited the British embassy where she met the staff
and businessmen over coffee hosted by Ivor Lucas,
the ambassador. She then went upstairs to the private
sitting-room with Lucas for a fifteen-minute meeting.
They did not see eye-to-eye on Oman. Lucas, in his
understated, diplomatic manner, was critical of the
sultan's regime. 'The sultan is spending too much
on defence and on the city of Muscat,' he told her,
'and not enough on economic development for the
majority of his people in the villages.'[18] He argued
that Qaboos needed to make democratic concessions
to ensure stability, otherwise political unrest would

threaten British trade and strategic interests in the Gulf. Mrs Thatcher, who was in a restless mood and did not appear to be listening too intently, disagreed fundamentally. She replied that she thought the Soviet threat was more important than the way the sultan ran his country. Consequently, she argued, Oman needed to build up its arsenal and buy strategic defence equipment.

Her preoccupation with communist encroachment was noted by the *Times* correspondent Robert Fisk, who reported on her visit: 'Mrs Thatcher – sitting in a cane chair at the edge of a 2,000-feet precipice – peered with concern into the impenetrable bank of cold mist and fog that obscured South Yemen. The Marxist enemy may have been invisible, but there was little doubt that she could identify it.'[19]

The prime minister's attitude to Ambassador Lucas's views was noticed by her aides. 'She was dismissive and unhappy about his analysis,' recalled one. 'It was almost as if she was already receiving advice from others close to the sultan,' said another source. This tense, impatient mood lasted throughout the tour. During her stay in Oman, she telephoned Sir Kenneth Clucas, the permanent secretary at the Department of Trade. She harangued him over the arrangements for the Oman trip and wanted more support from his department. She seemed even more highly strung than usual, and Sir Kenneth, a diffident, quietly spoken mandarin, withstood the verbal barrage with some dignity. When he put down the telephone, he turned to a colleague and said in classic *Yes, Minister* tones: 'Prime ministers should take a holiday during parliamentary recesses.'[20]

After her visit to the embassy, Mrs Thatcher and her party flew down to Salalah, capital of Dhofar, the southern province of Oman. Accompanied by Denis and Carol Thatcher, Douglas Hurd and Ivor Lucas, the Prime Minister was escorted in a convoy of armoured limousines with inch-thick bullet-proof windows for a private lunch at his State Guest House, built by Taylor Woodrow. Just as the guests sat down for lunch, Mark Thatcher suddenly arrived. He had flown into Muscat at 10am that day on a Gulf Air flight to Muscat and then on to Salalah by an Omani air force plane. 'He was a CIP – Commercially Important Passenger,' said Steve Lowes, a Gulf Air duty officer. 'An Omani Minister on the incoming flight was telling me that he had just dined with Mrs Thatcher and I thought, "Oh, Mark must be off to meet his Mum."'[21]

When Mark walked into the dining-room Ambassador Lucas was shocked to see him, as nobody had informed him that the prime minister's son was going to be in Oman. Nor was he aware of Thatcher's consultancy with Cementation. Privately, Lucas was angry about the underhand way this occurred, but he maintained his diplomatic silence. The main topic of conversation over lunch was the balance of power in the Gulf and the possible repercussions for the region of the Iran–Iraq war, which had broken out eight months earlier. Then Mark abruptly changed the subject and argued with his mother over his participation in the Nuremberg car rally. He was very keen to race but she was not happy about his competing and expressed her displeasure. The university project was not discussed, according to an official who was present.

Before lunch the prime minister had an involved private talk with Sultan Qaboos, which lasted just over an hour. She saw him as 'one of Britain's closest friends in the Gulf'. During their meeting they discussed the 'Sultan of Oman's requirements for military equipment'. She suggested he purchase the ground-attack Hawk aircraft rather than the more expensive Tornado.[22]

By her own account, she also raised the university project. 'I was advised to raise the matter of the whole University contract with the government of Oman,' she said later. 'I did it. I believed in it very forcefully because I wanted the business to come to Britain.'[23] She denied that she specifically asked for Cementation to be awarded the contract. However, as Cementation was the only British company allowed to bid, she was lobbying for them anyway – *de facto*.

In the meantime, Mark Thatcher was flying back to Muscat to meet Jamil Amyuni, Cementation's marketing director. Amyuni was very familiar with what made the country tick, according to John Townsend, a former chief economic adviser to the Omani government who knew the Lebanese businessman for ten years. Townsend, who visited Oman for over fifteen years as a businessman and consultant, was later asked how the arrival of Mark Thatcher would have led to certain assumptions in the minds of government ministers.

Interviewed by Granada TV's *World In Action* programme, he was asked: 'Would Omanis assume if the relative was in the country, then the head of government expected the contract to go to the relative?'

'They would certainly assume that,' he replied. 'That would be normal practice.'

'Why is that?'

'They would say that it's a normal part of business. It is recognized as normal in the Arab world for people in positions of authority to use that position for their own business interests. They would regard that as perfectly normal for other people as well.'[24]

Once Mark Thatcher's presence was confirmed, the
prime minister's private office became concerned.
They were not aware that he was a paid consultant
to Cementation International, but it was no secret in
Whitehall that he had business interests in the Gulf.
Clearly, as the prime minister had identified her trip
as a commercial hard sell on behalf of British firms
seeking export orders, there was a potential conflict of
interests – at the very least.

One of her civil servant advisers realized this and
spoke to her. 'I was aware that Mark Thatcher was
involved in oil trading, although I did not know then he
was working for Cementation,' he told us. 'I suggested
that her son's presence created a potential problem. I
said it would be perceived in the wrong way. She
replied that she was sensitive to the situation and
would take my advice on board. But I have to say she
was besotted by Mark and there was a blind spot, so
whether she said anything to him I just don't know.'

The prime minister, unlike the British ambassador,
knew full well that her son was going to be in Oman
at the same time. Her daughter, Carol, told Gordon
Martin, a BBC correspondent covering the trip, on the
beach in Salalah that Mark was flying in for 'a family
reunion'.[25]

Later that evening, Thursday, 23 April, Mrs Thatcher
attended a formal state banquet as the guest of the
sultan. There are conflicting accounts of what was
said during that dinner. After the *Observer* exposed
Mark's relationship with Cementation and his visit
to Oman, the paper received a letter written by a
British army officer serving in the Omani Ministry of
Defence. Written from Bait al Falaj, a military camp
near Muscat, it stated: 'During dinner Mrs Thatcher
asked the Sultan about the next five year plan. The

Sultan explained that most of the capital expenditure would be for civil engineering works, at which Mrs Thatcher remarked that she hoped the Sultan would bear her son in mind as he was involved with a British contractor, Cementation. It did not go unnoticed that the Sultan showed some surprise at the remark.'[26] Diplomatic sources say that she did press the sultan on the contract but did not mention Cementation.

When questioned about her lobbying for Cementation, the prime minister replied vigorously, 'I bat for Britain. I don't distinguish between British companies. When I'm trying to secure contracts it is to try to get business for British companies and not overseas companies.'[27] 'Batting for Britain' became her stock answer during the Oman affair. It was a phrase devised for her by Bernard (now Sir Bernard) Ingham, her press secretary, to counter growing criticism.

Whitehall also defended her. Officials briefed the press, arguing that as Cementation was the only UK company seeking the university order, the prime minister could not be accused of favouring one firm over another. But this only made her case less credible. Firstly, the contract was never put out to tender, which made it illegal under Omani law. Secondly, if Cementation was the only British company bidding, then Margaret Thatcher was obviously lobbying for Cementation! As Mark was on Cementation's payroll she was also 'batting for Mark Thatcher Ltd'.

On 24 April 1981, the morning after the state banquet, the prime minister was given a helicopter tour of the Dhofar mountains and visited the military units there. Just before noon, she had another meeting with Sultan Qaboos and then a private lunch at Mamurah, the sultan's farm just outside Salalah. This was a very restricted gathering, which did not include the

British ambassador, Ivor Lucas, but did include some of the sultan's closest advisers. Later that afternoon Mrs Thatcher returned to Muscat; she flew back to London the next morning.

It was the vital, pivotal role of the sultan's inner circle of confidants and courtiers that ensured the contract went to Cementation. It was a back-door deal, done through a coterie of British security counsellors, construction middlemen and Omani ministers – all with direct access to Sultan Qaboos. Mark Thatcher was, of course, indispensable to them. He was representing the right corporation and was in the right place at the right time. The company has always maintained that it secured the order before the prime minister's visit. But even one of their most loyal senior directors conceded to us, 'The University deal was won by a lot of hard work by us months before Mark was in Oman. There is no doubt he helped but I would say it was a combination of factors.'

A clue as to the source of real power and influence in Oman lies in the guest list of a special lunch at 10 Downing Street hosted by Margaret Thatcher on 17 March 1982. The lunch was in honour of Sultan Qaboos as part of his state visit. But its significance was that it took place the day after the university contract was publicly unveiled as 'one of the largest overseas orders to be won by a single building contractor'.[28] The Downing Street function was a therefore celebratory affair, with the guests including British academics who were consulted over the project, such as Peter Morice, a professor of civil engineering, and also Nigel Broackes, chairman of Trafalgar House, the holding company of Cementation.

Mark Thatcher, who was seated opposite Morice, had suddenly cancelled an appearance in a celebrity golf tournament in Spain in order to attend. 'I have learnt there is to be a State visit during that week,' he wrote to the tournament organizers, 'so I hope you will understand this has to take precedence.'[29] For the prime minister's son to be a guest at an official state function was, in fact, most unusual, as Buckingham Palace pointed out. 'Mark Thatcher seldom takes part in state visits,' said a spokesperson, 'so there's no reason why he should do so this time.'[30]

However, the most important guest was the little-known Brigadier J. T. W. Landon, the sultan's shadowy special adviser and a close associate of the prime minister's son. Before Margaret Thatcher embarked on her 'batting for Britain' tour in April 1981, Tim Landon met both Mark and Denis at 10 Downing Street.[31] The brigadier was known to be strongly in favour of Cementation for the university contract. This was effectively recognized at the Downing Street lunch, when ministers and officials adjourned upstairs. At the sultan's request, Landon was awarded an honorary knighthood – a KCVO (Knight Commander of the Royal Victorian Order) – for 'services to British exports' by the prime minister. Such were his access and closeness to 10 Downing Street that Landon and Sultan Qaboos had private meetings with Margaret Thatcher at Chequers which were not attended by any civil servants. According to one of her most senior foreign policy advisers, these tête-à-têtes were viewed with 'disquiet and concern' by Foreign Office officials.

These secret meetings were confirmed to us by two of Mrs Thatcher's private secretaries, who served her in the early 1980s. Landon's proximity to the affairs of state was such that an associate was once given a London telephone number to call him and was amazed to discover it was in the Cabinet Office.

In Oman he was known as 'the White Sultan', such were his authority and status. 'Nothing can be done in Oman without Landon's knowledge and approval,' said an Arab businessman with interests in the region. A Buddhist, the brigadier is a cold, unsmiling man, who never relaxes and is rarely rattled. 'He is the ultimate control freak,' said a source who knows him well. 'Everything Tim Landon does is calculated and premeditated. Nothing is left to chance.'

Landon's unparalleled influence over Sultan Qaboos can be traced back to the late 1950s when they were friends at Sandhurst. In 1965, their friendship was rekindled when the brigadier was seconded to Oman during the Dhofar rebellion as a desert intelligence officer. Two years later, after a brief course in military intelligence in London, he returned to Oman as the chief intelligence officer for the sultan's armed forces.

It was the 1970 coup that established Landon's power base. As the senior intelligence officer, he was in a unique position to help Qaboos overthrow his hated, despotic father, Sayyid bin Taimur. One account of the coup says that Landon led the military assault on the palace and was one of those who confronted the sultan at the top of the stairs. They began firing and Sayyid bin Taimur was twice wounded. He then locked himself in a room and shouted, 'I will only give myself up to a British officer.' But he then managed to shoot himself in the foot and surrendered, and he later reluctantly abdicated. After leaving hospital he was installed in the Dorchester Hotel, where he died two years later. When two former aides visited him near the end of his life, he was asked what was his greatest regret. 'Not killing Brigadier Landon,' the old man replied instantly.

After the coup Landon helped install Qaboos. The new, grateful, twenty-nine-year-old sultan rewarded the brigadier by making him his equerry, special adviser and chief military counsellor, and by awarding him an Omani diplomatic passport. He was now by far the most powerful official in the Omani government. An indication of his influence was that the Foreign Office official responsible for Oman had behind his desk a picture not of the sultan but of the brigadier.[32]

Part of Landon's duties was to build up the sultan's armed forces, and in the next decade he helped transform them into one of the best small armies in the Middle East. Defence became big business and by 1980 the budget for military equipment was £400 million. The problem was that Landon had no business acumen. Fortunately for him he was introduced to Ronald Cheeseman, then managing director of Cogswell and Harrison Ltd, Britain's oldest arms manufacturer, which held a prohibited-weapons licence from the Ministry of Defence.

Cheeseman was an experienced arms dealer and supplied the guns, usually from the United States, and the brigadier helped to sell them to Oman. They would meet at Cogswell and Harrison's office at 168 Piccadilly, central London, where orders were placed and negotiations conducted.

Landon's chief business partner in Oman was David Bayley, a former army officer who had learned to speak Arabic while serving in North Yemen. Bayley had moved to Oman in 1971, just after the coup. According to Lieutenant-Colonel Johnny Cooper, a founder member of the SAS who served in the sultan's armed forces, Bayley set up a private office in Muscat as an arms dealer. Working with Colonel Jim Johnson, he then bought weapons for the Omani élite special forces. Landon found him useful because of his connections in South Africa and Rhodesia and they began facilitating arms sales – working alongside Sayyid Fahr bin Taimur, the sultan's uncle and Oman's defence minister. Their market was largely southern Africa and Afghanistan.

The sultan also took a shine to the flamboyant Bayley and gave the young arms dealer a chauffeur-driven Rolls-Royce and paid for him to stay in the Hyde Park Hotel, Knightsbridge, whenever he was in London. It was not long before Bayley could afford to pay his own bill at the Hyde Park Hotel. By the 1980s he was reaping rich rewards as one of the four directors of Gulf Aviation Services Ltd, an Omani company which received some £2 million a year in commission fees from foreign companies to secure contracts. One of Landon and Bayley's unofficial agents was Mark Thatcher. In the mid-1980s they hired him to represent them on some arms deals in the United States and visited him many times in Dallas, Texas, according to a former business associate who worked closely with Landon and Bayley during that period. Simon Sloane met Thatcher twice – once with Bayley at the Mirabelle restaurant in London in 1986, and then in the company of Landon and Bayley at the Ritz Hotel in Paris in 1989. 'Mark Thatcher was asked to find prices and products in the States for us for armoured personnel carriers, tanks, spare parts and other kinds of weapons,' said the source. 'He was very enthusiastic but was always late on delivery and the work was incomplete.' Bayley, in particular, found it frustrating to deal with him: 'Mark is useful but a complete idiot. He is so incompetent,' the arms dealer once said during a drinks party at Doyley Manor, his former Hampshire country mansion.

Bayley and Landon became fabulously wealthy from their Omani exploits. But while Landon conducts business with a ruthless, brutal logic, Bayley is emotional and temperamental. He spends most of his time in France as a tax exile. He is an exhibitionist, and when he walks into the Ritz Hotel in Paris the staff react as if he were the Prince of Wales. 'I have never seen such sycophancy,' said an eyewitness. 'The hotel staff and waiters fawn all over him. He gets the royalty treatment because he tips them £150 a time. He is always trying to impress and craves the attention and recognition.'

Landon's fortune was based more directly on the sultan's patronage. After the coup the brigadier received a 'thank you' payment from Qaboos. The exact amount is disputed. One source is adamant that it was £6 million tax-free. Others say it was at least £3 million. Whatever the exact fee, Landon's vast wealth is apparent from his properties and life-style.

In 1978, he returned to Britain as a senior counsellor in the Omani embassy and immediately bought Faccombe Manor, a 100-acre country estate near Andover, north Hampshire. It cost him £2 million, paid through a Liechtenstein company, Etablissement Landon Co, and Mark and Denis Thatcher would spend weekends there at pheasant-shooting parties. It was no coincidence that the mansion was only a few miles from Wargrave Manor, the Sultan of Oman's country estate in a Thames-side hamlet near Reading, Berkshire. Qaboos had bought the residence three years earlier for £800,000 from Nigel (later Sir Nigel) Broackes, chairman of Trafalgar House plc, Cementation's holding company.[33]

Apart from Faccombe Manor, the brigadier runs a town house in London's Wilton Crescent, which is also used to accommodate visiting foreign guests, and

an office in Green Street, Mayfair. He owns land in
Cyprus and the south of France, a farm in Scotland and
a 40,000-acre ranch in Zimbabwe. In 1994 Landon was
able to pay £10 million for Gunnerside, a magnificent
36,000-acre north Yorkshire estate previously owned
by Earl Peel.[34] His fortune was also visible through his
own yacht – the *Katalina*, named after his Hungarian
princess wife – the joint use of a private Boeing 707 and
his own helicopter, which he later gave to the wealthy
property developers David and Frederick Barclay.

In the summer of 1980, Landon officially 'retired'
from the Omani government. He set up business
as a 'consultant for Middle East clients' with an
office in Mayfair's Upper Brook Street and another
in Washington, where he hired Chet Nagel, a former
CIA officer. But Landon remained Sultan Qaboos's
most trusted and influential adviser and confidant.
This was demonstrated by a letter written by Richard
Helms, a former director of the CIA, who knew the
brigadier well. Helms made enquiries about Landon's
status and on 5 January 1981, three months before
Margaret Thatcher's visit to Oman, he wrote to an
American businessman: 'He is still the most influential
individual on policy matters with the Sultan. The latter
consults with him constantly. In fact, the Sultan has
kept Landon on as chairman of his Planning Review
Committee, which is the group making military policy
and plans in Oman. To sum up, Tim Landon still has
a most influential position in respect to the Sultan of
Oman.'[35]

By the time Margaret and Mark Thatcher arrived in
Oman on 23 April 1981, Cementation International
was confident of winning the £300 million university
contract. Its agents say they already had a letter of

intent. But the sultan, a solitary and indecisive man, had not decided, and so access to and influence over him became the crucial factor. Nobody could provide that better than Tim Landon. And so it proved.

For Mark Thatcher and Jamil Amyuni a swift entrée to Qaboos was vital, and Landon was the door-opener. Within twenty-four hours of arriving in Muscat, Thatcher and Amyuni were meeting the head of state. 'Mark was able to get us to see the princes and rulers,' a former senior Cementation director told us. 'That's where he was useful and that's how Jamil used him on the Oman deal. He had the access to the sultan.' In later years the prime minister's son looked back with gratitude. 'The Sultan treated me like a son,' he told business associate Gary Smith on 4 December 1987. 'I saw him about six weeks ago and it was obvious we have gone as far as we can go in Oman. Too many people had gone on about the Cementation deal. It's a pity because I really liked him, a lovely man. He was very pro-British, you know.'

Timothy Landon was not the only facilitator on the university project. Ghassan Shaker, from Cementation Saudi Arabia Ltd, who first introduced Mark Thatcher to Oman, was influential in the early part of the negotiations. Shaker had known Sultan Qaboos since the early 1970s and remained close to him; he also knew Landon and Bayley. But when it was discovered he was looking for a very high commission, his role was substantially reduced. Fortunately for Shaker, he had a separate private agreement with Amyuni, which allowed for smaller commissions to be paid through a Swiss company they had set up and registered at the President's Hotel, Geneva.

The person who effectively replaced Shaker was Dr Omar Zawawi, a personal adviser to the sultan since

1975, whose brother Qais was deputy prime minister. Zawawi, who was active in oil deals, moved in amidst anxiety about the slow progress of the contract and counselled Qaboos about the merits of favouring Cementation. Eventually, in September 1981, the sultan awarded the order to Cementation International to build the university. Within days, on 9 September, the company activated its Omani-registered subsidiary, Cementation SICO Ltd, to represent its interests as a joint-venture agreement. Four Omani ministers owned 35 per cent of SICO, including two foreign affairs ministers – Yousef al-Alawi Abdullah and Salim Ahmed Khalfan – and Abdel Aziz al-Rowas, the minister for information. All four later sold their stakes.[36]

The business was originally worth £215 million to Cementation. This rose to £300 million when they also secured a hospital contract. Part of the deal was underwritten by British public money, as the Export Credit Guarantee Department guaranteed a £150 million loan provided by a syndicate of banks.

On 23 November 1981, two months after the sultan had chosen Cementation, the Export Group for the Construction Industry held its annual luncheon at the Savoy Hotel. The guest speaker was Margaret Thatcher. Also present were her husband, Denis, and son, Mark, accompanied by Jamil Amyuni. As the guests gathered, Mark spoke to Lord Matthews, chief executive of Trafalgar House, which owned Cementation. Matthews then took his place at the luncheon table, seated next to the prime minister on her left.

Her speech was apposite and full of irony. 'I was down in the Gulf recently,' she told the construction executives. 'I sometimes wonder if I missed a vocation. I should have been a head salesman of a company, where I would be a jolly sight better paid than I am now. So long as I get the orders for you and so long as you go on putting me back where I am now [i.e. electing her], so that I can go on getting orders for you, that will be absolutely marvellous.'[37]

Lord Matthews now says he was surprised to see her son at the lunch. 'I was surprised to see Mark Thatcher at the Savoy lunch,' he said from his retirement home in Jersey. 'I knew Mrs Thatcher would be there, of course, but I had not expected her son to attend.'[38]

Three months later, in February 1982, details of the Qaboos University contract were finalized and signed. Cementation was delighted and paid tribute to the 'keen interest in the negotiations' shown by the prime minister.[39] In March the sultan came to London for a state visit and celebrated the deal with a lunch at Downing Street, attended by Mark Thatcher and Nigel Broackes, chairman of Trafalgar House.

Details of the subsequent payments to Mark Thatcher have never appeared in the accounts of Trafalgar House, Cementation International or Monteagle Marketing, his own company. One of the more detailed press reports stated that he received, via Monteagle, a retainer of £34,000 a year, paid in quarterly instalments of £8,500.[40] These were paid into Monteagle's Barclays bank account at 415 The Strand. The co-signatories to the account were Steve Tipping, Mark's business partner, and Denis Thatcher.[41]

Tipping later claimed that their fees would be published in Monteagle's annual returns. 'The Omani money will appear in our accounts,' he said. 'There will be a queue at the door for the company's returns.' But this never happened as the money was not accounted for in the 1981–82 returns. Instead, Thatcher's friends briefed the press that Cementation paid him only £59,000.[42] This amount is disputed by Gulf sources, who say that Mark would also have received a commission – normal practice on Middle East construction deals – as high as £3 million (or 1 per cent of the contract price).

A clue as to how he was paid is contained in a memo by Alastair Brett, company solicitor of Times Newspapers, based on a lunch he had with Ian Sayer, a friend and former employer of Mark Thatcher. In early 1984, when Mark's relationship with Cementation in Oman was under public scrutiny, Thatcher drove down to see Sayer at his house in West Drive, Wentworth, Surrey. The prime minister's son had always admired the wealthy transport businessman. He was exactly the kind of young, self-made entrepreneur Mark aspired to be. A man of extreme right-wing views, whose huge Volvo trucks had been instrumental in strike-breaking in the 1970s, Sayer was thrilled to be part of the Thatcher golden circle. He loved going to 10 Downing Street for drinks parties. He was also a deft hand at tax avoidance and it was on this delicate topic that Mark came to ask his advice.

According to Brett's memo, Mark told Sayer he was worried about the tax implications of the commission fee he was paid by Cementation for the university contract. Mark then described in some detail how the fee was channelled through a Swiss company. Brett accepts he wrote the document but has only 'a hazy recollection of the memo and the circumstances under which it was written'.[43] Sayer told the authors: 'I have met Alastair Brett over the years and have met him for lunch, but that account does not accord with my memory. To be honest, I just can't remember.' Eventually the transport executive rediscovered his memory. When pressed by Barrie Penrose of the

Sunday Express, he said, 'I accept that Alastair Brett's memo is accurate.'

The Oman affair affected Margaret Thatcher deeply. Ever since Mark was a young boy, she had tried to compartmentalize her life so that her children were separate from her public duties. For her, Mark's business activities bore no relevance to her being prime minister. She resented what she saw as the intrusion into her private family concerns. 'She would arrive in Finchley,' said Andrew Thomson, then her constituency agent, 'and very occasionally complain how badly he [Mark] was being treated by the media. But this was said not as an encouragement to further conversation on the subject, more as a mutter to herself.'[44]

Colleagues, including supportive cabinet ministers, were astonished at how sensitive and protective the prime minister was towards Mark.[45] 'She's very sensitive about the boy,' said Edward (now Sir Edward) du Cann, a senior MP and chairman of the Conservative 1922 back-benchers' committee.[46] Alan Clark, a former defence minister and close ally of Margaret Thatcher, recorded in his diary after talking to her in the Commons during the Oman controversy: 'He [Mark] must be a source of anxiety.'[47]

For the prime minister, criticism of Mark was a personal attack on her. 'What was important to Margaret Thatcher during the entire affair,' said Andrew Thomson, 'was that she was being challenged not just as a politician, but as a mother.'[48] It was this inability or unwillingness to understand how her son's private commercial interests conflicted with her role as prime minister that would later undermine her credibility among colleagues and friends. 'It was a complete blind spot,' said one former Downing Street

aide who dealt with Mark at the time of the Oman affair.
'She just could not come to terms with the implications
of what he was doing and how it could have affected
her politically. None of us could talk to her about it.
She just wouldn't listen,' he told us.

The key question which Mrs Thatcher never answered
in parliament or in the media is whether she knew at the
time of her Oman visit about her son's consultancy with
Cementation. When directly and repeatedly asked this
by Sir Robin Day on BBC TV, she refused to answer
and would only say, 'I answer for what I do. . . . I don't
mention the names of particular companies and didn't
on that occasion. I said it was vitally important that
the business comes to Britain.'[49] When asked in the
Commons to state categorically 'yes' or 'no' whether
she knew, she again refused.[50]

During her BBC interview Thatcher said that the
full facts of the Oman affair could not be made public
because 'discussions between heads of governments
are confidential', particularly on 'commercial contracts'. She added that they would be published in
thirty years when government records were released.[51]
However, this was incorrect, as she was later forced
to admit. In a letter to Peter Shore, shadow leader of
the commons, she acknowledged that the government
documents did not contain the information which she
refused to give parliament. 'No reasonable person
would expect the public record to cover the matters
in those questions,' she wrote.[52] Consequently, the
papers released in the year 2011 will not reveal the
truth of what happened in Oman.

Despite being repeatedly asked to account fully for
her actions (twenty-three times in all), Mrs Thatcher
stonewalled. One former trade minister was bemused
by her approach. 'The curious aspect of the Oman

business was that she intervened at all in foreign contracts,' he recalled. 'I mean, in 1981 most of us were monetarists and we couldn't understand why she kept going on about "batting for Britain". Let the market decide was our view. . . . I could understand she was upset because it involved her family, but I felt she was a seasoned street fighter and she was being over-sensitive about it.'

Mrs Thatcher's parliamentary replies were drafted by Robin (now Sir Robin) Butler, then her principal private secretary and now the cabinet secretary. 'That's the way to handle it, Prime Minister,' he told her in 10 Downing Street. 'We don't need to go further than that.' It was the time-honoured method of answering tricky Commons questions – provide just enough information to enable the prime minister to refer to previous answers.

Her standard response was 'batting for Britain'. 'As part of my public duties,' she told the Commons in her first parliamentary statement on the Oman saga, 'I make strenuous efforts to secure contracts for this country. I do not decide upon those contracts. The decisions are made by the governments which give them. I do not distinguish between companies in this country. My job is to see that we get the contracts and the business here. As a result of that particular tour, hundreds of millions of pounds' worth of contracts came to this country.'[53] After that initial answer, she blocked further questions by saying, 'I have nothing to add to what I said on this matter in the House of Commons yesterday.'[54] She also refused to set up an enquiry, make a statement to the House or issue guidelines to ministers who are seeking contracts when their children have a financial interest in the outcome.[55]

Her only substantial attempt to justify refusing to answer the charge that her son benefited financially from her 'batting for Britain' was to argue that her family was entitled to privacy. 'I answer for my public duties from this dispatch box,' she said, 'and members of my family are as much entitled to privacy in going about their private duties as any other citizen. I hope we have not reached the stage when parents and their sons have to report everything to the authorities. If it comes to that, 1984 will be here.'[56]

Eventually, the prime minister did respond to the central issue when she was asked 'whether there was a conflict between her private family interests and her public duties on the Oman University deal'. But she chose to ignore the reference to 'private family interests' and replied, 'There was no question of conflict arising between my private interests and public duties.'[57] This, of course, did not answer the question. The issue was her family's private interests, not specifically her own.

Mark Thatcher only twice surfaced to comment on the controversy. In an interview with the *Sunday Times*, he confirmed his financial involvement in the university contract and that he had met his mother while she was in Oman. 'I played a very small part in a very successful British contract,' he said. He was unconcerned that the contract was not put out to tender: 'It is the prerogative of the client to decide the method of awarding the contract.'[58]

In a later interview with his friend Rodney Tyler, published in the *Mail on Sunday*, he was more defensive and emotional: 'I have done nothing wrong — nothing I should be ashamed of. So I don't have to stand up and answer questions about my private affairs. It's all innuendo and speculation. . . . I suppose I have

been naive. I have only ever been Mark Thatcher so I
don't know what it is like to be anyone else. I grew
up with my mother as she is, though I realise now I
have been naive about it. . . . Naive to think that this
business was just to do with me and my partner and
nothing to do with my mother. I see now how they
have used me to get at her.'[59]

Friends and colleagues of the prime minister became
increasingly concerned about the political consequences
of Mark's business affairs. 'It was a time-bomb ticking
away inside 10 Downing Street,' said one close associate. 'I can tell you without any reservation that we
were very worried about Mr Thatcher's activities,' Sir
Edward du Cann told us. Sir Edward had direct access
to the Tory chief whip and the prime minister and was
extremely influential within the party. 'I was receiving
reports from mainly Conservative MPs which disturbed
me,' he said. 'I would say there were two phases. The
first stage was when he was doing things that could
embarrass the prime minister by associating with the
wrong type of people. At the time I discounted this to
some extent because he was a bit of a joke figure. But
then there was a second stage where I was receiving
reports about how he was trading off her office.'

Sir Edward was sufficiently concerned to make two
formal verbal reports to two separate chief whips
during the Thatcher years. 'Thank you very much
for the information. Noted,' replied one of them
in the time-honoured Tory way of receiving such
representations. It is not known whether they discussed
Mark's activities with the prime minister.

Mark's activities also created anxiety at Tory Central Office. 'The problem we had was that she [Mrs
Thatcher] used to put up such a stonewall whenever
anyone raised it, so the Mark Factor became out of

bounds for us,' a former senior party official told us. 'I was very close to Margaret during one election campaign, and I saw that she and Denis had difficulties with regard to Mark. He was kept away from things, yet she was edgy and felt guilty when he was not around. I think it was very draining on her personally.'

A senior Conservative MP who was anxious about the situation was Ian Gow, Margaret Thatcher's parliamentary private secretary from 1979 until the 1983 election. Gow was almost universally admired and respected in the Tory Party and was in love, politically, with the prime minister. He saw her son's commercial activities as potentially extremely damaging. 'It's very serious,' he told a colleague. Gow used to have regular informal meetings with senior MPs on what he called political 'trip-wires' and 'elephant traps'. A recurrent topic was what he called 'the Mark problem'.

One incident which disturbed Gow occurred just after the 1983 election. It concerned a naval architect called Commander Peter Thornycroft who had designed a new boat for the Royal Navy known as the 'short fat frigate' (the S90). In the early 1980s Thornycroft became embroiled in a long-running dispute with the Ministry of Defence, which was resistant to the project. Thornycroft and his company, TT Boat Designs Ltd, claimed they were being deliberately obstructed and victimized by MoD civil servants and the naval establishment.

By the summer of 1983, Thornycroft and his partners had been awarded a development contract for a programme of testing of the hull. However, they desperately needed to get approval for the building of the frigate. And so they needed all the political muscle they could acquire. In September 1983, Thornycroft thought his luck had changed. One of his supporters

was a director of the Frank Williams racing team, and
offered to act as an intermediary and lobby on his
behalf. One of the people he approached was Mark
Thatcher, who was courting Williams at the time.

One Saturday, Thatcher turned to the intermediary
and said, 'All this stuff about the frigate. Doesn't it
depend on whether the tank testing will work?'

'That's right,' said the Williams director.

'Well, why don't you get Thornycroft to write a
one-page memo on the testing and I will put it in
front of my mother,' said Mark.

The intermediary told Thornycroft and his associates, who were very excited. Their initial enthusiasm
was tempered with caution when they consulted Ian
Gow. 'Be careful when you deal with Mark Thatcher,'
Gow counselled. 'He is her Achilles' heel.' But then
they spoke to Captain John Moore, a former controller
of the navy, who told them about the prime minister's views on the Ministry of Defence. Moore had
recently met Mrs Thatcher at Chequers. 'The place that
bothers me more than anywhere else is the Ministry of
Defence,' she told him. 'It's like a concrete bunker. If
you give me a bomb, I'll put it in there.'

Armed with this knowledge, the naval architect
realized that appealing direct to 10 Downing Street was
the ideal way of bypassing the MoD. On 21 September
1983, he wrote a one-page memo entitled 'Tank Testing – The S90 Frigate', and attached a covering letter
to his influential supporter. The note, which is in our
possession, stated: 'I enclose an envelope addressed to
Mark Thatcher inside which is a memorandum which
I think may explain some of the misunderstandings
over the way the Ministry of Defence are judging our
results. . . . If you happen to have a chance of passing
this over to him when you next see him I feel that this

may help when consideration is being given to our S90 proposals.'

Thornycroft's eager anticipation was shown by a letter he wrote the following day to Holst Sørensen, a Danish shipbuilder. 'As regards the S90, I have written a brief memo,' he said. 'This memo is, in fact, for Mark Thatcher, the Prime Minister's son, in the hope that it may find its way on to Mrs Thatcher's desk. . . . Mark Thatcher is to be a spectator at the British Grand Prix and has asked to have some information about the tank testing results of the S90.'

By early March 1984, at the climax of the Oman affair, such stories were being logged in the upper echelons of the prime minister's inner circle. Many of her courtiers were concerned about the effect her son's activities could have on her political credibility and public image. The most prominent was Tim (now Sir Timothy) Bell, her media guru and one of her most influential advisers. As managing director of Saatchi & Saatchi, Bell had masterminded the Conservative Party's advertising campaign during the 1983 election and had become a close confidant of Margaret Thatcher. He also became friendly with Mark and advised him informally, though not as a client, on his media relations. But this was done as a favour and out of loyalty to his mother, rather than from any admiration for Mark personally.

Publicly, Margaret Thatcher's favourite advertising executive defended him. 'He is tenacious, hardworking and has never courted publicity,' said Bell. 'I respect him enormously.'[60] 'I think what has been happening is that the media has been trying to get at Mrs Thatcher through her son,' he told the Sunday Times. 'It is nothing more nor less than a vendetta. The poor man is not a public figure but he has been rubbished left, right and centre. Why should he have anything but contempt for the media?'[61] (Privately, Bell had a rather different view of the misunderstood prodigal son. In the summer of 1983, during a birthday dinner party which was tape-recorded by an enterprising journalist, he remarked, 'Mark Thatcher is a twit. In my opinion, he has nothing to offer the world.'[62])

Despite his staunch public rearguard action, Bell was a shrewd strategist and knew Mark's commercial activities were politically explosive. 'Tim thought he was a bomb just waiting to go off,' said a political source close to him at the time. This resulted in Bell secretly co-ordinating a public relations operation on behalf of the prime minister's son to limit the damage caused by the Oman disclosures. Late one Friday night in March 1984, he telephoned David Boddy, the former director of publicity at Tory Central Office, who had worked closely with Margaret Thatcher during the 1979 election. He asked him to come over to his house the following afternoon. The topic for discussion was the media treatment of Mark Thatcher. Bell told Boddy that the prime minister had 'requested his assistance' in dealing with the press and television coverage of her son.

Boddy, who had left Central Office to set up his own private company, Capital Publishing, agreed and was hired on a one-month contract for a fee of £18,000. He was paid by Bell, who secured the funds from Conservative-supporting businessmen. But Boddy received only £5,000 and never saw the remaining £13,000. It was never disclosed who bankrolled the 'Save Mark operation'. When asked, Boddy replied: 'A group of senior Conservatives. They were not based at Central Office but they were connected with it.'[63]

Under Boddy's tutelage, a small informal group was

formed, including Michael Dobbs, a Saatchi & Saatchi executive. Sir Gordon Reece, another of Margaret Thatcher's media Svengalis, was also consulted for strategic advice. Their brief was to engage in 'crisis management'. The basic idea was to keep Mark out of the newspapers and remove him from the news agenda; but, when there were press enquiries, to ensure questions were answered and statements released.

At first Mark co-operated. He called in when arriving at Heathrow airport so that photo opportunities could be arranged. But then he began to act irrationally and showed signs of stress. His moods swung dramatically – from anger to despair to persecution complexes. 'It's become "Get Mark Thatcher Time" in certain sections of the media,' he said. 'And they don't care how they do it.'[64]

This resulted in bouts of manic and unstable behaviour. One night he attended the Miss World dinner at the Grosvenor House ballroom. After the main course, he suddenly stood up and started throwing sugar lumps at the journalists covering the beauty contest, shouting obscenities at them. 'He was on the verge of cracking up,' said one PR aide who witnessed this spectacle.

For one Conservative operative close to Mark Thatcher at the time, the more heat the media and parliament generated the more arrogant and paranoid he became. 'I remember getting a phone call from Mark on a Sunday afternoon,' our source recalled. 'He had just arrived at Heathrow airport and his main concern was that he was getting Special Branch protection. He sounded absolutely frantic.'

It did not help that Thatcher was surly and suspicious of David Boddy and made it almost impossible for him to do his job. He was always late for appointments, he never responded to questions with a straight answer, and Boddy had to talk privately to Steve Tipping, Mark's business partner, to find out what was going on.

The major problem for the crisis-management team was that Thatcher and Tipping refused to disclose any detailed information or answer questions about the Oman contract. 'The press are out to get me' was all Mark could offer and so Boddy was reduced to issuing bland, meaningless denials. This, of course, made it extremely difficult to defuse the situation and only kept Thatcher in the firing line – rather than out of it. The Mark time-bomb continued to tick away underneath 10 Downing Street. It was only a matter of time before it exploded. Something more drastic than effective public relations was required.

Chapter Five

Exile in the USA

*'There's nothing wrong with having a lot of
money. It is not the fact of having money that
is wrong, it is when it becomes the sole and the
only thing in your life.'*

Margaret Thatcher[1]

Mark's hasty retreat to the United States of America
was due mainly to counsel from the prime minister's
inner circle of advisers and friends. They believed
that 'the Mark factor' was highly damaging to the
government and undermined her authority. 'There was
a real problem and real cause for concern,' recalled one
of Mrs Thatcher's aides, who was also close to her son.
'We thought the stakes were very high. Some of us felt
his activities could really hurt her.'

And so at the height of the Oman crisis, Sir
Tim Bell and Sir Gordon Reece, her media advisers,
Lord McAlpine, the Tory Party treasurer, and Denis
Thatcher attended a secret meeting at 19 Flood Street,
the family's Chelsea home. It was essentially a 'What
to do about Mark' summit. They discussed the situation
and realized that damage-limitation was not sufficient
and something more drastic was required. Denis then

suggested he should talk to David Wickins, a business associate and family friend, about arranging a job for Mark, preferably overseas. He telephoned Wickins and a lunch at Chequers was arranged at short notice, also attended by Margaret Thatcher and Sir Tim Bell. They agreed that Mark needed to leave the country. The deed was done.

Wickins, king of the second-hand-car auctions, knew Denis because he owned a 36 per cent shareholding in Attwoods, the waste-disposal company of which Denis was deputy chairman. 'I was a friend of the Thatcher family,' recalled Wickins, speaking from his retirement home in Ibiza. 'What happened was that I was watching the grand prix in Detroit at a roof-top party. Mark was there with some people from Team Lotus and that's when I offered him a job.'

Mark did not need long to make up his mind. 'It makes sense to move away,' he told his friend Rodney Tyler, 'keep a low profile for a while and pull out of most of my present commitments – if only to examine each one from top to bottom. I have made this decision to live in the United States not least to show how sorry I am for the totally unnecessary aggravation all this business has caused my mother.'[2] He also knew Wickins well, as British Car Auctions had sponsored his motor racing by paying him £6,000 for at least a year.[3]

Within a few days, on 20 March 1984, Thatcher's company, Monteagle Marketing Ltd, had been closed down and he had resigned his consultancy with Cementation International Ltd. His secretary, Brenda Sanger, continued to work for him for a further three years but mainly part-time. She now lives in Chesterfield and has a house in Florida. 'I cannot talk to you without Mark's permission,' she told us.

Mark's mood was one of angry resignation. 'It's been twelve bloody weeks when they've slung every bit of mud at me they can,' he said. 'Twelve weeks when they've accused me of being just about everything from a crook to a con man. . . . If my partner Steve Tipping and I had robbed the Bank of England of £20 million, Mum would not have been to blame. But they would have tried.'[4]

But he was hardly going to be destitute and in late March 1984, he flew by Concorde with David Wickins, his new boss, to New York, his new home for the time being.

Thatcher was hired as a consultant to Anglo-American Auto Auctions (AAAA) Inc, a subsidiary of British Car Auctions, on a salary of £45,000 a year. Based in Nashville, Tennessee, AAAA Inc was a second-hand-car company set up in 1982 and run by Mike Richardson, an expatriate Yorkshireman.

Two weeks earlier, Richardson had received a telephone call from David Wickins. 'David said Mark Thatcher was moving to America and would be joining the company,' recalled Richardson. 'He said Mark was very good with numbers and would be useful to us on new acquisitions. He didn't have anything to do with the running of the existing twelve car auction sites. But if we were looking at new auctions, I sent him off to look at the locations and he advised me if the business was worth acquiring. I found him a level-headed, sensitive businessman, but his personality changed when he was faced with the press. He became a different person and just couldn't handle it.'[5]

Essentially, his job was to promote and advise AAAA Inc throughout the United States. But favourable publicity and Mark Thatcher are not often mentioned in the same sentence. David Wickins was clearly mindful of this. 'I appreciate that some people think he's an arrogant sod,' he said at the time. 'But I'm sure Mark will be a great asset. What I have to do perhaps is to persuade him to calm down a bit . . . to teach him to be a bit less aggressive with people. I suppose that is a thing of youth and you can't really blame him for being so uppity. He comes over very well as an upstanding young Englishman and that goes down particularly well in the sunshine states.'[6]

Clearly, for a British consultant selling and promoting expensive Lotus sports cars in the USA, personality was a key factor. But Mark seemed relatively unconcerned about his charm bypass. 'Some would call it arrogance,' he said. 'Some do. I would say, arrogantly, that I tend to be short with people. I don't tolerate fools. Period. It's something I've got from my parents. Neither of them tolerates idiots easily – what I have to do is learn to be a little softer about it.'[7]

Thatcher also worked in some capacity for Lotus Cars. One report stated he was 'an associate director'.[8] The company denied he was on the Lotus payroll, and said he was merely working for one of their US subsidiaries. But the confusion was caused by Mark himself, who publicly proclaimed that he was 'selling Lotus' in the USA and referred to 'the Lotus job'.[9] Whatever the exact arrangement, he was certainly involved in building a chain of Lotus dealerships across the USA and Canada in preparation for a North American sales drive in 1985 to promote the new X100 car.

'His name is worth quite a few motor cars,' said Wickins, who was by then also chairman of Lotus.[10] The company's managing director, Michael Kimberley, was more explicit: 'He helps establish dealer points and arranges wine and cheese parties, to which he brings the right sort of people.'[11]

Mark was indebted to Wickins. He saw it as 'a real responsibility and a chance for which I am grateful'.[12] But he was not short of self-confidence. 'The Lotus job is a great challenge and one where I intend to use my name ruthlessly to win orders for Britain – my name, that is, as a racing commentator and sports car expert,' he declared. 'People in the performance car world in America just don't give a damn who my mother is. They know me for my expertise and experience.'[13]

Thatcher had already been working for the company behind the scenes for over three years. 'Mark has been a very good friend to Lotus for some time,' said Alan Curtis, the company's deputy chairman.[14] Mark and Curtis became close associates. According to Gerald James, former chairman of the arms manufacturer Astra Holdings, the Lotus boss regularly spoke of his friendship with the prime minister and her son. 'He told me on more than one occasion how he would visit 10 Downing Street at "Slipper Time",' recalled James. 'This was after 10.30pm when Margaret Thatcher liked a chat with her favourite industrialists over a glass of whisky.'[15]

Mark Thatcher shamelessly used his position to promote the Lotus product. He had been given a free Lotus, and on one occasion deliberately parked his car outside 10 Downing Street when he knew the photographers and camera crews were waiting to film his mother leave. Norman Luck, the *Daily Express* journalist who had been fed stories by Mark in the mid-1970s, recalls being telephoned by Mark. 'He told me he was trying out new Lotus cars in the West End of London,' said Luck. 'But when I arrived I was surprised to find Margaret Thatcher sitting in a Lotus Esprit promoting the company.'[16]

By late 1982, despite Mark Thatcher's efforts, Lotus

was in desperate trouble. It was losing money and
was in a bitter dispute with the Inland Revenue over
protective tax assessments totalling £84 million. This
was calculated as part of the Revenue's enquiry into
missing money from the failed DeLorean venture.
Lotus had received funds from DeLorean, the supercar
manufacturer, to prepare production of its new gull-
winged car. But the cash had disappeared and senior
executives were being investigated for theft.

Colin Chapman, chairman of Lotus, who was the
prime suspect and later accused of embezzlement,
approached Alan Curtis, who had enjoyed a successful
career at Aston Martin and just sold his shareholding
there. 'Lotus needs to change its image,' said Chapman over lunch. 'We need to revamp the corporate
side of the company and we're having trouble with
the DeLorean business. Will you join us and help
restructure the company?' Curtis accepted and joined
the board. Two days later Fred Bushell, the managing
director later convicted of fraud over the DeLorean
affair, telephoned to say Chapman had died.

For the first six months of 1983 Curtis and Michael
Kimberley, the new managing director, worked day
and night to rescue Lotus. The company was in crisis,
often on the brink of being sold to the Japanese. In
July, Curtis consulted Mark Thatcher and discussed
the situation. Thatcher responded by setting up a
meeting with David Wickins, chairman of British
Car Auctions and a business associate of his father.
Five days later Wickins bought a 29 per cent stake in
Lotus and became chairman, with Curtis as his deputy.
'If David had not invested, then Lotus would have gone
under,' Curtis told us over coffee at the Savoy.

Mark Thatcher played an active role as a middleman, massaging people on both sides and acting as

a facilitator for new investors. He was not paid a
retainer during this period, but did receive expenses
and free use of a Lotus. 'He helped us a great deal,'
recalled Curtis. 'He used his clout and opened up all
the right doors in Detroit and all the right top people
in the motor industry.'[17] Using the Thatcher name,
Mark then introduced Lotus to the chief executives
and chairmen of General Motors and Chrysler. The
key move was in 1984, when Thatcher introduced
Curtis to Robert Eaton, a senior vice-president of
General Motors (GM).

Eaton, Thatcher, Curtis and David Wickins met for
dinner at the Savoy Hotel, where the long-term future
of the company was discussed. It was this connection
with Eaton which paved the way for the successful
friendly take-over of Lotus by GM. By late 1985 an
initial list of thirty-two companies had been reduced
to five (two American and three British) before GM
was chosen. In a deal which valued the company at
£22.7 million, GM bought 58 per cent of the shares,
including Wickins's 29 per cent stake. The take-over
was completed in January 1986 and Mark Thatcher
resigned his consultancy with both Lotus Performance
Cars and Anglo-American Auto Auctions. By then he
was settled in the United States, where other business
activities awaited him.

In Exile

Mark Thatcher's stay in New York was always likely
to be temporary. He lived at the Regency Hotel in
Manhattan and his job with Anglo-American Auto
Auctions meant travelling throughout the United States.

But it was a blind date in Texas four months earlier that precipitated his permanent move south. On 22 December 1983, he had flown down to Dallas to watch the Cowboys play the Washington Redskins at American football. That evening he was having dinner with oil billionaire Perry Bass and his wife, Nancy, when he found himself sitting next to Karen Fortson, a stunning twenty-four-year-old brunette from Fort Worth, Texas, who was one of the wealthiest and most eligible women in the South. She was the daughter of Ben Fortson, a multimillionaire from oil and cattle-ranching stock, and Kay (née Carter), who had inherited a fortune from her own family based on grain, insurance and oil. The Fortsons were the arbiters of Fort Worth's old-moneyed aristocracy, keen to add dignity and culture to their wealth, in contrast to what they saw as the brash, flash *nouveau riche* crowd in Dallas.[18]

Karen, who worked in a New York art auction house, was conservative, introvert, rich, well-bred, radiant and, above all, very discreet. Mark was attracted to her immediately. 'I was struck by her poise and beauty,' he said. Karen was equally impressed. 'I don't make a habit of blind dates,' she remarked, 'but I was intrigued to know what Mark Thatcher was like. My first impression was that he was nice and rather reserved. I'm quite reserved myself, so it's good to meet someone else like that.'[19]

Romance soon blossomed and Mark became a frequent visitor to the family's palatial mansion in Westover Hill, just outside Fort Worth. The house boasted a vestibule the size of a Greek temple – a symbol of the family fortune estimated at £100 million.[20] The couple became very close and Mark even turned down some driving offers. 'Karen isn't very keen on motor racing,' he explained.[21] Their courtship was very low-key and they once cancelled a weekend party at a Fort Worth night-club to 'stay out of the limelight'.[22]

Their relationship was tested barely a month after they met, with the Oman revelations. 'Karen was an enormous support to me. I don't know how I'd have got through without her,' said Mark. 'Things haven't been easy for him,' she said loyally, 'but he's really pulled himself together and coped with the problems. . . . I felt the pressures too but his must have been a hundred times greater.'[23]

In the midst of the crisis, on Saturday, 18 February 1984, Mark took her to Chequers to spend the weekend with his parents. That evening they entertained oil magnate Perry Bass and his wife, Nancy, for dinner. In the morning the couple and Margaret and Denis attended service at St Peter's Church in the Buckinghamshire village of Ellesborough. By pure chance, but with remarkably apposite irony, the service happened to focus on the evils of wealth. '"Wisdom cannot be bought with silver or gold,"' the church warden Bill Mitton read from the Gospel of St Luke to the congregation. '"How blessed are you who are poor, the Kingdom of God is yours. Alas for you who are rich, you have had your time of happiness."'[24] Mark and Karen then joined the prime minister for an official lunch for Crown Prince Naruhito of Japan, at which the guests included Princess Alexandra, Angus Ogilvy, Clive Sinclair and political friends. A sensitive Margaret Thatcher paid the bill out of her own purse for her son and girlfriend.

Karen and Mrs Thatcher established an immediate rapport. 'I found her so warm and pleasant,' said the Texan heiress.[25] 'She makes you feel so warm and comfortable.' This was apparent when the prime minister invited Mark, Karen, Karen's twin brother, Ben, and her mother for Sunday lunch at Chequers. On the morning of 13 May 1984, the party flew in from Paris and posed for photographers, arranged by Mark's friend Rodney Tyler. 'Come on, hurry up,' he snapped glaring at the cameras. 'We will be late for lunch.'[26] He then drove Karen to his mother's country residence in his silver Lotus Esprit while her family followed in their Daimler.

The lunch went well and Karen gave only a cautious denial of any wedding plans. It seemed marriage was only a matter of time, particularly when Mark moved to Dallas – a mere thirty miles west of Fort Worth, Karen's home town – six weeks later. On 1 June 1984, he moved into a one-bedroom rented apartment at Terrace House in the élite Turtle Creek area for $1,000 a month.

However, by mid-July 1984, his romance with Karen Fortson had rather abruptly wilted. 'Anyone waiting for an engagement is going to wait for a very long time,' she said caustically.[27] It was never clear why she broke off the relationship so soon after Mark arrived in Dallas. 'She thought it would be entertaining and glamorous to date him,' said a Fortson family friend. 'But she didn't know he wouldn't be socially acceptable in Dallas.'[28] Another view is that 'He was getting too much heat from the British tabloids and old man Fortson didn't like it,' according to a Dallas social commentator. 'When they started to suggest that Mark was a fortune hunter the shit really hit the fan and suddenly it was all over.'[29] From a source close to Mark Thatcher comes a different view: 'Basically Karen rumbled him. She saw through all the bullshit and realized he was always going to be on edge and paranoid. There was no way she could live with him.'

Karen herself is now married with children and living back in Fort Worth. At first she appeared willing to talk and asked for a list of questions, which were faxed to her. But she then changed her mind. 'I have the utmost respect and admiration for the Thatcher family,' she told us politely. 'I am afraid I would rather not say anything.'

When Mark moved permanently to Dallas, he was relatively friendless and short on business contacts. Publicly, he denied being banished to America. 'I know this is what my enemies are saying,' he said.[30] But privately he wrote home to friends signing off 'In exile', and felt he had been dispatched to the colonies. Margaret Thatcher also saw it in those terms. 'He's in exile, you know,' she remarked to the Tory MP Jeremy Hanley, Mark's old accountancy tutor.

The prime minister's son arrived in Texas, aged thirty, with ambitions to accumulate a pot of gold. 'I have a very high success criterion,' he said at the time, 'and I don't think I will have been successful until I reach what I see as success in my own mind – to have achieved something. Monetary values come into it, because I like to live well and have to earn a lot. I'll become less hungry once I do.'[31]

For Mark, business success was dependent almost exclusively on political connections. He already knew oil billionaire Perry Bass. And it was through the Texan oil network, which included Vice-President George Bush, that Mark became friends with entrepreneur Bruce Leadbetter and John Tower, the late senator for Texas.

Senator Tower, whose nomination as defense secretary by the President in 1988 was rejected by the

US Senate because of his reputation as an alcoholic and womanizer, became Mark's mentor in Texas. He introduced him to his business partner, veteran lawyer Paul Eggers, who has remained a close associate of Mark's. 'Mark has got a tremendous feel for business and finely tuned political antennae,' said Eggers, who has twice sought the governorship of Texas. 'He could have a political career of his own. It's a pity he wasn't born in this country and could run for office here.'[32]

Tower and Thatcher became close friends and associates. 'He [Mark] has had many meetings with John Tower,' said Eggers. 'They talk to each other on the same high plane.'[33] The two were often seen lunching and dining together at the luxurious Mansion on the Creek Hotel or drinking in the Library Bar. So much so that when Mark attended the senator's birthday dinner party at the Mansion on the Creek, on 19 September 1989, it became a joint celebration as Mark's birthday was the previous month.

The senator was one of those who came to Mark's aid when he was asked to vacate his apartment after fellow residents expressed concern that he was 'a target of international terrorism'. Margaret Thatcher had been the only Western leader to support the Americans' bombing of Libya shortly before, and her son had received anonymous death threats. 'The national interest and the honour of Texas were poorly served by this action,' said Tower. 'It reflects on my state. I'm terribly embarrassed. We have a moral obligation to this young man.'[34] Mark then received round-the-clock protection from armed FBI agents and a month's grace before moving to a new apartment in Turtle Creek.

Tower was a useful potential business contact for Thatcher, not least in the arms field. In 1985 he retired from Congress and set up his own defence consulting firm, advising contractors on how to secure orders in Washington. His clients included Martin Marietta, Rockwell International and Textron. For two years, 1986–8, he also acted for the American subsidiary of British Aerospace. Tower was paid a total of $250,000 by the company to 'work the system' in trying to sell Hawk and Tornado jets and Rapier anti-aircraft missiles to the Pentagon. He resigned the consultancy as soon as he became a candidate for defense secretary.[35]

Another close association was with Richard Fisher, a Dallas investment banker who befriended Mark and Denis Thatcher in the mid-1980s. 'I think Mark is extremely bright and loyal to his mother,' said Fisher. 'I think he realises that great people can serve and then be forgotten and their offspring amount to nothing.'[36] Mark described Fisher as 'a family friend who has had a number of private meetings with Lady Thatcher over the years'.[37] But he was more than that, according to the investment banker. 'For three years [1988–91], I had the honour of having been drawn into Prime Minister Thatcher's circle of private advisers, usually briefing her on financial markets.'[38]

Despite these useful entrées to Texas, Margaret Thatcher was concerned about her beloved son's activities, so she arranged for Calman L. Donsky, a lawyer and partner with the Dallas firm of Garderra and Wynne, to look after his interests. 'There was an agreement that whenever Mark launched a new business project, it would be cleared with Donsky,' said a Thatcher friend. 'Margaret provided her private telephone number so she could be reached at any time. It was a strange situation where she would not

admit he needed looking after but she did everything
she could to make sure he was.'

An example of this crisis management was when
Mark wanted to set up a financial services company
which would manage and co-ordinate investors' funds.
The problem was that he had not approached the
Securities and Exchange Commission (SEC) for authorization and did not seem to realize that investment
management firms were strictly regulated in the USA.
His proposed company would have operated outside
the SEC laws. Donsky was aghast, as he knew this was
a criminal offence and the British prime minister's son
could end up in jail. So he blocked the project just in
time, despite Mark's protests. 'But why can't I run the
company in this way?' he asked.

Mark was keen to be accepted in Dallas society. But
what he failed to realize was that social acceptance had
to be earned by civic duty. According to prominent
Texans, he did not pay his social dues because he
believed it was a free ride. Mark thought that being the
prime minister's son was enough and that he would be
automatically accepted. For example, he was desperate
to be a member of the exclusive Dallas Country Club,
not least for its lush golf course, but his application was
rejected. This was not necessarily because the leaders
of Dallas society disapproved of him. More relevant
was his lacklustre support for charities like the Jewel
Gala benefit for the Northwood Institute in Dallas.

In social terms Mark blew it and never recovered.
He tried to impress them by boasting that he knew
the royal family intimately (he did know the Duke
and Duchess of York, but that was about it). He also
loudly told friends and anyone within earshot that he
would later need to be addressed as 'Sir Mark' (this
would only apply, of course, after his baronet father

died). But it was his stand-offish behaviour that did not endear him to the talkative Texans. 'He's quite friendly to meet in private,' said John Haynsworth, Dallas's leading society photographer, 'but if you go to a party he's at, you'll see him walking around looking very aloof.'[39] 'I hate people who look down their noses,' said Caroline Rose Hunt, the owner of two luxury hotels in Dallas. She wasn't referring directly to Thatcher, but the implication was clear.

Thatcher's obsession with secrecy and his paranoia also did not rest well with Dallas's friendly and open society, particularly after his treasure chest began to fill. 'He had suddenly become a big fish,' said a school friend who visited him in America. 'I remember having lunch with him and he kept hiding behind a huge pot plant because he was worried who might see him. He told me he used to get dozens of death threats and that he had eight armed guards protecting him. He was rather proud of the fact. I came away thinking that Mark Thatcher was locked into himself and couldn't get out.'[40]

The focus of Thatcher's social and business activities was the Mansion on the Creek, the most expensive and luxurious hotel in town. He stayed there for six weeks when he first arrived in Texas and was remembered chiefly for insisting that his car be driven to just a few feet from the hotel kerb, so he did not need to walk the extra yards. He often holds business dinners and lunches there and hosted a private New Year's Eve party on 31 December 1992, in the wine cellar.

Dallas society came to see through him, and soon his arrogant manner led him to be known in some quarters as 'White Trash'. This came as quite a shock to Thatcher. He was noticeably irritated when asked about this. 'No, I don't get involved with Dallas society,' he replied with a trace of what the Hong Kong *Tatler* described as 'his famous sneer'.[41]

Mark responded by associating with an altogether different social set – young, flash, racy, aggressive entrepreneurs, often in the oil, automobile and property businesses. They were very much the 'new money' crowd and some of them were guests at Thatcher's wedding. They included Taylor Boyd, Bruce Leadbetter, Bob Franklin, Forrest Germany and David Davidson, a real-estate broker who was later convicted of eight counts of bank fraud and jailed for six months.[42]

An indication of Mark's new social crowd was the new woman in his life. Diane Burgdorf was very different from Karen Fortson in almost every way. They were both bright twenty-four-year-olds when they met him, but there the similarity ended. Diane was blonde and vivacious. She was also intelligent, reserved, old-fashioned and very religious. Very much an all-American girl, she was a cheer-leader and often competed in local beauty contests. After attending Bethany Lutheran College in Minnesota, she received a degree in business administration from the Southern Methodist University in Dallas. She then worked for a real-estate firm before joining the Cornerstone National Bank in Dallas where her job was to open new accounts for customers.[43]

Diane's family was very much part of the 'new dollar' set in Dallas as opposed to the 'old dollar' clique of Fort Worth. Her father, Ted Burgdorf, was wealthy but not by Texan standards. His millions were derived from being the owner of Uptown Auto Sales in Garland and Burgdorf Chevrolet in Pittsburg, Texas. He was also chairman of the Mary Miler company which converts vans into 'recreation vehicles (RVs)'. Diane lived with her parents at their house ('smart not

swanky') on Yacht Club Drive in Chandler's Landing,
just by the Sam Rayburn lake, a thirty-minute drive east
of Dallas. 'She's just an ordinary Texan millionairess,'
said her father of Diane, but he added that underneath
her shyness, 'She's a hell of a tough little lady in a
crisis.'[44]

Mark was introduced to her at a Dallas Christmas
party in December 1984, by a real-estate colleague. He
was mesmerized by her and soon bouquets of flowers
began arriving at her office. On their first date Diane
loved the way Mark constantly talked about Mummy.
'I figured that anyone who loved his mother so much
must have been raised well,' she recalled.[45] But it was
many months before passion entered the relationship.
When the couple first stayed overnight at 10 Downing
Street in April 1985, while Margaret Thatcher was
abroad, Diane's mother, Lois Burgdorf, said, 'My
daughter Diane is a real Southern Belle. And good
Baptist girls from Texas don't go in for hanky-panky
before they get married.'[46]

Their courtship was a quiet affair. Mark was
obsessed with keeping their romance confidential
and was furious their trip to London was leaked to
the press. When first approached by British reporters
in Texas, she replied: 'You know very well I'm not
allowed to say anything.'[47] He responded by calling
the Dallas police.

Even at the couple's first major social function
together – the 1985 Cattle Barons' Ball – Mark
was paranoid about secrecy. While they mingled with
guests at Southfork Ranch, where the *Dallas* TV series
was filmed, he was recognized by the photographer
Akhtar Hussein. 'Can I ask, who is your escort,
sir?' he said politely. Bizarrely, Mark tried to avoid
him by adopting a loud, fake Texan drawl. This

less-than-subtle tactic failed to work because Hussein knew exactly who he was and so turned to Diane. 'Just call me Mark Thatcher's mystery blonde,' she joked. Mark immediately turned on Diane and scolded her, ordering her never to talk to the media. After that, Mark would always withdraw on seeing Hussein at parties.

This incident typified his future relations with the press. On 5 March 1988, the couple flew to California to attend a charity lunch in Palm Springs, hosted by the Duke and Duchess of York. It was a typical celebrity event, attended mainly by media stars, including Victoria Principal from the *Dallas* TV series. The night before the lunch, Mark and Diane walked into the hotel lobby for a reception. Margaret Hall, who was covering the story for the *News of the World*, was among the waiting reporters. She had no intention of asking any questions but decided to introduce herself. She approached Mark, stretched out her hand and said, 'Maggie Hall, *News of the World*.' The journalists were then astonished to see the prime minister's son take off and literally run away, sprinting around the pillars and then down the corridor. Hall stared, shocked and open-mouthed, and turned to Diane: 'I just wanted to say hello.' Diane shrugged her shoulders. 'What can you do?' she replied.

The next day Thatcher and his wife attended the lunch in the VIP marquee at the El Dorado polo club in Palm Springs. Mark seemed happy enough, if moody, sitting next to Walter Annenberg, the billionaire former US ambassador to Britain, and at the same table as the Duchess of York. But then after lunch a club official approached his table and asked him to move his limousine because it was blocking the other cars. 'I am the passenger, not the chauffeur,' he sniffed, scowling at the 'impertinence' of the man. Much to the surprise of the other guests and watching reporters, Mark then drove off with Diane at full speed.[48]

The remarkable irony of his time in Texas was that Mark wanted to venture into public relations. One day an experienced PR consultant based in Dallas received a telephone call from a distant relative, who told her that Mark Thatcher wanted to 'get into public relations'. She was asked if she could offer any advice. After catching her breath, she politely declined. It would be hard to find someone less suited to PR, she thought to herself after replacing the receiver.

Despite Thatcher's penchant for secrecy, his romance with Diane prospered. They visited London periodically –– either to see Margaret and Denis at Chequers or staying at the Carlton Tower Hotel in Knightsbridge. They would then fly to Paris, where Mark had an apartment and spent a lot of time in the mid-1980s. He also began introducing her to his English friends. 'This is Diane Burgdorf, of Burgdorf-Goodman, you know,' said Mark. This did not impress the friend who knew she was Burgdorf – the car dealers from Texas – not Bergdorf – the prestigious New York store chain.

After initial doubts, Margaret Thatcher was won over by Diane's good nature and sincerity, and on 12 November 1986 Mark announced their engagement. The Burgdorf family were delighted. 'We have a very high regard for Mrs Thatcher, despite her critics,' said Diane's grandfather, Paul Burgdorf. 'As a preacher I myself have been taking a stand against Communism since the 1930s.'[49] Her father, Ted, was telephoned by the prime minister, who said she was 'thrilled by the engagement and adored' her future daughter-in-law. 'We are very proud to have a family connection with Mrs Thatcher,' said Ted. 'It's a great honour. I am looking forward to meeting Mrs Thatcher, but I don't plan to capitalise on it.'[50]

However, even Diane's father let slip Mark's obsession with security, with which the family originally found it difficult to cope. 'Every time we saw him he had his guards with him,' said Ted. 'The security guard was constantly in attendance and he went with them on dates. There was one time when we went water-skiing and one of his guards even came in the boat. It seemed very strange at first but we eventually got used to it.'[51]

Another revealing glimpse – and perhaps a warning signal to the family – of Mark's personality arose during the official photo call at 10 Downing Street, the day after the engagement announcement. Margaret and Denis beamed at the cameras while Diane and Mark grimaced and then stood stony-faced, only smiling briefly at the end of the five-minute picture session. When photographers asked to take pictures of Diane's engagement ring, Mark pulled her hand behind his back so that they could not see what looked like a diamond solitaire. 'It's a family thing,' he told them, much to the consternation of Bernard Ingham, the prime minister's press secretary.[52]

Having said that, Ted Burgdorf seemed genuinely happy at the time with his prospective son-in-law. 'I was impressed with him right away,' he said. 'He is a gentleman and has always treated our daughter like the princess we feel she is. We couldn't wish for a finer son-in-law.'[53]

Margaret Thatcher liked Diane, particularly as she saw her as a calming influence on Mark's volatile personality, and she was keen to have grandchildren. But she viewed his marriage as her precious little boy being taken away from her, despite the fact that he

was thirty-three years old. This was noticed by Diane's
family and close friends at a private dinner, on Monday,
9 February 1987, five days before the wedding. The
party for thirty guests was given in honour of the couple
by Charles Price, the American ambassador in London,
and held at his home in Regent's Park.

During the dinner, attended by BBC chairman
Marmaduke Hussey and cabinet minister Cecil (now
Lord) Parkinson, Lois Burgdorf, Diane's mother, said
to a fellow guest, 'I've been here for three days and she
[Mrs Thatcher] has not spoken one word to me.' When
this was pointed out to the prime minister, she shrugged
it off and moved to the other side of the room. She did
see Lois Burgdorf and Diane the following evening at
10 Downing Street. But her behaviour at the dinner
was a measure of her emotions at the time. Later she
was to have a warm but formal relationship with her
daughter-in-law who would often refer to her as 'Lady
Thatcher'. 'I have tons of admiration for the woman,'
said Diane.[54]

Meanwhile, Mark was enjoying himself at his stag
party in the wine cellar of the elegant Stafford Hotel,
St James's. Among the twenty-eight guests were nine
Texans, John Webb, owner of the Brands Hatch racing
circuit, Tim Bell, his unofficial public relations adviser,
Alan Curtis, chairman of Lotus Cars, and Steve Tipping, Mark's best man and business partner.[55] It was
a high-spirited, bubbly affair with Mark an engaging
and amusing host. One of the guests arrived with
thirty pairs of Groucho Marx spectacles and false
noses, enough for the whole crowd.[56]

But it was also very much a 'Boys Own' occasion.
Among the guests was a Top Gun pilot who was talking
in a jocular way about flying. 'Helicopter-flying is like
masturbation,' he quipped. 'It feels good but looks

funny to anyone looking on.' Mark, who had heard only the reference to helicopters, piped up and bragged, 'I've done 400 hours in a helicopter.' Everyone cracked up laughing.

The following evening, 12 February, the prime minister hosted a pre-wedding party at 10 Downing Street for 200 friends, relatives and political colleagues. The two-hour reception appeared to be dominated by the Burgdorf family, who arrived in two black limousines. But it was notable for the presence of several high-powered industrialists. One of the guests recalls observing the prominence of Lord Hanson and the late Lord White. 'The thing I always remember about that night,' he said, 'was Mrs Thatcher speaking to Lord Hanson on six separate occasions. I watched them very carefully. He was standing very upright with a foot on one of the pillars as if he owned a slice of the place. She spoke to him in an almost earnest way and then Mark twice went over to his mother after she broke off her conversation with Hanson.'[57]

Two days later, on Saturday, 14 February 1987, Mark and Diane were married at the Savoy Chapel, a sixteenth-century church that seats only 150 people. That meant several close friends and relatives of the families were not invited. Officially, this was for 'security reasons', so when the couple walked down the aisle armed Special Branch detectives were watching their every move. Trained marksmen mingled with the guests and travelled with the bride and groom and their families. They also checked out staff at the Savoy Hotel where the reception was being held.[58] Over the two days 240 police officers were assigned to the event, at a cost of £7,000.[59]

On the wedding day the press tried to provoke Mark. One newspaper dubbed it the 'St Valentine's

Day Massacre' and 'The Bride and Gloom'.[60] Another paper published a detailed street map for Mark to find his way to the chapel – as a less than gentle reminder of his being lost in the Sahara desert.[61]

But Mark, after being spoken to by his mother, was on his best behaviour. He arrived fifteen minutes early, providing a rare smile for the cameras. It was a simple service based on the revised prayer book which meant that Diane did not undertake to 'obey' her husband. Margaret was noticeably emotional when Mark recited his marriage vows. 'There were tears in my eyes more than once,' she said.[62] Diane wore a traditional white satin dress with a five-foot train, at a cost of $2,000 from Nieman Marcus.

After the ceremony the newly-weds got into a red Rolls-Royce which drove them to the reception at the Savoy Hotel 200 yards away. The party was a grand affair, with 300 guests, including seventy Texans. But Mark Thatcher could not resist trying to use even this romantic occasion for commercial purposes. 'It was quite extraordinary,' recalled one businessman who was present. 'He was even using his wedding to hustle for business. I particularly remember him introducing Steve Tipping to people saying, "We do a lot together, you know." That didn't go down too well.' Mark's bride shared this view. During a dinner party hosted by Wafic Said in Marbella, in 1992, a guest told Diane about his daughter's impending wedding. 'Well, don't make the mistake I made,' she said. 'There were 300 guests at my wedding and the bulk of them were my husband's business contacts that he wanted to impress.'

Two days later Mark and Diane Thatcher flew first-class on a Qantas 747 jet to Sydney, Australia, for a month-long honeymoon. The couple were driven

to the airport in an armoured chauffeur-driven black
Jaguar. The prime minister then picked up the £70 bill
for their use of the VIP Hillingdon Suite at Heathrow.[63]
Mark was back to his pre-wedding mood. 'I do not
pose for pictures,' he told waiting photographers.[64]
The couple were booked into the Regency Hotel in
Sydney as 'Mr and Mrs Green' but Mark was soon
recognized, much to his fury. 'He looks as if he's
spent a month on vinegar and lemon juice,' quipped
one Australian journalist.[65]

On their return to Texas, Mark and Diane moved
into their new home in Fairfax Avenue, Highland Park,
one of the most fashionable and prestigious parts of
Dallas. The area is known as 'the Bubble' because the
atmosphere is so rarefied only millionaires can breathe
easily.[66] Mark paid £415,000 in cash, using a bank
loan from Luxembourg, for the neo-Georgian house,
relatively small but built like a fortress. He installed
an intricate security system, complete with a black iron
security gate and an underground bunker room in the
basement known as 'the war room'. In the centre of
this room is a vault into which Mark, his wife and
two children can retreat at times of 'security alerts'
or, perhaps, other forms of human threat.

An estimated £110,000 has been spent on a separate
flat for the nanny at the back of the property, a new
hallway with Italian marble floors and a new annexe
to the sitting-room. Mark has also employed a Mexican
housekeeper and a personal English valet, Graham
Henderson, who travelled with him on many of his
trips to London.

Unfortunately, the house became so cluttered that,
when they hosted dinner parties, the numerous servants
made the occasion resemble a scene from the Keystone
Cops. Perhaps the most significant feature of the house

is that when Mark is abroad people passing by can see an imposing illuminated portrait of his mother above the mantelpiece in his drawing-room. Just in case they miss it, potential business clients are reminded of her presence in his office on the thirty-eighth floor of the Texas Commerce Bank building in Houston, nicknamed 'Maggie's hall of fame'. Portraits of Margaret Thatcher stare down imposingly from every wall on to any visitor. Her son has even framed the original hand-written notes of a speech she delivered to the Dallas Chamber of Commerce in 1991.[67]

Unlike his wife, Diane, Mark is not a popular neighbour in Fairfax Avenue. When he drives his BMW 735 saloon or black Porsche Carrera (bought for $78,000 from his father-in-law), he barely acknowledges fellow residents. 'They do have parties,' said one woman who lives opposite, 'but Mark picks one person – usually someone important to his business – and talks to them all night. He says good evening to the rest of the guests, then ignores them. I'm not real fond of him. One day, after I had just moved here, I turned round to find him all the way back in my bedroom. I had parked my car across the street and he didn't like it and told me to move. I stuck out my hand to introduce myself, but he just wanted me to move, quick.'[68]

Mark's behaviour towards his wife has also attracted comment in the neighbourhood and Dallas society. Diane's reasons for marrying Mark have never been clear. 'I always figured I'd marry the typical boy next door,' she said, laughing. 'But I guess God had something different in mind.'[69] Friends have often wondered what they have in common. Certainly, they are both very conventional socially and like to live discreet, secluded lives. They are also both devoted to their parents and children. But it's difficult to point to other mutual interests. More sceptical sources say the celebrity factor was crucial. 'Diane thought she was marrying British royalty,' said a friend of the couple. Mark played up to this by telling her he was close friends with the royal family. But this was only partly true as he only knew the Duke and Duchess of York (they had met at a polo match in California in 1986).

During their marriage Mark was as aloof and arrogant with his wife as he was with almost everyone else. This was noted on Sunday mornings after church when Thatcher liked to breakfast at the Mansion on the Creek Hotel. According to a fellow guest, his head would be hidden behind a newspaper for over an hour and hardly any conversation would take place. On another occasion the couple were in a helicopter owned by Wafic Said, the Syrian financier. Because of drizzling rain, it was a rocky flight with considerable turbulence and suddenly Diane's foot was pierced by her umbrella. Although the cut drew blood and she was limping and clearly in some pain, on landing Mark gave her no more than a cursory glance. 'That seems to be all right,' he said, and walked on.

At home Mark behaves with a curious combination of petulance and imperial aloofness. He treats Diane more like a glorified domestic servant than a wife, according to house-guests. 'He would bark orders like "Where's the breakfast? I want it now," and was unbelievably rude to her,' said one long-standing friend who stayed in the bedroom specially kept for Margaret Thatcher.

Diane has responded by trying to calm him down by adopting a soothing, serene southern belle tone of voice. 'Oh, Maaark, don't be so aggressive,' she would say when he went into his pugnacious, wide-boy routine in front of friends. She is also not without a mischievous sense of humour. In the summer of 1992, while attending a dinner party at Wafic Said's house in Marbella, she confided in a fellow guest about her marital problems. She said one of their disputes was over her cat. She was deeply attached to it: Mark, however, was not. He asked her to find it another home, but Diane refused. She told the guest that she returned home one day to find her pet missing. When she confronted her husband, he told her that he had ordered some Mexican workmen – who were building an extension to the Thatcher home – to bury the animal alive in the wall. Diane denied this when we spoke to her in August 1994. 'No, that's not true,' she said. 'Mark didn't like my cat but my cat passed away from natural causes about two months ago. It was not my husband's fault.'

Perhaps it was Diane's strict religious upbringing that caused her to endure her husband's antics for so long. For many years she has been a devout member of the Calvary Lutheran Church in Dallas. Founded in the 1960s by her father and part of the Wisconsin Evangelical Lutheran Synod, and now with some 500,000 members, it is very conservative and strict, and is devoted to the ideas of Martin Luther. Her brother, Dale, is an elder. 'Diane is a Bible girl and she's not afraid to tell anyone,' said Paul Burgdorf, her grandfather.[70]

Mark was converted to the Lutheran faith after a twenty-week course of one hour a week, which included a section on ethics. The couple attend a Sunday morning service whenever they are in town. 'We believe that the husband should be the head of the household,' the pastor, John Vieths, told us. 'That does not mean that he can behave like a monster. But wives are encouraged to follow his lead.' When asked by *Today* newspaper what the Church's attitude was towards monetary wealth, Pastor Vieths replied, 'If God blesses you with a lot, that's fine. There are some rich people in the Bible too. Some end up with more, some with less.' And Mark Thatcher? 'The Lord has blessed him, certainly.'[71]

Diane herself told us from her home in Dallas: 'I'm a Christian woman. I'm raising my children with the same upbringing that I was raised. I'm a Bible-believing person and I exercise the virtues of the fruits of the Spirit as much as I can – love, joy, peace, patience, kindness, faithfulness, goodness, gentleness and self-control. That's how I would like myself described. I don't have any personal vendettas against anyone. If they come after me, I just pity them. . . . I serve my Lord, I obey his commands and I think he has blessed me abundantly in this life because of it.'

The Church has strict, ascetic rules on moral behaviour. Smoking and gambling are discouraged, and drinking permitted only in moderation. Abortions are strictly forbidden and divorce is allowed only in cases of adultery or 'malicious desertion'.

On 28 February 1989, Diane gave birth to a son, Michael, at the Presbyterian Hospital in Dallas. The baby was then baptized in the Calvary Lutheran Church in a ceremony attended by his godparents, Steve Tipping and Carol Thatcher. Margaret Thatcher was elated. Three days after the birth, she strode out of 10 Downing Street and proclaimed to waiting reporters and cameramen: 'We have become a grandmother. It is just marvellous and Denis is thrilled too.'[72]

Mark's Dallas friends were equally delighted. One even suggested young Michael would make a future state governor. 'He's a solid little Texan all right,' said

Paul Eggers, the influential lawyer. 'If he turns out like his father and his grandfather, he'll be just the sort of guy we'll need in the next century.'[73]

Two months later, Mark and Diane flew to London to present their son to Mrs Thatcher, who was celebrating ten years as prime minister. 'He looks like Mark did at the same age,' she said as she cradled the boy in her arms on the steps of 10 Downing Street.[74] Within four years she was celebrating again, when Diane produced a granddaughter for her. Mark named his new child Amanda Margaret; she is a lively little girl, who soon became known as 'the Iron Baby'.

Despite being wealthy enough to afford nannies, Diane chose not to work during her marriage. 'Although I loved the intellectual stimulation and drive at work, I thought, "What's the point of marrying someone if you never see him?"' she said three years into the marriage.[75]

The problem was that her worst fears came true. Diane did accompany her husband on some trips to Hong Kong, New Zealand and France. But for the most part she stayed in Dallas while Mark travelled three continents. He is abroad for three months a year. 'I have three homes, one in Dallas, one in London – and one on a Jumbo jet over the Atlantic,' she said, only half joking.[76]

The result of her husband's endless overseas business excursions was that the couple gradually grew apart. Mark has always been addicted to travel and saw no reason to change his habits to suit his wife. This led to considerable tension in the marriage and they began to lead separate lives. Diane wanted to lead a normal family life, but he was simply never at home. So she would go skiing in Aspen, Colorado, alone, while Mark would usually be on an aeroplane somewhere, or staying overnight in Houston, where he moved his office.

What was worse was that Diane suspected her husband was spending time with other women on his overseas excursions. In 1989 she even hired private detectives to follow him during a weekend trip to London. She believed he was spending evenings with Sarah-Jane Clemence, the twenty-three-year-old daughter of property millionaire Terry Clemence, at her flat in Knightsbridge. Mark knew the family through their mutual interests in real estate and car dealing. 'He's a friend of the family, that's all,' said Sarah in 1994. 'I had no idea his wife was suspicious about me. . . . I'm the victim of his wife's jealousy. Diane is not a very nice person. She is unhappy and suspicious.'[77]

More recently, in February 1994, he was trying to charm a female American air force pilot at an exclusive health resort in Ashram, just outside Los Angeles. Mark was at the $1,500-a-week retreat to lose weight but seemed more interested in thirty-one-year-old Sheila O'Grady, according to two of the trainers. 'During hikes she would let him catch up then steam off like a rocket,' said Karin Solo. 'He was rather arrogant and I don't think she was that interested.'[78] 'Mark pushed himself just to be near her – he was really keen,' agreed fellow trainer Geo Moskios. 'I saw him chase her, but never saw him catch her.'[79]

When we asked Diane about her marital problems in August 1994, she replied with polite candour: 'I have no comment to make but I will not deny that things are not sympathetic at this time. He travels an awful lot. I can handle it myself, but I do feel sorry for my children. They love their father and they don't see enough of him. I once said, "What's the point of marrying someone if you never see him?" and I still hold to that point. I'm not going to speak unkindly of him. He is the father of my children, but I think some of the reporting in the press has some truth to it.'

By January 1994, the marriage was in deep trouble and disintegrating. Diane was unable to cope with Mark being away so much, his treatment of her as an appendage of his personal staff and his aloof behaviour. But, instead of just meekly accepting his antics, she began to criticize him regularly. On occasion she has refused to sleep with him and he has had to stay in the 'nanny's flat' above the garage. 'I've seen them together many times,' said a friend of the couple, 'and Mark just shows no affection or warmth towards her. But what's worse is that there's hardly any communication between them, even when he's in the house. I would say Diane is suffering from lack of emotional support, that's the crux of it.' Which makes Mark's comment that 'you have to work at family relationships' rather ironic.[80]

This was confirmed by Sarah-Jane Clemence, who first met the couple while she was on holiday with her family in 1989, staying at the Hôtel du Cap at Cap d'Antibes in the south of France. 'They were like Mr and Mrs Glum,' she recalled. 'They had their baby with them and joined us for dinner a few times. . . . She didn't seem to like being with us. My two sisters are very pretty and she continually stared at them and seemed to be keeping an eye on Mark.'[81]

An exasperated Diane has taken solace in her Church and told her husband the marriage could only be saved if he undertook religious counselling. 'Her everyday decisions are influenced by her faith,' said a close friend of the couple. 'If there is anyone else involved then it is God. Diane is having an affair with God.'[82]

Mark has been unable to deal with the situation and spends more and more time away from home.

He was already commuting 250 miles to his new office in Houston, and since 1993 has increasingly stayed overnight at the Omni Hotel, often returning only at weekends. For Diane, an absentee husband is not good enough. She has made up her mind and their relationship is irretrievable. Divorce is inevitable and only a matter of time. Publicly, Mark denied this. 'No divorce, and any speculation of it is just fanciful,' he said.[83]

However, by October 1994, the marriage was in such a precarious state that Lady Thatcher herself decided to intervene. During a visit to Texas that month she spoke to Mark and offered to pay for a family Christmas. According to a source close to the family, he complained that his wife wanted an expensive holiday in the Bahamas. So she called Diane who replied, 'No, that's not true. I just wanted a quiet family Christmas at home. It's Mark who wants to go to the Bahamas.' Margaret Thatcher was shocked by such deception and is virtually resigned to her son's marriage breakdown. 'I don't want to divorce him,' Diane told her, 'but it may be the only way to live a normal life.' Their marriage has, almost miraculously, survived. They currently live in South Africa.

American Gold

Although Mark has respected and accommodated his wife's strong religious faith, he has always worshipped at a different altar, namely, the pursuit of wealth; and Texas, USA, was the perfect church in which to continue his devotion to his brand of spirituality. 'My brother-in-law used to say that anyone worth their salt could come to Dallas, fall over in the street, and get up with a mouthful of money,' said Mark Seal, a local writer.[84]

Publicly, Thatcher's vehicle for his American business interests is the Grantham Company. Named in homage to his mother's birthplace, Grantham must be one of the most secretive commercial outfits in America. It is unlisted in any business directory and not registered with the Dallas Chamber of Commerce. Until 1992, the office was on the eighteenth floor of the Lincoln Center on LBJ Freeway in Richardson, a northern suburb of Dallas. It contained little more than a name-plate, a reception desk and a small boardroom. The secretary, Debbie Milner, was under instructions not to disclose the function of the company.[85] Even Paul Eggers, a very close friend of Thatcher in Dallas, was unaware of Grantham. 'I know he has some offshore things in Europe, but that's all,' he said.[86]

Although companies with offices in Texas are required by law to register in that state, Grantham has been allowed to keep its activities secret. It seems this is because it is structured as a partnership rather than a corporation and so is not obliged to file accounts. But that remains an incomplete explanation. What is known is that it was founded in the summer of 1987 after the general election in which Margaret Thatcher secured a 101-seat majority. Set up by Mark and Dallas-based financier Bruce Leadbetter, Grantham 'looks at investment opportunities, makes direct investments on behalf of the partners and brings in other investors'.[87]

One of its early projects was setting up a printing company in Mexico. David Wallace, a partner in Grantham, later said this firm operated and made money partly because goods and services were provided 'at lower wages'.[88] Later Grantham looked at financial leasing in the telecommunications industry, real-estate development and the processing of health-care claims.[89]

It also acts as a consultant to corporations, and in June 1987 was hired by Electronic Data Systems Inc (EDS), the computer company formerly owned by Ross Perot, the wealthy tycoon and 1993 presidential candidate. Perot had befriended Mark when he was asked to leave his apartment because of fears that he was a terrorist target. The billionaire businessman arranged for Thatcher to live in a bungalow near his Dallas house and the two became acquainted.[90]

It was a transitional period for Perot. EDS had just been taken over by General Motors and he was looking to break into international markets. It was in that context that Mark and Grantham were hired. The two-year EDS contract was for Thatcher to develop marketing plans for selling their data-processing facilities in South-East Asia, particularly in Hong Kong, China and Korea, 'and to the exclusion of all activities directly or indirectly related to the UK'.[91] 'They were door-openers and advisers for us,' recalled Roger Still, an EDS regional director of public relations.

Despite the UK exclusion clause, the consultancy was highly sensitive, because at the time EDS was bidding for a £1.6 billion contract with the British government to run a privatized National Insurance and social security system. It was also interested in a Ministry of Defence computer project worth £500 million. EDS staff had also been discovered by the Home Office to have obtained employment in Britain 'without the necessary authority . . . some EDS employees entered by deception'.[92]

And so when Sir Robert (now Lord) Armstrong, then cabinet secretary, discovered the EDS consultancy

he was not best pleased. He had been informed by
Sallingbury Casey, a UK lobbying firm acting for EDS,
and immediately told the prime minister. Sir Robert
was surprised to be told that she 'knew nothing of the
links'.[93]

The cabinet secretary and his senior civil servants were uneasy about Mark's commercial activities.
Bernard Ingham, the prime minister's press secretary
for eleven years, was particularly concerned that they
would damage her politically. In May 1987, at the out-
set of the general election campaign, Mark approached
Ingham and asked him what he could do to help his
mother's campaign. 'Leave the country,' the blunt
Yorkshireman responded.[94] Thatcher promptly flew
back to Dallas and returned to London only during
the final week of the campaign. He was in 10 Downing
Street on election night and joined in the celebrations.
But it was clear he was not welcomed by her staff and
was soon back in Dallas.

Four months later, Margaret Thatcher visited Dallas
for the first time. Ostensibly, her trip was a private,
family occasion to see her son and daughter-in-law.
But the visit had another agenda which Mark and his
associates tried in vain to keep confidential – she was
being used to entice some of America's most powerful
businessmen to a dinner in Dallas, thereby promoting
her son's commercial interests.

Margaret Thatcher had been attending the Commonwealth Conference in Vancouver. But instead of returning to London, she flew to Dallas in a US government
DC-9 jet. At 2.30am on Sunday, 18 October 1987,
she arrived at Mark's house in Highland Park like an
empress visiting her crown prince. Residents on Fairfax
Avenue were woken to see her appear in a twenty-
car convoy led by eight steel-helmeted motorcycle

police. To complete the performance, a Dallas police helicopter hovered low overhead, aiming a dazzling searchlight.[95]

Mark and Diane then greeted Margaret and Denis Thatcher on their doorstep, watched by armed guards. After five hours' sleep, the prime minister went on an impromptu walkabout to the nearby Flippen Park. She was accompanied by secret service agents, carrying concealed machine-guns, loaned to her by Vice-President George Bush. Her son walked beside her, looking distinctly uneasy as she chatted to local people and posed with bemused children for photographers. When asked about her schedule by a local reporter, Mark replied that was secret. 'I want to save everything as a surprise for her,' he said.[96]

Mark was unhappy about the attention, and naively thought her two-day stay could be kept confidential. 'We don't know how it got out that she's even coming here,' said Paul Eggers, the Dallas lawyer and close friend of Mark. 'I took an oath of secrecy.'[97] The reason for such reticence was the main motive for the trip – the private banquet the following evening on the first floor of the Verandah Club in the luxurious Loews Anatole Hotel in Dallas. Mark had invited a staggering selection of America's corporate and banking élite, stating that the British prime minister would be the guest of honour. Clearly, it was a device to attract many of the country's most powerful and influential to his dinner table and hence potentially benefit his newly established Grantham Company. Margaret Thatcher, basking in the triumph of her third successive election victory, and by then one of the world's most influential politicians, was being used to enhance Mark's business prospects.

On Monday, 19 October 1987 the forty guests flew

in from Washington, London, Boston and New York. The all-male guest list, marked 'Absolutely Private and Confidential', can be divided into two sections. The first consisted of prominent industrialists and merchant bankers. They were Robert Abboud, chief executive (CEO) of First City Bankcorp; Andrew L. Lewis Jr, president of Union Pacific; Alvin V. Shoemaker, chairman of First Boston Corporation; Robert Anderson, chairman of Rockwell International; Roger Smith, chairman of General Motors; L. William Seidman, chairman of Federal Deposit Insurance Corporation; Bill Schmeid, president of the Singer Company; Robert T. Daniel, CEO of United Technologies; Jack Moseley, chairman of US Fidelity and Guaranty Corporation; Allen Shepherd, chairman of Grand Metropolitan plc; Fernando Solana, director-general of Banco Nacional de México; Ira Harris, director of Salomon Brothers; Malcolm Forbes, proprietor of *Forbes* magazine; William A. Wilson, former US ambassador to the Vatican; Walter H. Annenberg, former US ambassador to Britain; Tan Kat Hock, chairman of Johan Holdings in Malaysia; John Thompson, chairman of Southland Corporation; the late Lord White, chairman of Hanson Industries; and last, but certainly not least, Wafic Said, the Syrian financier who was a broker on the Al Yamamah arms deal.[98]

Then there were Mark Thatcher's own commercial and legal associates – Steve Tipping, his business partner; Hugh Thurston, his personal banker and a director of Citicorp; Calman Donsky, his Texas lawyer; and Bruce Leadbetter, his partner at the Grantham Company. Other close business friends included Alan Curtis, chairman of Lotus Cars, Vester Hughes, a Dallas lawyer, Jay Pritzker, chairman of the Hyatt

Group, and Joe Refsnes, vice-chairman of the law
and brokering firm Rauscher Pierce and Refsnes.[99]

The event was hosted by Mark and the lawyer Paul
Eggers. But all attention was on the prime minister.
She was accompanied by Charles (now Sir Charles)
Powell, her private secretary for foreign affairs, and
her husband, Denis. At her table sat Roger Smith,
Malcolm Forbes, Walter Annenberg, Robert Anderson,
William Wilson, John Thompson, Jay Pritzker and
Wafic Said.

Whether any business was discussed is not clear.
The main topic of conversation was the dramatic
developments that day, later known as 'Black Monday'. The UK stock market had collapsed, precipitated by a dramatic fall in share prices on Wall
Street. Margaret Thatcher discussed the situation
with the businessmen at her table, who argued that
'we were not about to see a meltdown of the world
economy'.[100]

'A Born Businessman'

One of the eight lucky businessmen who sat at the
prime minister's table was Jay Pritzker, a multimillionaire whose Chicago-based family owns the Hyatt
chain of hotels. Pritzker was the leading investor in
a company which many people, including Margaret
Thatcher, wrongly believed was the source of Mark's
fortune.

The corporation was Emergency Networks Inc
(ENI), founded in 1981. Its basic function was to
buy cheap off-the-shelf security equipment, install it
in the home, and then charge a monthly fee for a

monitoring service. It was an attempt to undercut the expensive early-warning alarm systems then sold to largely affluent homeowners. ENI realized a profit only once the customer agreed to continue the monitoring service after the three-year minimum contract ended. Its strategy was to sacrifice short-term profits and go for rapid expansion and long term customers.[101]

The problem was that the company did not allow for high operating costs and was massively under-capitalized. By 1987, ENI was facing financial ruin. The two founders, David Stull and Scott Gurley, approached their banker, Bob Davenport of the Gateway National Bank in Dallas, for advice. They decided they needed new capital and so Davenport contacted his friend Bruce Leadbetter, a Dallas-based financier originally from Flagstaff, Arizona, and at the time Mark Thatcher's business partner in the Grantham Company. Leadbetter agreed to assemble an invest-ment rescue package worth $1.5 million and discussed it with Mark. 'Bruce and I sat down and worked out what we wanted to raise and wrote out a list of people and got on airplanes,' recalled Mark.[102] They set up Xpart Inc, an investment consortium which would purchase over 50 per cent of the share capital of Emergency Networks.

Near the top of their list of potential investors was Hanson plc, the industrial conglomerate which has donated more than £500,000 to the Conservative Party since 1987. The company's chairman was Lord Hanson, a close friend, supporter and influential unoffi-cial adviser to Margaret Thatcher. He was her favourite tycoon and had been a guest at her son's wedding earlier that year. His company agreed to invest as a limited partner in Mark's business scheme. A US subsidiary of Hanson plc paid $100,000 for a stake in Xpart and hence Emergency Networks. 'We knew that Mark Thatcher was involved when we agreed to make an investment,' said Martin Taylor, a Hanson vice-chairman. 'It was the only time we invested with him.'[103]

Another name on Mark Thatcher's target list was Li Ka-Shing, the powerful Hong Kong tycoon, who had also handed over substantial payments to the Conservative Party and who later pledged a donation to the Margaret Thatcher Foundation. Like Hanson, Li invested $100,000 in Emergency Networks via Xpart Inc.[104] Mark denied exploiting Tory Party benefactors. 'If the whole thing was funded by the *Who's Who* contributors to the party, then that would have been a different game,' he said. 'But for them to subscribe two-fifteenths of the investment, I do not regard that as significant.'[105]

Other investors included Jay Pritzker, who provided a seven-figure sum, Bruce Babbit (later US interior secretary) and Joe Refsnes (who attended the famous Margaret Thatcher dinner in Dallas that year). As for Mark Thatcher, he joined in and became a non-executive director of Emergency Networks Inc. He was also a shareholder, although his stake was never higher than 5 per cent.

The Thatcher-Leadbetter investment group, code-named 'Renaissance 5', was not a success, and another $10 million was required. So Mark returned to Hanson, who invested another $300,000 in an interest-bearing debenture. The new capital enabled Emergency Networks to expand, and by 1991 it had installed alarms in almost 200,000 homes and generated annual sales of $80 million a year. But the company, in which the Pritzker family had the controlling interest, was badly run. The new executives were paying themselves large management fees beyond what was reasonable, despite raising more investment, and the losses mounted up.

Even more seriously, millions of dollars of employees' tax were not being paid to the US Internal Revenue Service. On 27 May 1992, David Wallace, an investor and at the time Mark Thatcher's business partner, wrote a memo recording the situation. He stated that some $2.3 million had been deducted from employees' salaries on a PAYE basis, but had not been passed on to the IRS. According to Wallace, taxes had not been paid for the previous three weeks, the company was trading near insolvently and bankruptcy was not far off the horizon.

The following month a last-gasp effort was made to inject more capital. On 24 June 1992, a meeting took place at the Dallas offices of Electronic Data Systems (EDS) to discuss their outstanding $8 million loan to Emergency Networks. EDS executives made it clear to Wallace and Stull that further loan advances would not be forthcoming unless this $8 million was resolved. Despite this precarious position, Wallace and other executives did not file for Chapter 11 bankruptcy, which apparently would have saved the company.

Instead, Emergency Networks continued to trade, holding out to attract extra investment. Stull and Scott Gurley, his co-founder and president of operations, remained concerned about the non-payment of tax. But when Stull and Gurley again demanded that the funds be transmitted to the IRS, they were sacked as officers and removed as directors. As a farewell salvo, on 4 August 1992, they wrote a memorandum to Bill Moore, chairman, and Bruce Leadbetter, a director and former business partner and close associate of Mark Thatcher. 'We strongly recommend the company's payroll liability be paid immediately from *all* available

company funds,' they said. 'We consider the payment
of all the company's past, present and future tax
obligations to be the responsibility of you and the
present management.'

EDS were again approached for a cash infusion,
but it was a financial shot in the dark. In September 1992, Emergency Networks Inc finally called it
a day and filed for Chapter 11 bankruptcy, with
assets of $1 million and liabilities of $7.4 million.
The court-appointed trustees noticed the apparently
excessive executive fees almost immediately. 'The
fact that management was taking out so much in
salaries while other expenses were going unpaid was
very troublesome,' said George McElreath, a US
government trustee.[106]

It was only a matter of time before the more
serious allegation – the non-payment of tax extracted
from their employees – was investigated. David Stull,
president of sales, was always aware of this danger and
made strenuous efforts to effect the payments. This did
not prevent detection and on 10 December 1993, the
IRS Criminal Investigations Office issued proceedings
against six former directors and investors of Emergency Networks. One of them was Mark Thatcher.
Other defendants included his business partner, David
Wallace, who was a director and shareholder, and his
former colleague in Grantham, Bruce Leadbetter.

The total claim was for $2,661,496 on the basis
that the defendants 'were all responsible persons of
Emergency Networks, who willfully failed to collect,
truthfully account for, or pay over to the USA . . . taxes
for wages paid to the employees'.[107] According to the
IRS, they have 'neglected, failed or refused to pay the
full amount of the assessment . . . and are jointly and
severally liable to the United States' for the amount.

Mark Thatcher was quick to respond. On 18 January 1994, through the Dallas law firm Garderra and Wynne, he said he was not a responsible person in the company and denied all knowledge of the tax negligence. He 'further denies that he willfully failed to collect, [and] truthfully account for' taxes due to the IRS. Consequently, he claimed he should not be liable and the claim should be dismissed. But the case shows no sign of being settled out of court.

In 1994 a proposal for mediation was rejected by the IRS and the case was set for trial some time in 1996. An out of court settlement was reached in Dallas with Thatcher paying his own costs. According to his Dallas based lawyers he incurred no penalties. When asked why, if it was indeed the case that Thatcher incurred no penalties, he was not pursuing the IRS for the recovery of his costs, his lawyer claimed that they were irrecoverable.

Despite his protestations, Mark Thatcher was closely involved in Emergency Networks – as an investor and leading fund-raiser. He was ever-present as a director until July 1992, and even lent $1.1 million to the company. Through Grantham, Thatcher and David Wallace 'spent a great deal of time on various Emergency Networks related matters' while it was expanding.[108] Thatcher's participation can also be gleaned from the bankruptcy records: one of the creditors, owed $750,000, was Diversified Capital Ltd. This was one of Mark's companies, registered in Jersey and controlled by his banker, Hugh Thurston, and his accountant, Leonard Day.

Mark Thatcher made very little money out of Emergency Networks. He sold his shares to David Wallace (his close associate at Grantham), and bailed out in

1990 – just before the storm broke – but continued as a director for two more years. This was confirmed by Bruce Leadbetter, his former business partner in Grantham and former president of Emergency Networks. 'We all lost a lot of money in the company, including Mark,' he said. 'No one got rich out of it. . . . Mark resigned because he could see what the problems were. He could see the writing on the wall and he didn't have the time to sort out the problems.'[109] Mark was reluctant to admit the failure of this venture. 'I did make money out of Emergency Networks,' he said. 'I made in percentage terms a reasonable return on my investment.'[110]

The interesting feature of Thatcher's role in this ambitious but doomed home-security corporation was the way the prime minister, her political friends and two of her newspaper supporters portrayed it as a financial triumph. Margaret Thatcher has always been convinced her son is a commercial wizard. 'Mark could sell snow to the Eskimos and sand to the Arabs,' she told a friend. 'Wonderful salesman, but he will not learn to say "please" and "thank you".' For some reason she believed Emergency Networks was a shining example of her son's entrepreneurial expertise. 'He is a very, very good businessman,' she said. 'He's a born businessman, as indeed my husband was. He built up his own business and he managed to sell part of his interest in it. . . . It's a big concern for security, the best possible kind of home-security systems.'[111]

Fleet Street went further and claimed the 'profit' from the Emergency Networks investment was the source of Mark's multimillion-pound fortune! On 2 January 1990, the *Daily Mail* stated he made a 'killing' and 'stands to put around $10 million in his bank account'. The next day the *Sun* reported that the company was sold for $50 million and Mark's shareholding was 20 per cent, therefore he made a profit of $10 million. The paper quoted an unnamed Thatcher friend who said: 'He [Mark] bought just at the right time and the firm took off in a phenomenal way.'[112]

This, of course, was pure fantasy. The whole company was worth barely $10 million and so it was inconceivable that Mark could have collected such a financial windfall. But the stories were left uncorrected and Margaret Thatcher's friends continued to brief the press, notably the *Financial Times*, that his US interests were the source of his vast wealth. This was misinformation and it served a very useful purpose. By that stage, late 1989, Mark really was piling up Thatcher's gold. But the loot did not emanate from installing burglar alarms in Texas. It was derived from much more lucrative ventures – international arms deals.

Chapter Six

Arms and the Man

'Mark Thatcher was trying to cash in on the (al Yamama) deal. . . . in the arms business we had met many people, royal hangers on. We called them "Black Princes" and sometimes they had to be bought off. . . . Thatcher was acting in the same way, as a kind of British Black Prince, but it was surely not the proper role for a British Prime Minister's son.'

Alex Sanson, former Managing Director of
British Aerospace, Dynamics Division,
talking to the *Mail on Sunday*, 16.4.95[1]

Mark Thatcher loves to travel. It's almost a compulsion. Soon after his mother became prime minister he was on jet planes – jumbos, Concorde, anything that would propel him to countries that looked favourably on doing business with the son of the British prime minister. By 1981, he was flying 400 hours a year, or eight to ten hours a week, and that continued throughout the decade.[2] He used to boast to his Special Branch detectives that he never stayed in the same hotel twice, and his sister, Carol, remarked how her brother always called her from a different airport.

When he arrived in the first-class departure lounge, Mark was always immaculately dressed in a stiff, almost military style. Airline officials recall that he often drew attention to himself, ensuring he would be recognized. 'Mark reminded me of a former Sandhurst army officer,' said one. 'He talked in that clipped, brisk way and expected everything to be perfect. I didn't mind that, but he has no sense of humour so when anything went even slightly wrong he was very difficult to deal with.'

Despite his obsession with security, Mark would explode when airport staff asked to inspect his hand baggage. 'What are you talking about?' he shouted on one occasion. 'Don't you know who I am?' before reluctantly allowing his bags to be checked.[3] Another of his habits was to leave the Heathrow executive lounge through a secret route like a catering workers' exit.[4] He also used the code-name 'M. Teacher' when making airline reservations on commercially sensitive trips.

Mark usually flew either first- or business-class. On American Airlines, one of his favourites, he was always upgraded to first-class. But he was not a popular passenger, according to stewardesses who flew with him. Just as some Dallas waiters flinched on seeing Mark enter their restaurant, so did the aircraft staff. One senior flight attendant who encountered him was Jeannie Kovascy. Her first engagement with him was when she did her usual check-list in the first-class area. She did not recognize Mark by sight so she had to check. 'Are you Mark Thatcher?' asked Jeannie. 'Of course I am,' he replied as if he had been asked if he was the Prince of Wales. 'Who else would I be?'

As soon as the passengers were settled, Mark ostentatiously stood up, looked around and surveyed the other travellers. It was classic celebrity body language, according to the stewardesses. 'He seemed to want everyone to know who he was,' said one. 'He also treated the cabin staff as if we were inferior serfs and he was lord of the manor in medieval England. Nobody liked him, but his wife was very different. She flew with us on her own with their son and was very nice. A lovely person.'

On many of his overseas trips he was accompanied by Special Branch detectives. Mark had wanted bodyguards as soon as his mother was elected prime minister. On Monday, 7 May 1979, three days after her general election victory, he drove to Scotland Yard, walked into the office for the prime minister's Special Branch personal protection and slumped into a chair.

'Well, I know I'm something of a hero,' he said with a straight face. 'But I really do think that Scotland Yard should be providing me with some form of personal protection.'

The Branch officers were stunned by such pretentiousness and his application was turned down. 'It got nowhere because I didn't pass on the message,' said one of the officers present. 'If I'd thought he was vulnerable, I would have done so. But that kind of protection would have needed special funding by the Home Office and it didn't warrant it. He just wanted bodyguards for his own self-aggrandizement and self-esteem and that's how it turned out later on.'

Despite Scotland Yard's refusal, Mark was insistent and continued to request them. 'How can I get bodyguards?' he later asked an officer at a racing meeting. Eventually, in early 1982, the Yard agreed that a Special Branch minder be assigned to him and that he should have the use of a Jaguar or an armour-plated Rolls-Royce saloon.[5]

The official reason why Thatcher received personal protection was that there was 'a very serious IRA threat to his life. The IRA had plans to kidnap him and deprive him of food so that he could suffer in the same way Bobby Sands [the hunger striker] suffered.' This was the explanation given to Sir John Junor, then editor of the *Sunday Express* and a close friend of Margaret Thatcher, by Sir David McNee, then commissioner of the Metropolitan Police.[6] There were also anonymous notes being sent to the newspapers.

However, some former Special Branch officers were sceptical about why he needed them. 'In my opinion, he just wanted them so that he could swan around and feel important,' said one. 'He loved having them around and got a real buzz out of it.' Carol Thatcher, who always refused to have a minder, was also dubious about their necessity. When asked why he warranted them, she replied dismissively, 'Oh, I don't know, he's had some death threat or something.'[7] It was not the only time she expressed doubt about his use of bodyguards.[8]

Mark's first major trip with Special Branch protection was on 27 March 1982, when he flew to California for the Long Beach grand prix. He was there to take part in a celebrity saloon-car race. 'The detective is going along to protect me,' he said. 'There is an IRA trial going on in San Francisco. I won't be going there, but you can't be too careful.'[9] In fact, the extradition hearing had already been adjourned four days earlier, to 14 May 1982, but Thatcher retained his bodyguard.

While Mark was in California, Argentina invaded the Falkland Islands and his mother ordered the mobilization of troops. At first Mark responded flippantly. 'That's all we need just before Easter,' he said on being told the news.[10] Then he became more aggressive.

LEFT: *MARK, aged six, and his twin sister Carol, shortly after his mother was elected the MP for Finchley in 1959 (Press Association)*

ABOVE: *SCHOOLDAYS. Mark at Harrow, the prestigious but status-ridden public school. He was there between the ages of 13 and 17 (Harrow School)*

BELOW: *MARK (second from right on second row) as member of his house football team (Harrow School)*

ABOVE: *A NEW ERA.* At their country home in Lamberhurst, Kent, in 1970, just before Margaret entered the Cabinet as Education Secretary (Keystone Press Agency)

LEFT: *REJOICE.* Mark with his mother at Tory Central Office on the night she was elected Prime Minister for the first time in May 1979 (Press Association)

ABOVE: *PORN GOLD. Mark, after a meeting with Paul Raymond, the soft-porn publisher. They discussed* Men Only *sponsoring Mark's motor racing (Solo Syndication)*

BELOW: *PROMOTING LOTUS: From left to right: Colin Chapman, then chairman of Lotus; David Thieme, head of Essex Petroleum; Margaret, Mark and an unknown French racing driver (Focalpoint Pictures)*

UPPER RIGHT: *TAKING THE STRAIN. At Heathrow Airport after being lost in the desert for six days while competing in the Paris to Dakar motor rally (Press Association)*

RIGHT: *BREAKDOWN. A gaunt-looking Margaret Thatcher at the time Mark was lost in the desert (Press Association)*

ABOVE: *PARTNERS. Mark with his business partner Steve Tipping. Just after the 1979 election, they had set up their own company together (Solo Syndication)*

LEFT: *THE BANKER. Hugh Thurston, the Jersey banker who has been the personal financial advisor to Mark and Margaret for many years (Jersey Evening Post)*

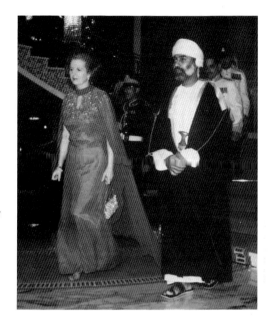

IN OMAN. Margaret Thatcher and the Sultan of Oman, Qaboos bin Said, arriving for a state banquet in Muscat, the capital, in 1981. (Rex Features)

THE BOSS. Chatting to Lord Matthews, chairman of Trafalgar House plc, whose subsidiary, Cementation International retained Mark as a consultant (Tomas Jaski)

Steik Zayed   *8 Nov.*

I have asked my son to convey to you my personal message of warm regards and good wishes. Margaret Thatcher

ABOVE: *OUT OF AFRICA. Welcoming Ibrahim Babangida, president of Nigeria, for talks at 10 Downing Street in May 1989 (Press Association)*

LEFT: *GREETINGS FROM DOWNING STREET. The letter to Sheik Zayed by Margaret, delivered by Mark who had business connections in the area.*

BELOW: *GREETINGS FROM THE GULF. Margaret Thatcher with Sheik Zayed, president of the United Arab Emirates (on her left) at Downing Street (Rex Features)*

ABOVE: *HAPPY FAMILIES. From left: Wafic Said, Denis Thatcher, Rosemary Said, Margaret, Mark, his wife Diane and below Wafic's son (Rex Features)*

RIGHT: *LEON WALGER. An Argentinian businessman and racing driver, who used Mark's name in a proposed deal to sell arms to Peru (LAT Photographic)*

LEFT: *ARMS AND THE WOMAN. Formally greeting King Fahd, ruler of Saudi Arabia, during a four-day state visit to Britain on 25 March 1987. (Press Association)*

ABOVE: *WE ARE A GRANDMOTHER*. *Margaret holding her new-born grandson, Michael, outside 10 Downing Street (Press Association)*

LEFT: *FAREWELL. Mark leaving 10 Downing Street for the last time on 27 November 1990, after his mother resigned as Prime Minister (Press Association)*

While a business associate was talking to Carlos Reuteman, an Argentine racing driver, at the Long Beach grand prix, Thatcher rushed over and blurted out: 'I've just been speaking to the Boss. We're going to whip those dago bastards' arses.' He apparently had not seen Reuteman and his associate, an adviser to Frank Williams, admonished him: 'Mark that's very tactless.' But he just shrugged his shoulders.

Mark was not popular among most of his Special Branch minders. 'He loved us being around,' said one, 'but he was so bloody arrogant. He was always so sarcastic and treated us like domestic servants. He would stop in the middle of the road, chuck the keys at us and shout, "Park the car." I was with him once when he parked the car on a double yellow line. When a traffic warden came across, he just leaned out of the window and said, "You can't give me a ticket, I'm Mark Thatcher." Most of us hated him but we got good money because of the overtime.'

Friends of Mark's also testify to the way he behaved towards his bodyguards. Jim Paterson, a Scottish businessman and farmer, knew him well and was a regular visitor to 10 Downing Street. He was once finishing lunch with Mark at the Dragon Inn restaurant in Gerrard Street, Soho, when his Special Branch detective approached the table and politely reminded him about a 3pm appointment. 'I'll fucking make up my own mind when I'm going,' flashed young Thatcher. Paterson was appalled and leaned across the table. 'Mark, if you think that impresses me, you can forget it.'[11]

On another occasion, in 1986, he arrived at Singapore airport to discover that his personal detectives were not there to escort him. 'Where are my Special Branch guys?' he shouted. 'Do you know who I am? Do you know who my mother is?' An airport official tried to placate him. 'This is Singapore, sir. We do things differently here.' But Mark was unimpressed. 'I want my Special Branch guys.'

Eventually, he was persuaded to accept an elaborate security system in his bedroom at the Raffles Hotel. 'After you go to bed, switch it on,' he was told. 'If there is an intruder you will receive help within seconds.' That night Mark was drinking in the hotel bar when he encountered a remarkably striking young lady. The two became instant friends and she took a note of his room number.

Thatcher then stumbled up to bed. Forgetting about his spontaneous invitation to the young woman, he switched on the security system. Within a few minutes, his new friend entered his room and slipped into bed beside him. Almost immediately, all hell broke loose. In a flash the finest of Singapore's security services burst through the door, guns cocked, shouting and pointing at the bed – ready to defend the son of the British prime minister. But all they found was a bleary-eyed Mark Thatcher and his innocent lady companion, blinking in fear and confusion![12]

Mark continued to use armed Special Branch detectives when it suited him. His obsession with security did not prevent him from dismissing them and travelling alone, or discarding them when with someone whom he clearly did not want identified. However, when he did retain them the cost was met by the taxpayer.

For example, in August 1982 he travelled to New York City for a three-day business trip. Before the visit a detective travelled to the USA by jumbo jet to make the 'security arrangements'. Then Mark and another bodyguard flew by Concorde to join him. Thatcher paid his own fare of £1,124. But the total cost in fares and accommodation for the two officers was an estimated £5,000, paid out of police funds.[13]

From then on, Mark was escorted by at least two detective sergeants, usually travelling business-class. On one occasion two officers had flown to Los Angeles to check the security arrangements, but were left languishing in the Californian sun for four days because Thatcher twice postponed his trip.[14] The official cost to the taxpayer was £3,200.[15] Labour MPs claimed it was a 'scandalous waste of public money'.[16] But Margaret Thatcher responded resolutely. 'Both the form of protection and the resources deployed are directly related to the nature of the assessed threat,' she said. 'In the case of my son's recent trip to the United States, the police judged it necessary that he should be accompanied. . . . It is not the practice to disclose details of arrangements of this kind.'[17]

By early 1983, Mark was being shadowed by three bodyguards and a police car. They seemed to follow him everywhere – when he played golf and even on visits to Annabel's nightclub. Two dinner-jacketed officers would watch him inside the club while another stayed in a Rover outside.[18]

As more detectives were assigned to him, the cost spiralled to about £50,000 a year. This extraordinary level of police attention was illustrated by the 1983 election campaign when he abruptly left the country. There was considerable unease about Mark being around. 'We felt he was trading too much off his mother's name,' recalled one former senior official at Tory Central Office, 'and so there was a move to keep him under wraps during that election because of the potential damage he might cause the party and her.'

During the first week of the campaign Mark was

accompanied by three Special Branch officers and attended his mother's adoption meeting in Finchley, north London. He then told startled friends that he was leaving for America and would be away for at least a fortnight. Just over a week later, on 26 May 1983, Thatcher flew out of Heathrow first-class on a Pan Am flight to New York. He was escorted by no fewer than eight plain-clothes police officers to the BA VIP lounge in Terminal 3 and kept away from journalists. When his flight was ready to board, police and airline officials virtually smuggled Mark out of the side exit and down the back steps from the VIP suite – normally only used by royalty, foreign heads of state and cabinet ministers. He passed through the suite to a waiting police Rover and was driven to the jet. The car circled the plane as the police tried to find a way on to the aircraft without being seen by the watching cameramen. But they were unsuccessful and, much to Mark's annoyance, his car was caught by the photographers.[19]

Airline officials said that this elaborate route was for 'security reasons'. Yet when he flew back to Heathrow ten days later, forty-eight hours before the poll, there was another police reception, usually reserved for royalty. When he left the BA aircraft he had so many bodyguards waiting that there was a crush in the car ride back to the airport terminal. He was then met by another plain-clothes detective and two armed uniformed officers. Watching airport workers were amazed to see all five squeeze into an Austin Allegro police panda car to drive to the passenger building. As he was escorted through Customs, a reporter half-heartedly suggested Mark was a 'don't-know' voter. 'That is almost an insulting question,' he replied sharply. 'There is such a thing as family unity, you know.'[20]

Mark Thatcher retained his Special Branch minders until 1992 – two years after his mother left 10 Downing Street.[21] For a decade he had been granted an unprecedented privilege, as only about twenty other people in Britain are given such police protection. It is usually reserved only for senior cabinet ministers and current and former Northern Ireland secretaries of state.[22]

Thatcher's request and unparalleled use of them was partly due to his deep-seated insecurity. But it was also an indication of his habit of exploiting the benefits of his mother's public office for potential private gain. This was reflected in his dealings with the Foreign Office and British embassies abroad.

Foreign Affairs

Mark Thatcher's relationship with the Foreign Office and overseas embassies was frosty and frictional. As he travelled throughout the Gulf, the Middle East and Africa, Mark walked into British embassies and foreign government offices, expecting VIP treatment to promote his commercial interests. He was, of course, entitled to use the embassy facilities. But several diplomats were concerned about the way he went about it and the extent to which he was allowed to exploit his position. 'He had no scruples and would do anything that was asked of him,' one Gulf diplomat told us. 'He would bring out blank 10 Downing Street note-paper and invite business associates to draft their own letters on it to suit their purpose.'

His favourite approach was to arrive at a British embassy and announce to the senior mandarin: 'I've got some business clients to entertain. I want access

to your facilities. It will be good business for Britain.'
This happened in South Africa in the mid-1980s. Mark
arrived at the embassy in Pretoria and demanded
introductions, immediate access to facilities and information to help his business interests. Soon after the
visit, the chairman of a major public company was
briefed about the incident by an angry diplomat.
On his return to London, the businessman reported
this, via his political contacts, to the Conservative
Party whips' office. He also informed Ian Gow, then
Margaret Thatcher's parliamentary private secretary.
'This needs to be watched,' the company chairman,
who was a Conservative Party supporter, told him.
'Yes, I know there is a problem,' replied Gow.

On another occasion, Mark visited Jordan on behalf
of Cementation International Ltd as they were bidding
for a contract to build an extension to a hotel. Mark
went straight to the king's palace rather than to the
British embassy and began lobbying on behalf of his
client. The ambassador became concerned about the
type of businessmen he was dealing with during his
stay in Amman. 'They were not the kind of people the
son of the prime minister should have been involved
with,' he told us. The ambassador then told a senior
director of Cementation International, 'Do be careful
about Mark Thatcher.'

The prime minister was judicious enough not to
allow her son to attend many official overseas functions. He was present at a dinner given by the British
ambassador, Oliver Wright, in Washington, during her
visit to the United States in September 1983.[23] But,
unlike her husband, Denis, Mark never appeared, in
an official capacity, during her overseas tours.

That did not stop him complaining bitterly about the
Foreign Office and British embassies after returning

to London. This was music to Margaret Thatcher's anti-Foreign Office ears. In 1981, she harangued a ministerial meeting about what she saw as the Foreign Office's ineffectiveness. 'My son, Mark, has just been out in the Gulf and had a lot of trouble with our embassies,' she said. 'The clear implication of what she was saying,' recalled one cabinet minister who was present, 'was that the Foreign Office was useless and Mark could run it better.' This was confirmed by one of the prime minister's foreign policy advisers in the early 1980s. 'Yes, he was reporting back about what he claimed were badly run British embassies,' he recalled. 'It was all nonsense but she believed anything he said.'

The consequence of Mrs Thatcher's stance was that her son secured considerable power and influence. This was demonstrated when the wife of Sheikh Zayed, the president of the United Arab Emirates (UAE), where Mark had business interests, visited London and wanted to see 10 Downing Street at short notice. Instead of the visit's being arranged through the Foreign Office who might have expressed reservations, Mark was asked to fix it. 'No problem,' he replied and a few hours later he telephoned back. 'Everything is fine.' The next day Sheikh Zayed's wife arrived at 10 Downing Street and received the red-carpet treatment.

The main source of anxiety among some British diplomats about Mark Thatcher was not that he was a businessman using their embassies. It was the nature of the commercial deals, his associates and the exploitation of the prime ministerial office that concerned them.

By far the most politically explosive and controversial was Mark's involvement in international arms dealing. This has always been denied by Thatcher's friends. Some of them admit he played a role in major defence contracts by acting as an intermediary and providing introductions between manufacturer and customer. But they contend he never actually sold the military hardware as such. 'He was only involved in those deals indirectly,' said one close friend of the Thatcher family.

However, businessmen on both sides of the Atlantic insist he was more directly involved. This was asserted in the UK by two former senior executives of Astra Holdings plc, an arms and munitions manufacturer. Its former chairman, Gerald James, said that he was told by Richard Unwin, one of his consultants, on more than one occasion: 'If you want to get on in the defence world, then the one person you need to get hold of is Mark Thatcher.'[24]

This was corroborated by Christopher Gumbley, Astra's managing director from 1986 until 1990. During that period he had several meetings with Unwin to discuss making contact with Steve Tipping, Mark's former business partner, and Alan Curtis, former chairman of Lotus Cars. 'It was quite clear from those discussions,' recalled Gumbley, 'that in order to promote the interests of Astra and obtain more customers and contracts it was important to include Mark Thatcher.'[25]

James also points to an encounter in July 1988, during the Army Air Corps exhibition at Middle Wallop near Andover, Hampshire. As he was walking towards the Astra chalet, James met Unwin, who was accompanied by Mark Thatcher, Denis Thatcher, Steve Tipping and Alan Curtis. The Astra chairman was introduced to each member of the party. They exchanged civilities and moved on.

Unwin has been an active player in the defence arena. In 1985, his company, Unwin Pyrotechnics Ltd, was involved in supplying mortar-fire-simulators to the Nigerian army in a contract in which substantial commissions were paid.[26] However, he denies that he ever said that Mark Thatcher was useful in the arms business. 'I never said that,' he told us. But he accepts that he met Mark at the Army Air Show and again at the Savoy Hotel with Alan Curtis in 1990. Unwin also confirmed meeting Steve Tipping: 'He came to see me in about 1984 or 1985 when I had my fireworks company, but I can't really remember what it was about. He was wheeling and dealing at the time.'[27]

Across the Atlantic more direct testimony comes from Jay Laughlin, who from January 1993 to January 1994 was one of Mark's business partners in Houston (see Chapter Eight). Laughlin was president of Ameristar Fuels, which traded in aviation fuel, and in December 1992 was negotiating with Mark, who was interested in investing in the company. As part of his due diligence (the necessary research into a potential investor's financial background), Laughlin asked Mark about his resources. He assumed that Thatcher's wealth was derived from his parents through trusts: 'So you've got your money from your parents.'

'I've got more money than my father or mother combined,' replied Mark indignantly.

'How? In what sort of business?'

'I brokered deals. I also have a construction company.'

'What sort of deals?'

'I brokered deals involving military equipment.'[28]

South America

One of Mark Thatcher's first forays into the world of

facilitating the buying and selling of military equipment was through a chance personal contact. In early 1982, he was going out with a girl who knew Colonel Henry 'Jim' Johnson, an insurance broker who was very well-connected in the security and defence arena. He was a director and shareholder of Saladin Security Ltd, a private security company, and was well placed, partly because of his friendship with the mercenary soldier Major David Walker.

At the time Mark was working on a project to sell surplus RAF aircraft to South America and so he wanted to sound Johnson out. A meeting was set up and he visited Johnson at his home in Sloane Avenue, Chelsea. 'He [Thatcher] had a girlfriend that I knew and she introduced me to him,' recalled the security consultant. 'He came to see me and we discussed it. He said he had a contact out there and wanted my advice. But he was very much fly-by-night and nothing ever came of it. I was supposed to receive some letters, but when they arrived they were late and incomplete, so we never got any further.'[29]

The prime minister's son never lost his interest in pursuing business in South America. His chief contact was an Argentine commodity broker called Leonardis Walger, who also acted as a middleman and, many years later, was convicted of cocaine-trafficking. Born in 1944, the son of a judge, Walger was a colourful operator, whose influence and connections stretched throughout the continent. A qualified lawyer, he was a private secretary to President Juan Carlos Onganía in the mid-1960s, responsible for liaising with Córdoba province, the country's most industrialized and sophisticated area. Walger then became an active member of the Montoneros, a right-wing Peronist guerrilla group in Argentina. As their financial adviser, Walger was responsible for fund-raising and the movement of cash, most of which came from General Manuel Noriega, president of Panama. But he grew disillusioned with the Peronistas and, in May 1974, left Argentina for England. For a brief period he remained on the payroll of the Montoneros, who, he admitted to us, were bandits.

The Argentinian decided to set up shop in the commodities business. His first break was meeting Sandy Harper, a futures trader who was well-connected in London society as a one-time boyfriend of Princess Anne. Walger had contacts in Paraguay, one of the crucial markets in the commodities business, and so in 1977 they joined forces. Based in a top-floor City office at 3 Lloyd's Avenue, off Fenchurch Street, the two ran a commodity futures company called Cominter UK Ltd, which had been a corporate front for the Montoneros. Dealing in coffee, sugar and cocoa, Cominter secured new investment capital from Paraguay and their business took off. In 1980 they were able to move into new offices at 79 Eccleston Square, Pimlico, and Walger bought a house for £200,000 at 2 Kensington Gate, near Hyde Park. He also owned homes in Peru and Uruguay.

Cash became readily available and much of it was spent on Walger's budding career as a Formula One racing driver. But commodity futures is a risky business. Essentially it is gambling and investors can win or lose a fortune. This was in tune with Walger's personality – adventurous, independent-minded and a commercial risk-taker.

When he met Mark Thatcher in the summer of 1981, the Argentinian was at the height of his financial success. The two had much in common. Their lives were dominated by dual passions – making money

and motor racing. As self-styled entrepreneurs, they
were looking for the main chance. At first they were
just social acquaintances. But then the silver market
collapsed and it hit Cominter hard. They paid off
their losses but were left penniless in terms of cash,
if not credit.

Walger and the prime minister's son then started
talking business, mainly international ventures. The
South American saw him as useful for opening markets, because he knew the senior executives of several
top UK companies. 'I had a commodity called Mark
Thatcher,' recalled Walger when we met him in
London in 1994. The 'commodity' in turn viewed
Walger as a beneficial front for his activities – someone to represent him. 'I was an ideal pioneer for his
marketing interests,' said the Argentinian.[30]

Their first joint project was to lobby Société Minière,
a Belgian mining company, which was interested in
selling its minerals – gold, silver and copper. Thatcher
knew their top executives and Walger had sources in
Spain who were potential purchasers, so in October
1981 the two men flew to Brussels for a meeting.
It was successful, though eventually the deal fell
through because the Spanish would not pay enough
for the minerals.

South America was the next commercial target in
their sights. The itinerary was Paraguay (railways),
Colombia (sugar) and Peru (aluminium). They also
devised a scheme, using the Thatcher name, to raise
sponsorship funds for their plans to drive in the Le
Mans race in June 1982. The Argentinian contacted
potential benefactors far and wide seeking £70,000. He
approached ¡Holá! magazine, the Spanish equivalent
of Hello!, for £35,000 and even travelled to Bogotá,
Colombia. But it was all to no avail. Their sponsorship

drive and business trip to South America were abruptly
interrupted by the outbreak of the Falklands war. The
British embassy told the prime minister's son it was
'too dangerous' for him to visit Peru.

On 4 April 1982, two days after Argentine forces
invaded the Falklands, Walger received a telephone
call from Argentina. Two days later he was on a plane
to Peru and while in Lima he volunteered for service as
an interpreter. He was not required for duty, but after
the war he received a certificate signed by General
Galtieri, thanking him for his offer to help recover
the islands, which he proudly hung on the wall of his
London home.

Despite the war Thatcher and Walger continued to
communicate, though not on commercial matters. A
week after the invasion Mark telephoned his Argentine
friend and said with a mixture of respect and fear:
'You've got no idea what my mother is like. She is
going to give your people such hell. You should tell
the Peruvian government.' They exchanged telexes,
discussing their ideas on racing. Two of them were
apologies for not being able to drive in the June
1982 Le Mans race because of the South Atlantic
campaign.

After the Falklands conflict, Walger returned to
London and resumed his business career and friendship
with Thatcher. Within two months of the war ending,
he used the prime minister's son in an arms deal that
was as bizarre as it was controversial. Mark seemed
unaware of the potential repercussions of helping an
Argentine middleman in a weapons transaction, which
was surprising in view of the political and personal
importance of the Falklands war to his mother.

The origins of the deal lay in a visit to Peru in
the summer of 1981 by Ian Smalley, a notorious

London-based arms trader and bankrupt, also known as 'Dr Doom' and 'the Fat Man'. Smalley's personal assistant, a bogus 'Russian princess' called Natasha Boldero (real name Cynthia Anne Mitchell), had useful Peruvian connections and suggested they cultivate them. Her most useful contact was Dr Juan Antonio Azula de la Guerra, a former boyfriend, who was a well-connected middleman based in Lima. He was also Leon Walger's Peru consultant.

Boldero arranged a meeting in Lima between Azula de la Guerra and Smalley. The Peruvian explained that his government was looking to buy weapons for its élite special forces, the Sinchis. He asked the British arms dealer whether he could supply them. Smalley said he could and returned to London. On 25 September 1981, Azula sent a telex to Smalley with a list of requirements and requested a price list. The dealer responded with a cost breakdown for 170,000 rounds of ammunition and explosives.

But negotiations became fractious and so Smalley decided to bring in Dick Meadows, his US contact, a retired Special Forces major and a former security consultant to Ross Perot. Meadows was director of marketing of Peregrine International Associates Inc, a Dallas-based company formed in 1981 to promote private security, arms sales and counter-terrorist training. It was modelled on the British firm, Keeni-Meeni Services (KMS) – *keeni-meeni* is a Swahili word describing a snake's movement through grass – which employed former SAS officers on operations deemed too sensitive for direct government involvement. Peregrine operated in much the same way, as a private arm of US Intelligence. Its personnel worked as contract undercover agents for the US Customs Service, infiltrating illegal international arms deals and reporting back inside information to customs officers. They were also directed by the Defense Intelligence Agency's (DIA) Forward Operating Group, commanded by Colonel Wayne Long.[31]

Peregrine, named after the falcon, was set up by Gary Howard and Ronnie Tucker, both Vietnam veterans and former federal agents and state police officers in Texas. They were later joined by Meadows and Charles Odorizzi, a former director of training for Delta Force. The company was geared up for arms deals with South America, mainly because the DIA had given it a list of countries where it could operate. At its peak, it employed over twenty agents.

As it happened, one of the arms dealers Peregrine was secretly investigating on behalf of US Customs, the CIA and the DIA was one Dr Ian Smalley. Howard and Tucker were hired to run a 'sting' operation against him because of his alleged involvement in illegal arms sales to Libya, Iran and Iraq. Known as 'Houston III', it involved setting up front companies to entice Smalley into delivering anti-tank missiles to Iraq and tanks to Iran. Peregrine would then receive a 'moiety' – a percentage-based commission on the captured military equipment. So when 'Dr Doom' Smalley and 'Princess' Natasha Boldero approached Howard and Meadows about the Peruvian business, they were delighted.

Meanwhile, on the other side of the deal, Azula talked to Leon Walger about the proposed business with Smalley and Meadows. Walger was interested because he had excellent connections in the Peruvian government. The family of his then wife, Malena Prado, was the most powerful in Peru. Her father was the founder of the National Bank and an uncle was a former president. Even more useful was Walger's friendship with Celso Pastor, legal adviser to the Prado family, the president's brother-in-law and the Peruvian ambassador to the United Nations. Pastor was an *éminence grise* and fixer for the Peruvian government. He was a perfect channel for any defence contract.

Walger agreed to proceed, and his office in Lima was used as a base for the deal. On 14 July 1982, Azula met Meadows and Odorizzi at a Dallas hotel. The Peruvian briefed them on how his government was now in favour of buying weapons from America rather than the Soviet Union. Meadows replied that he needed introductions in Peru for the transaction to succeed. 'No problem,' said Azula, and he described Walger's credentials. He also, for the first time, mentioned Mark Thatcher's friendship with the Argentinian.

Azula was ecstatic about his meeting with Meadows. He reported back to Walger that the former Special Forces major was 'a super-hero and a very impressive man'. A highly decorated Vietnam war commando, Meadows had just appeared on the cover of *Newsweek* magazine. The article described how he had slipped into Tehran undercover in 1980 to provide crucial on-site intelligence for the failed raid to rescue the hostages in Iran. The Argentinian was also impressed by the major's reputation and record.

On 22 July 1982, Meadows and Odorizzi flew to London and met Walger at the Montcalm Hotel in Cumberland Place, central London. Through the State Department's Office of Munitions Control, the DIA had arranged an export licence for Peregrine to sell arms to Peru. This gave Meadows the authority to tell Walger that Peregrine could fulfil Peru's requirements. The Argentinian responded by sending a telex to Celso

Pastor, Peru's ambassador to the UN, introducing Meadows.

Two days later Walger met Mark Thatcher for a drink at his Kensington Gate home and told him about his meeting with Meadows. The prime minister's son was excited because he had also just read about the Special Forces major in *Newsweek*. 'What are you doing with him?' he asked. Walger explained how he was facilitating a combined arms, anti-kidnapping and military training deal. 'I'm introducing him to the Peruvian government,' he said. 'Well, I'm very close to the Marcos family,' replied Thatcher. 'I can do the same deal in the Philippines. They have the same trouble with rebels and guerrillas.'

Nothing came of it, but Mark Thatcher's close association with the Marcos regime was confirmed by a source who used to work for him. 'I know there was a Philippines connection,' he said, 'because Steve Tipping went out there and was entertained by one of the Marcos sons.'

When Meadows returned to Texas on 27 July 1982, a telex from Walger was waiting for him at his office in Dallas. The telex (number 266978) outlined his commitment to the deal and introduced a new participant: 'Dr Azula has briefed me on your interests re: certain particular countries in which we are well connected and in which we might be able to help selling your ideas and or equipment. I would also like to point out that I am a close friend and associate of Mr Mark Thatcher who, for obvious reasons, is also highly well connected in other parts of the world. Last night Dr Azula and I unsuccessfully tried to contact you. We will try to call between 8 and 8.45pm London time. This time Mark will also be with us.'

The following afternoon Azula and Walger did

indeed telephone from London with Mark Thatcher in
attendance, in a conference call which the Texans tape-
recorded. 'We can do some good business together,
Dick,' Walger told Meadows. The Argentinian then
asked Thatcher to come to the phone. 'No, no,' said
Mark in a very panicky, almost frightened voice. 'For
Christ's sake, don't use my name.'

Gary Howard, Meadows's employer at Peregrine,
read the telex and listened in on the telephone call.
He was surprised but impressed by the Thatcher
connection. 'That name definitely added credibility
to the deal,' he recalled. 'No one would figure that
the prime minister's son would be involved in such a
deal.'[32]

Meadows, who died in 1995, confirmed Thatcher's
role. 'His name was mentioned as a point of reference,'
he recalled. 'Walger and Azula wanted me to know
that they had connections in the British government
and they had some authority. They wanted to do some
business and Mark Thatcher was part of it, but I don't
know how. I had daily liaison with them.'

At the time Meadows was sufficiently impressed to
fly back to London with his deputy, Charles Odorizzi,
for a more substantial discussion with the South
Americans on the arms supply. The meeting, which
took place at 2 Kensington Gate, was successful.
Meadows told them their political connections added
weight to the deal. 'We are using Thatcher simply
because of his name and the credibility it holds,'
replied Walger. 'He is not very bright and has to be
instructed on what to do. But his name does carry a
lot of weight.'

Walger wanted a commission of up to 18 per cent
on the deal. But that did not deter the Texans, and
it was agreed to draw up a contract for Peregrine

International to provide $30 million-worth of weapons for the Peruvian counter-insurgency forces. 'The sky's the limit on this contract,' Meadows wrote in a memo afterwards. He thought that the deal was worth $200 million but was instructed by the DIA that he could supply only about $100 million-worth of hardware.

Peregrine immediately drew up a 100-page inventory of weapons and support equipment and Meadows contacted the State Department to obtain authorization. A Washington law firm – Arent, Fox, Kintner, Plotkin and Kahn – then drew up a five-page draft contract and Charles Odorizzi went to Lima for a meeting with the Ministry of the Interior. Everything seemed to be progressing smoothly. On 21 October 1982, Meadows told Howard that the deal had the blessing of the DIA and he would stay on contract for another twelve months with no pay to see it through. But five days later Meadows suddenly resigned from Peregrine. He claimed it was 'due to internal disagreements'. In fact, the DIA instructed him to leave the company because they were on the trail of Smalley for arms offences, and Meadows was to be a witness at the trial.

Howard continued to liaise with Azula and Walger. But progress was slow and Peregrine was perplexed by the lack of action. Its formal bid had been finalized and freight costs were calculated. So, on 1 December 1982, Howard telexed the Argentinian: 'Due to circumstances beyond our control we are unable to make contact with you. Should we now make contact with Mark Thatcher through our British associate?' Walger did not respond and now says he was cut out of the deal. This has some credibility, as Meadows continued to work quietly for the DIA on the Peruvian order by setting up Gavilon, a private company he ran with Monza Bilbesi, a Jordanian arms dealer.

Despite Meadows's best endeavours, the Peruvians never received their weapons. It was later claimed that the Peruvian president, Fernando Belaúnde, rejected the deal because it was 'too complicated'.[33] Reflecting on it twelve years later, Walger believed Peru simply did not have the money. 'I don't think they could afford it,' he said.

Howard strongly disputed both explanations, claiming that the contract was cancelled because Meadows was tipped off that the arms were going not to Peru but to Argentina. Although he had no hard evidence to support this allegation, it was based on his personal involvement in and knowledge of the deal. 'After our meeting with Walger and Azula in London, which occurred after the Falklands conflict (which had left the Argentine army in a state of disarray), the whole tone of the telexes from them changed,' he told us. 'Peru wasn't mentioned any more. They were talking about Argentina now, not Peru, and here was Thatcher's son possibly involved in a deal with a country that Mrs Thatcher had declared war on.

'Part of the deal concerned mobile training teams. This was anything military – from medics to parachuting to armoured cars. It was obvious from the telexes these teams were destined for Argentina. On the weapons list, items jumped out at you to show that these were not arms for Peru. One was 36,000 riot batons. I mean, 36,000 riot batons! Peru doesn't have as many people as that in its defence force. Argentina does. There was an awful lot of cold-weather gear too. The Argentinians lost their cold-weather gear in the Falklands.'[34]

Walger later appeared anxious to protect Thatcher when the story broke. 'Mark was totally unaware that I had named him in the telex,' he said. 'It was wrong of me to do so and I regret having mentioned his name.'[35]

It was no surprise when his business relationship with Mark was abruptly terminated. In 1984 Walger sold his Knightsbridge house, closed down Cominter UK Ltd and returned to Buenos Aires. Three years later he resurfaced on the southern coast of Spain and became part of the Marbella jet-set. On 16 January 1987, Walger arrived in Madrid with two metal boxes containing 347 grams of cocaine with a 48 per cent purity which 'a friend from Peru' had handed him. Needing a buyer for the drugs, he hooked up with a notorious local playboy. But the Argentinian was then caught in possession of 247 grams of cocaine, valued at £10,000. Two months later he was convicted of drugs trafficking and sentenced to two years in jail. He served fourteen months of his sentence. After his prison term he returned to Buenos Aires, where he now resides.

Walger's lawyer, Dr Azula, also faded from the scene but still lives in Lima. The other 'Doctor', Ian Smalley, whose visit to Peru was the first episode in this curious tale, was eventually charged with arms smuggling but acquitted. It was claimed by Howard and Tucker, the Customs agents on his case, that this was because of what Smalley knew about covert and illicit weapons shipments by the US and UK governments. Smalley now lives in Houston and has always refused to talk about his time as an arms dealer. There is an outstanding warrant for his arrest and he cannot return to the UK.

His former personal assistant, Natasha Boldero, a.k.a. Cynthia Mitchell, fell out with her boss and stayed in Kensington. She got a job at Arabesk, an up-market jewellery shop in Walton Road, Knightsbridge, but no longer works there. She has cut herself off from the twilight world of arms dealing, and is believed to be living in Greece. Dick Meadows continued to work for the DIA until his retirement to Florida.

As for the prime minister's son, he was scared to death about his involvement with an Argentine arms broker being known, as the tape-recording proves. When it was disclosed by *Private Eye*, he rang Walger in a panic. 'Mum is going bananas,' he said. 'I was not involved. You've got to clear my name.'

At the very least, his association with Walger so soon after the Falklands war showed an extraordinary lack of judgement. It was a clear demonstration of Mark's indiscriminate choice of business associates. But what this episode revealed most of all was how Thatcher secured an entrée to the military-equipment business – through the motor-racing circuit. That was his introduction to South America. And it was originally via the Formula One grand prix racing scene that Mark acquired his largest sack of gold.

Saudi Arabia – Paying for the Doves of War

Mark Thatcher's largest commission payment was from the largest arms deal in history. Known as Al Yamamah (Arabic for 'the Dove of Peace'), this contract to supply military equipment to Saudi Arabia was negotiated at the very highest level. Batting for Britain was the prime minister, Margaret Thatcher, and for Saudi Arabia, Prince Bandar Sultan ibn Abdulaziz al-Saud, Saudi ambassador to the United States and King Fahd's most trusted envoy.

Mrs Thatcher took a close and active interest in Al Yamamah. In the spring of 1985, she held several meetings with Prince Bandar, the son of Prince Sultan ibn Abdulaziz, the Saudi minister of defence and aviation. At one of their early meetings, according to Adel Jubeir, an aide to the Saudi prince, she said to Bandar, 'What do you want? Planes, ships, tanks? They're yours. Anything short of nuclear. No problem.'[36]

Prince Bandar, only thirty-six years old when the negotiations took place, was King Fahd's nephew, most influential adviser and an ambassador in more ways than one. His diplomatic secret is that he is bi-cultural. A Koran-quoting Muslim, he is extremely adept at making all the right chess moves in the intriguing and conspiratorial world of rivalry between the Saudi princes. Yet at the same time he is a Scotch-drinking, US-trained fighter pilot, who is also a poker player and a graduate of the School of Advanced International Studies, John Hopkins University, in Washington, DC.[37]

It is a remarkable combination of qualities but he also brought to the negotiations a knowledge of commissions to intermediaries on major arms sales. This was largely because of his father's experience as the Saudi defence minister. Whether such payments were referred to during his often unscheduled and periodic meetings with the prime minister at 10 Downing Street is not known. But the multibillion-pound order was only awarded to Britain, according to Nihad Ghadry, a former adviser to King Faisal and successive monarchs, once Margaret Thatcher agreed to keep the details of the order secret and to allow the Saudis to handle the contract in their own way.

In August 1985, Mrs Thatcher interrupted her annual holiday in Switzerland and drove to the house of the British consul in Salzburg, Austria. There to meet her was Prince Bandar, armed with a confidential letter from King Fahd, and a memorandum of understanding was drawn up. A month later this document was signed in London by Bandar's father, Prince Sultan, and Michael Heseltine, then defence secretary, who said the prime minister's role 'cannot be overstated'.[38] The contract was formally authorized in Riyadh in February 1986.

One reason why the prime minister played a direct role in Al Yamamah was its massive value – about £40 billion to its contractor, British Aerospace plc. It was also a government-to-government deal which had diplomatic and political benefits in cementing alliances. This was underlined by David Gore-Booth, former assistant under-secretary at the Foreign Office, who was appointed UK ambassador in Saudi Arabia in 1993. He described the kingdom as 'easily Britain's most important partner in the Middle East, whether politically, commercially or militarily. . . . We have no intention of depriving our friends of the means to defend themselves.'[39]

'The Dove of Peace' developed into a 'wish-list' of defence equipment for the Saudi armed forces, with priorities and delivery varied to suit their requirements, plus the availability of funding.[40] The contract was then divided up into two phases, Al Yamamah 1 and 2.

The first order, in 1985, was for forty-eight Tornado GR1 strike fighter bombers, twenty-four Tornado F3 air-defence aircraft, thirty Hawk 60 series advanced training aircraft and thirty Pilatus PC9 basic training aircraft. The second stage, three years later, was for more Tornados and Hawks, plus six minehunters (from Vosper Thornycroft), up to eighty-eight Black Hawk helicopters (from Westland), a large air base and an air-defence command and control system.[41]

Al Yamamah was initially a gold-mine for British Aerospace plc as it was paid in oil. Under the contract, the Saudis delivered to British Petroleum (BP) and Shell 300,000 barrels of oil per day. This was later increased to 500,000 a day to compensate for the weak oil price and to enable equipment deliveries to remain on schedule. BP and Shell sell the crude on the open market. The proceeds are then paid into a special London bank account owned by the Saudi government and administered by the Ministry of Defence, which also receives an undisclosed commission. This MoD account is then drawn on by British Aerospace as the arms are delivered. However, the oil-derived revenues did not cover the full costs of supplying the equipment and so Saudi made several large cash payments to enable their delivery to be made.

Apart from its size, Al Yamamah's most notable characteristic was the extreme secrecy that surrounded the details of the deal. The Saudis were particularly keen on the confidentiality clause, and the UK government readily agreed, not wanting to jeopardize such a key contribution to its balance of payments. According to a report by stockbrokers Phillips & Drew, Al Yamamah was governed by what is known in the USA as 'a black defence programme' – whereby information is withheld from the public and parliamentary scrutiny. A three-year investigation of the contract, which included the use of commission payments, by the National Audit Office, the watchdog on government spending, has never been published.

A notable characteristic of the deal was the huge commission fees paid out to an assortment of brokers, middlemen, politicians and diplomats. British Aerospace documents on pay-offs are held in a Swiss bank. 'Commission contracts are often written so

that no one party can remove them from a bank,'
said Major-General Kenneth Perkins, former British
Aerospace marketing director for the Middle East.
'The contract requires both parties to be present
before it can be removed. Any party can go in and
make photocopies of the contract. But the party has
to cut off any letterheads and signatures before he can
take the photocopies out of the bank.'[42]

There is, of course, nothing unusual in intermediaries playing key roles in major arms deals. Quite
the reverse, in fact. Business in the Arab world is
often conducted on the basis of personal trust and
recommendations. In the Middle East many contracts
are sealed with a handshake not a fountain pen. All the
Saudi princes have their own middlemen, although they
are often little more than chiefs-of-staff. In the West,
the brokers are more sophisticated. Their fundamental
role is to bypass the formal lines of communication and
structures and connect their client directly to the prime
minister, head of state or chief executive – depending
on whom they are representing.

The difference with Al Yamamah is that the son
of the British prime minister who negotiated the
multibillion contract was one of those middlemen
who benefited financially.

Meeting the Middlemen

The origins of Mark Thatcher's involvement lay in his
friendship with Mansour Ojjeh, a wealthy American-
educated Saudi businessman and fellow racing fan.
They met in 1980 when Mark was invited to the
Frank Williams base at Didcot, Oxfordshire, and was

introduced to Mansour, whose family sponsored the
Williams Formula One racing team. The two became
friends. Mark would visit Mansour at his home in
Monaco and in turn invite his fellow car enthusiast
to Lotus promotional events.

Mansour introduced Mark to his father, the late
Akram Ojjeh, then procurement agent for the Saudi
royal family on all key military contracts. Born in
Syria, brought up in Iraq and educated in France,
Akram Ojjeh established his first arms-trading company in Switzerland in 1956. By that time he had also
set up Saudi Arabia's first weapons factory.[43]

The next decade saw Ojjeh rebase himself in Paris
and represent French defence firms like Dassault,
selling their Mirage jets and Matra's missile systems
in the Middle East; at one point he hired Adnan
Khashoggi as a consultant. Often under scrutiny by
the French authorities, he created a new business
vehicle in 1977 – the Geneva-registered TAG Group,
otherwise known as Technique d'Avant Garde or the
Trans-Arabian Group. By that stage, Akram Ojjeh had
unrivalled access to and influence with the Saudi royal
family on major defence projects. He was particularly
close to Prince Sultan ibn Abdulaziz, the defence and
aviation minister. Such connections also brought vast
wealth – enough to own the *QE2*, a large ranch in
Paraguay, houses in Paris and Monte Carlo and give
£1 million a year to the Frank Williams racing team
as sponsorship.

After meeting Mark Thatcher, the generous Arab
began to cultivate him as a useful contact and lent him
a car from the Saudi racing team. From 1980 onwards
the prime minister's son acted as a TAG introductory
agent, flying on their BAC1–11 private aircraft to Haiti
among other places. He was seen as potentially useful

in 1983, when a major contract became available in Saudi Arabia for the equipping and construction of two hospitals for the National Guard, in Riyadh and Mecca. The staffing and equipment orders were handled by the British Ministry of Defence and they entertained bids from interested firms.

Ojjeh was interested in acting for any of the bidding contractors and dispatched young Thatcher to work on the project. He approached Christopher Chataway, the former Conservative minister who was chairman of United Medical Enterprises UK (UME). At Mark's invitation, Chataway flew to Paris for a meeting with Ojjeh to discuss the tender, but nothing came of it.[44] Instead, UME hired the Saudi-based Project Development Company.

Unperturbed, Ojjeh and TAG represented a rival prospective contractor, American Hospitals International Inc. Ojjeh then used Mark Thatcher to lobby the Ministry of Defence on his behalf. This was not a wise move as the civil servants resented being approached by the prime minister's son acting on behalf of an American company. Despite the fact that UME secured the order, there was considerable disquiet inside the MoD about the episode.

When asked about his business relationship with Akram Ojjeh a year later (in 1984), Mark admitted meeting him on four occasions but played down the association. 'I know his son and he likes the same things I do, like cars,' he said.[45]

What Thatcher did not mention was that his friend Akram Ojjeh played a pivotal role in the crucial early stages of Al Yamamah on behalf of British Aerospace. Ojjeh was in a very powerful position because of his long-standing record as a procurement agent for the Saudi government.

The veteran arms fixer then helped deliver Al Yamamah 1. But his relationship with British Aerospace deteriorated when it was disclosed he was also the agent for the French company Dassault, a competitor on the deal. This was discovered by Alex Sanson, managing director of British Aerospace's Dynamics Division, who saw it as a conflict of interests. Ojjeh was sacked by Aerospace, but paid some compensation through Lebanese sources.

The person who benefited most from Ojjeh's removal from the Dassault contract was Wafic Said, a flamboyant, wealthy Syrian financier who was the UK director of Ojjeh's TAG company. He succeeded his former boss both as a key middleman on the Al Yamamah deal and as the chief courtier to the House of Saud. 'It [replacing Ojjeh] put Wafic in an embarrassing position, but then he was really the master of ceremonies,' said Sanson. He also became close to Mark Thatcher, who was his principal contact at 10 Downing Street.

Born in Damascus in 1939, Wafic Rida Said is the son of an eminent eye surgeon who held several ministerial posts in the Syrian government. He went to school in Lebanon and in 1960 moved to Britain to complete his education. After short spells in the Syrian foreign service and as a banker in Geneva, Wafic returned to London. By the late 1960s he was drifting and his prospects were not promising. He spent most of his days helping his brother Rafic run Caravanserai, an Arab kebab restaurant in High Street Kensington. A meeting-place for Arab students, Caravanserai operated more like a club than a business.[46]

In the evenings Wafic would hang out in the Christopher and Dean coffee house opposite Whiteleys in Bayswater, west London. It was there that he first met two young Saudi Arabian princes, Bandar and

Khalid, sons of Prince Sultan ibn Abdulaziz, who was a brother of King Fahd. It was a crucial connection, as both brothers were to become powerful figures in the Saudi government and the Al Yamamah negotiations.

Wafic's first break was in 1969 when an old family friend, Dr Rashad Pharaon, arranged a job for him in the Saudi Arabian government. Pharaon had been the personal doctor to King Saud ibn Abdul Aziz of Saudi Arabia, and headed an influential Syrian clique which was used by the Saudi royal family as a conduit to the outside world.[47] Wafic, reunited with Prince Sultan's sons, throve in Saudi Arabia, working long hours in the Ministry of Municipalities, responsible for construction and maintenance operations.

His link-up with fellow Syrian-born businessman Akram Ojjeh was Wafic's next smart move. In 1973 he became president of TAG Systems Construction SA in Paris and was soon brokering major building deals for defence-related projects. He was the agent for Raytheon, a US company that makes advanced anti-missile systems. Wafic's involvement with contracts to supply military equipment was confirmed to us by Alex Sanson, the former corporate marketing director of British Aerospace. Sanson recalls having lunch with him at Harry's Bar, an exclusive Mayfair restaurant in South Audley Street. 'Wafic told me he had a personal relationship with Prince Sultan [the Saudi defence minister],' he said, 'and that they had completed a large contract with Raytheon for the supply of Hawk missiles to Saudi.'

Financially, Wafic's real coup was in 1979, when he secured a $200 million sub-contract for TAG Liechtenstein from the US firm Litton Industries Inc to construct the infrastructure for a command and control system for the Saudi Ministry of Defence. He was on his way.

Wafic saw financial power as a passport to social and political respectability. 'I understand the value of money,' he said. 'I believe it is like a two-edged sword which can be used either for good or for destroying people.'[48] His wealth was derived largely from well-placed investments in the early 1980s. His chief corporate vehicle was Saudi (later Strategic) Investment and Finance Corporation (SIFCORP), which he formed with Ziad Idilby, a fellow Syrian banker. SIFCORP was registered in Bermuda and controlled by the Said Trust, Wafic's holding company based in Luxembourg.

One of his investments was a 30 per cent controlling stake in Aitken Hume International plc, the financial services company, whose founder and deputy chairman was Jonathan Aitken, the Tory MP. Aitken was also, until April 1992, a director of Al Bilad (UK) Ltd, a subsidiary of a Saudi parent company 'which received payments from contracts with Saudi Arabian royal family interests and government agencies'.[49] He became minister for defence procurement in April 1992, and two years later was made chief secretary to the Treasury. In 1995 Aitken resigned to fight libel actions over a variety of allegations concerning Saudi Arabia and other matters.

But it was Wafic's close friendship with Saudi royal princes that elevated him into that country's inner circle of influence. A measure of this was the award of Saudi citizenship in 1981 – a rare honour. That year an incident took place that Arab observers claim cemented Wafic's relationship with the royal family. Wafic and his family went to Riyadh for the ceremony at which the citizenship award was made. It was hosted by Prince Sultan at his home. Just before the ceremony, Karim, Wafic's thirteen-year-old son, drowned in the prince's swimming pool in a tragic accident. According to Islamic custom, a death in such circumstances incurs a moral obligation on the part of the host. It was claimed that in this case the moral debtor was the defence minister, the creditor was Wafic, and this created an extra bond between the Syrian financier and the Saudi princes.

Wafic finds this analysis 'offensive and entirely misplaced. . . . This fabrication is as insulting to my Saudi host as it is to me. What happened was a tragic accident, no more and no less. My friendships in Saudi Arabia date back to the early 1960s and have nothing to do with that accident.'[50] What is not in dispute is that Wafic became a confidant of key members of the Saudi royal family.

But his original entrée into Al Yamamah was his familiarity with the AWACS – a controversial order to provide Saudi Arabia with an Airborne Warning and Control System. Although this was passed by the US Congress in 1981, the Reagan administration prevaricated over selling dynamic F15 Eagle fighters to the Saudis. Their equivocation resulted in a battle between Britain and France to supply the Saudis with sophisticated military aircraft. The UK was offering Aerospace's Tornado and the French Dassault's Mirage 2000 and it was this competition that eventually lead to Al Yamamah.[51]

By the time the Al Yamamah negotiations were in full swing, Wafic was sufficiently well-connected to be a crucial intermediary between British Aerospace and the UK government and the Saudi royal family. His principal contact was Prince Bandar, the Saudi ambassador in Washington and chief negotiator with Margaret Thatcher. An indication of their closeness was that Wafic helped Bandar purchase Glympton, a vast estate-village in Oxfordshire, for £8 million from the bankrupt Australian businessman Alan Bond. It is just a few miles from his own 2,000-acre estate, Tusmore House, near Banbury, where he hosts pheasant-shooting parties.[52]

In 1994, Wafic was given planning permission to build a new stately home on his estate which will be on a larger scale than any other country home since the Second World War.[53] He also owns a large apartment in Eaton Square, Belgravia, which he bought in 1992 for £9 million, and a house on Avenue Princesse Grace in Monte Carlo, where he took residency in March 1991. Although he has been publicly extravagant with his wealth, he has also been generous. He has made substantial donations to charities, both in the UK and abroad, and has endowed scholarships at Oxford University.

One person who knew both the Syrian financier and the Saudi ambassador well at the time is Luther H. Hodges, former chairman of Washington Bankcorp while Wafic owned 27 per cent of that bank's holding company stock. 'I would bet anything on the strength of that relationship,' recalled Hodges. 'I was involved with Wafic Said and Prince Bandar in Washington on a few occasions. I think they were extremely close. Certainly, Wafic is known to have been close to Prince Sultan [Bandar's father]. . . . Wafic saw Prince Bandar every time he came to Washington and at some points that would be with some regularity. . . . In fact, the first time I myself ever met Prince Bandar was when Wafic Said took me to the embassy and introduced me to him to get some Saudi Arabian business for the bank.'[54]

Hodges is convinced that Wafic played an intermediary role on Al Yamamah: 'While I was visiting Wafic's home in Marbella, I had conversations with people as to why he was in London. What was it that was so important? It became my understanding that it was the arms transactions between the British government and Saudi Arabia that he was working on.'[55]

Wafic is not an arms dealer as such. 'I have never even sold a penknife,' he said.[56] But he was very much a facilitator, and in early 1985 he helped arrange Prince Bandar's letter of intent with British Aerospace which confirmed the contract.[57] Essentially, his role was to persuade the Saudis to buy the military aircraft from the British rather than the French. That was why Sir Dennis Walters, a former Tory MP and a well-connected Arabist, said that he 'has made a great contribution to British interests in Saudi Arabia'.[58]

Wafic himself acknowledges that he was an adviser on Al Yamamah, but maintains he was active only in the £2 billion offset programme. This involved British Aerospace reinvesting 25 per cent of the contract's value in 'offset' joint-venture industrial projects in Saudi. Because of his experience in the Saudi building industry, said Wafic, he advised British Aerospace on this scheme. His participation was verified by Mike Rouse, managing director of Aerospace's Systems and Services Division, which oversees the Al Yamamah project. But Rouse said his company has no 'direct link' with Wafic and refused to comment further.[59]

There is no evidence that Wafic Said received a commission payment from this arms deal, and he has always denied it. 'I did not receive any commissions from the Al Yamamah programme and nor am I an agent for British Aerospace,' he said.[60] He added that 'the agent for British Aerospace is the British Government' and the contract was a 'government-to-government project'.[61]

Indeed it was, and the paramount negotiator for UK plc was Margaret Thatcher. Just a few steps behind her was her son, Mark, and it was his extremely close association with Wafic Said that enabled him to act as a broker on Al Yamamah.

Mark first met Wafic in 1984 through their mutual acquaintance Akram Ojjeh, who at the time was still mediating with the Saudis on arms deals. They became 'good friends' through the racing circuit, said Wafic.[62] But it was more than a social acquaintance-ship. 'Wafic was using Mark for intelligence,' said Adnan Khashoggi, the international arms broker, who was also involved in Al Yamamah. 'His value to Wafic was his name, of course, and that whenever Wafic needed a question answered, Mark could go directly to his mother for the answer. He would pick up things unofficially.'[63]

This was confirmed by two of Mark's closest friends and associates. Wafic and Prince Bandar needed direct access and a channel to the prime minister. They wanted to bypass the official civil-service route and so they would ring Mark, who then arranged the meetings, either dinner at Chequers or a day-time meeting at 10 Downing Street. 'I know for a fact that on one occasion Wafic rang Mark, who then arranged for him to fly to Chequers by helicopter to see Margaret,' said one of our sources.

Wafic, who has given nearly £300,000 to the Conservative Party, was a fervent admirer of Margaret Thatcher and kept her picture on the wall of his office at 49 Park Lane, Mayfair, opposite the Dorchester Hotel. He first met her on 19 March 1987, the première of the film *The Fourth Protocol*, based on the novel by Frederick Forsyth, which the Syrian businessman helped finance. Mark Thatcher and his wife also attended, two days after returning from their honeymoon.[64]

Three months later, in the early hours of 12 June 1987, Wafic was to be found in an emotional state in Aspinall's, the exclusive gaming club in Curzon Street, Mayfair, celebrating Mrs Thatcher's third successive election victory. Every time a Conservative constituency victory was flashed on to the television screen, an ecstatic Wafic raised his glass and cried out loudly, 'Bless you, Maggie. Bless you!'[65]

The period after the 1987 general election triumph was a busy time for Al Yamamah. Negotiations were renewed about a further supply of Tornado combat aircraft to Saudi Arabia. Eventually, on 21 October 1987, George (now Lord) Younger, then defence secretary, signed an agreement for extra Tornados worth £7 billion – the largest single export order ever secured by the British aerospace industry. Two days earlier, on the night of 19 October, Margaret Thatcher had been guest of honour at a special dinner in Dallas organized by Mark. In attendance were many of the top American tycoons. Only eight of them sat at the prime minister's table. One of them was Wafic Said (see pages 177–180 for details of Dallas dinner).

Despite the October 1987 agreement, the full requirements of Al Yamamah 2 were still to be finalized. This involved further supplies, including aircraft, ships and military installations. Largely because of the sheer size, complexity and value of the contract, negotiations dragged on for another eighteen months. And it was during this period that Wafic Said and Mark Thatcher met regularly. They would lunch together at Harry's Bar, or have dinner at Claridge's in Brook Street. Sometimes they were alone, occasionally in the company of mutual friends like the Duke and

Duchess of Kent. Mark was also a house-guest at Wafic's palatial home in Marbella and would fly by helicopter to Glympton, Wafic's Oxfordshire estate, for a day's pheasant-shooting.

However, it was the purchasing of Mark's first British house that clearly demonstrated that his relationship with Wafic was more than social. In the autumn of 1987, Mark instructed two London estate agents to find him a suitable property in Mayfair. He told them he could afford to spend about £1 million.[66] Two months later he bought a house at 34 Eaton Terrace, Belgravia, for £800,000. He wanted to spend another £300,000 but was persuaded not to.

Mark paid for the property using an offshore company called Formigol SA, registered in the Bank of America building in Panama and incorporated on 19 October 1987 (ironically the same day of the famous dinner in Dallas). Formigol's registered office in London was the fifth floor of 49 Park Lane, London W1. This was Wafic Said's business address and the head office of one of his companies, Safingest Services UK Ltd.

The connection was strengthened further as the payment for the household bills at 34 Eaton Terrace was arranged by the law firm of Simmons & Simmons, then also representing Wafic. They helped settle Mark's domestic expenses by arranging for them to be paid by Mark's client account which was funded by a Swiss bank. It was certainly a strange way to pay the gas, electricity and telephone bills!

The solicitor who handled this arrangement was William Heard, who then left to become Wafic's lawyer and financial adviser, based at the 49 Park Lane office, and working for Safingest Services UK Ltd. 'Heard is very close to Wafic,' said a former executive. 'He was his chief adviser and always on call. He also travelled with him to the Middle East.' When we spoke to Heard, who is also a director of the Said Trust, Wafic's holding company, he refused to comment. 'We have a robust reputation for dealing with journalists in court,' he added darkly. 'I am well aware of your reputation, Mr Heard,' replied Paul Halloran, equally darkly, 'and I am totally unfazed by it.' Heard's former employers, Simmons & Simmons, are now Mark Thatcher's solicitors.

As for 34 Eaton Terrace, Mark lived there for barely two years. In March 1990, he sold it for £1.3 million, claiming it was 'a little too poky' for his tastes. Almost immediately, Wafic's short-lived Panama company, Formigol SA, was dissolved. But his dealings with Mark continued.

The Syrian financier gave the prime minister's son a £14,000 Rolex watch, presumably to express his appreciation of his friendship.[67] More significantly, Wafic Said was one of the businessmen who placed funds in one of Thatcher's pooled investment schemes controlled by his Grantham Company in Texas.

One person who knows Wafic well is Ghassan Zakaria, editor of *Sourakia*, an Arabic-language magazine based in London. He recalled that in April 1988, he was returning from the United States and happened to be on the same flight as Wafic. They chatted away amiably enough. But when they arrived at Heathrow airport and walked off the plane, Wafic was greeted by Mark Thatcher and two bodyguards, who whisked him through the VIP lounge while Zakaria was obliged to go through Customs.

The summer of 1988 was a crucial time for Al Yamamah. On 13 June 1988, Prince Sultan, the Saudi defence minister, met Mrs Thatcher for an hour and

a half at 10 Downing Street to review the contract. During his four-day visit to Britain, he also
saw Lord Trefgarne, minister for defence procurement, to discuss the problems surrounding the offset
aspects of the original deal. The Saudis were concerned about the slow pace of UK investment in their
country.

But this seemed to be resolved in July 1988, when
the prime minister and her defence secretary, George
Younger, flew to Bermuda to agree terms on Al
Yamamah 2. This new agreement, worth £10 billion-
plus, meant that British Aerospace would provide
forty-eight more Tornados, sixty Hawk military aircraft, eighty-eight Westland Black Hawk helicopters,
six minesweepers and two new air bases. Dubbed
'the arms sale of the century', it was dependent on
the offset programme being implemented. Apart from
establishing a missile-engineering facility in Saudi
Arabia, British Aerospace had also agreed to invest
in an aluminium-smelting plant.[68]

For Wafic Said, an Al Yamamah adviser, business
was thriving. On 24 June 1989, his wealth was
extravagantly displayed with a lavish party at his
£10 million home in Chester Terrace overlooking
Regent's Park. Friends and business associates were
amazed by the house's opulence, particularly the
paintings by Renoir, Picasso and Monet. 'I must
have passed £30 million-worth on the way to the
drawing-room,' said one.[69] Among the 150 guests at
the party, which cost £50,000, were Mark Thatcher,
Frederick Forsyth, Mark Birley (owner of Harry's
Bar), several British Aerospace executives and two
arms-dealing Arab middlemen, Baha Bassatne and
Yashir Kutay.

Meanwhile, progress on 'the Dove of Peace' was

slow. In its early stages, Al Yamamah was ultra-profitable for British Aerospace and resulted in considerable cash surpluses. This was due largely to oil revenues exceeding deliveries of military aircraft and interest income accrued from the pre-payments. But then there were production problems with the Tornados, and British Aerospace began to face serious cash shortfalls. Oil revenues were running behind their requirements by several hundred million pounds and so, in December 1989, the Saudis injected a special £2 billion payment.[70]

However, this seemed to be only a short-term solution. From the spring of 1991, refinancing again became a problem because of low oil prices and the cost of the Gulf war to the Saudi exchequer, estimated at $6 billion. Protracted negotiations continued through the rest of the year and British Aerospace's share price was adversely affected by the delay.

Eventually, on 3 April 1992, six days before the general election, John Major, who had succeeded Mrs Thatcher as prime minister in 1990, helped salvage Al Yamamah. Major had intimate knowledge of the arms deal as chief secretary to the Treasury (1987–9), then foreign secretary for three months, and then chancellor of the exchequer until November 1990. He announced that British Aerospace would receive an extra £1.5 billion cash instalment from the Saudis. This was arranged, almost uniquely, as a fifteen-month loan through a consortium of Saudi banks, rather than as a direct payment from government funds.[71] The contract was effectively rescued by this funding, although Al Yamamah 2 was not formally signed until 28 January 1993, after John Major visited King Fahd in Riyadh.

Mark Thatcher's role in securing Al Yamamah was,

like that of his close friend Wafic Said, as a facilitator. He supplied a conduit and direct route for Wafic and Bandar to negotiate with the prime minister, bypassing official channels. From the Saudi vantage-point, Mark's involvement – and even his mere presence in the deal – provided comfort and reassurance. In that sense, he was useful.

For the Saudi princes the fact that the prime minister's son was a middleman on Al Yamamah was not unusual. Most Arab countries are run by families. Their allegiance is quite often to their relatives rather than to their nation-state or social class. So Mark would be perceived as a crown prince and for him to play a role would not raise any eyebrows in the Saudi royal family.

An insight into how the Saudis saw the Thatcher family on this arms deal was furnished by Nihad Ghadry, a former adviser to Saudi monarchs and now an author, based in Paris. In February 1987, he visited Prince Bandar at the Saudi embassy during one of his regular trips to Washington. During one of his meetings, Ghadry raised the subject of the Al Yamamah project and the issue of large commissions. 'Only a few people, including myself, know the whole truth,' replied Bandar. 'As in politics, in order to successfully complete commercial deals, you need to communicate directly with the Head. . . . I myself delivered a personal and confidential letter from King Fahd to the Prime Minister, Mrs Thatcher. I told her that this deal is between us directly, between the two countries. It should go no further. Whatever is related to us is our concern and no one else's. . . . I also told her that we are a Royal Family and around us are a lot of people and a lot of responsibilities. My conversation with

Mrs Thatcher ended with her understanding what I meant.'[72]

Margaret Thatcher's instinctive understanding of Prince Bandar's carefully chosen words was born out of her long-held views. 'There is no such thing as society,' she said while she was prime minister. 'There are individual men and women, and there are families. And no government can do anything except through people, and people must look to themselves. It's our duty to look after ourselves and then to look after our neighbours.'[73]

Given that philosophy, perhaps it was not surprising that Mark Thatcher made money out of the largest arms deal in history. It was Thatcherism in action.

A Financial Interest

Evidence of Mrs Thatcher's son's commercial involvement in Al Yamamah comes from a variety of sources. Mark's former business partner Steve Tipping, described it in characteristically earthy terms. 'I specialize in defence,' he told former business associate Gary Smith over lunch at the Savoy Grill. 'But I was never involved in Saudi Arabia. That was Mark's business. In the world of defence, Saudi Arabia is an essential market because you can make the silly rag-headed buggers buy anything.'

An equally compelling source is Alex Sanson, who was managing director of British Aerospace's Dynamics Division during the Al Yamamah period. An Armenian Turk, he had joined the company's guided-weapons section in 1977 and rose through the executive ranks to be group sales and marketing director. In 1983, Sanson was promoted to be Aerospace's corporate marketing director under Admiral Raymond Lygo. But it was as MD of the Dynamics Division – the prime contractor for Al Yamamah – that he became intimately involved in the deal. For example, he was responsible for the first sale of Tornado aircraft.

We interviewed Sanson, who has retired to Biddenden, Kent, four times over the telephone. He was guarded but decisive in his remarks. When asked about Mark Thatcher in general terms, he said, 'Well, he was involved in the Tornado deal.'

'How was he involved?' we enquired.

'Well, when we [British Aerospace] realized that he was sniffing around in the classic way as he has done before, we simply made it clear [to him] that he get out of it. But I don't think he ever did because that's where he made all his money. The amazing thing is that he has survived all this time.'

'Whom was he representing on Al Yamamah?'

'Let's face it, he managed to climb aboard. . . . He was very close to Wafic Said and Prince Bandar, the indestructible ambassador for Saudi Arabia, who is, by the way, a very, very fine chap. . . . A number of people were aware that he [Mark Thatcher] was involved. He is bad news. He was a user of people to make connections. I don't think there is any doubt about it. That was his technique and with the image of his mother at the time it was a useful asset at the time.'

'What was the attitude of British Aerospace towards Mark Thatcher?'

'We were very guarded but that did not stop the fact that he had got his fingers in there with certain Saudis and there was no getting out of it.'

'So he was working for the Saudis?'

'Oh, yes, yes, definitely, once he got his connections there.'

Documents relating to Mark Thatcher's commercial involvement were compiled by the Saudi Arabian intelligence agency, Istakbarat. In 1984, during the early stages of the Al Yamamah negotiations, they secretly recorded telephone conversations between some of the leading participants – arms dealers and agents representing the Saudi royal family. Translated transcripts of those discussions were shown – but not given – to the *Sunday Times* by Mohammed al-Khilewi, a senior Saudi diplomat. He was a first secretary at the United Nations in New York until June 1994 when, disillusioned with the Saudi regime, he defected, taking with him thousands of documents.

The taped conversations took place at a time when the Saudis were monitoring and analysing the various bids by Britain, France and the United States to supply the weapons. They focus on the prospective merits of two influential British middlemen with inside knowledge and government connections. One was referred to as 'John'. The other was Mark Thatcher.

The first discussion was between Abdel Aziz al-Ibrahim, King Fahd's brother-in-law and his chief agent in major arms deals, and an unnamed Arab middleman. The prime minister's son had a rival in 'John' as the Saudis' intermediary to the British government. 'Don't forget to tell him we are already in contact with John in Britain,' said al-Ibrahim, 'through Turki [Prince Turki bin Nasser, who was a conduit to British Aerospace] and Manquour [Sheikh Nasir Hamad al-Manquour, then the Saudi ambassador in London] and John's offer is excellent and the cost is less than Mark is offering us.' The Arab arms broker replied: 'I think you are right, but Mark is more in power and he has influence with the military group and the government.' He added, 'These people will sell their families for money.' The two Saudis concluded by agreeing that the commission payments should be deposited into either a Swiss or a Saudi bank.[74]

Al-Ibrahim then consulted Prince Turki bin Nasser. 'I think Mark's connections regarding the military equipment . . . we can't compare it with John's connections,' said the prince. Al-Ibrahim responded: 'Yes, but Mark has excellent connections with the government and he has good information.' He later observed, 'We have to make a decision quickly because we can't keep dealing with both of them at the same time. And Tawil al-Omar [King Fahd] is more comfortable with Mark.'

The king's choice for facilitating the biggest arms deal in history was decisive. The Saudis chose the British crown prince, the son of Queen Thatcher.

Mark Thatcher's commercial interest in Al Yamamah was also being monitored in the United States. One senior government official who did this was Howard Teicher, head of the National Security Council's (NSC) Near East Section from March 1982 until May 1986. He then became the NSC's senior director of political and military affairs until his departure in March 1987. Teicher was a specialist on the Middle East and responsible for monitoring arms sales to that area. 'Any application of military power and arms sales to the Middle East was a responsibility of mine,' he said. 'It was incumbent upon me to co-ordinate the positions of the disparate US government agencies in an effort to work out a common position on when, what and how to sell in terms of major weapons systems to our friendly countries in the Middle East.'[75]

Between May 1986 and March 1987, Teicher read
several documents, classified intelligence cables and
diplomatic dispatches from US embassies in Europe
that included details about the activities of middlemen
in Al Yamamah. 'They were arms-dealers who were
not necessarily known to us, but obviously individuals
who made their living selling arms and living off the
commissions on the transactions,' he recalled. 'It was
quite clear to me that this group believed that their
ability to make the sale to the Saudis would be
enhanced by the involvement of a political member
of the group like Mark Thatcher.'[76]

Detailed data on Thatcher's commercial participation in the arms deal were contained in diplomatic
dispatches by the defence attaché at the US Embassy
in Saudi Arabia. The information was also contained
in CIA and Defense Intelligence Agency reports from
Saudi Arabia and Europe, and in diplomatic cables
from other European capitals. 'I considered these
dispatches totally reliable and totally accurate,' Teicher
told Channel 4's *Dispatches* programme. 'I did not
think that people would loosely accuse the son of the
prime minister of being involved in such a transaction
unless they were certain that it was the case. Also the
fact that I saw his name appear in a number of different
sourced documents convinced me of the authenticity of
at least the basic information regarding some measure
of involvement on Mark Thatcher's part. When I say
"involvement" I mean a business involvement. He was
clearly playing some sort of business role to help
facilitate the completion of a transaction between the
two governments.'[77]

Teicher reaffirmed his analysis to us. 'He was
playing an active role in the arms transaction and it
was unambiguous that he was involved in a business

capacity,' he said. 'He seemed to have no specific role except that he was suggesting that he could get the job done. In my view, there was no way he was doing it for the love of his country.' He added: 'I surmised that his role was to facilitate the communications between the UK manufacturer and the buyer in Saudi Arabia. The role that someone like him would play typically would be to ensure that the buyer was confident that the other side was genuine, legitimate and able to deliver the goods. I had no reason to believe that Mark Thatcher had any particular expertise with advanced weapons systems or Tornados.'[78]

After reading the intelligence and diplomatic documents, Teicher went to the British embassy in Washington to talk to two diplomats about young Thatcher's activities. 'They just looked at the ceiling,' recalled the former senior NSC director. 'They were very polite and diplomatic but were not happy to talk about it. Their view seemed to be "You are not surprised, are you?"'

Teicher then discussed the issue with a fellow member of the National Security bureaucracy in the US Defense Department: 'I asked him if he was confident that Mark Thatcher was actually playing a role. He said that he was quite confident that Thatcher was involved and that this showed him that the British were extremely serious about selling these aircraft.'[79]

The prime minister's son has been typically bullish in his denials. 'The idea that I run around peddling Kalashnikovs or second-hand MiG jets is ridiculous,' he told *Today* newspaper in 1994. When asked point-blank whether he had received any payments in any way from the sale of weapons, he replied: 'No, I haven't even sold a penknife. . . . There were allegations of CIA documents to say that I had been involved and subpoenas were flying around. At the end, absolutely nothing happened. Nothing at all. . . . My position on the supposed Al Yamamah agreement is that the people I am supposed to have been involved with – that is to say Mr Said – have denied, on any number of occasions that there's any link.'[80] More specifically, he said: 'Merely because I know this man [Wafic Said] does not mean to say that he is going to pay me £12 million because I am a nice guy.'[81]

But privately he did refer to his role in Saudi Arabia during business meetings with Gary Smith, the international oil trader. In April 1987, when asked about business prospects in Saudi Arabia, Mark Thatcher replied, 'I have a perfect channel there [a favourite euphemism for 'connection']. He is A1 and tops for me.' He did not elaborate. But eight months later, on 4 December 1987, he was more forthcoming. 'It [Saudi Arabia] is a backward, feudal country,' he told Smith over dinner at Harry's Bar in Mayfair. 'But it's paradise for doing defence deals, because spare parts have no limits in a country where commissions have no limits.'

Fixing a Fee

The precise amount the prime minister's son was paid for helping the British sell weapons to the Saudis is not known. Even Mark's friends admit it was considerable. 'I was told it was an enormous amount of money, an eight-figure sum,' said one. The commission fee would certainly not have been paid directly by British Aerospace or the Saudi Arabian government. It would have been channelled through one of the seemingly countless Al Yamamah middlemen and brokers who received lucrative pay-offs. Our sources state that Mark's commission was a minimum of £12 million, but probably closer to £20 million.

Evidence for the payment is in a transcript of the taped conversation between al-Ibrahim, King Fahd's agent, and an unnamed Arab middleman in Riyadh, the Saudi capital. 'The important thing is that they [the British companies bidding for the order] have to do it by our conditions,' said al-Ibrahim. 'Also to agree with us to increase the costs of the bills.' This meant increasing the cost of the contract to accommodate the commissions. The Arab intermediary agreed: 'I'll talk to Mark today and I will confirm to him the money will never be more than $500 million [£400 million at 1984 exchange rates] for him and his group.'

It is perfectly legal in Britain for a defence contractor or foreign government to pay a commission to an individual on an arms deal – unlike in the United States where it is a criminal offence under the Foreign Corrupt Practices Act.

On Al Yamamah, the commissions, estimated at between 10 and 30 per cent of the contract's total price, were so huge that they created cash-flow problems and delayed delivery of the weapons and aircraft. Indeed, one reason for Al Yamamah's spiralling £20 billion-plus 'value' was the inflated kickback fees that were added on top of the actual cost of the equipment. For example, it was claimed that the Tornados were sold at £25 million each, about double their real value, allowing for extra money to be distributed to middlemen. Excessive shipments of oil for sale on the spot market in Rotterdam were also favoured. This activity took place alongside those genuine oil exports which were used to pay for

the Al Yamama weapons under the Government to
Government contract.

Intermediaries are part of commercial life in the
Arab world and commissions are always spread widely.
This is why the size is often astronomical to those who
do not understand this simple economic fact.

The British and Saudis have always insisted officially
that no commissions were paid on Al Yamamah. It was
such a sensitive issue that the Ministry of Defence
was even asked by Saudi Arabia to write a letter
denying their existence. They claimed that as it was
a government-to-government deal, there was no need
for kickbacks. It is true that senior cabinet ministers
and diplomats did negotiate the contract. But it was
also indisputably the case that Al Yamamah was in
a constant state of uncertainty and it took no less
than eight years for the deal to be officially signed
and sealed.

A more compelling argument that commissions
were paid is the simple reality of doing business in
the Middle East. 'When you sell to Saudi Arabia,
you are really selling to the Saudi royal family –
a limited company with 200 shareholders,' said one
senior executive involved in Al Yamamah. 'It is quite
simple. In some countries you pay import duties of 30
per cent, in others you pay commissions.'[82]

Mark Thatcher knew, at the very least, many of
these advisers. Apart from Wafic Said, one of his
closest associates was Jean-Pierre Yonan, a Lebanese-
born businessman based in Paris. Fabulously wealthy,
Yonan has homes in Beaulieu in the south of France,
Rio de Janeiro and Geneva. In the 1970s he had
a powerful commercial presence in Oman and then
became close, like Wafic, to the pertinent Saudi prince.
Yonan was part of the bridgehead between the UK

government, British Aerospace and the Saudis on Al Yamamah 1. He once laid on an impressive fleet of cars for Sir James Blyth, then head of defence sales, on his arrival in Riyadh. The Lebanese arms broker also flew with the prime minister's son on his private 727 jet to Saudi Arabia as a way of impressing on the Saudis the fact that he was well connected. 'Yonan knew [Mark] Thatcher very well,' recalled Alex Sanson, British Aerospace's former marketing director.[83]

Arms and the Woman

The crucial factor, of course, was whether the prime minister knew that her son received payment for the epic arms deal she negotiated. It was an issue she consistently and repeatedly refused to answer over the Oman University contract.

On Al Yamamah, she adopted the same approach. In October 1994, she said she was 'absolutely satisfied that the Al Yamamah contract was properly negotiated . . . and proud that, after a great deal of hard work by ministers and officials, it brought thousands of jobs and billions of pounds to this country.'[84] Lady Thatcher (she had become a baroness in June 1992) again declined to say whether she knew her son was paid a commission.

However, her private office staff were certainly told – and they were duty-bound to inform her – because British Aerospace executives became very concerned about what they called Mark's 'meddling' in the arms deal of the century. They knew that if his role were exposed, the consequences would be disastrous. The Saudis, renowned for their distaste for public scandal and critical publicity, might cancel the whole deal and negotiate instead with the French or the Americans.

Senior British Aerospace executives discussed the potential crisis. They decided that the prime minister needed to be informed, in what, in a reference to *Macbeth*, was nicknamed the 'witches' warning'. And so Admiral Raymond (now Sir Raymond) Lygo, the company's chief executive and chairman, and Alex Sanson, corporate marketing director, went to see Clive (now Sir Clive) Whitmore, permanent secretary at the Ministry of Defence from 1983 until 1988. During this period Lygo met Whitmore regularly at the MoD to brief him on Al Yamamah's progress, and at one of their meetings talked to him about Mark Thatcher's 'interference'. Whitmore was especially close to the prime minister, having been her principal private secretary from 1979 until 1982, so it was perhaps easier for him to talk to Madam about her son in a 'nudge-and-a-wink way'.[85]

Admiral Lygo told Whitmore that Mark's business interests in the Middle East were 'dangerous for British industry' and asked him to inform Margaret Thatcher about Aerospace's anxieties. 'This happened because we got very concerned about Mark Thatcher's interference in the Saudi Tornados deal,' Sanson told us. 'It was felt that if this matter came out, it could be exceedingly damaging to the prime minister.' The 'witches' warning' was duly delivered but Whitmore's former boss refused, as usual, to address herself to the problem.

When asked about this, Lygo confirmed meeting Whitmore 'at least once a month' but denied discussing the prime minister's son. 'I remember Mark Thatcher being mentioned in the office but whether that specific meeting took place, I couldn't really say,' he said.[86] Sir

Clive, now a director of Morgan Crucible plc and N. M. Rothschild, declined to comment. 'I do not believe there is anything I can do to help you,' he said.[87]

Howard Teicher, the US National Security Council's former director of political and military affairs for the Middle East, confirmed that, at the very least, her closest civil servants knew: 'I find it difficult to believe that Margaret Thatcher would not be aware that he [Mark] might have been playing a role,' he said. 'Certainly the senior officials in the British Ministry of Defence and the British arms industry would have been aware of the role that he was playing. Is it possible that she might somehow be insulated from that kind of information? It's possible. . . . Over a period of years Mark Thatcher's involvement, in my mind, certainly seemed to be something that officials in London would have been aware of.'[88]

Mrs Thatcher's friends often argue that she might have been informed about her son's business activities but she would have disbelieved the information. 'Oh, that could not have happened,' she once responded after receiving a report about Mark, according to a family friend.

However, the difference with Al Yamamah was that Mark helped arrange meetings for her with Wafic Said and Prince Bandar. So she could hardly shut her eyes and ears to that reality. As with Cementation's contract in Oman, her son was a shadowy figure one step behind her while she helped British Aerospace negotiate in Saudi Arabia. Al Yamamah was the pay-day that Mark Thatcher had been looking for. Now he could look further east to exploit the business interests and contacts he had cultivated in the early 1980s.

Chapter Seven

Far Eastern Promise

*'My mother loved me too, but she knew when I
was being a bloody idiot – and she said so.'*

Thatcher Peer[1]

The Far East was an ideal commercial hunting ground
for Mark Thatcher. It is a continent full of lands of
opportunity and the prime minister's son was the ultimate
opportunist. Business is conducted in an uncluttered,
unregulated market where money talks and contacts are
everything. For Mark, who has always found it difficult
to work in a structured environment, the Asian enterprise
culture suited the way he liked to operate. In opera terms,
he was a *primo uomo*: he was not interested in being part
of the chorus.

Nowhere is the materialistic, money-obsessed ethos
more clearly exemplified than Hong Kong – the Wall
Street of the Far East. The colony appealed to Mark
Thatcher because many of its inhabitants shared his
pursuit-of-wealth attitude to life. 'The great thing about
Hong Kong is its enterprise and ambition,' he said in
1991. 'Less government is one of the reasons for Hong
Kong's success. . . . It is one of the few places I look
forward to coming to.'[2]

Mark also genuinely enjoyed visiting the colony. He had worked there as a trainee for Jardine Matheson in 1971 and had been treated well. He liked the polite, deferential Hong Kong society, where he was sought after as an honoured guest at dinner parties. He would stay at the Mandarin Hotel and drink at the Hilton's Dragon Boat bar. Best of all, businessmen were discreet and even the hated newspapers were relatively sympathetic to him.

His first excursion to Hong Kong was in November 1977, driving in a major race in the nearby Portuguese enclave of Macao. He failed to finish, but later competed three times at Macao for the Crown Motors Toyota team, usually driving a 1300cc Starlet in which he had moderate success.[3]

The 1981 Macao grand prix brought the first glimpse of Thatcher's business interests in Hong Kong. While preparing for the race Mark was filmed wearing a smart green-striped Giordano sports shirt. It was part of a television commercial for the Hong Kong-based fashion label, later broadcast on the local ATV and TVB stations. The thirty-second advertisement showed the British prime minister's son donning a shining silver cat-suit with 'Mark Thatcher' blazoned across it; he slowly zipped it up and put on his helmet. Then, after posing in the sports shirt, he smoothed his hands down his chest and body. At the climax, he stood beside a long red car, again with the brand-name 'Mark Thatcher' written on it, and a husky Chinese voice said, 'Giordano, every inch a man.'

Mark had been hired as a male model as part of a £100,000 advertising campaign by Giordano. 'He exactly fits the image of the shirts. Very sporty,' said Antony Chow, director of account services at the Hong Kong office of Young & Rubicam, the agency which made the commercial. It was broadcast in the summer of 1982 but was last shown on 20 September that year. The next evening the advert mysteriously disappeared from the TV screens, just as Margaret Thatcher was about to bid farewell to Japan on her way to China for delicate discussions over the future of Hong Kong. The commercial's absence was 'a complete coincidence', said Chow.[4]

Gold, Jewellery and Commodity Trading

It was also through competing in the Macao grand prix that Mark Thatcher secured his entrée into the Hong Kong business community. In November 1979, he met Tony Zie, alias Chin Kwok Chung, one of the race's promoters and an ambitious financier. They became friends and Mark introduced Zie to his business partner, Steve Tipping. The three then set up various joint commercial projects.

Their first venture was Ulferts Services Company Ltd, incorporated in Hong Kong in February 1981, and set up to 'import consumer durables and sales promotion items', particularly furniture. Thatcher, Tipping and Zie were all directors, with Mark holding 30 per cent of the shares. His financial stake was later expanded to a controlling HK$ 30,000 as the capital of the company was increased to HK$ 100,000.[5]

The company was launched with a dinner party at Maxim's Palace restaurant and printed invitations were issued to guests on behalf of Ulferts 'to meet our chairman, Mr Mark Thatcher'. A holding company, Ulferts Services UK Ltd, was established in the UK 'to extend the trade, not only in the Far East but worldwide'.[6] But the two firms never traded and both folded after two years, with the Inland Revenue chasing the British parent for a notional corporation tax assessment. It was not an auspicious start to Mark's Far Eastern commercial career.

He was strangely sensitive about his involvement with Ulferts. When asked later whether he still had an interest in the company, he reacted angrily: 'Absolutely not. Why do you have to mention Ulferts? I just happen to know some of the Ulferts people.'[7]

Within a few months of the collapse of Ulferts, Mark became chairman of Hon Hing Trivest Group, one of the largest commodities traders in Hong Kong – itself the third largest bullion market in the world. In the summer of 1982, the company issued a glossy booklet and distributed it to potential clients overseas, including Canada. It enclosed a signed statement by Mark, accompanied by his photograph. Hon Hing, he wrote, is 'supported by an extensive network of international offices specialising in commodity-based investments. This group has amongst its members specialists in practically every form of commodity investment.' He concluded by saying the company had 'a reputation of which we are justifiably proud'.

However, the group's reputation was far from unsullied. During the period that Thatcher was chairman, three of its subsidiaries were under investigation for financial irregularities. One of them was Yearcome Commodities Ltd, a subsidiary based in Vancouver, British Columbia, Canada. Between 1982 and 1984, the Superintendent of Brokers, Investment and Real Estate of the British Columbian government (BIRE) and the police received numerous complaints about the company. This led to BIRE, the Royal Canadian Mounted Police and the Canadian Ministry of Consumer Affairs conducting an enquiry to trace missing money paid to Yearcome Commodities to invest overseas.[8]

The investigation was also embraced by the Hong Kong Securities Commission. 'We have attempted to establish whether the [investment] orders came through,' said Alan Mills, an assistant commissioner. 'They were specified in the loco London Market here. We're continuing to look into it.'[9] But Hon Hing, which means 'Chinese prosperity', refused to co-operate with the regulators as there was no law governing commodity traders, although one senior partner was interviewed.[10] No action was taken against Yearcome, but in January 1984 it stopped trading.

Another Hon Hing subsidiary, Yearcome Pte Ltd, based in Singapore, was forced to shut down for financial offences after an investigation by police and the Singapore Monetary Authority. An inspectors' enquiry, held while Mark Thatcher was chairman of the holding company, resulted in a court order to close it for 'conducting its business in a manner detrimental to the interests of its clients'. The firm did not appeal against the ruling.[11]

The third subsidiary to be probed by regulatory authorities was another Singapore company, Trivest Bullion Enterprises Pte Ltd (TBE). A report by Singapore government inspectors stated that the firm's local directors had 'acted in concert with Hon Hing Hong to deceive the authorities'. The inspectors concluded that TBE failed to control their brokers, clients were tricked into giving brokers discretionary control over their accounts and that this control was abused by brokers who ordered unnecessary transactions to increase their commission payments.[12] It was recommended that TBE be closed by court order and this was granted.

Mark Thatcher maintains he was a 'non-executive

chairman of Hon Hing Trivest for a short period' until he relinquished it in December 1982. He added that he 'had no involvement in the running of the company and was not aware of the brochure being circulated after he resigned the position'.[13] He also 'totally rejected' any suggestion that he should be linked to the financial irregularities of Hon Hing's subsidiary companies.

However, Mark was not quite the passive company chairman he would like to appear. On 7 September 1982, he opened a new gold-dealer branch for Hon Hing Trivest in Kowloon, flanked by his bodyguards and his close business associate Tony Zie. The ribbon-cutting ceremony was conducted with some aplomb and fanfare. Every announcement began: 'Mark Thatcher, son of the British Prime Minister . . .' Local businessmen noticed that this occurred only a few days after Mrs Thatcher had paid an official visit to Hong Kong for talks on the future sovereignty of the colony. 'It is not what he is but who he represents,' said one observer.[14]

Mark's claim that he 'had no involvement in the running of the company' was further weakened by his attendance at a private meeting in early 1983 with the president of the Chinese Gold and Silver Exchange, Woo Hon-Fai. He was accompanied by John Kit, managing director of Hon Hing Trivest, and Tony Zie, at the time his fellow director at Ulferts. All three refused to talk about the meeting.[15]

The Emperor's Dirty Clothes

A mere month before the two Singapore subsidiaries of Hon Hing Trivest were closed down for fraud, they were bought by a Hong Kong-based company called Emperor Investment Holdings Ltd (EIH). The affiliates were then renamed and traded on the gold market.

It was Mark Thatcher's direct involvement with EIH that was to prove the most controversial of his business dealings in Hong Kong. The bullion and commodities futures trading firm has a chequered history. It was originally owned by Marvellous Investments, a property and jewellery company which collapsed in the early 1980s after writs were issued for the repayment of debts totalling HK$ 250 million.

In early 1983, Emperor Investment Holdings was set free after Marvellous sold its 52 per cent stake in the company. It was then resurrected by Albert Yeung Shou-Shing, the chairman, a leading shareholder and one of Hong Kong's most controversial businessmen. He relaunched Emperor with a capital of HK$ 70 million and 10 million shares. 'It rose like a phoenix from burning ash,' according to one local analyst. Yeung had a strong desire to make Emperor a powerful and prestigious force and spoke to Tony Zie about how to achieve this. Zie suggested recruiting the British prime minister's son and his business partner, Steve Tipping.[16] And so on 27 June 1983, two weeks after Mrs Thatcher's second general election victory, Mark Thatcher and Steve Tipping became directors of Emperor Investment Holdings, with an arrangement to be paid a slice of any future profits.

Emperor executives were not shy of explaining why Thatcher was hired. 'We are using his name because he is well-known through car racing and his advertising here,' said Ho-Pak Kong at the time (he was the chief shareholder, who bought Yeung's stake just before Mark joined the board). 'The fact that he is the son of the Prime Minister carries some weight.'[17] Looking back ten years later, Ho-Pak Kong has not changed his view. 'Mark was made a director because he was the prime minister's son and Albert [Yeung] thought it would add prestige to the company.'[18]

It showed an extraordinary lack of judgement to forge such a close business association with Albert Yeung. Emperor's chairman was not allowed even to be on the board because of his recent criminal past, which was well-documented and widely reported. Just two years earlier, Yeung had been convicted and jailed for nine months for attempting to pervert the course of justice. The case involved Tony Cruz, a young jockey, who was charged with assaulting Wai Kin-Bong, manager of the *Tin Tin Daily News*. Yeung, a high-flying racehorse owner and watch dealer, was a close friend of Cruz and decided to intervene on his behalf. He approached Wai, introduced himself as 'the boss of Tony Cruz' and offered Wai 'up to HK$ 2 million' for not giving evidence against his jockey friend. Yeung added that he could 'fix up the police officers at the Shatin station' and there would be no further trouble. Another witness, Lau Tinchau, testified that the Emperor executive told him he would pay 'up to HK$ 10,000' as Wai's medical fees if the matter could be forgotten.[19]

At first, Yeung was given only a two-month suspended sentence, which caused such shock and outrage that when he lodged an appeal the judges increased it to nine months' imprisonment. As he was managing director of a number of companies, Yeung was allowed a few days' grace before he was taken away to Ma Hang prison, where he served six months. Tony Cruz later pleaded guilty to the assault charge against Wai Kin-Bong, whose injuries required him to remain in hospital for eighteen days.

The Emperor chairman's criminal activities did not end there. In July 1986, he was convicted of bookmaking offences and sentenced to six months' imprisonment, suspended for two years. He was also fined HK$ 50,000. Yeung, a well-known gambler, and two associates were found in a Kowloon flat when police from the Organised and Serious Crimes Bureau raided the premises. They discovered two telephone units which were used to receive calls from people who wanted to place bets on races or check their winnings. One police officer later claimed she had been obstructed by Yeung, but this charge was later withdrawn.[20]

After his conviction for trying to bribe Wai Kin-Bong, Yeung was disqualified as a director and banned from the Hong Kong Jockey Club. But that did not appear to concern Mark Thatcher. Not only did he join the board of Emperor Investment Holdings, but he also became deputy chairman of Andrope Commodities Ltd, a wholly owned subsidiary. To launch his involvement, Mark co-hosted a cocktail party at the Hilton Hotel. All directors of Hong Kong government departments, civil servants responsible for the futures and securities business and several journalists were invited. Several of them were introduced to Thatcher.[21]

He was enthusiastic about his participation in Emperor and its subsidiaries, which he described as a 'gold futures trading operation'. He added: 'We make available to the man in the street the ability to trade in gold and gold futures. We write an incredible amount of business. I mean 20, 30, 40 million dollars is not exceptional. It's a very good little business.'[22] He also acknowledged his active interest in the company. 'I will look at each month's management report, balance sheet and will attend all the business meetings,' he said proudly.[23]

One of Emperor's most controversial subsidiaries was Gainsborough Holdings Ltd, an unlicensed offshore commodity-broking company registered in Guernsey. Incorporated in May 1983, a month before Mark Thatcher joined Emperor, its function was to act on behalf of speculators who wished to gamble on the price of commodities. Funds were accepted from Hong Kong and British investors to speculate in futures on the New York commodities exchange. Clients made a 10 per cent deposit to buy or sell gold, tin, cocoa or sugar at a price set months ahead.[24] Emperor in Hong Kong then charged a commission for placing these bids on their behalf. But it was a highly risky operation, as investors could often lose large amounts of money overnight. Commodity-broking was, said an Old Bailey judge at the time, 'a jungle . . . in which the small animal is gravely at risk'.[25]

Mark Thatcher's connection with Gainsborough Holdings was that his name was used as a 'selling point' for clients. For example, he was introduced to Alec McDade, a director of the company, at Les Ambassadeurs club in Hamilton Place, Mayfair, by Andrew Chan, Emperor's managing director. At the time McDade, a haulage executive from Wakefield, Yorkshire, was considering investing 'a very considerable sum' in Gainsborough. While he was negotiating this shareholding, he was informed by Uisden McInnes, a director of Emperor Investments and former head of the Hong Kong Securities Commission, that Mark Thatcher was a director of the parent company. McDade proceeded with this investment but later withdrew from the company. 'It was just gambling,' he recalled.[26]

Despite McDade's departure, Gainsborough continued to operate and remained an Emperor subsidiary. On 4 October 1983, newspaper advertisements were placed soliciting funds for 'investment purposes'. But there was little, if any, trading taking place and clients were becoming concerned about their money. Five weeks later a saviour appeared at hand when City financier Robert Knight walked into Gainsborough's London office in Buckingham Palace Road, Victoria, and announced, according to a former employee, that he had 'bought the company'.

However, he was far from dressed in shining armour. At that precise moment, Knight was facing criminal charges of attempting to defraud financial institutions by trafficking in fraudulent Eurodollar bonds. He was also charged with defrauding his own company, Sturla Holdings, and was being sued for an outstanding debt of £115,000. Known as 'the Conjurer', Knight was a director of numerous companies. Two of the firms he had acquired were put into receivership.

Gainsborough fared little better. Its clients became anxious about the way their funds were being handled, particularly as their bids were not being placed in New York. Within two months, in January 1984, the firm had collapsed and this led to several complaints to the police. Almost immediately, the City of London Fraud Squad launched an investigation into Gainsborough Holdings – both during Emperor's ownership and while Knight controlled the company.

Mark Thatcher and his business partner, Steve Tipping, went to great pains to say that 'as directors of Emperor Holdings they were in no way involved in the business activities of Gainsborough Holdings'.[27] However, apart from Mark's business link with the holding company, there was a further connection which has remained undisclosed until now. Thatcher knew Robert 'the Conjurer' Knight and had had a previous commercial association with him.

This connection can be traced back at least until late 1979. At the time Knight was chairman of Tiger Securities Ltd, his private investment vehicle specializing in sport. He adorned the board with some influential figures. One was Sir David Checketts, former private secretary to Prince Charles and later a director of arms firm International Signal and Control Technologies. Another was George Magnus, later a senior executive in the corporate empire of Li Ka-Shing, one of Hong Kong's most powerful businessmen.

In late 1979, Knight was looking to invest money he had made in the Far East and spoke to Mark Thatcher about it. Mark suggested CSS Promotions Ltd, who were his marketing and promotions agents at the time. Knight agreed and so Mark spoke to his friend Barrie Gill, joint managing director of CSS, about the proposal. Gill was enthusiastic and told a fellow senior director, 'There is an opportunity for us to expand through a company called Tiger Securities. They have a lot of money from the Far East which they want to invest.'

Two weeks later, Gill and the director went to see Knight at his office at 78 South Audley Street, Mayfair. 'I would like Tiger to invest in your company,' Knight told them. 'In return, I have some sports stars I would like you to look after.' But the meeting was not a success, as Gill's colleague was not impressed by his prospective investor. 'Almost from the first moment I knew I could not deal with him,' he recalled. 'He was shooting his diamond and gold cuff-links and decorated his office in a ridiculously flashy way with two huge stuffed China tigers in the foyer.'[28]

Drawing on his extensive commercial experience, Gill's colleague instinctively felt that Knight was bent. 'We're not having anything to do with an outfit like that,' he said to Gill as they walked down South Audley Street after the meeting. 'I can't stand the man. He's not reliable.' His partner disagreed: 'But he's very wealthy and comes highly recommended as a respectable investor. Anyway, I'm sure Mark would not be involved with them [Tiger Securities] if there was anything dodgy about them.'

It seemed to CSS Promotions that Mark Thatcher was acting as if he were an introductory agent for Knight. As it turned out, Tiger Securities' proposals were so vague and indecisive that the investment never occurred. But Gill's colleague proved to be correct. Two years later, in 1981, Tiger Securities went bankrupt. In 1985, Knight was charged and convicted of conspiracy to defraud and jailed for twelve months. He now lives in the Canary Islands.

Robert Knight and Gainsborough Holdings might have lost their way, but another of Mark Thatcher's friends with a criminal record, Albert Yeung, prospered. His company, the Emperor Group, former owner of Gainsborough, expanded by mergers and take-overs, and by 1993 its assets had risen to over HK$ 2 billion. Its principal sectors of business are property investment, gold and securities, jewellery and overseas investments. The company was also awarded a licence to open a bank in Cambodia. Yeung is now fabulously wealthy and owns Hong Kong's most expensive car licence plate – the prized 'lucky' Number Nine, which he bought for HK$ 13 million.[29]

But he remains a notorious figure in the colony. On 11 December 1994, after an investigation by the Organised Crime and Triads Bureau, Yeung was

arrested by police officers at 1am in the karaoke
bar of the Happy Valley Hotel. He was accused of
detaining Lam Yih-Jun, a rival businessman, against
his will at the Mandarin Hotel and inside a room in
the Emperor International Exchange office. The next
day he was charged with criminal intimidation and
unlawful punishment.[30]

The Emperor chairman has also lost none of his knack
of hiring political muscle to strengthen his sprawling
business empire. In 1994, he recruited Bob Hawke, who
until his replacement by Paul Keating in December 1991
had been Australia's longest-serving prime minister, as a
non-executive director, largely to develop the company's
racing and casino interests. 'I know the region well and
the political and business leaders in the region,' said the
former premier. 'I've been able to help them out with
some introductions.' Yeung confirmed this role: 'Mr
Hawke has introduced a lot of friends to me and he
has a lot of connections.'[31] This, of course, was why
the Emperor chairman had hired Mark Thatcher a decade
earlier and the two were, according to one Hong Kong
source, 'very friendly'.

The Profits of Diplomacy

Mark's commercial interests in Hong Kong, particularly in Emperor Investment Holdings, led to concern
among some Foreign Office civil servants about a
potential conflict of interests. At the time (1982–3) Mrs
Thatcher was conducting sensitive and decisive negotiations with China over the future sovereignty over
the colony. It was argued that the prime minister's son
could benefit commercially from inside information

about the state of the Sino–British talks. This was because the price of gold was exceptionally vulnerable to reports about the state of those discussions. As Mark Thatcher was a director of a company that traded in gold futures in Hong Kong, London and New York, there was a possible conflict of interests.

'That's utter crap,' was Mark's characteristic response in 1984. 'We're open in Hong Kong for 20 hours a day and anyone can walk in and take a gold position on the Hong Kong market or the London, New York or Chicago exchanges. There is no way that Hong Kong lease negotiations can possibly affect the gold futures price in, say, Chicago.'[32]

However, his Foreign Office critics point to an incident which reveals how easy it was for him to be on the inside track during the Hong Kong negotiations. In 1983, a senior diplomat called on the prime minister to brief her on the latest developments in the colony. To his surprise, he found her son sitting in the room. According to two press reports, the diplomat waited uneasily while he thought personal family business would be disposed of and Mark would depart. But, much to his discomfort, Margaret Thatcher told him to continue his briefing while her son remained. 'It's only Mark,' she reportedly said reassuringly.[33]

More first-hand information can be derived from a remarkable interview Mark Thatcher gave in late 1983 to a reporter from *Ming Pao Weekly* in Hong Kong. Despite arranging and agreeing the meeting in advance, the Chinese journalist was told he could have fifteen minutes on the street while the prime minister's son waited for his car, accompanied by his security guard. The reporter first asked about the nature of Mark's business interests. 'Nothing special, I just don't like to disclose,' sniffed Mark. The conversation then turned to Hong Kong.

'Do you talk to your mother about Hong Kong?' asked the journalist.

'Of course I do,' replied Thatcher.

'Are your views about Hong Kong the same?'

'She likes Hong Kong too. Naturally, she is not as familiar with the place as I am. She has only been here two or three times. Of course, we often talk about Hong Kong, but this is only between us – mother and son.'

'Have you any intention of doing business in China?'

'Just taking a look. Many friends invited me to go. Perhaps I will accept their invitation in the future. China is a place really worth going to.'[34] (His commercial interest in China was as chairman of Couvin Ltd, a Hong Kong company that advised firms on doing business on the mainland.[35])

'Does the reason for your affinity with Hong Kong have anything to do with China?'

'Definitely not. Hong Kong will not become better or worse just because of China. You can never see Hong Kong and China as two separate matters.'

The interview was notable for the candour with which he spoke about his relationship with the prime minister. 'My mother is perfect,' he said. 'She will support me 100 per cent, no matter what I do. We talk about virtually everything, but this is strictly between my mother and me.'[36]

The depth and extent of Mark's conversations with the prime minister on Hong Kong are not known. However, by his own account in late 1983, 'we often talk about Hong Kong' and it was the one international issue he commented on. 'She fought very hard for the agreement,' he said in 1991. 'She feels a great affinity

with Hong Kong. It has such self-reliance, adaptability
and self-determination.'[37]

How much money Mark Thatcher made out of Hong
Kong is in some dispute. The Hong Kong press estimated it at £100,000 a year but that seems unlikely.
Apart from Emperor, most of the companies that
hired him were not a success and it is unlikely he
reaped much reward from them. Tony Zie, his former
business partner, who has since become embroiled in
a series of civil law suits over control of the Jademan
comics publishing company, later played down Mark's
activities: 'He was rarely here. I used mainly to deal
with Steve Tipping. Mark seemed more interested in
the Middle East.'[38]

The last statement was certainly true but the first
was not. Throughout the 1980s Mark visited Hong
Kong every three months. After delving into the gold
and commodities market, he opted for the investment
business. One of his main contacts was Robert V.
Wang, chairman of the United Overseas Bank Group.
He met Wang through Suntech Investments, a hugely
powerful investment consortium dominated by six of
Hong Kong's top ten business tycoons and controller
of 35 per cent of the colony's capitalization. 'He comes
here fairly regularly to touch base and sniff around for
business,' the banker said in 1993. 'When my company
started we looked at some of his proposals for mobile
telephones and hi-tech equipment, but we didn't go
ahead because it was for an American market.'[39]

However, despite his mother's boasts about Mark
being 'a born businessman',[40] his foray into the investment game brought him few, if any, financial suc-
cesses. 'I would say Mark wanted to be an entrepreneur
and an investment syndicator for different companies,'

said the managing director of a Hong Kong investment company that deals mainly with middle-ranking
Chinese businessmen. 'He is a man of tremendous
energy but he wished to play in a finance and investment world which is an unforgiving environment in
Hong Kong for people who are short on skill and Mark
is lacking in wisdom, I'm afraid. He is more likely to
have succeeded in marketing, sales and promotion.'

For Margaret Thatcher's son, Hong Kong was not
the place where he acquired sacks of gold. As in
many of his commercial adventures of the early 1980s,
he found there was much Eastern promise but not
much fulfilment. Considerable energy and activity
were invested and generated but there is precious
little evidence of much in the way of cash returns.
His business record in the colony is summed up by
an old Chinese proverb: 'The chap who sits on a hot
cooker once learns. But the chap who does it twice is
stupid.' Mark sat on the cooker several times and so
decided to look elsewhere in South East Asia.

Arming Malaysia

In February 1994, Hugh Thurston, the personal banker
to Mark and Margaret Thatcher, flew from his home
in St Helier, Jersey, to Belgravia, London. He had
been asked to make the journey by the former prime
minister for a special reason. They spoke periodically,
of course, but this time there was an urgent matter.
According to a source close to the Thatcher family,
she asked Thurston about the family finances: 'Are
they in order, Hugh?' After being reassured, she then
expressed fears about Mark's possible implication in

a looming scandal – his involvement in an arms deal with Malaysia which she negotiated and signed as prime minister in 1988. Her anxiety was fuelled by the disclosure that millions of pounds of taxpayers' money, designated as aid for Third World countries, were handed to Malaysia as a 'sweetener' to secure the £1.3 billion defence contract. This policy, confirmed by former defence secretary George (now Lord) Younger in early 1994, was particularly controversial as Malaysia was seen as a wealthy country.

The origins of the deal lay in Margaret Thatcher's assertive and aggressive arms-sales policy in the Far East. Briefed by Sir Colin Chandler, head of defence sales, she was told that Malaysia could be a sequel to Al Yamamah. It was ripe for an arms deal as the country had laid plans and allocated a multi-billion-pound budget to turn its armed forces into a tough fighting outfit by re-equipping all three major service branches by the year 2000. As a bonus, the deal had the advantage of restoring diplomatic relations with the country after a dispute over university fees for overseas students in the UK.

Malaysia's prime minister, Dr Mahathir Mohamed, was keen to pursue rearmament because of disputes with China, the Philippines and Vietnam over islands in the South China Sea. Defence-spending cuts had taken their toll and so he welcomed Mrs Thatcher's approach, particularly as he admired her political and economic policies. The result was direct and intimate negotiations between the two prime ministers. They began with Dr Mahathir's visit to London in 1987 and culminated when Mrs Thatcher went to Kuala Lumpur on 6 August 1988.

A month later, on 27 September 1988, the two leaders signed a Memorandum of Understanding (MOU) in the Cabinet Room at 10 Downing Street. The terms of the MOU were not released for 'reasons of commercial confidentiality'.[41] But the essence of the document was that Malaysia agreed to buy from Britain twelve Tornado jet fighter aircraft, air-defence radars, artillery guns, two Oberon-class submarines and Rapier anti-aircraft missile systems worth £1.3 billion. Mrs Thatcher said the signing marked a new phase in their improved relationship, which showed their 'confidence in one another'.[42] It transformed Britain into the world's second largest arms exporter during her tenure in 10 Downing Street.

She set up a special unit in the Ministry of Defence in support of the deal. But negotiations were at first stalled by a dispute over air landing rights. The UK government had promised to grant Malaysia Airlines extra flights between Kuala Lumpur and London but this was not implemented. Mrs Thatcher intervened and an accord was reached on 10 March 1989 after British Airways was paid £1 million in compensation.[43] Detailed arms discussions then began between British Aerospace and the Malaysian Defence Ministry.

By the autumn of 1990, it had been decided that the Tornados were 'too costly' and Malaysia opted for the cheaper Hawks.[44] Eventually, on 10 December 1990, a contract was signed for Malaysia to purchase twenty-eight Hawk fighter aircraft, a Martello radar system and two frigates from Yarrow, a GEC subsidiary, for a total of £450 million. The deal was dependent, like the Al Yamamah deal with Saudi Arabia, on an offset programme worth about £110 million. This included the transfer of technology from British Aerospace to Airod, a Malaysian-Lockheed joint-venture firm which performed all maintenance work on the Hawk.

The similarity with Al Yamamah continued in its method of payment. The weapons were to be paid for partly in cash and partly by the sale of crude oil, natural gas and other commodities. Apart from using Britain's Overseas Aid Budget to sweeten the deal, Mrs Thatcher also offered the Malaysian government cheap loans to subsidize their arms purchase. Under 'Funding', the Memorandum of Understanding stated: 'In the event there is any shortfall in the funding, the UK government will assist in the arrangement of financial facilities provided by a UK bank or a group of UK banks and the UK will ensure that the interest to be charged will be at concessionary rates.' In other words, the British government was subsidizing the arms deal by paying the difference between the banks' commercial rates and their concessionary interest rates.[45]

The role of Mark Thatcher in this massive military order was first alleged by two Malaysian MPs, Lim Kit Siang and Dr Kua Kia Soong, members of the opposition Democratic Action Party. In December 1991 they claimed (and they have since repeated the claim) that Mark was linked to the deal through a local company called Bakti Udara. They encountered strong denials from the Malaysian Ministry of Defence.

However, two major segments of the contract provided clues to the extent of the involvement of Margaret Thatcher's son. The first was the sale for £70 million of a top-secret Starburst laser-guided missile system, made by Short Brothers in Belfast. This missile was carried by British troops during the Gulf war and is highly regarded as an anti-aircraft device. The middleman who helped broker this deal on behalf of Short Brothers was one Stephen W. Tipping, Mark Thatcher's business partner since 1979 and best man at his wedding. Tipping represents Short Brothers in the Far East and it was confirmed by the Malaysian MoD that he was 'a facilitator' on the Starburst deal.[46] The ministry spokesman added that he understood Mark's best friend 'was influential with the Thatcher family'.[47]

Tipping acted as an intermediary by arranging and attending meetings in London between Alex Roberts, managing director and executive vice-president of Short Brothers, and Najib tun Razak, the Malaysian defence minister. He also visited Kuala Lumpur frequently, sometimes accompanied by Roberts. Between 1988 and 1993, he made over thirty trips, staying at least 169 nights at the Shangri-La Hotel, one of the most luxurious in South-East Asia.[48] He also based himself at the Oriental Hotel in Singapore. Razak has said that he met Tipping several times to discuss the Starburst contract and knew him as a 'friend of Mark Thatcher'. However, he denied that the prime minister's son had influenced the deal.[49]

Secondly, and more fundamentally, Tipping was involved in providing parts for the British Aerospace Hawk fighter. This was consistent with Tipping's own policy as an arms fixer. 'The secret of defence deals is the engines,' he later told business associate Gary Smith. 'On the spare parts you can name your number.'

Tipping's direct commercial connection with British Aerospace was verified by his friend Sir Tim Bell, who also has a public relations contract with the Malaysian government. 'Tipping has a relationship with Dick Evans, chief executive of British Aerospace,' Sir Tim told the *Sunday Times*. 'He has either acted as an agent for British Aerospace in their negotiations with Malaysia or he has attempted to be involved in the BAe contracts. He certainly has interests in various contractual arrangements to do with BAe and Malaysia.' When asked by the paper to clarify his specific role, Sir Tim replied: 'What he does for a living is introduce people to each other.'[50]

The secret of Tipping's success in selling weapons to Malaysia is his cultivation of bankers, businessmen, brokers and politicians. One of his closest contacts was Harbhajan, an Indian. On 18 December 1989, Tipping wrote to a friend: 'Regarding Malaysia, Harbhajan is over for a few days over Christmas and I will have a long talk with him.' Another important associate was Mohamad Haji Hassan, who at the time was general manager of the Bank Bumiputra Malaysia. Hassan attended a reception with the English arms middleman at the Hilton ballroom in December 1990, just after the final contract to supply the Hawks was signed. The banker, like Tipping, was a keen golfer and they played together at Wentworth.

Perhaps more important in what became known as Thatcher's 'golden magic circle' of influence in Malaysia was Tan Sri Arumugam, a very close associate of Dr Mahathir, the prime minister. An Indian by birth, Arumugam controls GEC Malaysia, which was awarded contracts as part of the 1988 agreement. Both Mark Thatcher and Steve Tipping knew him as someone who could provide direct access to Mahathir. Arumugam, who is also represented by Sir Tim Bell, played a key role in the arms deal. Such was his close involvement in the deal that he stood behind Mrs Thatcher and Dr Mahathir when they signed the Memorandum of Understanding in 1988. Arumugam remains influential, and on 11 May 1992 he attended a dinner in honour of Mahathir, hosted by John Major at 10 Downing Street.[51]

However, Tipping's most significant relationship is

with Najib tun Razak, the Malaysian defence minister, who was given prime responsibility by Mahathir for the Hawks contract which was signed on 10 December 1990. Razak shares Tipping's passion for golf and they spend as much time on the fairways and putting greens of Malaysia as they do in the ministry office.

Steve Tipping has continued to broker arms deals since the 1988 agreement. 'I've just arranged the sale of six Sikorsky helicopters to Malaysia,' he told Gary Smith in October 1993. 'Mahathir is a good friend of mine and when the Malaysians come to England I fly them around all the golf courses in my private jet. I've done a lot of big defence deals in Malaysia. They were daft enough to buy MiG 28s from the Russians so I told them, "You had better check in case you buy toy ones!"' Tipping has always disputed this version of events.

Tipping's comment that the Malaysian prime minister was a close friend was no idle boast. In 1991, he attended a dinner at the Savoy Hotel to celebrate the birthday of Dr Mahathir's son. It was attended by Denis Thatcher, Alan Curtis, chairman of Lotus, and Alex Roberts, managing director of Short Brothers. The dinner, said one of the guests, was notable for Denis's remark that his wife regretted endorsing John Major as prime minister and that 'intellectually, he was just not up to the job'. But it also illustrated Tipping's Malaysian connections at the highest level.

The extent of Mark Thatcher's direct involvement in facilitating the supply of weapons to Malaysia is difficult to ascertain. Certainly Tipping's sales pitch to the Malaysian government was that he was connected to 'the Thatcher family'. He has also used

Hugh Thurston, Mark's personal banker, to prepare the commercial papers on Short Brothers' military contracts with Malaysia.

In an attempt to distance Mark from the Malaysian arms deal, the Thatcher camp have sent out the message that Steve Tipping's business partnership with the prime minister's son ended in 1984. Consequently, say Thatcher's friends, Mark could not have been involved in the contract. Tipping himself has repeated this assertion – both to the authors and to *Financial Times* – claiming he departed after the liquidation of Monteagle Marketing Ltd in 1985.

It is certainly true that from 1985 onwards, Mark concentrated more on Saudi Arabia and Tipping devoted his time largely to the Far East. But as late as 1987, Mark recounted to Gary Smith, the oil trader, over supper at Claridge's how he had just visited Malaysia and dealt with an Indian consultant out there. Tipping has always disputed Smith's account.

But Smith claims that Tipping continued to be aware of various of Mark's commercial projects in the late 1980s. While their relationship no longer retained its Siamese twins character, they remained linked. This was demonstrated in August 1986, when Mark introduced Tipping to Gary Smith as my 'closest confidant'. He added: 'I do all my business with him. When you talk to Steve, you are talking to me. He is my eyes and ears in the business world.'[52]

For the next eighteen months, until the spring of 1988, Smith attended a series of meetings with both Mark Thatcher and Steve Tipping on a proposed oil deal in Nigeria (see Chapter Eight for details). According to Smith, it is beyond any doubt that the two remained, at the very least, business associates until the summer of 1988. And even in the early 1990s they continued to discuss investment propositions. In October 1993, Tipping had dinner with David Wallace, who represented Thatcher's interests in Ameristar, an aviation fuel company. They discussed 'the areas in which I [Wallace] feel you can assist' (see Chapter Eight for details).

Tipping also remained close friends with the prime minister and particularly with her husband. They share the same brand of right-wing Golf Club politics. 'If the Paddies, Jocks and Taffies want to go it alone, then that's bloody fine by me,' Tipping once remarked. A regular visitor to 10 Downing Street, he often spent late mornings with Denis Thatcher drinking gin and tonics. Early one morning, Tipping telephoned a business associate to arrange a meeting. 'Can we make our appointment lunch at 12.30?' he said. 'I'll need a meal by then because I'm seeing Denis in the morning.'

Margaret Thatcher saw Tipping as a moderating influence on her wayward son. He often saw her at 10 Downing Street and was a lunch guest at Chequers, particularly at Christmas. She once sent him a framed photograph of herself and signed it, 'To Stephen. Warm regards. Margaret.' Indeed, Lady Thatcher even consulted her son's former business partner about this book. On the evening of 12 July 1993, she confided in him: 'I am very worried about this book being written about Mark.'

When asked to contribute to this biography, Tipping responded: 'Despite considerable provocation and temptation over the years, I have never discussed my business in public. I see no reason to change this habit of a lifetime as far as my own affairs are concerned; and certainly no justification whatsoever in talking about those of a friend and former colleague. I am sorry, therefore, to have to turn you down.'[53]

Stephen Tipping has come a long way from his days working for the family garage company in Yateley, Surrey, in the early 1970s. The Malaysian arms deal was the culmination of seizing the main chance in 1979 when he linked up with the prime minister's son. He now bears and wears all the trappings of his millionaire status. Since 1986 he has lived in a sprawling mansion in Fleet, Hampshire, with several garages containing his collection of classic cars. He owns a BMW Sports car, a Mercedes 600 SEL, chauffeur-driven by a former Scotland Yard officer, a Vauxhall jeep and another Mercedes for his wife, Lynda. Most of his business meetings are held at the Savoy Hotel, where all the waiters address him as 'Mr Tipping, sir'. He also drops by at the St James's Club and the Lanesborough, London's most expensive hotel, which is run and owned by Texans, for a drink when he is in town.

Mark Thatcher's business partner for almost ten years is now an immensely wealthy man. Like Mark, Tipping uses Hugh Thurston to look after his financial affairs. 'I have made more money than I think I can spend,' he told Gary Smith in 1993.

'Where do you bank it all?' he was asked.

'It's buried deep, man. Very deep.'

Stephen Tipping has consistently disputed the accuracy of the authors' sources for this account of his relationship with Mark Thatcher.

Flying into Sri Lanka

To the west of Malaysia, about 1,600 miles across

the Indian Ocean, lies the tropical paradise of Sri Lanka. A mountainous, largely agricultural island – known as the 'Teardrop of India' – Sri Lanka has been experiencing an economic revolution. For thirty years the country's basic utilities and industries have been state-owned. But the early 1990s saw a sea change, with a programme of privatization and industrialization of its infrastructure. The process has been supported by the British government. Sri Lanka will be the 'Malaysia of South Asia within a few years', said Richard Needham, the trade minister. But the programme has been besmirched by allegations of corruption, including the misuse of financial aid from the United Kingdom.

It was to this once peaceful, neutral island that Mark Thatcher next turned his gaze in the Far East. His chief contact point was Ravinora B. Wethasinghe, a thirty-two-year-old British-educated entrepreneur and aviation enthusiast. Wethasinghe is exactly the type of businessman Thatcher likes to associate with. Like Mark he is a car fanatic, owning eight Ferraris and a Lamborghini. A secretive man, for many years he preferred to hire a private jet and fly alone on his regular trips between England and Sri Lanka, rather than on a normal commercial flight. He owns two planes. One is a private executive Gulfstream jet, kept at the Osprey Aviation hangar in Southampton, for his own use. The other is chartered out to high-powered business delegations.

In his earlier years Wethasinghe had been an arms dealer and supplied guns to the Sri Lankan government during the civil war with the Tamil Tigers. He also liked to have weapons for his own use. On 24 June 1989, he was convicted and fined £1,550 at West London Magistrates Court for the illegal possession of ninety-six rounds of long ammunition and a high-calibre Ruger .22 semi-automatic combat rifle. Yet such was his influence in the Sri Lankan high commission that just two and a half weeks later he was a guest at a Buckingham Palace garden party, mingling with the royal family.[54]

Despite his criminal conviction, Wethasinghe has remained a powerful and wealthy business operator. In 1992 he secured a 600-million-rupee (£7.6 million) contract with the Sri Lankan government to supply 2,500 buses to a country which was in desperate need of public transport. Wethasinghe had set up a company, Latec Engineering and Management Services Ltd, to facilitate the deal and manufacture the buses in Sri Lanka, based on imported parts and engines made by Duple Metsec Ltd, a Birmingham-based company. He had also persuaded the Department of Trade and Industry to provide an aid and provision grant of £2.65m – 30 per cent of the total cost – for the project and acquired funding from the Sri Lankan government.

But the problem was that hardly any buses were actually built and the contract was heavily criticized for its high cost and overheads. One diplomat compiled a report entitled 'The Sri Lanka Bus Deal – How to Rob a Country'. Local politicians were also furious. On 17 June 1993, a Sri Lankan MP told parliament: 'The Duple Metsec–Lanka Agents collaboration has a sordid record in the supply of the earlier 600-bus-kit contract. The local businessman involved in the collaboration . . . has been fined in the British courts.'[55]

One of the executives whom Wethasinghe hired to promote the contract was Kate Roy, his communications manager. The project appealed to Kate because it provided much-needed employment for Sri Lankans and involved local people as investors. She was also a pacifist and a strong critic of Margaret Thatcher, whom she saw as promoting the arms trade. So when she first started working for Wethasinghe she made her views crystal-clear. 'I have to know where your money comes from,' she told him. 'If it comes from arms or drugs I cannot work for you.' Wethasinghe appeared upset. 'Kate, I have to tell you that a few years ago I was involved in arms,' he said. 'It was lucrative, but I now want to put the money back into this project and change things in my country.'

Wethasinghe was not a political animal but he could see the value of politicians. 'I'm going to get Mrs Thatcher to open the factory,' he often said. 'Well, I'm not going to be there,' replied Kate. 'You'll have to get Babu [his security guard] to hold me down to shake her hand.' Wethasinghe laughed and teased her about her views. But his links with the Thatchers were no idle boast, according to Kate. Wethasinghe later telephoned to ask her advice on the best medical treatment for his father. 'He told me that when he flew his father from Colombo to London after his stroke he had dinner with Lady Thatcher,' recalled Kate. 'Ravi [Wethasinghe] said she was very kind because she introduced him to her personal physician and private clinic. She has been very helpful to [him] and she has been a good friend.'

By late August 1993, Wethasinghe's attitude towards Kate changed. 'It's so difficult to make a living this way,' he told her. 'I'm going back to my old business.' Kate, who knew what this meant, replied: 'Well, you know we had an agreement. I will resign if that happens.' Suddenly Wethasinghe started making life in the company very difficult for her and on one occasion his staff tried to stop her entering her own office. The reason for this behaviour became apparent five days later on Thursday, 9 September 1993. Kate was sitting on the porch outside her office when she was stunned to see Mark Thatcher and Wethasinghe arriving together. She was introduced to Mark, who then entered the office and used the fax and telephone.

'I immediately thought, "All is lost," because it was obvious to me that they were doing some kind of business together,' she recalled.[56] She told Wethasinghe she was resigning because of the Thatcher association. 'Mark is a friend of mine,' he replied, 'and if you don't like the way things are done around here you should go.' Kate then returned to her hotel, packed her bags and flew back to England.

Mark Thatcher and Wethasinghe had met through a mutual passion for aviation. Mark has been a keen helicopter flyer since 1982 when he qualified as a pilot after being instructed at Blackbushe Airport, Surrey, in an American-built Enstrom helicopter. He paid £5,000 for the thirty-five-hour training course and at the time he said he did it 'just for fun'.[57]

Ten years later, in July 1992, Thatcher was able to buy a B206 Bell jet ranger helicopter from Skyline Ltd for £185,500 (he occasionally leases it back to them for commercial projects). He then spent £70,000 on its interior. 'It looked like the inside of a Ford Escort,' said film-maker Tim Cooper, who has flown in it.

In July 1992, the helicopter was purchased through a company called Newbury International Ltd, based in the Isle of Man. Six weeks later the helicopter's registration was transferred to another Isle of Man firm called Corporate Enterprises Ltd. This appears as the owner in Civil Aviation Authority (CAA) records as of 10 August 1992. However, this was a misleading CAA registration, because five days earlier, on 5 August 1992, Mark Thatcher's nominee directors had changed the name of the helicopter's owner to Newbury Aviation Ltd. Consequently, his declared CAA declaration is incorrect because Corporate Enterprises Ltd does not exist! Such a convoluted method of registering a helicopter is a classic example of Thatcher's secretive and intricate business methods.

The following spring Ravi Wethasinghe also bought a B206 jet ranger helicopter from Skyline and it was at their aerodrome in Booker, near High Wycombe, Buckinghamshire, that he first met Mark Thatcher in July 1993. 'Any dealings we had with Mr Wethasinghe and Mr Thatcher are confidential,' said former Skyline director Trevor Taylor. 'I cannot talk to you without their permission.'

But when Mark arrived in Sri Lanka two months later he was on a different kind of business mission. He was acting on behalf of American firms who were keen to bid for the state-owned Lanka Petroleum Corporation, other state-owned corporations being privatized, and contracts to supply equipment to the electricity-generating board. Mark needed introductions to the very top of the Sri Lankan government and Wethasinghe was the ideal facilitator. Wethasinghe used his chairman, D. S. Jayawickrema, to make the background enquiries. Jayawickrema asked Kate Roy to bring over brochures of British electricity companies that might be interested in bidding for the contracts.

Mark had flown into Colombo from Bombay, on a private British Aerospace 125 jet hired by Wethasinghe and leased from Osprey Aviation. The pilots were told

that this trip was 'highly confidential' and ordered not
to tell anyone whom they were picking up. If asked,
they should say 'an engineer'. Mark stayed at the
Ramada Renaissance Hotel and his bill was paid by
Swiss Lloyd Ltd, a travel firm. Swiss Lloyd paid all
the residential expenses for all Ravi Wethasinghe's
employees and business associates, said Kate Roy.
'They paid all my hotel bills and Ravi then immediately
reimbursed them, so there is no doubt in my mind that
Ravi paid Mark Thatcher's hotel bill.'

For the next four days and three nights he gained
remarkable access to senior ministers and military
generals. He met President D. B. Wijetunga at the presidential secretariat with Wethasinghe and his brother
Gamini.[58] Mark also paid what was described as 'a
courtesy call' on Prime Minister Ranil Wickremasinghe
and the newly appointed military chief.[59]

On the first evening of his visit Mark was a guest
at a special dinner at the Ramada Renaissance Hotel
hosted by Wethasinghe. The twelve guests included Ian
Dallas, the commercial attaché at the British high commission, Scott Hamilton from Duple Metsec, Milinda
Ekanayake, a director of Latec and managing director
of Skyline Helicopters UK Ltd, which Wethasinghe
had just taken over, Jacquie Fance-Wheeler, another
Latec director, Latec's chairman, D. S. Jayawickrema,
and Wethasinghe's brother Gamini.

Officials at the British high commission were introduced to Thatcher and became increasingly concerned
about his business activities in Sri Lanka. They were
not informed about his visit and were particularly
anxious about how he obtained direct access to senior
ministers, while others had to wait or go through proper
channels. His visit was also noticed by a Conservative
MP with Sri Lankan connections, who happened to be

in Colombo at the same time. He was not happy. 'What
the hell was that man doing there?' he said. 'I don't
want to be associated with him.'

Chapter Eight

Black Gold

'I am a millionaire. That is my religion.'
George Bernard Shaw, *Major Barbara*

Mark Thatcher's introduction to the oil business was a chance meeting with Gary Smith, a well-connected international oil trader, on a 7am British Airways flight from Paris to London in August 1986. Mark often flew from the USA to London via Paris, to avoid what he called 'the nurks' (journalists who met him at Heathrow Airport by tracing his direct flights from Texas). He also had an apartment in Avenue Foch in Paris, which he used as a base to meet prominent Arabs.

But as he sat in the business-class compartment reading the newspapers, more political matters were on his mind. It was a time when the Conservative government was in trouble and the Labour Party (or 'the goons' as Mark liked to refer to them) was in contention for power. Suddenly Mark closed his newspaper and turned to Gary Smith. 'What are you going to do if the goons get in?' he said without introducing himself. 'I don't know,' replied the oilman. 'Mum must be supported or the country will have all kinds of problems,' said her son.

Smith then introduced himself formally and Mark began to chat away, particularly about the threat posed by 'the goons' and 'chief goon' Neil Kinnock.

'If I were you, I'd go and live in Switzerland like the rest of us will have to,' said the prime minister's son. 'In my opinion, Switzerland is by far the best place in the world.'

'I lived in Geneva for two years, which was very pleasant, but I prefer London because it's more vibrant,' replied the oilman.

'London is OK but Switzerland is where the dosh is,' said Mark.

The conversation then turned to the oil industry. 'A lot of politicians in nig-nog land [which Smith took to mean Africa and the Middle East] are creaming it off [making money] like crazy,' said Thatcher. Smith agreed and said the Saudi Arabian private businessmen were the most avaricious. He added that he had helped put together a deal in 1984 which involved exchanging Saudi oil for aircraft. 'King Fahd was persuaded to insert an extra 36 million barrels of oil into a market which was over-supplied, and huge commissions were paid,' said Smith. 'Sheikh Yamani had actually opposed these sort of deals.'

Mark was curious but not knowledgeable about the oil business. He was more interested in sponsorship for his motor-racing career. 'I would like to get sponsorship from oil companies for my racing cars,' he said. 'I'm looking at a minimum of $200,000, because my name has sponsorship value.'

Smith indicated he would be able to help.

'Good, I'll introduce you to my closest confidant, Stephen Tipping,' replied Thatcher. 'I do all my business with him. If he rings you, call him Steve as if you were talking to me. He is my eyes and ears

in the business world and will know what to do if any
really decent deal is on offer.'

Smith took 'decent' to mean profitable and said he
would make some enquiries.

'I hate time-wasters,' Mark added. 'I will need a lot
of money to retire on, at least £5 million.' He then
changed his mind. 'Well, £10 million would be safer
because it's a tough world.'

Smith thought to himself that this reflected Margaret
Thatcher's harsh view of the world. This was confirmed by her son's next remark: 'Life is short, brutish
and nasty.'

As the BA flight descended into Heathrow airport,
Mark handed Smith his business card, which read
simply, 'The Grantham Company, Dallas, Texas'.
'Please call me in Texas or on this number at 10
Downing Street. I usually stay there when I am in
London.' He then scribbled down the number 01–222
8141 (a direct 10 Downing Street line).

'Doesn't your mother mind if you do business from
there?' asked Smith.

'Mum wouldn't have it any other way,' replied
Mark. 'If you would like to meet my mother, I would
be happy to introduce you.'

As they walked through Terminal 4, Smith said he
would approach Swiss and German oil companies for
sponsorship of his motor racing. Mark was appreciative
and they began laughing about his getting lost in the
desert. 'Mum was really worried about that,' he said.
'It shows what a wonderful mum she really is.' As they
reached the end of the escalators of Terminal 4, Mark
was met by four security officers. 'Everything OK,
sir,' one said, and they went their separate ways.

That evening Mark Thatcher rang Smith at his West
Hampstead home. 'I am leaving soon for the States,'

he said, 'but me and Steve [Tipping] have an oil deal which we would like to talk to you about.' However, Tipping denies any involvement in this deal.

Three months later the oil trader heard from Mark again. 'We're on track for a big oil contract in Nigeria,' he said. But again things went quiet. Then, in April 1987, Smith says he was invited by Mark to dinner at Claridge's, the elegant hotel in Brook Street, Mayfair, where he was introduced to Steve Tipping. At first Thatcher recounted with great relish an episode when he was in Malaysia. 'An Indian I was dealing with offered me a pretty girl for the night,' related Mark. 'I told him, "No way. I am not that type," so the Indian offered me a pretty boy!' At this he burst into raucous laughter, so loudly that a waiter came over to their table and asked, 'Is everything all right, sir?'

The conversation turned to commercial matters. 'I know nothing at all about oil, except how it works in cars,' said Mark repeatedly. 'That doesn't matter,' interrupted Tipping in his distinctive Kent accent. 'Mr Smith knows about oil. Connections and the right channels make the world go around.' Over coffee the talk focused on which countries were ripe to do some business. Eventually they reached Nigeria, if rather obliquely. 'We don't want Oman, we've done that,' said Tipping to Smith. 'We don't want Saudi, because that's your speciality. So, let me ask you. What's black, big and messy?' 'Nigeria,' replied the oil businessman hesitantly. 'Bang on, clever boy,' laughed Tipping, who added that they were working on a deal with an 'important' Nigerian chief. 'We will introduce you to him soon,' he said.

Marc Rich, the fugitive oil trader, was the next topic. Mark Thatcher, who said he had done some work for him in New York, thought that the Swiss trader was 'too big' to get entangled with.

'Marc Rich made so much loot by defrauding the Americans,' remarked Smith, 'that if he squealed the whole Washington establishment would come crashing down, because so many top Americans were involved.'

Thatcher agreed: 'It's best left alone.'

The prime minister's son then made a remark which Smith found somewhat weird. 'Anyway, the Jews have Washington completely sewn up,' he said. 'My mother likes Jews a lot, especially their stress on family life.'

Tipping asked Smith: 'What do you think of Jews? Do you like them?'

Smith, somewhat taken aback by the question, replied that he lived in a Jewish area in north London. 'I have had no problems with them as neighbours,' he said.

'That's acceptable,' said Tipping quickly. 'It's important in our circle to like Jews, because Mark's mother likes them a lot, especially the members and officers in her constituency association.'

The dinner ended with Mark paying the bill, and with a brief exchange on the importance of family life. The three agreed to meet again to discuss the Nigerian deal in detail. That happened a month later over a late dinner at Claridge's. The essence of the plan was that Nigeria had substantial oil reserves which it was keen to sell to pay off its foreign debts. Thatcher and Tipping saw a golden opportunity and had hooked up with Chief Bola Abimbola, who ran a trading company called Interocean Petroleum Nigeria Ltd. The Chief was a controversial figure in the trade. From 1984 until 1986 he was the agent for Voest Alpine, the state-owned Austrian oil corporation, which was involved in a scam that lost the Austrian taxpayer millions of schillings. Its agents purchased crude oil from Egypt and Iran and then deliberately sold to traders at a loss in return for huge commissions.

Thatcher and Tipping saw Abimbola as their channel into oil-rich West Africa. The Chief would use his influence and broker a deal with the state-owned Nigerian National Petroleum Corporation to sell 50,000 barrels of oil a day through Euravia AG, represented by Gary Smith. Euravia, based in Zurich, was a private distribution company which bought crude oil directly from countries like Saudi Arabia, the United Arab Emirates and Libya. It had offices in eight west European countries, and Smith was their London manager, based at 37 Queen Anne Street, off Harley Street.

Thatcher and Tipping told Smith that 'Chiefy', as they half-mockingly called Abimbola, would deliver the contract for Euravia and everyone would 'get their cut'. Mark's role was to introduce Abimbola to Smith and help the chief lobby the Nigerian government. He added that Chiefy had a Scottish associate called James Lang, whose company supplied generators for the oil pipelines. Lang also became friendly with Mark Thatcher, despite being ten years older, and was a guest at his wedding. 'He's a nice guy,' said Mark, 'but he thinks the sun shines out of Chiefy's arse.' Tipping denies that these words were used. Unknown to Mark, Lang also became acquainted with the prime minister who asked him, 'to look after Mark and keep an eye on him'.

The second meeting at Claridge's was concluded by Mark's expressing confidence in Euravia, because they were 'cash-rich' and 'had the millions' to complete the deal. 'I have been told you are an acceptable name in the oil industry,' he said.

Six weeks later, shortly after the general election in late June 1987, the first set of negotiations took place, again over dinner at Claridge's. Gary Smith arrived first. Tipping then walked in and was greeted by the manager: 'Good evening, Mr Tipping.' He sat down next to the oil executive and pointed out the trio of elderly musicians dressed in eighteenth-century Austrian costumes. 'Wonderful thing is culture,' said Tipping, 'but they look as if they've been playing since the eighteenth century.' Tipping has always disputed his involvement in the Nigerian oil deal.

Chief Abimbola and James Lang then arrived. The chief was in a jolly mood and said their proposed business was progressing well. He added that he was very close to Nigeria's president, General Ibrahim Babangida, who was 'all-powerful'. 'Absolutely correct, sir,' said Lang rather obsequiously. Within twenty minutes Mark Thatcher and his wife, Diane, appeared. Mark was carrying a massive square briefcase of the type often used by architects. He passed it to the head waiter with instructions that it be kept safe because its contents were 'top secret'. He too was in a good mood and crowed about the large majority secured by the Conservative Party in the recent general election.

The group then moved to the adjoining restaurant for dinner. Smith sat next to the newly married Diane Thatcher. The oil executive found her a woman of happy disposition but the kind of person dependent on financial security. 'You cannot really enjoy life without money,' she said.

Tipping raised the subject of the oil deal. Lang said there was nothing that the Chief could not do in the oil business in Nigeria. 'We are all lucky to have his support,' he said. Tipping replied that Abimbola's influence was 'very much appreciated'.

He then introduced Smith as the person who could market the oil and guarantee the commissions from Switzerland. 'The commissions are *the* most important issue,' said the Chief [his emphasis]. 'My company is not the Salvation Army.' Mark Thatcher agreed and said all commissions would be paid through the Chief. 'He will look after everybody,' he said. Chief Abimbola concluded that he would ensure the Nigerian government would award the contract. The president, or 'IBB' as he referred to him, 'will push it through,' he said. Tipping strongly disputes this account of events.

However, negotiations in Nigeria were slow and the next meeting did not take place for another five months. At 6.30pm on 4 December 1987, Mark Thatcher and Gary Smith met for after-work drinks in the back bar of the Connaught Hotel, on the corner of Carlos Place in Mayfair. It was a regular and favourite 'watering hole' of Mark's. 'Decent place,' he said. 'If the day winds you up, the Scotch at the Connaught can wind you down.'

When they arrived Mark was greeted by Lord Young, then secretary of state for trade and industry, who was sitting at the bar surrounded by a large entourage. 'Evening, Mark,' he said. 'Lovely to see you, Mark. How's everything, Mark?' Smith thought to himself that the repeated use of Thatcher's first name reminded him of a headmaster addressing a pupil whose parents were paying a large part of his salary. 'Fine, fine,' replied Thatcher. 'Good,' said Lord Young. 'I'll talk to you in detail at a more appropriate time.' Smith pondered about the cabinet minister's relationship with Mark. 'What do you think of Lord Young?' he asked. 'Tops,' replied Thatcher. 'He is one of Mum's closest advisers.' After a brief chat, the two left the Connaught with Lord Young shouting out, 'Bye, Mark.'

Thatcher and Smith walked around the corner to have dinner at Harry's Bar. Mark was given an equally sycophantic welcome. 'Welcome back, sir,' said the manager. 'How is Madam [i.e. Diane]? Is she joining us tonight?' 'No,' said Mark, 'she is back in Dallas because I'm in London on special business.'

They were shown to a back table and it was not long before Thatcher spoke about the Nigerian oil deal. 'Everything is on course,' he said, 'and IBB is aware of the deal. The prospects are very good because he owes Mum a favour.' He did not elaborate, but it was no secret that Margaret Thatcher had assisted the Babangida government in its dealings with the International Monetary Fund (IMF) and the General was grateful. Her administration had also substantially increased overseas aid to Nigeria, from an average of £5.7 million a year in 1984–8 to £67.7 million in 1989–90.

The 'favour' can be traced to discussions the prime minister held with Babangida on 7 January 1985, during a visit to Lagos. 'He was a forceful, intelligent man,' she recalled in her memoirs, 'trying to put Nigeria's economy on to a sounder footing and in due course, we hoped, to create the conditions for a restoration of democracy. We had helped Nigeria in its dealings with the IMF and this was appreciated. General Babangida seemed to be open to my suggestions about the need to curb Nigeria's budget deficit, cut inflation and provide reassurances for foreign investors.'[1]

Margaret Thatcher returned to Nigeria on 7 January 1988, just five weeks after her son's dinner at Harry's Bar. She discovered that the General had taken her advice and embarked on a monetarist economic programme – even tougher than the measures she had advocated. 'With our support,' said Thatcher, 'Nigeria now had the approval of the IMF and its main Western creditors and had secured a rescheduling of debt to its public sector creditors.'[2] Nigeria is now a chaotic, corruption-ridden country plagued by civil unrest, and its economy is in dire straits.

Mark was clearly attempting to reap the commercial benefits of his mother's 'favour' to the Nigerian president. On this deal he was asking for a commission of $2 per barrel. Smith thought this was outrageous. The normal commission on 50,000 barrels a day was between 20 and 50 cents, unless it was something special. Thatcher was looking for a pay-off close to $2 million, based on 365 days of production. During the dinner at Harry's Bar, Smith told him this was 'unusually large' – even for Nigeria. 'It's not me who makes the rules,' replied Mark. 'Anyway, there are many mouths to feed and the president is unusually hungry. In Africa they all have to make hay while the sun shines.'

Thatcher made it clear he did not like the country. 'I'm not going near the dump,' he said, 'but it's a good place to make a hoot [sic] of cash which is what matters most.' He added that Chief Abimbola was working out the contract details. 'Don't worry about Euravia's profits,' he concluded. 'Chiefy is protecting us' (this was a euphemism for paying the commissions).

The conversation then changed to oil deals in other parts of the world. Smith suggested Oman and described how the tiny Gulf state had supplied oil to South Africa during the United Nations embargo. Mark saw nothing wrong in it. His view was that, if it happened during the republic's 'down times', then 'good old Oman' because South Africa was pro-British. In any case, he said, 'my sympathy is with the struggling white community'. As to future petroleum business in Oman, he said it was a 'non-starter' because of the problems created by the Cementation university contract. 'Why not see what we can do in Saudi and Iraq?' he added more hopefully. 'There are plenty of big fish in the pond. Go for it.'

They then talked about his mother. Mark repeated his statement that he stayed at and worked from 10 Downing Street and that 'Mum wouldn't have it any other way'. After a brief chat about the political scene, they left Harry's Bar. The next day Thatcher rang Smith and suggested drawing up a Heads of Agreement between Euravia AG and himself for future oil deals in Saudi Arabia and Nigeria. That afternoon he visited Smith at his office in Queen Anne Street to say that he was returning to Dallas. Before he walked in, his Special Branch detective came into the office to check it out. 'Got to do this, as his mum got back in,' he said.

After the Harry's Bar dinner the negotiations speeded up. Smith reported back to Switzerland Mark Thatcher's comment about President Babangida owing the prime minister a favour. Mark began to visit Smith's office more regularly and even delegated his wife, Diane, to type out the contract letters. In Nigeria Chief Ambimbola was lobbying the minister of petroleum resources, Rilwanu Lukman, who agreed on the 50,000 barrels of oil a day. On 7 March 1988, he delivered their proposals directly to Lukman, who instructed his officials to appraise them.

In Switzerland Euravia AG reluctantly agreed to pay the service fee (the industry phrase for commission). On 23 March 1988, Dr Erich Gayler, chairman of

Euravia AG in Zurich, signed a letter in anticipation of the 'refine and sell' agreement: 'This is to confirm that Euravia AG will pay to Interocean Petroleum Nigeria Ltd, a service fee of $2 for each barrel of oil lifted and refined under such an agreement.'

The following month Chief Abimbola returned to London and summoned the various parties to his UK residence, Obokum Castle. Beforehand, Mark Thatcher, Steve Tipping and Gary Smith met at the Connaught for a drink. Mark stressed that Abimbola was taking care of his commission. 'It's being dealt with by a separate letter between me and Chiefy,' he said. Tipping disputes that he was present at this meeting.

The three then drove up to Obokum Castle which turned out to be not a castle at all but a large detached house in Totteridge Lane, Hendon, north London. An unimpressive dwelling, it was in a state of some disrepair. They were greeted by a Nigerian man who ushered them into a sparsely furnished room. The Chief offered tea or beer but Mark was impatient. 'We need to move on and do the bloody deal,' he said. 'There has been far too much pissing about so far.' Tipping agreed. Smith responded by saying his letters guaranteeing the commissions were prepared and signed. 'Well then, the deal is ready,' said Mark. 'The ball is now in your court, Chief. You need to run with it.' The Chief appeared uneasy. 'Things take time in Lagos,' he said. 'The president and the minister were both very greedy.' Thatcher was irritated: 'He [Babangida] owes my Mum a favour and you should ask him to move his ass.'

Abimbola tried to reassure them. 'Don't worry, it will be OK.' But it was apparent to Smith that Abimbola lacked the finesse and resources of the other Nigerian middlemen he had dealt with in his trading days. Even the state of his 'castle' indicated that the Chief was short of cash. Despite the documents he had sent from Lagos it was not clear he could deliver the goods – quite literally. The deal was falling apart. Smith's superiors in Switzerland were also uneasy and losing interest, particularly in view of the size of the commission. In any case, they had their own connections and channels in Nigeria.

However, Mark Thatcher was hanging on. A week after the Obokum Castle summit, he telephoned Smith from his base at 10 Downing Street. The oil executive was out but returned his call that evening. He found Mark in angry mood. 'There has been too much delay on this business,' he said. 'If Euravia are not going to cover the Chief with the $2 commission, then we'll forget the whole fucking thing. I don't want to piss about any longer.' Smith replied that Euravia was serious about the deal but its management were reassessing it.

As it turned out, on this occasion Nigeria's black gold was not sold, partly because the Chief could not deliver, but also because of the massive commission fee demanded by Thatcher and his associates. This discouraged Euravia from further involvement.

Gary Smith continued in the oil business and worked for Sonangol, the national oil corporation of Angola. He became increasingly disillusioned with West Africa as it declined economically, and virtually gave up on Nigeria. James Lang suffered great financial strain from his association with Abimbola and died from a heart attack in tragic circumstances in 1989. The Chief, who had previously made a fortune from his oil exploits, lost all his money in a deal supplying crude to Guinea and Liberia. He went bankrupt and has since disappeared from the scene.

As for President Babangida, he was forced to resign in August 1993, after losing the June presidential elections. Known as a dictator with a keen eye for business, he was ousted largely because of the misuse of the vast wealth derived from Nigeria's oil. Babangida fled to Cairo, then Saudi Arabia, and for a time lived in exile in Jeddah, frightened for his safety as irate Nigerians want to know into whose pockets the oil revenue went. In the summer of 1994, Mark Thatcher was visiting Jeddah on business. Perhaps he dropped by to discuss that favour his mother had bestowed on Babangida all those years ago.

White Mischief – Drilling in Kenya

Margaret Thatcher saw Kenya as the most likely convert – even more likely than Nigeria – to her political and economic creed. She saw herself as a missionary for Thatcherism in the Third World. 'I wanted to spread the message,' she recalled in her memoirs, 'that a combination of limited government, financial orthodoxy and free enterprise would work for prosperity in under-developed countries as well as it did in the prosperous West. I chose Kenya and Nigeria for my first African political safari. In both cases with good reason. Kenya because it was the most pro-Western, most free enterprise of the important black African states.'[3]

Its president, Daniel Arap Moi, was also pro-Britain, not least because it was the largest investor in his country and provided the most overseas aid. So Margaret Thatcher was made particularly welcome by President Moi when she flew to

Nairobi on 4 January 1988, for a three-day visit.

Another member of the Thatcher family had a keen interest in Kenya. After the Nigerian deal collapsed in the summer of 1988, her son, Mark, and his partner, Steve Tipping, began cultivating channels into the prime minister's favourite African state. But there was nothing evangelical about their activities. It was, like everything they did, strictly business and very private.

Unlike Nigeria, Kenya was hungry for oil. According to Gary Smith, the oil executive who worked on the Nigerian deal, Thatcher and Tipping were keen to move into Kenya. Smith was not used on this occasion but was later told by Tipping that their principal business contact in Kenya was Ketan Somaia, the country's most powerful and wealthiest businessman. An Asian entrepreneur, Somaia is a former motor trader who became a millionaire by the age of thirty-six. His corporate vehicle is the Dolphin International Group, based in Dubai and registered in Bermuda. Worth about $120 million, its main interests are casinos, leisure centres, sugar plantations, car factories, oil and film-making. In August 1991, Dolphin bought the Kenyan and Mauritius subsidiaries of BCCI after the bank's collapse and changed the subsidiaries' names to the Delphis Group. But it was not an auspicious initial period of ownership. The following year Delphis was one of four banks to be investigated by the Kenyan Central Bank after complaints about their procedures were voiced by the IMF and Western aid donors.[4]

Somaia clearly felt he needed political muscle. In the autumn of 1992, Lord (Cecil) Parkinson, former energy secretary and close friend of the Thatcher family, became chairman of Dolphin. He spent a week in Dubai for a briefing on the company and then flew to Nairobi for a meeting with President Moi.[5] A year after his appointment, on 4 October 1993, Tipping had lunch with Gary Smith at the Savoy Grill and claimed, 'I fixed Cecil up with his job with Somaia because he was short of a few bob.' The appointment was confirmed by a separate source: 'Tipping introduced Parkinson to Somaia, because the Kenyan wanted a big name in the UK to be chairman of his company.'

Mark Thatcher's connection with Somaia was forged much earlier. No source can place a date on it, but he and Tipping certainly visited Kenya in May 1989. Officially, Mark was there to open a car rally in Kisumu, sponsored by the Dolphin Group, but few believe that was the only purpose. Indeed, Tipping told Gerald James, then chairman of the arms company Astra, at the Savoy Hotel in April 1989: 'I am going to Kenya next month on business. If you supply me with your brochures, I'll show them to the people I'm meeting.' The commercial nature of the visit was also borne out by the fact that Thatcher, Tipping and Ketan Somaia had two meetings with President Moi at his State Houses, one in Nairobi, the other in Nakuru.

On another occasion in 1988 Mark Thatcher and Tipping attended a meeting with Somaia at his north London house. Also present was the Kenyan finance minister, the head of Kenya's Central Reserve Bank, and influential Arabs. Somaia wanted introductions to wealthy Arabs in the Gulf, to advance his business operations there, but they were not impressed by Somaia's proposals and no substantial introductions were made.

When asked about Mark's links with Somaia, Lord Parkinson consulted with the Dolphin boss. Somaia said that he did discuss potential business with Thatcher but nothing came of it. But Tipping told Gary Smith: 'We've done some business with Somaia. I have to say he's done some stupid things. He once hosted a social function in Kenya but didn't invite any blacks. There were only Asians. That's just not on if you're aiming to make a few bob.' Tipping disputes this version of events.

Tipping continued to cultivate Somaia and arranged legal advice for him on how to base his company in Dubai. On 5 December 1990, he was one of the prominent guests at a reception arranged and paid for by Dolphin Promotions Ltd at the London Hilton ballroom. Gary Smith was also invited, and when he arrived Tipping told him, 'Somaia is the key boy in Kenya. He is very close to [President] Moi.' The oil executive was interested and introduced himself to Somaia. 'I met Nicholas Biwott [the energy minister] in Abu Dhabi recently,' said Smith. 'Biwott, good old Biwott,' Somaia replied, laughing. It may have been a knowing chuckle because Biwott, known as 'Tricky Nicky', was later sacked by President Moi for corruption. Smith added that he had approached Biwott to supply oil to Kenya more cheaply than the complex, more expensive, deal Biwott had negotiated. Somaia made no comment except, 'Talk to Steve about it.'

At the end of the evening Somaia went round the tables to shake hands and say goodnight. He sought out Smith and suggested a meeting in the New Year to discuss the oil business in Kenya. He then gave him his business card with his north London home address. Nothing came of it, but they continued to keep in touch. So did Tipping. He continued to talk about Somaia in terms of oil and had meetings with him in London in late 1992. However, their relationship fizzled out and in July 1993, Steve Tipping telephoned Gary Smith: 'I have just spoken to Somaia, but he's not as hungry as he used to be.'

Fuelling the Fortune

Despite his lack of success in Africa, Thatcher remained fascinated by the world's most valuable natural resource, especially aviation fuel. 'Mark is now into the oil business,' said Tipping in 1993. 'He calls it the stuff that goes into aircraft.' But for many years he did not have a commercial outlet for his ambitions.

The opportunity arrived fortuitously in the autumn of 1992, when Ameristar Fuels Corporation, which specialized in the sale of jet fuel, began looking for new investment. Founded in June 1990 by two enterprising Texans – Jay Laughlin, president, and Jim Swieter, vice-president and company secretary – Ameristar had a winning formula. It provided a special facility by buying, distributing and selling fuel direct to airlines, charter firms and private pilots on a tax-exempt basis in North America. There was also a division which marketed petroleum to non-airline customers in South America.

It was a simple operation. Clients and customers simply presented their Ameristar card at the airport and were then able to buy the fuel at fixed prices. This undercut established outlets like Esso, BP and Shell, and turnover soared. Initially, the company operated as a 30 per cent partner in a joint venture with a competitor. After May 1992, Ameristar was successful enough to go independent and was financially flying with profits of £4 million a year.

For the forty-year-old Laughlin, a pilot and former

commodities trader, it was a dream come true. Now he wanted to expand. That meant substantial extra investment and his deputy, Jim Swieter, believed he had the answer. He was friendly with David Wallace, a thirty-two-year-old Texan, who was junior partner in Mark Thatcher's Grantham Company and treasurer of the US Thatcher Foundation, set up by the former prime minister to promote her philosophy. When approached by Swieter, Wallace replied that he could facilitate the capital required through his associate, one Mark Thatcher.

A meeting was arranged, and in September 1992 Laughlin and Swieter flew to London. They stayed at the Number Sixteen Hotel on Sumner Place, South Kensington, where Thatcher books in a number of business guests. The negotiations took place at Mark's £2 million house at Tregunter Road, off The Boltons, and the Thatchers were generous hosts. They took the Texans out to dinner at their favourite restaurant, Formula Veneta in Hollywood Road, a 300-yard walk away. Laughlin and his girlfriend were also escorted to Ascot, and Mark flew the Texan in his own helicopter to the Farnborough air show in Hampshire.

Although the trip went well, Ameristar's founder was in no hurry to agree finalized terms that would bring extra capital into his company but also reduce his control. He owned 50 per cent of the shares and wanted time to think about it. But Thatcher was impatient and wanted him to sign a letter of intent quickly. When the Texan said he wanted more time to consider the proposals, Mark lost his temper. On the morning of 17 October 1992, in the garage connected to Ameristar's office in San Felipe, Houston, Laughlin repeated his request for more time. 'You'll sign now or there won't be a bloody deal,' Mark shouted, in a manner reminiscent of the Nigerian negotiations. 'Well, you can get in your little red rowing-boat and row all the way back to England,' Laughlin shouted back. 'It didn't bother me,' he recalled later, 'but I was kind of surprised at [Mark's] manner.'[6]

Despite Thatcher's outburst, that afternoon the Texan partly agreed to his demand and a Management Agreement was signed between the Grantham Company and Ameristar Fuels Inc. The deal was for Grantham (Thatcher and Wallace) to provide 'financial services' for a fee of $16,000 a month plus expenses for eighteen months.

Three months later, in January 1993, the investment agreement materialized. The deal was that Wallace provided capital of $500,000 on a certified deposit. This money came from Diversified Capital Ltd, one of Thatcher's offshore companies in Jersey overseen by his banker, Hugh Thurston, and his accountant, Leonard Day. The $500,000 was placed with the South-West Bank of Texas in Houston – as collateral for a loan, also of $500,000 – by Wallace, who acted as a 'messenger' for Thatcher's offshore firm. In return, Wallace acquired 20 per cent of Ameristar's stock, with an option for an additional 13 per cent if he brought in extra investment. He was also given control of the company's financial and accounting affairs.

Officially, Mark Thatcher did not hold any executive or corporate position in Ameristar. Rather bizarrely, a company spokesperson said he 'has never been involved with Ameristar as employee, director, shareholder, investor, anything'.[7] Yet Mark moved his Grantham Company from Dallas to Ameristar's office at the Texas Commerce Tower on San Felipe Drive in Houston. His own personal office was right next to Laughlin's. To cement the connection, Grantham,

whose plaque was placed alongside Ameristar's in
the foyer, received $16,000 a month in management
fees from Ameristar.[8] More significantly, the $500,000
investment capital was Thatcher's money. It came
from Jersey and was channelled through Grantham.
Effectively, Grantham played an active role in running
the prosperous jet fuel corporation and Mark was the
senior partner. Wallace was simply a front man.

Laughlin certainly saw Mark as his partner, particularly as he attended board meetings. Mark was
particularly energetic in trying to secure new business
– with mixed fortunes. He went with some Chinese-
American businessmen to Puerto Rico to buy an oil
refinery. But there were environmental problems. He
lobbied the Bahamas government for the contract to
supply fuel to Nassau airport. But when Prime Minister
Lynden Pindling lost the election, that failed.

In February 1993, Thatcher and Wallace travelled
to Alma Ata, capital of Kazakhstan, to start up an air
charter operation for the Kazakh oil industry. Before he
set off, Mark said in the Ameristar office, in Laughlin's
presence, that British Petroleum 'would help because
my mother was owed favours by BP and the Russian
[i.e. the former Soviet] government'.

The Far East proved more encouraging. Mark targeted Indonesia because for some years he had cultivated close links with the family of President Suharto,
who virtually run the country. He is especially friendly
with the president's son, who is a keen motor-racing
fan. It helped that General Suharto was an admirer of
Margaret Thatcher, whose government had sold his
regime ground-attack aircraft and other weapons. In
1992 she was presented with an award from Indonesia
for 'helping technology'. She replied, 'I am proud to
be one of you.'[9]

Mark Thatcher's former business partner, Steve Tipping, has also been busy in Jakarta, the capital. 'Indonesia is big, man, big,' he told Gary Smith in 1993. He said the prospects for making money there are 'endless' because the country will be a net importer of oil by the year 2000. 'With our Middle East connections,' Tipping remarked, 'there should be a few shekels in it for us.'

However, Ameristar's office in Jakarta was more interested in providing charter aircraft to transport Muslims on the annual pilgrimage to Mecca. 'About three to five million people go to Mecca, and Garuda [Indonesia's state airline] does not have enough planes to bring them all,' said Anton Mandagi, the office administrator, in 1994. 'They are negotiating for Mark to supply planes to bring them all, but we haven't got the answer yet.'[10]

Across the Indian Ocean in Malaysia, Ameristar International was also able to reap the benefits of Mrs Thatcher's legacy. In 1993 the company, based at Gatwick airport, secured a lucrative deal to distribute fuel to planes that land in Malaysia, supplied by Petronas, the country's state-owned oil corporation.[11]

As 1993 unfolded, the company was prospering. Gross sales amounted to $200 million a year, notably a lucrative fuel supply contract with Southwest Airlines. By the autumn Mark Thatcher had become almost totally preoccupied by Ameristar, his fascination for aviation and oil all-consuming. Privately, he began to view and even talk about it as 'his company'. For the first time he believed he was in a position to build, manage and expand his own firm, just as his father had done. After the failure of Monteagle Marketing Ltd in the mid-1980s, this was always his ambition. For all his millions, he wanted something tangible to show for all the years of 'brokering deals' and playing the middleman. But there was just one irritating snag. Ameristar did not belong to him. He was not even a director or shareholder. And its founder was not going to give it up easily.

The consequence, claimed Jay Laughlin, Ameristar's president, was that Mark and Wallace masterminded a carefully orchestrated operation to oust him. Their strategy, alleged Laughlin, was 'to suppress the actual state of the Ameristar entities' and engineer a cash crisis as a way of acquiring more of the shares.[12]

In September 1993, the Grantham duo informed Laughlin that outside capital investment was required to expand the company and increase profit margins. They claimed they could raise $10 million themselves. Their scheme was for the investment to be structured in the form of a 'limited partnership'. Controlled by Grantham, the various investors would be the limited partners. The partnership's principal asset would be a five-year senior secured-term loan note, as well as 25 per cent of Ameristar's equity. The prospectus, put together by Thatcher and Wallace, concluded: 'Having consideration to the [Ameristar] Group's sales and profit forecasts, the value of the warrants attached to the $10 million offering would provide prospective returns of greater than 30 per cent in the event of the Group accomplishing a public listing at very conservative multiples.'

Wallace and Thatcher immediately approached twenty-three potential investors in the USA, UK, Switzerland and Germany – bankers, fund managers, even Wallace's own law firm, Akin, Gump, Hauer and Feld in Dallas, Texas. Others were asked on the basis that they might secure the capital on behalf of Grantham. Dmitry Bosky of MITRA Private Equity Ltd, based in Paradise Walk,

Chelsea, was told by Wallace: 'As always, we will gladly discuss a fee arrangement and/or carried interest in this investment should you be able to arrange funding.'

An old favourite was also solicited 'to discuss a strategy for moving forward'. This was Steve Tipping. On 12 October 1993 he had dinner with David Wallace, and their discussion clearly indicated that Tipping had retained his commercial links with Mark Thatcher. After the meal, Wallace wrote to his predecessor 'to describe several ways in which I think you could assist the company'. He added, 'Ameristar would enter into a combination agreement to be mutually agreed upon for the creation of such business. The commission agreements presently in place generally provide for a percentage of the gross profit secured as to each particular transaction.' One of the sectors in which Tipping was asked to assist was privatization of the jet-fuel divisions of state oil companies. 'We would have an interest in looking at their airport refuelling operations,' said Wallace. 'This would need to include the negotiation of long-term supply contracts and would generally depend on other competitive market forces at the airport.'

Mark Thatcher was equally engaged in the fund-raising for the $10 million. In early November 1993, he was in Geneva on business and approached Claude Jourda of Aeroleasing for a half-hour meeting 'to explain the investment in greater detail'. He also approached Charles Wick, who was director of the US Information Agency under President Reagan in the mid-1980s.

As it turned out, only $1.25 million materialized. But Laughlin had agreed, on the basis of the proposed new investment, to reduce his stake to 25 per cent in return for the equity input. This enabled Wallace to

secure a 50 per cent controlling shareholding. 'Having
successfully reduced my share of ownership in the
Ameristar entities,' Laughlin later stated in a legal
petition, 'Wallace and Swieter [his former partner],
along with others, concocted a scheme to freeze me
out altogether.'[13]

Wallace's next device was to merge the various
Ameristar parent firms and form a new separate
holding company, Ameristar Consolidated Holdings
Inc. He then informed their president that the entire
stock of all the Ameristar firms would have to be
transferred to it. Laughlin was given until 31 December
1993 to sign documents agreeing to the new corporate
structure. He requested that this proposal be modified
to conform with the shareholder agreements and by-
laws of the Ameristar companies. Wallace agreed to
make the changes and amended the relevant company
documents. But, according to Laughlin, the finalized
executed papers were never delivered to him.

Instead, unknown to the Ameristar president, Wallace
had been devising a plan for Mark Thatcher to be the
kingpin and dominant force of this new corporate
structure. On 23 November 1993 Wallace wrote to
Grantham's tax lawyers, Simmons & Simmons, about
'the role that Mark Thatcher will play in the ongoing
operation'. He advocated: 'It is contemplated that
Ameristar Fuels will be wholly owned by a company
for which Mark Thatcher will be the chairman. It
is not contemplated that Mark will hold any officer
duties or other responsibilities. From an ongoing level
of activity, Mark Thatcher would assist in various
marketing efforts for both international and South
America.' In effect, this meant he would have a service
contract to market their international operations.

Wallace added, 'There are various matters that

could affect Mark Thatcher, and I would appreciate
your guidance.' He asked about any 'ramifications'
for Mark as chairman or shareholder of a holding
company which had an office at Gatwick airport.
Also what were the consequences if 'Mark Thatcher
actively solicits business' or was involved in its daily
activities? In other words, Wallace was enquiring
about the tax implications of Mark Thatcher playing
an executive role in Ameristar and being based at its
British office.

On 1 December 1993, the lawyer for Simmons
& Simmons, who specializes in tax avoidance and
offshore trusts, replied that it depended on 'the extent
to which Mark Thatcher will be working in the UK'.
If his time spent on Ameristar business in the UK was
'negligible', then there was no problem. 'However, if it
is envisaged that Mark Thatcher will either be working
in the UK, or for the office in Gatwick or in general for
the promotion of Ameristar Fuels in the UK – then I
would be concerned.'

Judgement day for Jay Laughlin came on 17 January
1994, the day of the Los Angeles earthquake. A
board meeting was called at the office of law firm
Fouts and Moore in Houston, ostensibly to discuss
pending litigation. What transpired was somewhat
different. When Ameristar's founder arrived for the
meeting, he was abruptly informed of his removal as
an officer and employee. Shell-shocked and stunned
by the manoeuvre, Laughlin immediately drove back
to his office on San Felipe Drive, anxious to collect
his papers, which he believed would prove that the
company had effectively been stolen from him.

However, as he was searching through his filing
cabinet, two heavily built men burst through his office
door. One was Mike Winton, a former British police

officer and Mark Thatcher's personal bodyguard, or
'special assistant', as he describes himself. The other
was Jay H. Olszewski, an armed off-duty policeman,
who was head of Houston's Criminal Intelligence
Division (one of his duties was to guard visiting
dignitaries like Lady Thatcher). 'Please do not touch
any property, and leave the building immediately, sir,'
said Winton threateningly. 'Otherwise we will have no
option but to arrest you for trespassing.'[14]

Within minutes Ameristar's president and found-
ing father was taken away from his corporate baby.
Laughlin had no choice and was escorted from the
premises. He could scarcely believe it and was devas-
tated as he drove home. 'This company was my hopes
and my dreams,' he said later.[15]

Wallace argues that he had set up the new holding
corporation to make a legitimate offer of $2 million to
Ameristar's president to buy him out. 'The purpose of
the merger company,' he said later, 'was to give Jay
Laughlin his fair value for the stock.'[16]

In Laughlin's view, this was a miserly offer for a
company which was valued at $20 million. He claimed
Wallace, fronting for Thatcher, effectively hijacked his
company. So he decided to fight back. In June 1994, he
filed a lawsuit alleging that Wallace and Swieter, using
Thatcher's money, 'fraudulently induced him to transfer his entire stock in the various entities to the holding
company'.[17] The writ also claimed that there was a
breach of their 'fiduciary obligations of trust and care to
the shareholders' to make 'all required disclosures' in
the management of Ameristar's affairs. It concluded by
alleging that 'the defendants fraudulently, maliciously
and intentionally converted the assets of the Ameristar
entities to their own personal use and benefit'.[18]
Wallace countered that Ameristar's former president

was removed because he 'inadequately performed various management duties'.[19]

As part of the case, a subpoena was issued for Mark Thatcher to supply a deposition on the details of his wealth and business transactions, including a videotaped sworn statement. Publicly, he was unruffled and denied all the claims. 'He needs to be very careful what he's alleging,' he said. 'Mr Laughlin or anybody else can allege whatever they want.'[20]

But underneath the bravado, he was very worried. According to Laughlin, in July 1994, he received a telephone call from his former partner. 'He told me that if I put the Thatcher name on trial, he would bring all the power he could raise and go for me,' recalled the Texan. 'He also said that his father, Denis, was upset about the situation.' When asked by the *Today* newspaper about this conversation, Mark replied: 'Poppycock! That is totally untrue. It is fallacious. I mean, I wouldn't ring up and threaten Jay – good God. Why would I want to do it? I categorically deny it. That is exactly the sort of thing that Jay would do. God!'[21]

Whatever the truth about what was said on the telephone, Mark was very nervous about what might emerge during the litigation. He faced the horrifying prospect of appearing as a witness in Houston County Court. Even worse, the proceedings would be recorded by video camera.

But then just three weeks before the court case, Ameristar filed for Chapter 11 bankruptcy, which protected it from over 100 creditors, including Mobil and Shell, who were owed £12 million. Under American bankruptcy laws, Ameristar was allowed to continue to trade and operate. But it was obliged to make provision to pay off its debts. In one swift manoeuvre, the law

suit was scuttled. With it sank any chance of Mark
Thatcher's being cross-examined for the first time
about the mystery of how he acquired his millions.

For Jay Laughlin, it was a devastating blow. 'The
news of the bankruptcy sickened me,' he said. 'It was
even worse because I heard it in a telephonic meeting
of directors. Wallace just announced it. He then said,
"Have a nice day, gentlemen," and hung up. It was all
over in 30 seconds. This is a company that was my
whole life. I built it up over four years and put all
my money into it. When I left it, it was in a profitable
state and the bankruptcy petition only makes me more
determined to win it back.'[22]

Mark was no doubt delighted by this sudden development and he promised to stand by Wallace, who had
effectively taken a fall for him. 'Because David is in
difficulty doesn't mean that I or anybody else is going
to run for the lifeboats,' he said. 'On the contrary, I
am going to do everything I can to show that I'm
supporting him personally – as a friend.'[23] It was
more than personal, of course. Wallace's dependence
on Thatcher was such that even his own house – 3318
Alcorn Crossing, Sugarlands, Texas – was owned by
Diversified Capital, a Jersey-based company controlled
by Hugh Thurston, Thatcher's banker, and Leonard
Day, his accountant.

However, if Thatcher thought he had disposed of
the Laughlin problem, he was very much mistaken.
In October 1994, the former Ameristar president filed
a further writ against him under the civil clauses of
the Racketeering Influenced Corrupt Organizations
(RICO) Act, which was originally enacted to fight
organized crime. Laughlin will claim that Thatcher
used fraudulent methods to 'hijack' his company.
Publicly, Mark was confident of surviving the legal

storm. 'Five or six people who are businessmen in the States – household names – have been ringing me up and saying "Don't worry about this," '[24] he said. Eventually, however, the pressure told and Thatcher settled the case out of court, paying a minimum amount in damages to Laughlin.

Wealth – 'It's all Comparative'

As well as by his long-held ambition to run his own company, Mark Thatcher's enthusiasm for Ameristar Fuels was governed by a desire for an outlet to invest his millions. How much he was able to call on from his Swiss-based funds, via Jersey, remains a puzzle that only Mark Thatcher and his bankers and accountants can solve.

Our sources close to Hugh Thurston indicate that at Mark's peak in the late 1980s he was worth at least £40 million, but that has dwindled dramatically in recent years. Certainly Mark is keeping mum, so to speak. When questioned by David Jones of *Today* in 1994, he described himself as a 'pauper' compared to fellow Dallas millionaires like Ross Perot. But he admitted he was 'doing well' in British terms. 'It's all comparative,' he reflected.[25]

The exact amount is to some extent inconsequential. What has became apparent is that material wealth is absolutely paramount in his life. 'Mark always wanted to be a tycoon and had a strong urge for recognition as a commercial force,' said a Hong Kong investment banker who dealt with him in the mid-1980s. 'But I would also say he was avaricious and craved the life-style of the rich and famous. He loved the glamour.

I don't think Mark has ever made a secret of wanting to be very rich or admiring those who are – on an indiscriminate basis. Money is what lures him rather than quality. If you look at who he knows around the world, they are invariably self-made wealthy people or heirs or heiresses. There is very little breadth in his address book. If they have money, they are [in it]. There are not many out-of-work painters or authors, or even politicians. He is only interested in politicians who could be useful for business.'

By 1988 his opulent life-style began to provide clues as to the size of the treasure we have been hunting. He had always sought and craved the high life. Only now did he possess the money to pay for it. He was living in a plush £1.3 million house in exclusive Belgravia. He was travelling extensively, sometimes chartering private jets, and staying in the most expensive hotels. Suddenly he was seen lunching at Harry's Bar, dining at Mirabelle, drinking at the Connaught Hotel. Driving a black Porsche Carrera, Mark wore a gold Rolex watch, took holidays on the Riviera and drank vintage champagne. He even retained a personal tailor, Dimmy Major, whom he shared with the comedian Ronnie Corbett.

At weekends he was visiting wealthy friends – shooting with Wafic Said or sailing with Sir David Gosling, chairman of National Car Parks, or a guest on the yacht of millionaire publisher Malcolm Forbes. Even at Chequers the prime minister's son was noticeably star-struck by his mother's favourite tycoons. At one lunch for captains of industry he continually muscled in on conversations, repeating things like, 'Gosh, $2 million.' This annoyed one of the guests, Alan Clark, then a trade and industry minister and a close friend and admirer of Margaret Thatcher. 'I got a bit sick

of this,' he recorded in his diaries, 'and said "That's
not much" (which it isn't), but people affected not to
hear.'[26]

Mark clearly saw himself as part of the new entrepreneurial Thatcherite jet-set, above and beyond ordinary
people. 'I remember having lunch with him at the
Dorchester Hotel,' said the financier Brian McHugo,
who met him in 1988. 'I remember it because Mark
had to sit at a particular angle so that his bodyguard
could see him. Also he kept using the phrase "the great
unwashed", which he said quite often. It was not said
in jest and was not an expression I liked.'[27]

The most ostentatious symbol of Mark's new-found
wealth was his hiring, in the summer of 1989, of a
personal valet, Graham Henderson. Recruited in Texas,
where such menservants can command salaries of up to
£50,000 a year, Henderson waited on Mark, laid out
his clothes, loaded his shotgun at shooting parties and
flew with him in his private jet.

When Mark stayed at the luxurious Claridge's Hotel
later that year, the staff had to make special arrangements for his valet. This was a curious request as
Claridge's is, of course, hardly the sort of place where
a guest might need a valet. But Thatcher was insistent.
While he moved into his £390-a-night suite, Henderson
was dispatched to the servants' quarters for a mere £25
a night.[28] At dinner fellow guests even saw his butler,
rather than the waiters, serve him. This so embarrassed
the *maître d'hôtel* that he arranged for Thatcher to be
seated in the restaurant's alcove, slightly hidden away.
Those who saw them together say Mark treated his
servant 'firmly but well, rather like an officer would
treat a batman in the Army'.[29]

Later that year, in October 1990, Margaret Thatcher's
son bought perhaps the most visible symbol of his fortune

– a house in The Boltons in South Kensington, one of the most exclusive residential areas of London. Among his neighbours are members of the Saudi royal family, the prime minister of Bahrain and the Sultan of Brunei. Many were astonished that he could afford to buy the £2.1 million property at 1 Tregunter Road from the financier Peter de Savary. 'If you can find out how he can afford a house in The Boltons, let me know,' said his sister, Carol.[30]

Four-storeyed, semi-detached, with a double garage, the house was most notable for its extraordinarily elaborate security system. Visitors were greeted by two security cameras – one on the gate and another above the front door – with a video remote-control entry system. Just in case anyone escaped the surveillance, another camera was placed above the back door, marked 'Tradesmen's Entrance'. Mark also inserted bomb-proof windows, steel shutters and blast-resistant curtains. 'He was worried that he might be a terrorist target and he showed me the new security system he had installed,' said Jay Laughlin, his former business associate. 'He pushed a button and a metal grille came down over the windows to guard against a rocket attack.'[31] According to one regular guest, the house is 'climate-controlled' and 'bugged and monitored for sound'.

Once inside, visitors see a marble-floored entrance lobby. Off to the right is a 28ft by 14ft drawing-room with marble mantel and hearth and thick bottle-green carpets. The walls are hung with silk, with the dining-room featuring a mural by P. M. Rudelle. There are four air-conditioned bedroom suites and three reception rooms, and one of the bathrooms is complete with more marble, murals and gold taps. Outside there is a 140ft garden. To accommodate his valet, there are separate servants' quarters with a housekeeper's flat. 'The staff are all locked away in the basement, which is jolly useful if you want to have an argument with your wife in the drawing-room upstairs,' said Andy Buchanan, the estate agent who handled the sale.[32]

Mark Thatcher spent £600,000 on 'improvements', notably the security devices, a Texas-style conservatory, a chiller unit in the garden, mahogany joinery in the drawing-room and a special television set that rises out of a box at the foot of the bed in the master bedroom. The house is dominated by gold and marble.

The acquisition of 1 Tregunter Road in October 1990 was a sure sign that Mark Thatcher was by then a rich man. But the purchase of the property provided clues not just about the value of Thatcher's gold, but also about the way the treasure has been handled.

The house was bought by Eastcoast Investments Ltd, an offshore company set up in January 1990 and registered in Jersey. The shares are jointly owned by Hugh Thurston, Thatcher's banker, and Leonard Day and his wife, Margery. Household bills, even Mark's poll tax, were paid using this Channel Island firm.

The ownership of his UK house by an offshore company highlighted Mark Thatcher's delicate and precarious relationship with the international tax authorities. His long years in Texas enabled him to secure non-residency status from the UK Inland Revenue. For most people that means they can spend only a stipulated, limited, number of days a year in Britain. It also requires that the individual does not own a UK property. Anyone found to have contravened either of those rules is liable to pay tax on his or her worldwide income.

As Mark Thatcher owned a UK property and was

spending several days a year in London, there was
clearly a case that he was resident for tax purposes. This
factor, plus his offshore companies and bank accounts,
naturally brought him under the scrutiny of the Inland
Revenue. He was petrified that he would have to pay
tax at the top rate. Fortunately for him, the Revenue
enquiry concluded that he would be exempt. In 1990
Mark Thatcher received a certificate of clearance
stating that for the previous six years he had been
non-resident in the UK for tax purposes, because of
his offshore status. Mark was delighted and promptly
threw a champagne party at the Dorchester Hotel in
Mayfair to celebrate. Thatcher's gold was safe – for
the time being, anyway.

Chapter Nine

A Family Business

*'If Margaret Thatcher had a motto on her desk,
it would have read "No Cheques Accepted".'*

Paul Johnson, Historian and conservative columnist[1]

During the dramatic palace coup which dethroned his
mother as prime minister, Mark stayed at Chequers and,
together with Carol, was a source of great emotional
support for his mother. He attended the dinner given
there, on Saturday, 17 November 1990, for her closest
confidants – Sir Tim Bell, Sir Gordon Reece and Lord
McAlpine – together with her campaign team.[2] It was
a crucial summit meeting and, unfortunately for her,
the atmosphere reeked of complacency. But Mark was
never a political animal and wisely steered clear of
advising her on election tactics.

However, he must have been surprised by his mother's resignation. For during the tense and traumatic
atmosphere following the first ballot – in the early
hours of Wednesday, 21 November – he was on a
flight home to Texas to take care of a business deal.
As soon as he landed at Dallas airport, he telephoned
London and was told her support was wavering. He
immediately caught an American Airlines DC10 and

flew back to Heathrow. When Mark arrived at 10 Downing Street later that day his mother was upset, confused and in disarray. She was shocked by what she saw as a calculated betrayal by her once-loyal cabinet ministers. 'It was treachery with a smile on its face,' she later remarked.[3] Mark comforted and consoled her and spent time with her. Even his many enemies conceded that he behaved with great care and compassion towards her.

During her final days in 10 Downing Street, Mark's mood changed from sadness to anger. When asked how his mother was spending her time, he snapped: 'She's doing what she always does on a Friday – running the country.'[4] His rage was barely concealed the following Wednesday morning when Mrs Thatcher finally left office. Mark was beside her in 10 Downing Street as she said a tearful farewell to her private staff. He then ushered her outside to read a short statement to the media. As he waited to drive her away a cameraman noticed how Mark glared and glowered across at the journalists and photographers. It was as if he blamed the newspapers and television for his mother's dramatic downfall.

Mark's former business partner, Steve Tipping, was also in 10 Downing Street on that last day in office. He looked on, stunned and shocked, as the removal vans arrived to collect the Thatchers' possessions. Tipping was upset at the prime minister's demise. This was partly because he was a genuine Thatcherite but also because he felt her policies benefited big business.

Tipping made his feelings clear the following Wednesday, 5 December 1990, when he attended a reception in the ballroom on the first floor of the London Hilton Hotel, Park Lane, Mayfair. It was on behalf of Dolphin Promotions Ltd, a trading company run by Ketan Somaia, the Kenyan businessman with close connections to President Moi and Mark Thatcher. Tipping was very depressed as he sat with Haji Hassan, a banker who worked with him in Malaysia, and other business associates, mainly Kenyan Asians.

'I've had a terrible week,' Tipping told the other guests. 'I've been sinking gin and tonics with Denis Thatcher.' 'Who was to blame for her downfall?' a guest asked. 'It was a Taffy Mafia that brought her down,' he replied, 'but at least Heseltine didn't get the leadership, so it worked out well in the end. Major is one of us.'5 According to Gary Smith, the international oil trader, who was present: 'Mark and Steve were naturally unhappy about Mrs Thatcher leaving office but they felt Major was a satisfactory choice because it preserved the status quo.'

Tipping and some of the other guests, including Gary Smith, then retired to Trader Vic's bar downstairs. Once they had sat down with their drinks, Tipping became more reflective. 'I suppose we've got to admit we've all done well out of the Thatcher government,' he said. 'We've made our pile of money so we can't complain too much. But things are going to be more difficult from now on. I suppose we're better off with Major than Heseltine.'

The Property

After leaving Downing Street, the Thatchers reluctantly drove to their neo-Georgian south London home at Hambledon Place, Dulwich, built by Barratt. They hated living there, mainly because it was so far from Westminster. 'A widow's house', as Denis aptly described it, unsuitable for a woman cut off in her prime. Even the local political landscape was an eyesore to him. 'The disadvantage, and I shouldn't say this, is that it falls into the communist "whatnot" of Southwark,' he remarked.[6]

It was not long before the couple put the property on the market and eventually it was bought by Edward Nassar, a Swiss-based businessman, for £595,000 – £85,000 less than the original asking price. Nassar knew Mark Thatcher because both had commercial interests in Lausanne, but was not keen to talk to us. 'I don't think it helps very much what you are doing,' he said from his office in Switzerland.

In the meantime the Thatchers moved into an apartment in Belgravia's Eaton Square lent to them by Kathleen Ford, the widow of Henry Ford II, and looked around for a new home. Mark decided that he would be his mother's estate agent. But an early suggestion was not warmly greeted – a £7.5 million house in Tite Street, Chelsea, built by Lord Glenconner. His idea was that a grateful and adoring businessman would buy the property and lease it back to her at a favourable rent. Denis was comfortably off but Margaret would receive only an allowance of £59,600 a year and a £25,600 annual pension. Even with her projected earnings from lecture tours and memoirs, it was way out of their price range. More significantly, such a sweetheart deal would look like a pay-off to the former prime minister. But her son, unruffled, escorted his parents around the Tite Street house, complaining loudly that the government had not done enough to help his mother adjust to life outside 10 Downing Street. He then offered £6 million but was £250,000 short of the asking price.

His sister, Carol, was furious about the idea and

saw it as a futile expedition. 'When I heard about Tite
Street I knew it was a ridiculous amount of money,'
she said.[7] Lord McAlpine, former Tory Party treasurer
and a close friend of the Thatcher family, was more
charitable and diplomatic. 'Mark's not a politician,' he
said. 'He doesn't understand these things. Whatever
Mark may have done was with the best intentions.'[8]

A more suitable property soon became available in
the form of 73 Chester Square, Belgravia, two doors
down from Tiny Rowland. It was owned by David
and Frederick Barclay, the secretive millionaire twins
based in Monte Carlo who had made their fortunes
during the Thatcher years. They offered the five-
storeyed terraced house to the former prime minister
for £700,000. The deal was arranged through the good
offices of Sir Tim Bell, her long-time media adviser
and confidant. But when her son was informed he
reacted petulantly. 'He told Tim that he wasn't going
to have a couple of businessmen just walk in and buy
up his mother like that,' said a Thatcher family friend.
'He implied that the Barclays were not fit to open the
door of her Daimler. He was pretty offensive.'[9]

After Mark Thatcher's intervention, the property
was sold to another buyer. But Bell was convinced
this was the ideal home for Margaret. So a few weeks
later he arranged for her to be shown the exterior as she
was being driven through Belgravia. She liked it and,
despite Mark's objections, asked the Barclay brothers
to reconsider. They agreed, bought back the house, and
in April 1991 sold it to the Thatchers for the original
price on a ten-year lease.

Finding an office was equally difficult. At first she
set up camp at 27 Great College Street, Westminster,
a seventeenth-century house kindly lent to her by its
owner, Lord McAlpine. That was converted into a

temporary base while Mark again played estate agent. One of the candidates was the head office of Sale Tilney plc, a mini-conglomerate, in Queen's Gate, Kensington, whose lease was up for sale. One day Dorothy Wyndham-Lewis, personal assistant to the chairman, was told that a VIP would be arriving to inspect the premises. 'Keep it under your hat,' said the estate agent.

The VIP turned out to be Mark Thatcher, who arrived with a bodyguard and was shown into the boardroom. Sale Tilney's chairman then walked into the room to greet his visitor. Mark looked him up and down, readjusted his huge cuff-links and asked: 'And *who* are you?' [his emphasis]. Stunned by such impertinence, the businessman replied he was in fact the chairman and chief executive. He then escorted Thatcher up to the executive office, which overlooked Horse Guards Parade and St James's Park. 'You have a wonderful view,' said Mark. 'We used to be at Number 10, you know.' After inspecting the rest of the premises, Mark left.

Two days later a black limousine drew up outside the office and two burly bodyguards stepped out, followed by a pale, weary-looking Margaret Thatcher, her son and an estate agent. The former prime minister, with Mark trailing sheepishly behind her, was given the same tour. She was impressed by the premises but decided against them and looked elsewhere. Eventually she moved into 35 Chesham Place, Belgravia, just across the road from the German embassy. Lady Thatcher rents the building from Chelsfield, a property company now owned by Elliott Bernerd and by Olayan, a Saudi Arabian investment institution, which have formed a joint venture to run the Chesham Place Estate.

The Legacy

In the first two months of her exile, the atmosphere inside her office was administrative chaos combined with Margaret Thatcher trying to come to terms emotionally with losing the premiership. The logistical problems were solved by hiring Andrew Bearpark, her capable former home affairs private secretary, as her chief of staff. But she also desperately needed sensible strategic advice. She had greatly relied on briefings from Charles (now Sir Charles) Powell, her foreign affairs private secretary, but that facility disappeared when he left Downing Street after the Gulf war.

The consequence of this vacuum was a private power struggle between Mark and Denis. 'Mark and Denis did not get on,' recalled one of her closest aides. 'I was present when Mark was extremely rude to his father in front of Margaret, sometimes even in public, and she just sided with her son. Denis continued to give her emotional support but she turned to Mark to manage and organize her financial affairs and speaking programme.' When asked by *Vanity Fair* how her son was qualified to do this job, Mrs Thatcher replied angrily: 'Look, my children are not children any more. They know about life. I find he is one of the most businesslike people I deal with. You want something done, he does it quickly – there's no "Oh well, I'll do it tomorrow."'[10]

By late February 1991, Mark was running the Margaret Thatcher revue. For the first time in his life, his mother needed him – rather than the other way around – and he revelled in his new-found power and freedom of action. He became her aide-de-camp,

financial adviser, literary and estate agent, tour operator, fund-raiser and, it appeared, anything else that
caught his fancy. One person he did consult was
the international marketing agent Mark McCormack,
who usually represents sports superstars. McCormack
is the author of *What They Don't Teach You at
Harvard Business School*, which contains the immortal
Thatcherite advice, 'Never underestimate the importance of money.'[11] 'She [Lady Thatcher] certainly has
complete and total confidence in Mark and that often
outweighs a lot of alternatives,' said McCormack. 'He
was speaking to us always on behalf of his mother. . . .
He decided he wanted to do different segments of her
commercial activities with different groups of people.
He was, as we say in America, the quarterback of the
team, who plans the entire situation.'[12]

Mark's first act was to pour in some of his own
private funds, acquired while she was prime minister.
'Now's the time to rally round and help Mummy,' he
said, and paid nearly £1.5 million into her coffers.
This was used for her initial expenses and also for
the refurbishment and renovation of her new house in
Chester Square.

A separate bank account was set up to handle
the cheques that flooded in from big business. The
early donations were for the Thatcher Foundation.
This had been announced, but as it did not yet
formally exist the money was used, with the donors'
permission, for running her office. Lord Hanson and
Bruce Gyngell, the former chief executive of TV-AM,
were among the early corporate backers who contributed some £250,000. Most of this money was
used to pay staff salaries. Sir Michael Richardson,
chairman of stockbrokers Smith New Court and a
long-time confidant, became her unofficial financial

adviser but it was Mark who controlled the Thatcher cheque-book.

While her son looked after the money, Margaret Thatcher had grander designs. After the shock of her enforced abdication she decided to establish three lasting monuments to her political legacy – her memoirs, a foundation and a series of overseas lectures and speeches. This had the advantage of keeping alive the creed of Thatcherism and raising revenue. And Mark was a willing crown prince to the Empress Margaret to keep her legend alive – and prospering.

The Privatization of Margaret Thatcher

It was not long before Margaret Thatcher was off abroad. The trips were meant to be partly evangelical crusades for Thatcherism and partly fund-raising for the stuttering Thatcher Foundation. Her beloved United States was to be a regular port of call. She was still worshipped there by conservatives, and there were plenty of willing congregations happy to pay handsomely for her ideological sermons.

Within a week of losing the premiership she was approached by Harry Rhoads, head of the prestigious Washington Speakers Bureau, dangling untold riches on the international lecture circuit. He was in a position to do so, as his agency had just made former president Ronald Reagan the highest-paid speaker in the world. The previous year Reagan had received a record $6 million fee for an eight-day speaking tour of Japan, although he later refused engagements unless they were less than an hour's flight from his California ranch.[13]

Margaret Thatcher was tempted but delayed her

decision for two weeks until she had talked about the
offer with her old friend Ronald. Over tea at Claridge's
on the afternoon of 6 December 1990, the dethroned
prime minister asked the former president and his wife,
Nancy, about the agency. They recommended acceptance, and the following month Margaret Thatcher
signed an exclusive contract with the Washington
Speakers Bureau. She charged $50,000 per lecture for
a minimum of thirty minutes, plus another half-hour for
a question-and-answer session. Then there was at least
$5,000 for travel and hotel expenses for herself and her
entourage. The fees were handled by her son, Mark,
liaising with her full-time agent, Sandra Warfield.

Three weeks later Margaret Thatcher flew to California
on the private jet of Lodwrick M. Cook, chairman of the
Atlantic Richfield Corporation (ARCO), for a week-
long visit. After inspecting an ARCO oil refinery, she
moved on to the principal reason for the trip, Ronald
Reagan's eightieth birthday party. Accompanied by
Denis and Mark, she was the guest of honour at the
Beverly Hills Hilton Hotel, Los Angeles. Among the
friends and celebrities, paying £1,250 a head at dinner,
were film stars, politicians and businessmen, notably
media tycoons Rupert Murdoch and Barry Diller.

During their stay in California, Mark and Denis
were entertained by Walter Annenberg, an old friend
and former US ambassador to Britain. One morning
Annenberg, one of America's wealthiest men and a
great philanthropist, showed his guests his stunning
new golf course on his Sunnylands Estate, specially
designed by Jack Nicklaus. 'Well, what do you think?'
he asked with undisguised pride. 'Marvellous,' replied
Denis. 'Can't wait to get out there.' Mark, who plays
an eight handicap to his father's sixteen, paused and
then sniffed: 'Bit Mickey Mouse, isn't it?' He was not

joking.[14] This story has been confirmed by two other sources, both friends of Margaret Thatcher.

The newly ennobled Lady Thatcher was the focus of celebration a month later on 7 March 1991, when she was awarded the Presidential Medal of Freedom at a special White House ceremony. President Bush praised the 'greengrocer's daughter who shaped a nation to her will'. The guests then retired to the president's private quarters for a lavish dinner party in her honour. Despite losing her crown, she was in her element. So was her son. Sitting next to Georgette Mosbacher, the flame-haired entrepreneuse and wife of the then US commerce secretary, he held forth on his 'successful' business career and how he had 'made millions' in the home-security business. Mosbacher, no wilting flower, responded by describing how she had made her fortune in the cosmetics business. The two then sparred with each other for the rest of the evening on their respective commercial prowess.[15]

Lady Thatcher's next stop on her US tour was Mark's home town of Dallas. On 11 March 1991, she was the guest speaker at the annual meeting of the North Dallas Chamber of Commerce at the Loews Anatole Hotel. 'We sold out the biggest ballroom in Dallas and they loved her,' said Steve Taylor, president of the chamber. Arranged by Mark, 1,850 members and guests paid over $100,000 to hear her views on the Gulf war, crediting former defence secretary Caspar Weinberger and ex-US Senator John Tower with having 'kept our defences strong and our technology ahead of the others'.[16]

The Texas trip was, according to Steve Taylor, 'a combination of business and pleasure'. That evening a more intimate gathering assembled at the Mansion on Turtle Creek Hotel, where Lady Thatcher was staying at $1,000 a night. The fifty-five guests paid $5,000 each to dine with the former prime minister, raising $175,000 for the Chamber of Commerce. Mark negotiated her five-figure fee, but only on the basis that her contract included a clause stipulating that the actual amount be kept confidential.

That event was hosted by Caroline Rose Hunt, the millionaire owner of the Mansion on Turtle Creek Hotel in Dallas and the Lansborough in London, as head of the Rosewood Corporation. Before dinner she hosted a drinks reception in the hotel's Pavilioni Room. All the guests were asked to wear name-tags. Mark Thatcher refused point-blank. 'If people don't know who I am by now, they never will,' he sniffed. Ironically, the truth was that much of Dallas society did *not* know who he was [our emphasis]. 'If Mark Thatcher walked into my office, I wouldn't recognize him,' said a local businessman.

Despite this act of petulance, Caroline Hunt was delighted with Lady Thatcher's appearance. She asked permission to be photographed with her, which was happily granted. So Hunt asked Wendy Strong, her PR consultant, to take a picture of herself and her honoured guest. Suddenly, just as Wendy clicked the instamatic camera, Mark pounced on her and yelled, 'You can't take pictures of my mother.' He then grabbed her left arm, dragged her away and tried to take the camera off her.

Mark looked around and there was an embarrassed silence. Lady Thatcher glared at him, stone-faced. Caroline Hunt looked away, mortified. Denis was also uncomfortable but tried to break the ice by laughing it off. 'Mark has always been like that,' he whispered to some nearby guests. 'He likes to be major-domo. We've always had problems with him.'

Another guest was aghast: 'He was acting like a South African bodyguard. I've never seen anything like it.'

The guests, who included Charles Simmons, a Fort Worth oilman, and Rosewood Hotels president Atef Mankarios, were shocked but proceeded in to dinner. It was not long before the conversation turned to politics. In a discussion about social inequities, the chief executive of the *Dallas Morning News* dared to mention the existence of a class structure. 'Any reference to class distinctions is a Marxist concept,' snapped Lady Thatcher.[17]

Two days later she was in the now-bankrupt Orange County, California. Dressed in royal purple, she arrived in a Costa Mesa mall with the band playing 'God Save The Queen'. 'You have come home to conservative country,' shouted her host, shopping magnate Henry Segerstrom. Later that evening she addressed a dinner, at which local businessmen paid $125 each to hear her. In return she was paid $50,000 plus expenses. Mark did not attend and instead sent David Wallace, his business partner.

Her next trip was almost like a state visit. In May 1991 she flew to South Africa at the invitation of President De Klerk, with all expenses paid by his government. On her first day she was presented with the Order of Good Hope (Grand Cross Class). Her son did not go but fixed the private plane and flights and arranged for her to stay with his friend Anton Rupert, a wealthy South African businessman and owner of Rembrandt Tobacco.

By June 1991, there was concern among some of her advisers and friends that too many of her overseas engagements were commercially rather than ideologically motivated – based on advice from her son. 'In the early weeks she was not paid for many of her trips or she would give the fee to charity,' one of her key aides told us. 'The strategy was that it would be partly free and partly financially rewarding. But later on it became nearly all commercial, because Mark wanted the tours to be run as a business proposition and purely as a money-making enterprise. We thought that could damage her and diminish her reputation as a world figure.'

Despite this disquiet, Mark's view prevailed. On one occasion Walter Annenberg hosted a special lunch and one of his guests invited Margaret and Mark. She attended and spoke at fairly short notice but Annenberg was shocked when approached by her son after the lunch. He asked the former ambassador for a contribution. Annenberg refused; another guest who entered was outraged.

One of Lady Thatcher's most lucrative trips was to the United States in June 1991. Eight carefully selected groups of wealthy businessmen and right-wing groups were addressed in exclusive private clubs. Six of her eight speeches were delivered in secret, with details not being divulged for 'security reasons'.[18] However, it has been possible to piece together much of her week-long lecture tour.

On 14 June 1991, she flew by private executive jet to the exclusive resort of Greenbriar, West Virginia, where she based herself. The next day she addressed a food wholesalers group, sponsored by the Heinz Corporation.

On Monday, 16 June, Lady Thatcher dined and lectured the Chicago Council on Foreign Relations with 4,000 guests paying $15 each – total $60,000. The next day she flew to New York to talk to 1,700 businessmen at the Economic Club; the lunch bill was $150 each – total $255,000. Those were the only public

engagements and her estimated fees for both functions
were $25,000.

The Thatcher camp then moved on to private meetings. Down in Atlantic City, New Jersey, she addressed
IBM executives. In North Carolina and Ohio, $300 a
head for dinner and speech was the going rate for 300
devotees. This took care of her fee of $30,000. Her rate
for each lecture varied enormously – from $10,000 up
to $60,000.[19] She also used the opportunity to solicit
much-needed funds for the Thatcher Foundation.

One of her private seminars was at the Washington
head office of Johnson & Johnson Inc, the huge US private medicare corporation. Executives and managing
directors from their parent and subsidiary companies
were specially flown in from all over the world for
the occasion. Lady Thatcher spoke for an hour on
the 'global market' and 'executive leadership' and
then took questions from the star-struck executives.
For two hours' work she was paid a cool $100,000
plus expenses. 'She was worth every cent,' said one
of those present.

However, some aspects of the privatization of Lady
Thatcher bordered on the ludicrous as well as the
lucrative. One organization that was keen to market
her name was the Richmond Forum, an organization
that arranges for celebrities to speak to Virginian
audiences. In 1991 they distributed a brochure entitled
'How Having Dinner with Margaret Thatcher Could Be
the Best $30,000 You Ever Spent'. It boasted: 'Con-
verse with Mrs Thatcher. Ask General Schwarzkopf
a strategy question. . . . We're not talking about just
getting to hear these people. We're talking about
getting to know them. An opportunity for one-on-one
conversation with some of the most important people
in the world.'

Investing in Thatcher plc was clearly seen as profitable by the Richmond Forum. 'Imagine the lasting impression you could make on clients when you introduce them to someone like Margaret Thatcher,' advised the Forum. 'Join Richmond's leading companies and corporations in providing five unforgettable evenings of information and entertainment. And don't forget. An evening that starts with "Pass the salt, Mrs Thatcher" could end up with "Maggie, the next time you and your husband come to Richmond, stay with us".'

The former prime minister returned to more serious promotional appearances on 7 August 1991. She flew to New York to help out an old friend, Lord (Jeffrey) Sterling, chairman of P&O, which was a substantial financial donor to the Tory Party. That evening she was guest of honour at dinner on board the *Regal Princess*, P&O's new 70,000-ton luxury cruise liner, to be based at Fort Lauderdale, Florida. The next day, Mrs Thatcher launched the *Princess*. Sterling paid her expenses and it was arranged as a tribute to her – co-hosted by Charles Price, the former US ambassador in London. When asked by the *Observer*'s Andrew Stephen why she was there, Lady Thatcher was uncharacteristically uncertain. 'Because I was invited,' she replied. 'Because I was asked by Lord Sterling. Because if I had been asked and not come, people would have . . .' Then she started stammering rather desperately and uncharacteristically – about the time of year, parliament in recess, etc, etc.[20]

The Margaret Thatcher financial flying circus then turned to the Far East. On 1 September 1991, sponsored by Nippon Telegraph and Telephone (NTT), the Japanese telecommunications company, she flew to Tokyo accompanied by Lord Archer and Mark, plus entourage. For a week she was treated as though she had almost divine status as she gave a series of lectures, attended private business dinners and granted interviews – forty-seven engagements in three cities. She was paid an estimated £50,000 a speech. Privatization was very much on the agenda as she had dinner with the presidents of Japan's leading privatized corporations in the airline, tobacco and railways industries.

Like her recent US tour, her visit to Japan was also used to raise funds for the recently launched Thatcher Foundation. This was the case two days later when she arrived in Hong Kong. It was the first time she had returned to the British colony since signing the joint declaration on sovereignty with China in 1984.

But since leaving 10 Downing Street she had developed financial interests in Hong Kong along with her son, Mark. One commercial connection was with Moss and Partners, a firm of investment consultants and property developers, based in Tilney Street, near the Dorchester Hotel. One former employee was amused to learn that the company's secret code-word for Lady Thatcher's overseas financial correspondence was 'Roofmaker'.

As the former prime minister and her son descended on Hong Kong in their private plane on 13 September 1991, it was unclear how she would be received by the local business community. 'Hong Kong is pretty ruthless and bourgeois about power,' said David Tsang, a prominent businessman who also raises money for the Conservative Party. 'Because of who she is there will still be interest in her, even though she is out of power. But if she is going there to raise money, she might find a lukewarm response. Everyone in Hong Kong will be thinking, "What's in it for me?"'[21]

Any doubts were immediately dismissed when she was greeted at the airport by George Magnus, deputy chairman of Cheung Kong Holdings, the giant property company owned by Li Ka-Shing. Before being whisked away in a stately Bentley limousine, Mark Thatcher said her visit was a 'private' matter. 'My mother has a lot of friends here,' he said. 'She will be renewing a lot of old friendships in the business world.'[22] His mother refused to comment. Instead she walked off to see Henry Kissinger, the former US secretary of state, whose private plane was on the tarmac just about to depart. He had been in Hong Kong on business for his own Kissinger Associates.

Li Ka-Shing was one of her strongest political supporters in the business world. He was also one of the most controversial. In 1986 a judicial tribunal concluded an investigation into insider dealing by one of his companies by stating: 'As to the degree of culpability to be attributed to Li Ka-Shing, we considered that it was high.' In Hong Kong insider dealing was at the time not a criminal offence. The only sanction was public disgrace.

This did not appear to concern Lady Thatcher. In March 1991, she had flown to Vancouver with her son to launch the HK$ 16.75 billion Pacific Place community complex, a waterfront park. The project was run by Concord Pacific Developments Ltd, a Canada-based company in which Li Ka-Shing had a controlling interest. During her visit Lady Thatcher and Mark had inspected the model of the park, accompanied by George Magnus and Victor Li, son of Li Ka-Shing and a senior vice-president of Concord Pacific Developments. She had then dedicated the project to David Lam, the first person of Chinese origin to become lieutenant-governor of a Canadian province.[23]

During her three-day stay in Hong Kong the former

prime minister and her son renewed their friendship with Li Ka-Shing, who also has interests in shipping and telecommunications. Mark stayed in the Presidential Suite of the Hilton Hotel, owned by Hong Kong's most powerful tycoon, while Margaret stayed in the Harbour Rooms at Government House.

After her only public appearance, as guest speaker at the Trade Development Council, she visited Li Ka-Shing's international container terminal by taking a trip on his boat in Hong Kong harbour. That evening, her final day in the colony, she was the guest of honour at a private dinner at the Albany penthouse of Baroness Lydia Dunn, chairwoman of Swire Pacific. The guests at what was billed as the 'Foundation Dinner' included top executives from Jardine Matheson and the Hongkong and Shanghai Banking Corporation. It was intended diplomatically to solicit donations. One businessman who pledged a six-figure sum was Li Ka-Shing.

Her next Far East benefactor was Citibank, one of whose directors was her own personal banker, Hugh Thurston. Almost a year later, in August 1992, she flew to Taipei, the capital of Taiwan, for a three-day visit. Her party of seven, including two bodyguards, took up eighteen rooms on two floors of the Sherwood Hotel at a cost of £26,000 for three nights.

On 31 August, she had a private breakfast with Citibank executives and major clients and then delivered the bank's 'Leadership Series In Asia' lecture at the Hilton Hotel. That evening she called on Taiwan, a country with the world's largest dollar reserves, to lift its remaining barriers against imports and foreign investment.[24]

This was a real money-spinning trip. 'Mr Gorbachev asked for a personal fee of £125,000 for one lecture and appearances. We put Lady Thatcher in that same pricing category,' said a Citibank spokesperson.[25] Her co-hosts, the United Daily News Group, paid a similar fee for their lecture. 'We had to pay a lot for the speech – but that was kept secret even from me,' said a spokesperson for the newspaper group. 'We were told we had to make a donation to the Thatcher Foundation.'[26]

Her next destination was Seoul, South Korea, where she was greeted by Kim Sang-Man, head of the powerful *Dong-A Ilbo* newspaper group. Kim donated £37,000 to the Thatcher Foundation. In return she gave his newspaper an exclusive interview, spoke at one of its public meetings and attended a gala dinner hosted by the media corporation.[27] Another £12,500 was picked up after she granted an interview to KBS, the television station.

The Far East tours were well-organized and even the donations were delivered in a relatively open way. But Lady Thatcher continued to attend and perform at functions, especially in the USA, which bordered on the evangelical. On 12 October 1994, she flew by a private jet, owned by right-wing property developer Harlan Crow, to Dallas for a charity lunch billed as 'A Conversation with a Living Legend'. An estimated 2,000 tickets, costing between $75 and $13,000, were sold. In Europe her lectures have been more serious and clearly money-making exercises. In June 1994, she spoke in London at the AGM of the Chase Manhattan Bank and was paid £60,000. She received the same fee in April 1995, when she addressed the AGM of the bank's European branch in Paris.

There has been nothing too surprising about Lady Thatcher's cashing in on her premiership. She was merely being consistent with her ideology. She was enacting the Thatcherite creed. 'Money is important,' said a former adviser. 'She always attached considerable importance to it and designed a society in which making money was one of the highest goals. It's a source of some satisfaction to her to be able to earn considerable quantities of it.'[28]

Making a Killing

'My mother must have money,' said Mark soon after the Thatchers left 10 Downing Street. Certainly, the allowances the former prime minister receives compare unfavourably with those of other ex-world leaders. Besides, she was not retiring from public life nor departing from the political arena. So funding for her private office and activities was crucial. The real question was: who was she going to take money from? And to what extent were her paymasters going to use her unparalleled contacts and influence with governments?

Multinational corporations were soon lining up to persuade her to join their boards of directors. Executive headhunters were hired, largely by American companies, to secure her services. One of them was the Egon Zhender company, based in Switzerland. 'We have clients who would very much like to talk to her,' said John Gumbar, the head of its London office. 'A number of world-class corporations would give anything to have her on their board. I don't have a blank cheque, but I do have several requests.'[29] They realized her international connections would enhance their commercial prospects as well as their prestige. 'This is seen as of enormous value to a company with a global strategy,' added Gumbar.[30]

One adoring businessman who approached her was Conrad Black, the Canadian owner of the *Daily Telegraph* and *Jerusalem Post*. He asked her to join his international advisory board, which included such luminaries as Giovanni Agnelli, chairman of Fiat, and William F. Buckley, editor-at-large of the *National Review*. Mrs Thatcher politely declined the offer but did agree to be an honorary senior international adviser to his holding company, Hollinger Inc.

It became apparent that the former prime minister was selective as to which companies she joined. Perhaps she thought boardrooms were too restrictive an environment. Whatever the reason, she weighed up the offers very carefully. The one commercial proposition she did accept could not have been more controversial. In January 1992, she became a consultant to Philip Morris Inc, the giant global tobacco corporation and manufacturers of Marlboro, the biggest-selling cigarette in the world. Although the company also owns Kraft Foods and Miller beer, cigarettes account for 43 per cent of its operating revenues and 69 per cent of profits. Mrs Thatcher signed a contract worth $1 million over three years. 'She is doing consultancy work for us on geo-political concerns on a world-wide basis,' said a Philip Morris vice-president of corporate communications.[31]

Details of what services she was providing the tobacco company were contained in an internal management memorandum, leaked to the *Sunday Times*. Written on 31 March 1992, by Geoffrey Bible, an executive vice-president of Philip Morris International, and circulated to thirteen other executives, it said:

'We have the ability to use Mrs Thatcher's services

and skills over the next few years. On the few occasions we have asked for her advice, she has provided very skilful help. However, we believe that we are not taking full advantage of all that she has to offer. As a result, I have attempted to summarize as many issues as I can think of where she may be able to offer guidance and assistance.'

Bible then listed the areas where Thatcher could use her influence. They were split into three areas. The first was the European Community. This included the advertising ban, lowering of tobacco tariffs and monopoly privatization in Spain, France and Portugal. The second was non-EC international, which encompassed the Swiss cartel, Turkish pricing, distribution in the independent republics of the former Soviet Union, and entry into South Africa. The third was Asia and the Pacific, comprising China entry strategy, monopoly privatization in Japan, Taiwan, Korea and Thailand, and legislation in Indonesia, Malaysia and Singapore.

Bible added: 'You will note that most of the points I have raised are skewed to Tobacco where we tend to have more governmental issues. But I would very much appreciate it if you could reflect intensively on food issues where she could also be of assistance.' He concluded by asking his executives for a 'one-page summary on each of the points so that I can discuss them with senior management, finalize those which qualify for discussion with Mrs Thatcher and then meet with her to map out a game plan of how she might be able to help us over the coming years.'[32]

Essentially, Philip Morris was concerned about the decline in Western tobacco sales and saw the newly privatized markets in Asia and Eastern Europe as an opportunity to maintain profitability. But not all governments were accommodating and regulatory barriers were in place. 'Cigarette prices in many international markets are government controlled,' stated its 1993 accounts. 'Excise, other tax increases, higher costs and government price restraints in a number of markets have restricted the sales and income attributable to Philip Morris.'

Enter Mrs Thatcher. She was the one person who could help the company break into troublesome foreign markets. Philip Morris already had Rupert Murdoch as a director and shareholder. But the former prime minister could provide that extra political leverage which would persuade the presidents of developing countries to remove any regulatory and legislative obstacles.

Asia and the Pacific is the region where Lady Thatcher is most likely to exert influence on Philip Morris's behalf. The massive untapped tobacco markets in the former Soviet republics and the Far East present golden sales opportunities. But the company is faced with significant government regulatory impediments – foreign ownership restrictions, monopoly privatization and import barriers. Who better than the revered Lady Thatcher to lobby the presidents and rulers and open up access to those markets for her client?

Nowhere was this more paramount than Taiwan, the most anti-tobacco country in the Far East. This twenty-million-strong island state off the coast of China presented a problem to Philip Morris. One out of five deaths in Taiwan is smoking-related and so in 1991 the government proposed a 'Law Governing the Prevention and Control of Damage from Tobacco Use'. This contained clauses banning cigarette sales through vending machines, restricting smoking in public places and banning all direct advertising and promotion of cigarettes.

Philip Morris was aghast. It immediately lobbied the US trade representative, complaining that the new law would have an adverse effect on its business. In public relations terms the company was initially successful and boasted, 'We have successfully made this a trade issue rather than one of health.'[33]

But there were serious negotiations to be conducted. Fortunately for the corporation, Lady Thatcher arrived on the island in August 1992 – on the eve of vital discussions between the Taiwanese and American governments about the planned advertising ban. She stayed at the luxurious Sherwood Hotel, where, ironically, she demanded that all the ashtrays and matches be removed from her suite.

Officially, she was in Taiwan to lecture and to raise funds for the Thatcher Foundation. But, according to a Philip Morris representative on the island, her presence was useful to the corporation because of her access to the highest echelons of government. 'She was seen by the president, who gave a state banquet,' the representative told Granada TV's *World In Action*. 'She had a private meeting with the prime minister and the foreign minister. She was accepted and seen at every level. She came at a very interesting juncture. The Taiwanese were addressing the issue of entering the World Trading Community. They were perhaps not clear which way they should go. But they got a very clear signal from her that this was what the rest of the trading world expected. It wasn't a lecture, it was a very friendly piece of advice.'[34]

In her main speech Lady Thatcher called for the removal of all import barriers. 'The faster you go, the more positively the rest of the world will respond,' she said. It was sweet music to Philip Morris's ears. S. Chung, the company's Taiwan-based executive, said she had made 'a very good point'.[35]

Taiwan's proposed anti-tobacco law has been delayed and at the end of 1994 was still not on the statute book. It was just one of several countries – including China, Korea, Kazakhstan and Japan – whose tobacco markets Philip Morris was keen on breaking into. And young teenagers were their target customers.

Lady Thatcher was a willing and active paid ambassador for their interests. Everyone who knows her testifies that her consultancy with Philip Morris was no passive affair. It was not in her nature to be laid-back and sanguine about a job of work. 'One thing you can be sure about,' said a friend, 'is that she has not been hired as some kind of ornament or decoration for the company.'

For anti-tobacco campaigners her $1 million contract was 'shameful'. The protests were long and loud; among her critics was Tory MP Roger Sims, who described her appointment as 'astonishing' and 'irresponsible'.[36] Doctors and cancer victims wrote to Mrs Thatcher requesting an explanation. None of them received a reply. The comedian Roy Castle, a life-long Conservative, who had campaigned for Margaret Thatcher, was shocked and dismayed. At an awards ceremony in November 1992, he refused to meet her. 'I would be accused of double standards if I shook her hand or posed with her,' he said. 'I'm very angry about cigarettes and what they do to young people in the Third World.'[37] In July 1994, Roy Castle died of lung cancer.

The great irony was not just that she was a non-smoker and did not even like other people in the same room to smoke. It was that while she was prime minister she actively sought to protect vulnerable young teenagers from companies like Philip Morris. In January 1989, she launched a government campaign aimed at halving the number of young smokers by 1993. 'It is for me to emphasise, particularly to young people,' she said, 'the message that smoking kills. Smoking kills. About 95 per cent of those who die from lung cancer are smokers and for most the habit is acquired before adulthood.'[38]

That she should take money from the manufacturers of Marlboro may have been shocking to anti-smoking campaigners. But to any serious student of Thatcherism it should not be too surprising. After all, she was merely lobbying for a company to operate in the open market-place. And being paid for it showed she had a market worth. She was being a Thatcherite. Her speeches in the Far East imploring governments to abolish import duties and open up markets may have helped Philip Morris Inc. But she would argue she was simply promoting the Thatcherite creed. She wanted to preserve her legacy, not just for her contemporary political reputation but also for the history books.

The Memoirs

As soon as Mrs Thatcher left 10 Downing Street, it was apparent that one of her most lasting monuments to Thatcherism would be her political memoirs. Her first thought was of revenge. 'We knew that there were voices close to her from the very start,' said literary agent Michael Sissons, 'who were trying to urge her to write a short-term, splenetic book, whacking the ice-pick into the people who had been responsible for her demise.'[39] But she decided against the idea. 'No,' she told ITN News in June 1991, 'I will one day be able to write it but it would be too hurtful to too many people.'

Instead, she chose a more considered approach. 'We are not dashing into the memoirs,' she said. 'We are making quite certain the memoirs will be a vigorous intellectual record of what we did and what happened.'[40]

However, the book was also lucrative. Every publisher was interested and a multimillion-pound advance on royalties beckoned. It needed delicate, decisive and astute negotiation skills to pull off the deal.

Margaret Thatcher immediately appointed Mark her chief adviser and appeared uninterested in the financial aspects of the project. 'Let Mark deal with it,' she said, waving her hand impatiently. This was not greeted with great glee by her friends. On 4 January 1991, six weeks after she had left Downing Street, Alan Clark, the former Conservative minister and military historian, went to see her in her temporary office at Great College Street, Westminster. A paid-up member of the 'One of Us' club, he was a front-runner to write the book. But she had second thoughts and so during their talk Clark changed the subject to finance. He had heard from agents that multimillion-pound figures were being bandied about like Monopoly money. 'Apparently Mark has been winding her up,' Clark later recorded in his diaries, and saying the book's value 'could be as much as £20 million'. Clark was uneasy about how it was being handled. 'I'm doubtful about all this,' he noted. 'It's tempting, I can see, to allow yourself to be regarded as a "property". But slightly demeaning for the premier politician of the western world.'[41]

Two days later a gathering of Mrs Thatcher's friends and confidants assembled for dinner at Alan Clark's magnificent home, Saltwood Castle, Kent. Among the guests were Richard Ryder, the Conservative chief whip, his wife, Caroline, a former secretary to Mrs Thatcher, Lord Deedes, former editor of the *Daily Telegraph*, and cabinet minister Michael Howard. Towards the end of the dinner the conversation turned to the thorny question of the memoirs. 'There was some desultory talk about "the book",' recalled Clark. 'There was agreement on the general "problem" of Mark.'[42]

The subsequent negotiations were a protracted and unhappy saga. Initially, Mark agreed that his mother needed a literary agent. So he arranged for a 'beauty contest' of four prospective agents to be interviewed by 'Three Wise Men' – himself, Lord McAlpine, former treasurer of the Tory Party, and Sir Michael Richardson, chairman of City stockbrokers Smith New Court. After the literary agents were sent an elaborate questionnaire, an all-day meeting was arranged for a Saturday in London. The participants were sworn to secrecy. It was postponed several times but eventually cancelled by Mark. 'I can get a better deal than any agent,' he boasted.

In fact, secret parallel negotiations were already under way with Macmillan Scribner books, an imprint of the American firm owned by Robert Maxwell. They had a reputation for publishing high-quality non-fiction books and saw their list as the ideal home for Margaret Thatcher's account of her years as prime minister.

Macmillan were ahead of the pack because of an introduction by Lord Brownlow, a wealthy Lincoln-shire landowner and close friend of the Thatchers. Brownlow, who once lent Margaret Thatcher a stunning silver plate collection worth £2 million while

she was prime minister, arranged for her to meet
Macmillan executives in mid-January 1991 to discuss the project. The meeting was a success. Mrs
Thatcher got on extremely well with Robert Stewart,
the commissioning editor, partly because of his knowledge of English history, and there was an immediate
personal rapport. She also liked Macmillan because
they had published the memoirs of George Shultz, the
former US secretary of state, whom she had met at a
dinner given in her honour at the White House. He
recommended them.

Margaret Thatcher was keen to proceed, and outlined
her view of the book. 'I want it to be a serious book
which will contribute to history,' she said. She concluded
the discussion by telling the Macmillan executives to
negotiate with her son. 'Mark manages all my business
affairs,' she said. She also informed them that Hugh
Thurston, her banker, and Leonard Day, her accountant,
would deal with the financial detail of the deal.

Stewart then had several conversations and meetings
with Mark about the book. 'What we found out fairly
quickly was that he didn't know what he was doing,'
recalled the editor. 'He didn't know how to be an
agent because he had no experience and did not
know what was involved in terms of planning a
schedule for negotiations. It made those negotiations
very difficult and vague. It was almost an attitude of
"Take it or leave it".' The legendary American literary
agent Irving 'Swifty' Lazar took the same view. 'The
son is a fly in the ointment,' he said at the time. 'The
son thinks he can be the agent. He's decided he knows
all about publishing, and he's an amateur.'[43]

Two weeks later Mark Thatcher, Steve Tipping and
Hugh Thurston flew to New York to meet Macmillan
to discuss the book. A special lunch was laid on by

the publishers, cooked by Maxwell's own chef. Mark dominated the conversation. He tends to babble when he is nervous and this occasion was no exception. He talked incessantly in his characteristic rapid-fire style, in between gulps of red wine.

'We want a great deal of money for this project,' he said. 'And I'm talking really big money.' He added that the book should be a monument to his mother.

'He was basking in her glory. He was also very imperious and sounded like a Saudi Arabian crown prince,' said a former Maxwell executive involved in the negotiations. Mark's attitude did not endear him to the Macmillan editors, who regularly dealt with former presidents and business tycoons. 'Genuinely successful people,' one said, 'don't need to boast about their achievements.'

Mark was Mrs Thatcher's principal agent but other members of her inner circle also became involved in the negotiations. Chief among them was Hugh Thurston, her Jersey-based banker. In March 1991, Thurston and Tipping flew to New York and met Maxwell himself at the Waldorf Astoria to discuss the financial aspects of the project. 'We don't want an agent, just a reputable publisher,' said Thurston. He told Maxwell that he wanted the advance payments and royalties to be paid into an offshore company, specially set up as a subsidiary of Macmillan. The publisher agreed. 'I would do anything to get my prime minister's book,' he told them. 'She is a wonderful patriot.'

But the negotiations were going painfully slowly because Mark continued to change his mind and shift the agenda. And so Jeffrey Archer brought in George Greenfield, the respected literary agent, as an adviser. Greenfield, a wily and highly experienced exponent of his craft, went with Lord Archer to see

Margaret Thatcher, Denis and Mark at their Belgravia home in Chester Square. It was a frustrating meeting. Denis leaned against the mantelpiece pouring gin and tonic while Mark sat silent, keeping his countenance. Greenfield did his best to provide astute counsel but was constantly interrupted by Mrs Thatcher in clipped, acerbic tones. He walked away from the meeting exasperated by her uncharacteristic indecisiveness. Still, they agreed with his recommendation that discussions with Macmillan should continue.

In April 1991, Robert Maxwell took over the negotiations for Macmillan. His stockbroker, Sir Michael Richardson, chairman of Smith New Court, telephoned the Macmillan office from the Lyford Cay country club in the Bahamas, of which Mark was also a member. Richardson, a long-time confidant of both Mrs Thatcher and Maxwell, said her son was unreliable and he would play an intermediary role to smooth the path.

Maxwell was desperately keen to win the commission and was often in a state of tension and anxiety. 'I must have this book. I want my prime minister,' the tycoon once shouted. 'He was so desperate to be accepted and he saw the Thatcher book as a route to that,' said a source close to him at the time.

The press baron had a close and curiously friendly relationship with Margaret Thatcher. 'Maxwell talked constantly about his respect and admiration for her,' said a source involved in the negotiations. 'He had done an important favour for her years ago and she was very grateful to him. He never said what it was but it was obviously quite significant.'

Another source said: 'Maxwell was keen but he thought it unlikely that Mrs Thatcher would want him as the publisher. He liked her and said how helpful she was to big business in the 1980s.'

As for Mrs Thatcher, 'She told me she had no problems in being published by Maxwell,' said a Macmillan source. 'She said she admired Maxwell as a businessman and was not concerned about the attacks on her by the Mirror newspapers.' Her only public comment was after the publisher's death in late 1991: 'Mr Maxwell kept me informed about what was happening in Eastern European countries and what their leaders were thinking.'[44]

It was not difficult to see why Maxwell and Margaret Thatcher admired each other. They saw each other as self-made people, outside the class-ridden British establishment. She respected wealthy, flamboyant and powerful business tycoons who fought their way up. Maxwell dealt with her as a head of government rather than as leader of the Tory Party. He was also commercially grateful to her for two key policies. The first was her reform of the trade-union laws which he applied ruthlessly to his own employees. The second was the privatization of British Airways, which enabled him to buy British Helicopters International from the government for £30 million.

Although Mark was acting for Mrs Thatcher, Maxwell treated him like a domestic servant or medium-rank aide. 'Come along, my boy,' he would say. Yet Mark continued to play the primary role and remained in charge of the financial arrangements. 'My mother must have money,' he said. He wanted $10 million for world rights, apart from Japan. He proposed $1.5 million on signature of contract, $4.25 million on delivery of the manuscript and $4.25 million on publication of the book. On royalties, he wanted 17 per cent for hardback sales and 15 per cent for paperback.

The self-appointed literary agent held out on the $10 million figure as late as 22 May 1991. But the delays were diminishing the book's value. This enabled Maxwell to offer $8 million plus 'editorial and research expenses' for three books, two volumes of political memoirs and an illustrated history book entitled *England's Heritage*. This was accepted, and on 28 May 1991 a 'handshake contract' was agreed between Mark Thatcher and Robert Maxwell.

A secret undertaking was that Mark Thatcher wanted a commission or 'finder's fee', as he called it. 'I want to be specific about this,' said a Maxwell executive directly involved in the deal. 'We never actually said "plus one million for Mark". We called it expenses or something like that. It was never spoken openly, but I knew Mark wanted a million dollars because this information was passed on to me. He wanted it as a finder's fee and so in a way there was nothing illegal about it.'

Macmillan drew up a draft agreement and on 4 June 1991 Mark Thatcher and George Greenfield met Maxwell and his executives at 10.30am in his penthouse suite at the Mirror Group offices, Holborn Circus, to finalize the deal. Mark made it clear that he was in charge of the tax provisions and financial arrangements. He said the Inland Revenue was happy with the advance and future royalties being paid into an offshore company. This was part of a complex arrangement to sell the copyright to the offshore firm. Maxwell confirmed his prior agreement, and a letter of intent was signed by Greenfield and Mark, on his mother's behalf. They then shook hands and the delighted Macmillan team trooped off for a celebration lunch.

On Wednesday, 12 June, Macmillan formally agreed to the conditions. But suddenly, the deal collapsed when Mark Thatcher received a fax that the deal was off. Valiant attempts by Macmillan to recover the deal were then sunk. Just as well really as five months later Cap'n Bob took his final plunge.

Mark Thatcher, quite wrongly, blamed Greenfield for the Maxwell débâcle and sacked him. The truth was that Mark and Sir Michael Richardson had been privately talking to Marvin Josephson, a high-powered New York literary agent and friend of former president Ronald Reagan, and conducting discreet parallel negotiations. This was borne out less than a week later, on 18 June 1991, when Josephson signed up Mrs Thatcher as a client of his company, International Creative Management Inc.

Within a few days publishers were invited to bid. Macmillan again entered the fray and in August offered $6 million. But Josephson would not even return Macmillan's telephone calls. Instead he went to Rupert Murdoch and cut a deal with HarperCollins for £3.5 million. Thurston was livid about the outcome because he believed the Macmillan proposal was excellent and he resented Mark's antics.

Other friends of Mrs Thatcher were also angry. They believed she could have secured a much better commission. 'We should have closed the deal in the first two weeks while people were being very silly indeed,' said Lord Archer. 'We could have got all the silly people in one room and made them bid against each other and I think we would have got a silly figure.'[45] Irving Lazar, the veteran literary agent, agreed: 'When [Mark] had the chance to strike he didn't. . . . What [Lady Thatcher] doesn't realize is that there's a hot moment when you can get a lot of money.'[46]

Michael Sissons, a seasoned literary agent with Peters, Fraser & Dunlop, summed it up best: 'This was, unquestionably, the most saleable autobiography of our times. Not since de Gaulle has anyone been involved in world affairs at the very highest level for such an extraordinary length of time. . . . So the project initially had enormous value and to see that frittered away was immensely depressing. The value just seemed to fade because of the bad publicity, the indecision and the aura that Mark Thatcher's involvement gave it.'[47]

The essence of the problem was that, as always with his mother's private affairs, Mark wanted to be major-domo, to use his father's apt description. Despite his minimal knowledge of how to be a literary agent, he was adamant that only he could faithfully represent and protect Mrs Thatcher's interests. And so, far from master-minding the operation, he master-meddled. The result was an atmosphere of indecision, unreality and confusion.

Eventually, Mrs Thatcher settled down to write the book, assisted by her staff. By late December 1992 a first draft was complete and she flew with Mark, Carol and Denis to the Bahamas, partly to celebrate Christmas but also to work on the manuscript. She did not enjoy her stay in the sun-soaked Caribbean, and would be seen sitting near the beach, impatiently tapping her fingers.

Her son loved the Bahamas. He had been visiting the tax haven since the spring of 1991 and enjoyed rubbing shoulders with the 'big rich'. It was his kind of place. 'It's the Guernsey of America and a pirates' cove,' said one banker.

Apart from the casinos, the central focus for the tax-avoiding tycoons is the Lyford Cay country club in Nassau, whose members include Mohamed Al-Fayed. Mark Thatcher was desperately keen to join the exclusive club. 'It's a very money-orientated place and very snooty,' said one member. 'It is gutted with billionaires. Very few members are worth less than £10 million, and the committee has to agree to your membership.'

Mark joined the club on the recommendation of Sir John Templeton, a multimillionaire financier knighted by Mrs Thatcher in 1986. Sir John, an active Christian and author of books like *Riches for the Mind and Spirit*, wrote a letter to the committee on her son's behalf and in the summer of 1991 Mark became a member. This caused some disquiet in the club, because his application was pushed through without consultation, but Mark was delighted. However, it was not long before he was indulging in some classic Thatcher Junior behaviour and alienating other members. 'I'm very annoyed with them,' he complained. 'They're not giving me prime starting times on the golf course.'

While Mark consorted with other wealthy visitors, his mother remained in her rented house completing her memoirs. She could not wait to return to London. *The Downing Street Years* was published in the autumn of 1993 and became both a best-seller and an enduring legacy of the former prime minister. But its success was despite rather than because of her son's involvement.

Gifts from the Gulf

Lady Thatcher wanted her memoirs to be more than just a history book. She viewed them as a political instrument to promote her views and preserve her power base. But she also had secret commercial ambitions and it was to the Gulf that she looked.

The United Arab Emirates had always been one of Margaret Thatcher's favourite regions, both politically and commercially. She was a great admirer of Sheikh Zayed bin Sultan al-Nahayan, the imperious Ruler of Abu Dhabi, and was a regular visitor, even after leaving 10 Downing Street. Her son also looked upon the region with some affection, as it was in nearby Oman that he had helped secure the university contract for his client Cementation International.

While prime minister, Margaret Thatcher occasionally cultivated her diplomatic ties with Sheikh Zayed, while assisting her son's business interests and connections in the Gulf. She had, after all, hand-written a letter to Zayed, accompanied by her signed photograph, introducing her son as her unofficial ambassador. 'I have asked my son to convey to you my personal message of warm regards and good wishes,' she wrote. The Ruler of Abu Dhabi responded by helping her son with his commercial activities in the Gulf.

Mrs Thatcher also developed close ties with other UAE ministers. In 1982 she was visited at her home in Flood Street, Chelsea, by Dr Mana bin Said al-Oteiba, the UAE oil minister. Al-Oteiba must have been keen to cultivate Margaret Thatcher as he gave her a Kutchinsky ruby and diamond necklace, then worth half a million pounds.

Most of Mrs Thatcher's jewellery gifts came from Arab dignitaries. During seventy-seven official foreign trips to fifty-four countries, she acquired a vast treasure of presents and trophies. Most notable were a heavy silver Omani coffee pot and a jewelled desk set from Abu Dhabi. She was also given a perfect pearl necklace by Prince Khalid of Saudi Arabia and, in 1985, a glittering gold bracelet, encrusted with diamonds and rubies, by the Sultan of Brunei.[48] Under government rules she was not allowed to keep the gifts, and many of them languish in a vault at 10 Downing Street, are available for use only by future prime ministers and their spouses.

One of Margaret Thatcher's favourite presents from a Gulf ruler was a stunning necklace worth £1.2 million from Sultan Qaboos of Oman. She was delighted with the gift and often wore it at state occasions. After leaving office, she was forced to hand it back to the sultan. So in November 1991, just before she visited the United Arab Emirates, she asked one of her trusted advisers to enquire whether the UAE would consider buying her another similar necklace from Asprey, as she loved the original so much. Her request was taken seriously by the UAE government, according to a source in the presidential court in Abu Dhabi. A meeting took place in Paris, but they could not agree terms and Lady Thatcher never received her beloved necklace.

Towards the end of her premiership, plans were laid to maintain her Gulf connections. There was speculation in Margaret Thatcher's inner circle as to what she might do after she left office. The consensus was that she would lead the Conservatives into a fourth successive administration and then bow out gracefully. One of their most extraordinary ideas was to make her the president of the Bank of Credit and Commerce International (BCCI).

In the late summer of 1990, while she was still in office, her financial advisers and Mark devised a secret plan to take over BCCI. They believed they could run it better themselves. They must have been unaware that the bank's other services included laundering drugs money, fraud, funding illegal arms deals and stealing customers' savings.

BCCI's fortunes were closely linked to and bound up with Sheikh Zayed. It was the dictatorial Ruler of Abu Dhabi who founded the bank in 1972 with Agha Hasan Abedi, a Pakistani financier. Zayed funded BCCI and was its head. He supplied $6.9 million of the $10m start-up capital and his family later held a 77 per cent controlling shareholding.

The crimes of BCCI were no great secret to the regulatory authorities in the 1980s. Billions of pounds of investors' funds were disappearing down financial black holes and laundered through the Cayman Islands. But the biggest bank fraud in world financial history was not made public until 1991. 'BCCI was operated as a corrupt, criminal organization throughout its entire 19-year history,' said Robert Morgenthau, the New York district attorney, on announcing the indictment against the bank. 'It systematically falsified its records. It knowingly allowed itself to be used to launder illegal income of drug sellers and other criminals and it paid bribes and kickbacks to other public officials.'[49]

Margaret Thatcher already had links with BCCI investors when she was prime minister. Her main contact was with Nazmi Virani, whose property and leisure company, Control Securities, was dependent largely on loans from BCCI. An Asian who settled in Britain after being expelled from Uganda, Virani made substantial donations to the Tory Party. 'I paid the money to Conservative Central Office over many years,' he said.[50] In 1986 he met Margaret Thatcher and Norman Tebbit, then Conservative Party chairman, on several occasions. She admired his entrepreneurial spirit, which had made him one of the richest people in Britain. 'Mrs Thatcher had a soft spot for Virani,' said one former BCCI official.[51]

Unfortunately, much of his wealth was accumulated by fraud and deception. In May 1994, Virani was jailed for two and a half years for seven offences – one of false accounting and six of furnishing false information to Price Waterhouse, BCCI's auditors. Essentially, he had conspired to help BCCI deceive the auditors into believing that the bank was solvent.

In return Virani received huge loans to prop up his companies and cash payments for himself.[52] Through Virani, Margaret Thatcher met several BCCI officials and investors.

Her financial aides believed she had the aptitude to run an investment and commercial bank. In order to facilitate the deal, Sheikh Zayed needed to be approached because his family owned 77 per cent of the shares. His approval was crucial for both the take-over and this new version of BCCI.

The Thatcher camp's approach was received with some enthusiasm in Abu Dhabi. This resulted in a remarkable meeting at the Inn on the Park Hotel in Mayfair in the late summer of 1990. From Mrs Thatcher's stable were her son, Mark, and Hugh Thurston, her banker. From Abu Dhabi was Ali Shorafa, a former director of the sheikh's court, a one-time BCCI shareholder and the closest confidant and adviser to Sheikh Zayed. He was also one of the founders of BCCI. According to sources in Sheikh Zayed's court, the purpose of the meeting was to discuss concrete terms with Ali Shorafa and to persuade him that their proposals were realistic and beneficial to the bank.

Mark Thatcher and Hugh Thurston were very keen on the idea. Thurston presented an outline of the plan. He said the first stage was to conduct an extensive internal audit and due diligence into BCCI. This would take a year and cost about £3–4 million. At first Ali Shorafa was keen on the idea and reported back to Sheikh Zayed. But sources close to Zayed say he was not happy and said the 'funds were not available' for such an investigation.

Unperturbed, the Thatchers proposed a new two-part deal whereby BCCI would enter into a joint-venture agreement with the Royal Bank of Scotland. This was because BCCI had lost a valuable ally when the Bank of America had dropped its corresponding-bank status with it, and was anxious to find a new partner. The idea was that the Royal Bank of Scotland should become the new corresponding bank. This meant they would introduce new business and clients to each other. A key figure would be Lord Younger, chairman of the Royal Bank of Scotland. As he had been Mrs Thatcher's defence secretary from 1986 until 1989 and her campaign manager in the 1990 Tory leadership election, her camp was confident he would agree to the deal. However, there is no evidence to suggest that the Royal Bank of Scotland or its officers had any knowledge of or were party to these negotiations.

The second stage was that Mrs Thatcher would become president of BCCI after she retired from public life. Sir Alan Walters and other financiers close to her would join her as directors. As part of this arrangement, BCCI would acquire a royal charter, which would have needed approval from the Queen (presumably it would have been known as the Royal British Bank of Commerce and Credit International!).

Ali Shorafa again responded with great interest and said he would need to discuss their proposals with Sheikh Zayed. But then Zayed withdrew co-operation before the Bank of England closed down BCCI in July 1991 for fraud, corruption and money-laundering. Zayed's decision caused much annoyance in the Thatcher camp, which was still enthusiastic about the idea. However, the truth was that Margaret Thatcher had been saved from a humiliating commercial and political catastrophe by Hugh Thurston's astute decision to insist on an investigation into BCCI.

Mrs Thatcher herself remained enamoured of BCCI. In November 1991, four months after the bank was closed down, she met Sheikh Zayed during her tour of the Gulf. During their meeting she told him she thought BCCI had been treated unfairly by the Bank of England and John Major: 'I believe you have been badly mistreated by my successor.' Their conversation was translated and a note of it was sent to 10 Downing Street.

Nearby Kuwait also had a special place in Mrs Thatcher's heart. She had been prime minister when Iraq invaded the oil-rich Gulf state in August 1990. And she was the politician who, according to President Bush, stiffened the allies' resolve during the build-up to the Gulf war. 'Remember, George,' she told him. 'This is no time to go wobbly.'[53] In return, the ruling al-Sabah royal family were eternally grateful to her. They named her '*Um*', an Arabic term meaning 'Mother of All' or 'Guardian of the Nation', and even named a street in Kuwait City after her. Mark, in contrast, was known as '*Um Quais' ah*' (prounounced 'Kissach').

The Kuwaitis were equally grateful to President Bush and his government. In April 1993, after losing the presidency, George Bush flew to Kuwait with his wife, his sons Neil and Marvin, and entourage to be awarded the country's highest medal by the emir. The al-Sabahs, most of whom had fled to the Bahamas when the Iraqi troops moved in, saw themselves as in Bush's debt. At official functions he was presented with dozens of expensive gifts, notably watches and necklaces, valued at thousands of dollars.[54]

The former president himself did not cash in on the spoils of war and returned to the United States. But his two sons had no such inhibitions. Neil was involved in two Houston oil-related firms – the Ultraflote Corporation, in which he is a partner, and the Link

Group – who were both seeking business in Kuwait. His older brother, Marvin, was hired by Murphy and Associates, a Washington-based consulting firm, as a lobbyist for defence firms seeking a contract to build an electronic fence.[55]

Kuwait's infrastructure might have been wrecked by the war, but its massive oil reserves meant that billion-dollar contracts to rebuild the country were there for the taking. The Bush sons and former US public officials did not wait long before attempting to exploit the financial fruits of military victory. But some refused to do so. Norman Schwarzkopf, commander-in-chief of the allied forces, was offered hundred-million-dollar commissions by US defence firms to lobby their case in Kuwait. He declined. 'In the Arab world, your position in the government may get you through the door, but it's the personal relationship that gets you the contract,' he told the *New Yorker*. 'I've developed that personal relationship in Kuwait. I know that all I've got to do is go to the Emir and say "Hey, I want you to do this" and he will. There are people who have made use of such special connections, and I don't begrudge them. But don't ask me to betray the trust these people have in me. I won't do it. American men and women were willing to die in Kuwait. Why should I profit from their sacrifice?'[56]

There were also opportunities for the Thatcher family to profit from the war dividend. But they were exploited in a different way. In October 1991, eight months after British and American troops drove Saddam Hussein's army out of Kuwait, the Emir of Kuwait visited London. He was anxious to see Mrs Thatcher to thank her for her steadfast support during the war. It was arranged that they would meet for breakfast at the Conrad Hotel on Chelsea harbour.

Mark Thatcher then telephoned the Kuwaiti embassy and said he wanted the meeting to be at his mother's house in Belgravia. The Gulf visitors were offended by this brash request and so the breakfast remained at the Conrad. The meeting was a success and the Emir invited Mrs Thatcher to Kuwait. The only blemish was Mark's abrupt manner, notably his insistence that non-Kuwaitis should be excluded from the room.

The following month the former prime minister and her son did indeed go to Kuwait on a triumphant three-day 'state visit'. Again Mark was prominent in the arrangements, running the show in his characteristically strident manner. Even the Kuwaitis found his behaviour difficult, to say the least. Apart from the gratitude bestowed on Mrs Thatcher, more tangible topics were discussed with the al-Sabahs. It was proposed that a 'Thatcher Committee' be established. This would consist of four Kuwaiti businessmen, four British businessmen and members of Mrs Thatcher's private office, including Mark. Its aim was to promote trade between the United Kingdom and Kuwait. But, according to a source in the Kuwaiti embassy, the Foreign Office expressed some disquiet about the idea, particularly about Mark's participation, and the project was shelved.

Mrs Thatcher and her son enjoyed the generous hospitality of the al-Sabahs and several introductions to the indigenous business community were arranged. One of the most prominent and influential was Souad M. al-Sabah, a very powerful businesswoman. She had created a successful career as chairwoman of Action International Consultancy Bureau Ltd, a firm of consultants based in Kuwait. Their clients include AT & T, General Dynamics, Marconi Space Systems, British Petroleum and construction firms Bovis and

AMEC. Unsurprisingly, oil was Souad al-Sabah's speciality, and well-placed Kuwaiti sources say commercial connections were forged with Mark Thatcher, or at least discussed.

During their visit Souad al-Sabah introduced the former prime minister and her son to her managing director, Ahmed El-Mokadem, an Egyptian economist. As El-Mokadem had a house in Guildford, Surrey, they kept in touch and the Egyptian monetarist attended private dinners with Mark and his mother. 'I do know Mark and have met him several times, but it has always been social,' El-Mokadem said in a telephone interview. 'There is no business relationship between us. We do not deal with wheelers and dealers. We don't operate in that way. We are a highly professional and serious company and in my opinion Mark Thatcher is not a good businessman.'[57]

It was no secret that Mrs Thatcher and her devoted son were also soliciting funds for an organization that, like a newly born political party, was struggling and stuttering into life: the Thatcher Foundation. Kuwait was a good location to secure the funds. Grateful local merchants were falling over themselves to hand over large amounts of cash to 'Um', second only to George Bush as the saviour of their nation – and businesses. The most enthusiastic group of financial donors were the al-Ghanims, the second most powerful family in Kuwait and political and commercial rivals to the al-Sabahs.

As the agents for Ford and Bayer in Kuwait, the al-Ghanims were fabulously, and ostentatiously, wealthy. Some pledged hundreds of thousands of pounds each to the foundation. 'Lady Thatcher is now part of our nation's family,' said Fouad al-Ghanim, a BMW car dealer with construction interests. 'I could call twenty businessmen right now and each would give £100,000.' Fouad himself agreed to donate £100,000. Strangely, his money was not collected. 'Mark Thatcher was supposed to be in contact with our people but our fund organiser has heard nothing from him,' he said.[58] But other Kuwaiti donations were banked. Mrs Thatcher may not have been prime minister when British forces bombed Baghdad and helped liberate Kuwait City, but her foundation was now reaping the rewards of her strong support for the war. And the way he amassed and presided over the gold filling up the coffers of her foundation would prove to be one of Mark Thatcher's most controversial deals.

The Foundation

Even before leaving 10 Downing Street, Margaret Thatcher envisaged the idea of a vehicle to preserve and continue her political vision. The foundation would have a dual function. It would spread the gospel of Thatcherism internationally, particularly in Eastern Europe. More significantly, from her point of view, the foundation would be a monument to her career and ideology. Her place in the history books has always been very important to Margaret Thatcher. And the notion of political immortality through Thatcherism living on beyond the grave has always appealed to her. That was the driving force behind the establishment of the Thatcher Foundation.

At first, some of her close friends questioned the need for a foundation. Charles Price, US ambassador to the UK from 1983 until 1989, and a director of British

Airways and Hanson plc, argued it was unnecessary and in the USA would face direct competition with countless other think-tanks. 'She could have put together a blue-ribbon panel of British businesspeople who would have helped her organize her office, get a staff and get it all done,' said Price. 'There were plenty of dynamic people around to help.'[59]

However, the former ambassador's advice was disregarded and the search for revenue began almost immediately. 'We've got to raise in excess of $20 million,' said Lord McAlpine, former Tory Party treasurer and head of the board of trustees of the UK Thatcher Foundation (other members included former arts minister Lord Gowrie and Sir Geoffrey Leigh, chairman of Allied Properties).[60]

As Mrs Thatcher had asked her son to handle all her financial affairs, he was the chief fund-raiser. But his style did not endear him to even her most devoted business admirers. One chief executive of a major American corporation turned him down flat. 'If my company donates to the Thatcher Foundation, we will give a donation on the basis of a proper approach by Mrs Thatcher,' he said at the time. 'We are not going to give money after being propositioned by her son.'

Mark's attitude when he approached senior Conservative businessmen and financiers was that it was now pay-back time. Margaret Thatcher had been generous to big business. Now it was the turn of big business to be generous to Margaret Thatcher. At one fund-raising meeting he read out a list of high-powered chairmen and chief executives who had made their fortunes in the 1980s and asked how much they were donating. When informed of the amounts, he replied, 'Chickenfeed. My mother made them. Now they have to pay up.'[61] Just before her trip to the Far East, he telephoned a Hong Kong millionaire tycoon and told him, 'It's time to pay up for Mumsie.'[62] When one leading industrialist offered to raise £7 million for the foundation, Mark was dismissive. 'That's not good enough,' he sniffed contemptuously. 'I have someone else who can offer more.'[63]

By the second week of April 1991, chairmen and chief executives were reporting back these horror stories to Margaret Thatcher's private office and her political friends. 'Our first thought was to talk to Margaret about him,' said one, 'because we felt his activities were preventing the foundation getting off the ground. But we knew she would not listen.' They were also scared to confront her, because of her usual stone-faced reaction. 'Some people have tried to do so,' said Charles Price, 'first questioning the wisdom of a foundation and then of having family members involved. It kind of goes into thin air.'[64]

As an alternative tactic, some of her closest disciples, notably a former senior Downing Street official and a minister, briefed the *Sunday Times*. The result was a front-page story on 21 April 1991 with a banner headline: 'Mark Is "Wrecking Your Life", Friends Tell Thatcher'. An accompanying feature article contained strong criticisms of him, on a non-attributable basis, of course.

This secret briefing had little effect as Mark continued on his insensitive path of propositioning usually sympathetic businessmen. But industrialists who normally handed over thousands of pounds of shareholders' money to the Conservative Party over lunch at the Savoy Grill, were not so happy to do the same for the foundation.

The Thatcher stalwarts Lord Hanson and Lord King were conspicuous by their absence as donors to the foundation. Lord King's BA was viewed as an almost automatic benefactor, but when the airline's director of public affairs, David Burnside, was asked whether it would contribute, he replied, 'Not on your life.' The result was a potentially catastrophic shortage of funds, which threatened to sink the vessel before it was even launched. Officially, the delay was blamed on problems with negotiations over its plans for charitable status. But the truth was that Mark's lobbying tactics were dramatically counter-productive.

By June 1991, prospects for the foundation were bleak. There was no money, office, staff or even any headed note-paper. It was a woeful failure, particularly when compared to its nearest model, the Konrad Adenauer Foundation, which by 1991 had a worldwide staff of 1,700 and a budget of £230 million. But Margaret Thatcher was determined to proceed. On 28 June 1991, the day that she announced she was standing down as MP for Finchley at the next election, she said that branch offices of the foundation would be set up in several European capitals. 'It is going to embody all of those things which I've explained and believe in,' she said. 'How to roll forward the frontiers of freedom and how to bring it about. Educating people about what it is all about, giving practical help to the people of Eastern Europe who are trying to do it.'[65]

A thirteen-page colour brochure was compiled and produced by Sir Tim Bell's company. But even then the shortage of funds delayed the grand opening. This was decided for them on 22 July 1991, when a secretary inadvertently sent out the foundation's manifesto to the press. The glossy document outlined the basic idea of the foundation – to teach Thatcherism to the former Communist states and developing nations. Backed by a £10 million budget, this would be realized by holding conferences and seminars, distributing grants and scholarships and commissioning research. The co-ordination and implementation of these services would be arranged by the branch offices in the capital cities of the various countries.

After its premature launch, the brochure was distributed to targeted Conservative businessmen with a discreet appeal for donations. Eventually, funds were forthcoming. But this was due to Margaret, rather than Mark, Thatcher. During her Far East tour in August and September, she secured donations from Li Ka-Shing and other Hong Kong magnates, the Sultan of Brunei, and several corporations in Japan, Korea and Taiwan.

How these funds were handled by the US branch of the foundation, in particular, would show just how dangerous it was for Mark Thatcher to be so influential in her financial affairs. As soon as she decided on the foundation, an application for charitable status was lodged with the UK Charity Commission. If granted, this would ensure tax relief and incentives for the donors and tax concessions for the foundation. The stumbling block was that the foundation would have to demonstrate that it did not have political objectives. Under the rules, 'A trust for the education of the public in one particular set of political principles is not charitable.' Clearly, for the Thatcher Foundation *not* to have political aims would be unthinkable, and it was no surprise that on 1 May 1991 the commission refused to grant charitable status.

Despite this setback, Mrs Thatcher's lawyers devised a plan whereby its financial backers could enjoy tax benefits. Six weeks after the Charity Commission's decision, on 10 June, the Margaret Thatcher Foundation Ltd, a company limited by guarantee, whose assets were held by trustees, was set up. The trustees included Lord McAlpine, Sir Tim Bell and Lord Gowrie.

Registered at the Mayfair law firm of Glover, this reconstituted version was used to channel its donations through the Charities Aid Foundation (CAF), a separate agency which acts as a fund manager for trusts. Essentially, the CAF was persuaded that some of the foundation's aims were charitable. This enabled donors to receive tax relief and the foundation to avoid paying tax on gifts deemed for charitable purposes. In return, the CAF is trustee of the money and 'content to act on instructions from our clients, in this case, the Thatcher Foundation'.[66]

This convenient new arrangement was confirmed on 22 November 1991, with the first official meeting of the UK Thatcher Foundation's trustees and members. Chaired by Mrs Thatcher at her new office in Chesham Place, the meeting agreed the objectives and accounting procedures. One person who was noticeably absent as a trustee or even adviser was Mark Thatcher, who had been so prominent in its inception and attempted fund-raising. He attended the celebratory lunch but it had been decided not to give him any official role. His friends said Mark was 'not interested' because he was 'neither a philosophical nor a political animal'.[67]

That was certainly true. But it did not stop him becoming an active president of the US Thatcher Foundation. In early 1991, Mark Thatcher telephoned Daniel Evans, an attorney with the Indianapolis law firm of Baker and Daniels. Evans was very much 'one of us'. In 1988 he had been chairman of the National 'Dan Quayle for Vice-President' Committee and he remained a close adviser to Quayle. Thatcher asked him to draw up the US foundation's articles of incorporation because his law firm specialized in representing non-profit-making far-right-wing think-tanks like the Hudson Institute.

Evans agreed, and applied for the US foundation to be granted charitable status by the Internal Revenue Service (IRS). Its aims were to 'promote the widest possible acceptance of the principles of economic and political freedom'. It also encouraged 'strong transatlantic links between Britain, Europe and North America' and would 'foster greater contact between Western nations and those of the Middle East'. Members of the executive advisory board include Charles Wick, director of the US Information Agency under President Reagan, Dwayne Andreas, former head of chemical giant Archer Daniels Midland, Timothy Forbes, son of billionaire publisher Malcolm Forbes, and Charles Price.

In May 1991, unknown to his mother's private office, Mark Thatcher secretly arranged for the Thatcher Foundation to be registered and run in the tiny state of Liechtenstein, a tax haven where financial donors can claim massive tax relief. Apart from Mark as president, the only trustees of the Liechtenstein arm are David Wallace, his business partner and later treasurer of the US foundation, and Cornelia Ritter, a local lawyer. Those three have sole signatory rights to the trust.

This was done just in case the US or UK foundations did not achieve charitable status. 'We formed this one in Liechtenstein to have a fall-back position, shall we say,' Mark told the *Sunday Mirror*. 'If you examine the articles of incorporation, you will find they are bloody nearly word for word the same as the application to the Charity Commission and the Charities Aid Foundation in the UK.' He claimed it was 'highly unlikely' that

the Liechtenstein Thatcher Foundation would ever
be used.[68]

Setting up the charity in Liechtenstein was arranged
in great secrecy. 'I was not aware of its existence,'
said Julian Seymour, director of the UK foundation,
and one of his colleagues insisted Mrs Thatcher had
no knowledge of the central European branch. But
the former prime minister not only knew about it, but
authorized it. 'It required the written consent of my
mother,' said Mark.[69]

It was also claimed that arrangements were made
for the receipt of funds in Switzerland. This would
have the benefit of concealing the origin and size
of the contributions.[70] Mark Worthington, project
director of the UK foundation, denied this but did
acknowledge having 'various arrangements for moving
money around'.[71]

In January 1992, the US foundation was awarded
charitable status by the IRS, which meant substantial
tax relief for its financial backers. Mark lent the
foundation $15,000 to pay for legal fees to register as a
charity. This made fund-raising much easier, although
in its first year donations amounted to only $448,229.
As the UK branch received only £254,000 in outside
funds, that raised questions about the disbursal of the
estimated £3 million fees paid to Mrs Thatcher during
her overseas tours in 1991. What happened to the rest of
the money? Nobody in her private office could provide
an answer, except: 'It was always accepted that not all
her earnings would go to the Foundation.'

In Washington, it was not long before the IRS began
preliminary investigations into the US foundation.
Officials believed it was contravening laws on political
activities. 'We don't care who they [the Thatcher
Foundation] give their money to,' said Denis Broze, a

specialist in tax-exempt organizations. 'What matters is
the purpose of the donation. If the Thatcher Foundation
is simply pushing out Margaret Thatcher's ideas, that
may be a difficulty. . . . If we're talking about the
views of one person, that counts as political.'[72] On
that basis, it is amazing that the US branch acquired
charitable status in the first place.

More significantly and seriously, the US foundation
became closely linked with the private commercial
interests of Mark Thatcher. Although it was based
in Washington, the foundation's registered office was
1850 Lincoln Center, 5420 LBJ Freeway, Dallas –
the same address as Mark's Grantham Company. In
1992, when he moved his corporate office to 5847 San
Felipe Drive, Houston, the foundation moved there too.
Mark remained president and spent one day a week on
foundation business. The treasurer was David Wallace,
his business partner in Grantham and other projects.

In 1992, Wallace was a thirty-year-old financier
looking for the main chance. A graduate of the University of Texas, with a degree in real estate finance,
he had no professional or commercial training or qualifications. 'I'm trying to get my pilot's licence,' he said,
'but beyond that, I really can't think of anything.'[73] His
first job was a three-year stint as a salesman with Equity
Management, a real-estate syndication company which
went bankrupt in 1986. He then became a consultant
to the Dalfort Corporation, the parent company of
Braniff Airlines. It was there he met Bruce Leadbetter,
chairman of Braniff Airlines, and they joined forces on
investment banking projects.

After the 1987 general election, Leadbetter set up the
Grantham Company with Mark Thatcher, and Wallace
came in later as a consultant. After Leadbetter left,
Grantham was reconstituted as a separate outfit, but

using the same name, and Wallace became a full equity partner and later chief executive. He was an active director and shareholder of Emergency Networks Inc, which went bankrupt in 1992. One of his responsibilities was to liaise with its chief customer, Denver-based Alert Security, but that company also ended in insolvency, owing up to $18 million. His next venture was as chief executive of Ameristar Fuels. This corporation filed for Chapter 11 bankruptcy in 1994.

This was the commercial record of Mark Thatcher's business partner, who in 1992 became treasurer of the US Thatcher Foundation. The following year Wallace became immersed in the affairs of Ameristar Fuels as a substantial shareholder and its accounting and financial officer. He was effectively fronting for Thatcher, according to Jay Laughlin, the company's president. It was during this period that the foundation and Ameristar became financially interconnected.

In October 1993, working alongside Mark Thatcher, Wallace approached several contacts to persuade them to invest in Ameristar Fuels. One of them was Robert Higdon, the $125,000-a-year director of the US foundation in Washington. Higdon was recruited into the White House in 1984 by Michael Deaver, then deputy chief of staff, who was later investigated for improper lobbying and received a suspended three-year jail sentence for lying about his business activities.[74] After his spell with Deaver, Higdon worked at the Library of Congress and as a fund-raiser for President Reagan.

On 12 October 1993, a copy of the Ameristar prospectus arrived on Higdon's desk at the US foundation's office. Enclosed was a letter from David Wallace: 'Please give me a call after you have had an opportunity to review the enclosed.' Higdon, despite being the full-time head of an educational charity

with strong political aims, was effectively being used
on a commercial project. He responded by introducing Wallace, then foundation treasurer, to Frank
Richardson of Westray Capital in New York and
Robert Gray of Gray and Company in Miami.

That year the US foundation was used in a more
direct way to support Ameristar Fuels Inc, in which
Lady Thatcher's son had invested, according to the
firm's former president, Jay Laughlin. In February
1993, Laughlin had arranged for Mark Thatcher and
David Wallace to meet Jean Baudois, a French banker
from Caisse Nationale de Crédit Agricole. The meeting
took place over tea in the lounge of the Carlisle Hotel,
New York, where Baroness Thatcher was also staying.
It was a long afternoon discussion, with Mark trying
to persuade Baudois to invest in Ameristar Fuels. But
when the $77 bill arrived it was charged to Mark's hotel
bill, which, according to Laughlin, was paid for by the
Thatcher Foundation. Ameristar Fuels later reimbursed
the foundation for these expenses.

To what extent foundation funds were used to pay
Mark Thatcher's business expenses is one of the
questions to which the IRS sought to find answers
in 1994 when it launched an investigation into the US
foundation. The enquiry will no doubt be given the
names of the funders of Margaret Thatcher's US and
UK 'charities'. This information has been kept secret
from the public. 'I don't really feel comfortable talking
precise figures,' said Robert Higdon, 'but we are not
thinking small. It relies, you could say, on a great deal
of generous support.'[75] In 1993 this amounted to $1.3
million in donations.

The UK foundation has even utilized a legal loop-
hole to ensure that only the barest minimum details of
its finances are published. Under the 1985 Companies

Act, small private companies are granted an exemption
which allows them to file only abbreviated, limited
accounts. Ironically, it was Margaret Thatcher who
introduced this measure, designed to cut bureaucracy,
while she was prime minister. As a company limited
by guarantee, the UK foundation was able to take
advantage of this useful clause. The 1993 accounts
merely state they have £467,000 in cash and net assets
of £452,000. What's more, the directors (trustees)
opted to cancel annual general meetings and no longer
present their accounts for inspection by foundation
members. The 1993 accounts for the US branch are not
much more informative, as the list of donors has also
been withheld from the public. What is noticeable is the
high 'fund-raising expenses' and 'administrative costs'
of $253,690 – twice as much as the $127,500 paid out
in grants. Revenue for the year was $1,321,706.

The brief lives of the Thatcher Foundations have not
been happy. Some grants have been awarded – £30,000
to Enterprise Europe, £10,500 for a scheme to educate
fifty-three students from the Eastern bloc in English
public schools and $100,000 for Russian librarians to
spend eight weeks in Washington. In 1993 a total of
just £216,687 was allocated to pro-Thatcherite groups,
mainly in Eastern Europe. An active office has also
been established in Warsaw.

However, it could have been so much better. By
1994 only £6 million of the projected £10 million had
been raised for both UK and US foundations after
three years of lobbying. Fund-raising was impeded
because of Mark's inept, insensitive approaches to
normally supportive businessmen. That brought what
was supposed to be a philanthropic monument to
Thatcherism into discredit and suspicion.

In the USA, donations were more forthcoming,

with Walter Annenberg, the former US ambassador to the UK, and *Forbes* magazine being prominent benefactors. But that relative success was undermined by the use of foundation money to support Mark's involvement in Ameristar Fuels and the funds were running dry.

As in the cash shortage of the autumn of 1991, it took the former prime minister herself to help fill up the coffers. 'On occasion Lady Thatcher will go and meet prospective donors and explain what she is trying to do,' said Robert Higdon, director of the US foundation. 'She never talks money with them. We ask them to donate, but don't ask for a certain sum. They write a cheque. She is very good at it.'[76] She has put some of her own money into the US foundation to 'keep it going', according to her friend and trustee Lord McAlpine.[77] And in June 1994, she flew to Abu Dhabi to see her old friend, Sheikh Zayed bin Sultan al-Nahayan. It was fourteen years, almost to the week, since her son had been to see the benevolent ally of the Thatchers, armed with a letter of introduction from the prime minister. This time she was asking for a donation for her impoverished US foundation, but it was not forthcoming.

A Swiss Retreat

In April 1991, Mark Thatcher took time out from his activities as the foundation's financial major-domo and his mother's business manager to fulfil a long-time aim – a commercial and residential base in Switzerland. His parents knew the country well. Every August for fifteen years they spent a two-week holiday at Freudenberg

Castle, on the shore of Lake Zug, near Geneva, as the guest of Lady Eleanor Glover, the wealthy widow of former Tory MP Sir Douglas Glover.

Mark was also familiar with the country and used to half-joke about moving there if a Labour government were elected. He had been travelling to Switzerland since 1980, when he flew to Zurich to lobby bankers for sponsorship of his racing activities. He had a Crédit Suisse bank account in Geneva. On 9 November 1987, Mark and Denis were spotted flying out of Heathrow on a private plane to Geneva.[78] It was a regular journey, for in the secret Swiss bank vaults of Geneva lies Thatcher's gold.

However, it was not until the spring of 1991 that Mark established a permanent presence in bankers' paradise. It was then that he became a consultant to Compagnie Financière Espírito Santo, based in Lausanne and a wholly owned investment subsidiary of the Portuguese-owned bank. Part of his contract with Espírito Santo was that they would arrange his Swiss residency and work permit.

Banco Espírito Santo, which means 'Bank of the Holy Ghost', has a mixed reputation in the business world. Set up in October 1937, it became Portugal's most powerful bank, with the Espírito Santo family owning a 70 per cent shareholding in the company. The late 1930s and 1940s was a time of great prosperity for the bank. It became a conduit for flight capital as persecuted Jews and wealthy European aristocrats sought refuge in Portugal and planned their escape to South or North America. The family itself became aristocratically conservative and often played host to titled visitors, notably King Karol of Romania and the Duke of Windsor, who spent several months in Portugal during the Second World War.[79]

By the early 1970s Espírito Santo was hugely successful, with deposits of about $2 billion and equity of $200 million.[80] But disaster struck in March 1975, when a Socialist–Communist coalition seized power from the military junta. One afternoon Espírito Santo managers returned from lunch to find troops armed with machine-guns in the lobby. Within three months the banks had been nationalized, with senior Espírito Santo executives thrown in jail. They were charged with 'economic sabotage' but later released. The key family members regrouped in London where they planned their come-back. They established a new holding company in Luxembourg and a bank in Brazil to look after the interests of Portuguese refugees.

By 1977 the Brazil bank was sufficiently profitable to provide the capital to set up a new fund-management and private banking company in Lausanne – Compagnie Financière Espírito Santo (CFES). Ironically it was the 1975 *coup d'état* that made CFES prosper, as wealthy expatriate Portuguese were looking for management of their money in Europe.

By 1991, when Mark Thatcher became a consultant, the bank's client base had expanded to 3,000 mainly private individuals of various nationalities. It supplied them with centralized portfolio and asset-management services, looking after $1.2 billion of funds. The investments are managed on a mainly discretionary basis and include international securities and gold and silver bullion.

The CFES consultancy was a useful arrangement for Mark. The financial benefits of living in Switzerland are well-known, with income tax averaging 20 per cent and ultra-secret banking rules. Mark's salary was £80,000 a year after tax. This easily covered the £25,000 annual rent for his four-bedroomed penthouse apartment, which overlooked Lake Geneva and was only half a mile from CFES's glass-fronted office.

Mark was allowed to spend a week in every month in Lausanne on a part-time two-year contract, shrouded in classic Swiss secrecy. When asked by a newspaper what services Mark provided, Frederic Strittmatter, a senior CFES executive, replied defensively, 'We have other sons of well-known people working in our group as well as him. He is no exception. I don't see him very often but he is an international man and he travels a lot. There is nothing unusual about having more than one job. I know a lot of people in his position who live in Switzerland.'[81] But Strittmatter was a little more forthcoming when we spoke to him in Lausanne. 'His brief was to develop business in the Far East,' he told us. 'But no clients came in.' When asked why, he replied: 'Perhaps our criteria were too high.' He added that he would be happy to discuss in more detail Mark's involvement with the bank if he received permission from Mark. Regrettably, that was not forthcoming.

CFES executives may have been happy with Mark's absences but the Swiss authorities were not so satisfied. By mid-June 1992, when his work and residency permits were due for renewal, the Swiss Federal Department of Justice and Police took an active interest in his affairs. They were concerned that he had not worked or spent enough days in Switzerland. 'It is not enough to simply bring money into Switzerland,' said Jourg Kistler, special counsellor to the minister of the interior. 'You must work in the bureau of a Swiss company to justify a resident's permit. There are only a limited number and we are besieged by requests for them every day.'[82]

Mark had been granted a 'B Permit', a *'permis de*

séjour', allowing him to make Switzerland his 'permanent home base' for one year until 1 June 1992. Despite his late application for renewal, this was granted for another twelve months. It was an astonishingly lenient decision. Under Swiss law, residents have to spend most of the year in the country. As Thatcher lived and worked in Texas and travelled abroad constantly, it was self-evident he did not meet that criterion. 'Mr Thatcher knows that he has been given the benefit of the doubt over his first year in the country,' said Kistler in the summer of 1992. 'He has been told there will be a check over the coming 12 months on his movements to ascertain that Switzerland is really his true home.'[83] Kistler added that the law stipulated he should have moved his wife and son into his Lausanne apartment.

Mark managed to keep his residency permit by telling the authorities he 'had problems moving'.[84] But his Swiss base came under threat in late 1992, after recurrent media claims about alleged arms deals in the Middle East. His employer, Espírito Santo SA, was anxious about how the allegations might affect their worldwide business. So in October 1992, Mark voluntarily handed in three months' notice and on 31 December his contract was terminated. In March 1993, Mark's Swiss excursion ended when he informed the local police that he was leaving the country, as he did not intend to take another job.

That was the official version. But the truth was that Mark left Switzerland voluntarily and for an entirely different reason – the spectre of his recurrent taxation problems had returned to haunt him. Hugh Thurston, his personal banker, always believed he 'sailed close to the wind' on his tax affairs. This was confirmed by outside legal advice in 1991, which argued he was in constant danger of investigation by the Inland Revenue.

Mark ignored this advice and thought he could outma-
noeuvre the authorities. At one stage he even told the
taxman that his net worth and declared assets were
only £600,000. This was greeted with almost universal
derision and by the summer of 1993 the Revenue were
again taking a close interest. Mark faced the frightening
prospect of declaring all his income from his fortune if
he were deemed to have UK residence for tax purposes.
Consequently, in August 1993 Thurston hired the City
law firm of Simmons & Simmons to examine and
advise on the tax implications of Mark Thatcher's
wealth (his tax documents are labelled 'MT Tax Advice
– M76209' and filed under 'Thurston'). Within two
months Mark was renting out his Kensington house
at £2,000 per week (while it was for sale) and had
moved permanently back to Texas.

It was true that Lady Thatcher's son thought that
the country had got into 'a bloody mess', since John
Major had become prime minister. But that was not the
motivation for his departure. He was not running away
from Major's Britain. He was moving permanently to
the US because he was concerned about his tax affairs
in the UK. Whether that anxiety was valid, only time
and the investigations of the US and UK tax authorities
will tell.

Chapter Ten

Λ True Thatcherite

'The answer to the question "Who disciplines the Prime Minister?" is that no one does.'

Lord Blake, Conservative Party historian[1]

On Monday, 12 October 1994, at a time when allegations about Mark Thatcher's commercial involvement in the Al Yamamah arms deal resurfaced, the former prime minister was talking to one of her closest confidants. She was very upset.

'I'll just go down in history as Mark's mother,' she said.

'No, no, Margaret,' replied the friend, a former Conservative cabinet minister. 'Your place in history is secure, really.'

'No, they want to do me down,' Lady Thatcher said repeatedly. 'They want to do me down.'

The former minister was so concerned about his mentor's state of mind that he decided she needed reassurance. So he asked for a special section to be inserted into the inaugural speech of Jeremy Hanley, the new Tory Party chairman, at the Tory Party conference in Bournemouth the following day. Sure enough, early in his address Hanley paid a distinctive tribute to her. Turning towards her he said : 'Mr Chairman, Margaret Thatcher's place in history is absolutely assured. She will be seen worldwide as one of the leading figures of the twentieth century, whoever writes the history books.'

Margaret Thatcher's place in history is, of course, very secure. On her tombstone, she will be remembered as one of the most remarkable and politically successful prime ministers of all time. Winning three successive general elections was no mean achievement. Historians will describe her as someone who broke with consensus politics and by sheer driving force and determination introduced waves of revolutionary legislation, notably privatization and trade-union reform.

But her legacy will be stained and besmirched. For the Thatcher years will also be known as a period when the prime minister's name was used to enrich her own son, when 10 Downing Street effectively became a registered office for a family business called Mark Thatcher Enterprises Ltd, and when Thatcherism began at home. For the most enthusiastic exponents of Thatcherism were the Thatchers. Mark was just the most vigorous and fervent disciple. Although he was not a political evangelist, he is a child of Margaret Thatcher's in every sense of the phrase. For the Thatcher family, money and material wealth are God. They worship at the temple of the almighty sterling (and often Swiss francs and US dollars).

Mark would, according to an Arab businessman who dealt with him, 'do anything for money. Anything that was asked of him.' Even Margaret Thatcher's political admirers accept there is a strong mercenary streak and bounty hunter mentality running through the family. 'She was a money snob,' said one former senior Conservative grandee. 'She admired people who made a lot of money. I didn't mind that, but her weakness was that she didn't seem to mind how the money was made. Money talks as far as she was concerned.'

It was not so much what Margaret Thatcher occasionally did to help her son in his commercial endeavours. It was that she did nothing to prevent him from capitalizing on her name and office. Officially, she professed ignorance of his activities. The standard line among her friends and admirers was: 'Well, yes, Mark may have done all those things and made all that money, but I can assure you that Margaret knew nothing about it.' But that argument is severely undermined by, for example, the letter of introduction she wrote to Sheikh Zayed for Mark in 1980.

At the heart of the 'What did she know and when did she know it?' issue lie Mark's relationships with his mother and, to a much lesser extent, his father and sister. From an early age, Mark, like most children, aimed to fulfil his parents' aspirations and expectations. But it was soon apparent he had neither the appetite nor the aptitude to achieve success at the level of his mother and father. 'Mark always wanted to be as big as them, but could never quite make it on his own,' said Andrew Thomson, Margaret Thatcher's constituency agent in Finchley from 1982 until 1987.[2] During his mother's tenure as prime minister, his behaviour was that of a man who could not cope with the fact that both his parents were successful in their own right. He set himself targets that were far beyond him and so he became chronically insecure. As a result, he was reduced to exaggerating his own importance, boasting and telling harassed shopkeepers: 'But don't you know who I am?'[3] Or ostentatiously pulling out his mobile telephone during dinner parties and speaking to his bodyguards.

Such arrogance, born of insecurity, was usually displayed more in public than in private. When he walked into a glass door by mistake at an architect's office, he wanted to sue the builders. When he leaned back in his chair and toppled over into the dessert trolley in a restaurant, he loudly announced that the management would have to pay his dry-cleaning bill.[4] 'I found that Mark's behaviour changed dramatically when he was with a group of people,' said Jim Paterson, who knew him in the mid-1980s. 'When I was on my own with him he was a decent guy – good company and could be quite funny. But when he was in a public place he could be very pompous and rude.'[5]

Ironically, in later years he appeared to acknowledge this reputation. 'Hello, I'm charmless Mark' was an occasional opening gambit at social functions.[6]

The other consequence of his insecurity was the constant need to promote and project himself by showing off his wealth (hence the valet). He would mix only with the rich, tycoons and celebrities, always with a swagger and an airy confidence. At parties unless the guest is wealthy and famous, Mark is not interested. 'He is far by the rudest person I have ever met,' said a friend of his sister, Carol. 'He just acts so superior as if he is so important and successful and you are a mere blip on the universe.' This contrasts with his actual business record, which shows that he was a failed accountant who never retained a job for more than a year.

Yet Mark Thatcher maintained a relentless desire to achieve, and make his mother proud. His chosen route was to accumulate a huge pot of gold. Nothing wrong with that, many people would say. But his insecurity also bred impatience and he cut corners. He became so driven by the desire to make money that he became an exponent of the 'get rich quick' school of wealth-creation. He was indiscriminate about his business associates and the type of deal he was brokering. He wanted cash and he wanted it fast. The problem was that he had no business prowess or even, at first, any decent contacts. So when his mother became prime minister in 1979, he exploited the one saleable asset at his disposal – his name – and, as several of his former associates have testified, he was brilliant at it. It was almost as if Mark believed he was an unofficial appendage of the government. One lunch-time in June 1993, he walked into the drawing-room of his Kensington house and saw John Major speaking on television. 'God, he's useless,' he said. 'It wasn't like this when we were in power.'[7]

From Margaret Thatcher's perspective, her son could do no wrong. He was her adored child and she bristled with indignation whenever anyone criticized him. Even while she was prime minister she pampered and doted on him when he stayed with her in 10 Downing Street. She hovered and fussed, indulging in what Mark called 'little spurts of mothering'. She would wash and iron his shirts, folding them into neat little squares and slipping them carefully into plastic bags for travelling.[8] In public, however, she appeared to gloss over her maternal over-indulgence. 'You can't just tie young men and women to their mother's apron strings,' she said. 'You just can't. You can't take all the challenge out of life for young people. It wouldn't be right to do so.'[9]

Margaret Thatcher allowed her son to use her position in his business ventures for two reasons. Firstly, she could not see anything wrong with it. He was merely being a Thatcherite. Secondly, she felt guilty and blamed herself for his inadequacies and flaws. 'My perspective is that she felt that when the twins were very young, she decided early to pursue a political career in the hope that it would not affect the kids,' said a former Tory official who worked closely with her in the early 1980s. 'Carol could handle it. But Mark's hang-ups were so bad that when his mother was away that only made him more insecure. After that, every time he screwed up – like his accountancy exams – she blamed herself. She reacted in exactly the same way when she was prime minister. She felt that if she had spent more time with him when he was younger, he would have turned out better.'

This resulted in Mark Thatcher being the prime minister's perpetual blind spot: even the most blinkered Thatcherites – there are still a few left – accept that. She could not see the implications of what was happening and would not hear any criticism of him. 'Margaret Thatcher's mind is very compartmentalized,' said a former long-serving senior Tory Central Office direc- tor. 'She would listen to advice and you could discuss anything with her, but you couldn't talk about Mark. It was just impossible. All of her friends or people on her political staff knew they could not broach the subject of Mark, because she saw it as a criticism of herself.' Consequently, the prime minister's son had licence to do almost anything, knowing she would not do anything. 'In Margaret Thatcher's eyes, there is nothing for which Mark requires forgiveness,' said Andrew Thomson.[10]

That raises the crucial question of how much knowl- edge she had about Mark's business activities. She knew for four reasons.

First, her relationship with her son, by their own and everyone else's account, was and remains extraordinar- ily close. During the mid-1980s he would telephone her every Sunday night regardless of where he was in the world. They discussed everything.

Second, nobody disputes that Margaret Thatcher was the most meticulous and punctilious of prime ministers. Her attention to detail and her thorough reading of almost every document that crossed her desk were unsurpassed, and her capacity for knowledge was unrivalled. It is inconceivable that she did not know what her own son was doing.

Third, her most senior ministers had, at the very least, some knowledge of what was going on. This was partly because of their departmental responsibilities but also because they received informal verbal reports from senior Conservative MPs. For example, John (now Lord) Wakeham, chief whip from 1983 until 1987, is known to have been given at least one such report, in 1984. It is possible that ministers did not inform Mrs Thatcher about her son's activities. If they did not, they should have done.

Fourth, and most crucially, she was informed by her own civil servants, ministers and security services. They could not fudge it. They were officially duty-bound to tell her. This occurred in 1984, at the height of the Oman contract controversy. A former minister was present in her room when a senior civil servant entered and presented to Margaret Thatcher a Secret Intelligence Service (MI6) report, collated in Vienna, on her son's commercial activities. Normally she was fascinated by security-service reports, especially those from the Joint Intelligence Committee. But on this occasion, as the prime minister stared at the document, she was almost in tears. 'I don't want to read it,' she said, her voice quivering. 'I don't want to read it. I can't.'

Mark was not slow to take advantage of his mother's

weakness. He knew how to exploit her self-imposed guilt and keep her under his psychological thumb. One of his favourite tactics while she was prime minister was to telephone 10 Downing Street at about 1.45pm on a Tuesday or Thursday afternoon. This, of course, was at the precise moment when she was being briefed and preparing herself for prime minister's question time in parliament and was under the most extreme pressure. When Mark's telephone call was put through to her private secretary, he would naturally be told she was too busy to talk to him at that time. Her son would then tell the official that if she didn't come to the phone immediately he would never talk to her again. When this message was relayed Margaret immediately came to the phone.

The remarkable inability or unwillingness of Margaret Thatcher to deal with her son and put him on the straight and narrow lies at the heart of the matter. Her defenders argue she was merely being a doting mother, who may have spoiled him a little. She did much more than that. But the issue was fundamental and best expressed by a former cabinet minister now in the House of Lords. 'My mother loved me too,' he said, 'but she knew when I was being a bloody idiot – and she said so.'[11]

Denis Thatcher did not fare much better in dealing with Mark. His relationship with his son has been cool and formal and has not warmed over the years. Privately, Denis is disappointed with Mark. 'I can spot a wrong 'un a mile off,' he would say. Denis would have liked him to have earned and worked for his money – the old-fashioned way. 'Doing favours for Arabs is not a proper job,' he once remarked.

His son has sensed his father's disapproval and has often reacted in a petulant way. During the last week of her premiership in November 1990, Denis and

Margaret were having dinner late one night. 'What do
you think about being a baronet?' she asked him. Denis
was taken aback but delighted. He thought it would
be particularly beneficial for his grandson Michael,
and accepted. 'That would be wonderful,' he replied.
Mark was less pleased. When told about the honour
by his father the next day in the upstairs flat in 10
Downing Street, Mark replied: 'I suppose that's what
you wanted.' He promptly walked out of the room
without a further word. One would have thought he
should be grateful. When Denis dies, Mark inherits his
title and becomes Sir Mark. According to Carol, the
honour was created by Margaret partly so that Mark
could inherit it.

There are conflicting views on who is the real
boss and chief executive in the Thatcher family.
Some of Mark's friends say Denis always has the
last word. Others are not so sure. One of them,
Charlie Crichton-Stuart, former sponsorship consultant
to Frank Williams Racing, recalls an incident which
illustrates what he saw as the true balance of power.

In 1982 Crichton-Stuart was having lunch with
Mark, when at 3.25pm Mark suddenly said: 'Would
you like to come up to the ranch?' The sponsorship
consultant agreed and off they trooped to 10 Downing
Street, where they met Denis in the top-floor flat. He
was in a jovial mood. 'Would you like a drink?' he
asked. Crichton-Stuart was not a drinker, as alcohol
did not agree with him, but he could hardly refuse
an invitation from the prime minister's husband in 10
Downing Street. So Denis went to the drinks cabinet,
prepared two large gin and tonics and lit a cigarette.
As he was handed the glass Crichton-Stuart heard an
unmistakable voice haranguing and abusing an official
as she walked up the stairs. 'The poor man was getting

a horrendous bollocking,' he recalled. 'I've never heard anything like it.'

Suddenly Denis gulped his double gin and tonic down in one movement and quickly stubbed out his cigarette just as Margaret passed by the room. For Crichton-Stuart, sitting petrified with a large gin in one hand and a cigarette in the other, it was a real eye-opener as to who had the clout in the Thatcher clan. As another member of the family reflected: 'It was Margaret who wore the trousers.'

How much Denis knows about his son's business activities is unclear. Certainly, they have been on business trips together. But at private social occasions he professes ignorance. 'I don't know how Mark made his money,' said Denis in January 1994. 'I made enough, but he's made a lot more.' He was no more forthcoming with the authors. Thanking us for our 'kind letter', he wrote: 'Some twenty odd years ago I made a rule for myself, namely, *never* to make speeches except at sports occasions, *never* to give interviews to the Press or others, *never* to write anything for publication except for sport, and *never* to "go on the box". By and large my "rule" has maintained me in a low profile (awful word) as befits my small position in public life. In my advanced years I see no reason to depart from it' [his emphasis].[12]

As for Carol Thatcher, she has been perennially frustrated by her mother favouring her twin brother in every way. 'Oh, she just *adores* Mark,' is a common remark by Carol to her friends. She has always been anxious for Margaret's love and affection. On one occasion she confronted her mother. 'Why does Mark get away with everything?' she asked. 'Why is *everything* he does all right? Don't you know I have feelings too?' The former prime minister replied: 'Because, darling, you and I are the strong ones.' In some ways Carol suffers from being Margaret Thatcher's daughter whereas Mark exists by being his mother's son.[13]

The differences between the Thatcher twins have only accentuated the favouritism shown to Mark. Carol is single with no children while Mark has a wife and two children – for the time being at any rate. Carol dresses informally while Mark always wears a formal suit and tie. Mark is a multimillionaire 'businessman' while Carol earns a modest living as a journalist. For Margaret Thatcher – whose only personal interests and hobbies are money, family and clothes – this is very important. It has little to do with who is the stronger personality.

The tension has been exacerbated by the way Lady Thatcher has often responded as if her daughter were a struggling subsidiary company in Thatcher plc. In early 1993, when Carol appeared depressed about her life, the former prime minister responded by handing over thousands of pounds for a large extension and decoration in her Fulham house.

The contrast between Carol and Mark is quite stark. He traded off his mother's name while she went to Australia to make her own living as a journalist. He lived in 10 Downing Street while Carol bought a house in Fulham. Professionally, she undoubtedly secured an advantage in gaining easy access to people and sources. But compared to Mark she did nothing to exploit her position as the prime minister's relative. Carol may have got some contacts but Mark obtained the contracts.

It is therefore not surprising that Carol and Mark have never been close. Virtually all they have in common is their fervent defence of their mother against criticism. It is not a warm relationship and several friends of Carol have told the authors of her intense dislike for her twin. 'I don't mind being described as Mrs Thatcher's daughter, but I get stroppy with "Mark's sister",' she once said.[14]

Despite her frustration Carol decided not to co-operate with this book. 'I'm afraid that I have to decline your invitation to be interviewed for your book on my brother,' she told us. 'I'm sure you'll appreciate that I got rather maxed out [weary] on the family interview scene during the eleven years my mother spent in Number 10.' In private and public she professes not to know how her brother acquired his millions. 'The only thing I don't want to comment on is Mark's money,' she told *Today* for a series of interviews six months after she refused our offer. 'I don't know how he made it, so it's not up to me to say anything. Besides, he's kind enough not to comment on my lack of it.'[15] She was more forthright to a friend: 'Of course, he has made a lot of money but God knows how.'

A Confusion of Interests

A key reason why the former prime minister did not prevent Mark from amassing his gold was that she did not seem to come to terms with either the notion or the danger of conflicts of interests. When asked whether she knew her son had a commercial interest in the Oman and Saudi Arabian contracts she negotiated, she refused to address the question. Instead, she denied there was any impropriety. Apart from evading the fundamental issue, she also missed the point. As Ronald Dworkin, professor of jurisprudence at Oxford

University, pointed out: 'A conflict of interest is a *situation* [his emphasis], not any particular piece of wrongdoing. The difference is very important, because avoiding conflicts means avoiding relationships and connections that might raise questions of improper motives.'[16]

The cabinet rules governing ministers' financial interests are quite clear. They were first laid down by Sir Winston Churchill in 1952: 'It is a principle of public life that Ministers must so order their affairs that no conflict arises or appears to arise between their private interests and their public duties.'[17]

Margaret Thatcher has never been able to reconcile that guideline with her own affairs. This was illustrated in 1986 when it was revealed that as a cabinet minister she had bought shares in her own name. In 1971, while education secretary, she purchased 348 shares for £2,142 in Broken Hill Pty, an Australian oil and steel conglomerate. After she joined the company's reinvestment scheme, her holding increased to 1,327 shares. Over the next fourteen years the stock, bought in her own name, increased in value through rights and dividend issues to £4,470.[18] She retained the shares when she became prime minister in 1979, and they appeared in Broken Hill's company register as 'The Hon. Mrs M. Thatcher c/o Miss J. Robillard [her constituency secretary], 10 Downing Street, London SW1'.

It was not until 1985 that the prime minister transferred her holding and other shares to nominee discretionary accounts, to be controlled by a firm of investment fund managers.[19] Thus for six years Margaret Thatcher held a direct stake in a company that was quoted on the Stock Exchange. As prime minister and first lord of the Treasury, she could theoretically have had access to a great deal of sensitive economic and industrial information. It was a potential conflict of interests, because she kept the shares under her own name from 1979 until 1985.

When questioned in parliament, Thatcher denied she had breached the cabinet office rules. 'Under those conventions,' she said, 'there is nothing which requires me, on assuming office, to dispose of my shares or to transfer them into a trust or in the name of investment managers.'[20] But *Questions of Procedure* states: 'There may be less clear-cut cases where a minister would feel it appropriate to place his holding in the hands of trustees.'

For close relatives and spouses, the cabinet office document is clear-cut and pertinent: 'It is a well established and recognised rule that no Minister or Public Servant should accept gifts, hospitality or services from anyone which would, or might appear to, place him or her under an obligation. The same principle applies if gifts, hospitality or services are offered to a member of their family.'[21]

Fortunately for Margaret Thatcher, she was the final judge and jury on the matter. It is, of course, the prime minister who is responsible for the conduct of ministers. 'The answer to the question "Who disciplines the prime minister?" is that no one does,' said Lord Blake, the historian of the Conservative Party. 'The other ministers, if in doubt, are enjoined to consult the prime minister. But the prime minister is on his or her own in this respect and not accountable, in that sense, to any particular person. But, of course, he or she is always in the last resort accountable to parliament.'[22]

The argument that the prime minister is answerable to the Commons is flawed, because it simply does not work in practice. In the Oman case, Margaret

Thatcher refused to make a statement to the House. She answered questions either by arguing it was a private issue or by saying that she was batting for the British company not her son. Lord Blake agreed with her: 'I think that the prime minister, in taking the line that in purely private matters she is not prepared to answer in public in parliament, is only doing what any other prime minister would have done.'[23] This was also her response to the authors when we requested an interview. 'Lady Thatcher has a standard policy not to comment on her family,' said her office.

However, it was much more than a private or family matter. In the Oman situation, her son was being paid by a public company for which she was lobbying for a multimillion-pound contract. Over in Saudi Arabia he received a commission fee for another public contract which she not only negotiated but also signed. The public-interest issue was recognized by Howard Teicher, a former senior US National Security Council official, who saw documents on Mark Thatcher's financial involvement in the Al Yamamah arms deal. 'I think it's totally inappropriate,' he said, 'for family members of elected officials to engage in commercial transactions involving governments where, even if the law permits such involvement, the appearance of impropriety is quite apparent and the family member is exploiting his family connection to the possible detriment of his own taxpayers. . . . In a democratic society, this is the worst form of nepotism – to see a member of a political family clearly exploit the connection to carve out power and influence in order to make money.'[24]

The perennial problem was that Mark Thatcher was never answerable or accountable for his actions. The only person, officially and personally, who was responsible was his mother, the prime minister. Yet she was often directly involved herself, so she was judge and jury in her own cause.

Very early in her premiership, her son claimed he was aware of the dangers of trading off his name. 'It seems a pompous thing to say but I now have a responsibility to Mum in how I behave,' he commented in February 1980. 'I have to deliberate about everything I contemplate doing and think of the possible repercussions. There have been times when I've known I've been guilty, and got it straight in the back of the neck. My mother is pretty efficient at shooting you down – there is no doubt about that.'[25]

Clearly, that never happened. Mark was never able to succeed on his own merits so he utilized his one asset – his name. And he never cared about what anyone thought. 'I am responsible to three people on this planet,' he said in 1984. 'One of them is my mother, the second is the Almighty and the third is me. My responsibility is to her as my mother, not as prime minister. To me, that is peripheral.'[26]

His defenders argue that Mark is merely a private businessman who has been attacked as a way of undermining his mother. That has been proved to be false by the fact that some of his strongest press critics have been her most ardent and sycophantic supporters, notably the *Sun* and *Daily Express*. He may be a private businessman but he is also the only child of a post-Second World War British prime minister to have traded off his name. When Sir Alec (later Lord) Douglas-Home became prime minister in 1963 (after being foreign secretary for three years), his son David worked for Morgan Grenfell International in Abu Dhabi. Not once did he or Lord Home exploit their positions to make money for their family or the merchant bank. Other children of prime ministers have virtually been invisible. Few people even knew Harold Wilson had two sons. John Major's son has barely made the press. The Thatcher experience is unique.

'Margaret Thatcher's blind-spot' has been a familiar phrase to describe her son. But it was much more than that. He was the one emotional and dangerous political chink in her otherwise impenetrable public armour. Some of her policies were unpopular and her critics attacked many of her decisions and actions. But, according to her closest confidants, it was Mark who could have brought her down. 'He was a threat to the stability and very survival of the prime minister herself,' said one. 'The only consolation I had when I left 10 Downing Street was that I was not there when the government fell apart over Mark Thatcher,' said one former senior Downing Street official. 'There was a real possibility that the government would fall because of him. It was that serious.'

As for Mark, he has continued to behave as if he were still the son of the prime minister. He has retained 10 Downing Street cards, which he has handed to people to impress them. On one occasion, in June 1993, he scribbled down his mobile telephone number on the card and presented it to his wife's maternity nurse. He retains a personal bodyguard. He has maintained an air of bravado about various enquiries into his business affairs and believes his gold is untouchable. 'They have nothing on me,' he said.[27]

Whether that remains the case is a question that only the current cabinet, many of whom served as senior ministers in Margaret Thatcher's administrations, can answer.

Notes and References

Preface

1 Saladin Holdings Ltd (SHL) 'provides management, marketing and technical services to clients', according to its accounts. It has two wholly owned subsidiary companies. On 15 May 1987, SHL bought 100 per cent of Saladin Security Ltd – 'a company active in the security field'. On 23 May 1988, SHL acquired 100 per cent of Saladin Trading Ltd – 'a UK company specialising in buying and selling military equipment', according to its latest accounts. On 1 October 1993, Sir Archie Hamilton, a Conservative MP, became a director of Saladin Holdings Ltd. Sir Archie was a junior minister for defence procurement, 1986–7, parliamentary private secretary to Margaret Thatcher, 1987–8 and minister for the armed forces, 1988–93. From 1978 until 1979 his political aide was David Hart.

2 David Walker, chairman of SHL, is also a director and shareholder of Saladin Security Ltd and Saladin Trading Ltd. A former Conservative councillor and SAS major, Walker was hired by Oliver North to implement 'certain special operations' in Nicaragua to support the Contras against the Sandinista government.

Chapter One

1 Andrew Thomson, *Margaret Thatcher – The Woman Within* (London: W. H. Allen, 1989), p 118.
2 *Jersey Evening Post*, 29 August 1973.
3 *Ibid.*
4 *Ibid.*

5 *Financial Times*, 31 October 1994.

6 Hugo Young, *One of Us* (London: Macmillan, 1989), p 4.

7 *Sunday Express*, 20 July 1975.

8 Christopher Ogden, *Maggie* (New York: Simon & Schuster, 1990), p 24.

9 Penny Junor, *Margaret Thatcher – Wife, Mother, Politician* (London: Sidgwick & Jackson, 1983), p 3.

10 Young, *One of Us*, p 22.

11 P. Junor, *Margaret Thatcher*, p 40.

12 Ogden, *Maggie*, pp 40–41.

13 P. Junor, *Margaret Thatcher*, p 12.

14 Hugo Young and Anne Sloman, *The Thatcher Phenomenon* (London: BBC Publications, 1986), p 17.

15 Ogden, *Maggie*, p 46.

16 P. Junor, *Margaret Thatcher*, p 26.

17 *Ibid*.

18 Interview with *The Times*, 5 October 1970.

19 Diana Farr, *Five At Ten* (London: André Deutsch, 1985), p 171.

20 *Ibid*, p 173.

21 *Ibid*, p 176.

22 *Ibid*, p 174.

23 *Ibid*, p 175.

24 *Ibid*, p 178.

25 *Ibid*, p 178.

26 *Ibid*, p 180.

27 Margaret Thatcher, *The Downing Street Years* (London: HarperCollins, 1993), p 22.

28 Farr, *Five at Ten*, p 180.

29 Nicholas Wapshott and George Brock, *Margaret Thatcher* (London: Macdonald & Co, 1983), p 57.

30 *Observer*, 29 May 1983.

31 *Independent on Sunday*, 25 November 1990.

32 Farr, *Five at Ten*, p 177.

33 Interview with *The Times*, 5 October 1970.

34 Interview with authors.

35 Ogden, *Maggie*, p 56.

36 George Gardiner, *Margaret Thatcher – From Childhood To Leadership* (London: William Kimber, 1975), p 46.

37 *Ibid*.

38 Wapshott and Brock, *Margaret Thatcher*, p 56.

39 Ogden, *Maggie*, p 60.

40 P. Junor, *Margaret Thatcher*, p 35.
41 *Ibid*, p 34.
42 Gardiner, *Margaret Thatcher*, p 51.
43 *Sunday Graphic*, February 1952. Quoted in Young, *One of Us*, p 36.
44 Ogden, *Maggie*, p 70.
45 *Ibid*.
46 *Daily Mirror*, 13 March 1981.
47 Farr, *Five at Ten*, p 189.
48 Ogden, *Maggie*, p 71.
49 Brock and Wapshott, *Margaret Thatcher*, p 60.
50 Gardiner, *Margaret Thatcher*, p 51.
51 Ogden, *Maggie*, p 71.
52 Gardiner, *Margaret Thatcher*, p 52.
53 P. Junor, *Margaret Thatcher*, p 40.
54 Gardiner, *Margaret Thatcher*, p 54.
55 P. Junor, *Margaret Thatcher*, p 41.
56 Interview with *The Times*, 5 October 1970.
57 *Spectator*, 7 May 1988.
58 Wapshott and Brock, *Margaret Thatcher*, p 60.
59 *London Evening News*, 10 October 1959.
60 *Sunday Times*, 24 November 1974.
61 Patricia Murray, *Margaret Thatcher* (London: W. H. Allen, 1980), p 59.
62 Interview with Carol Thatcher, *Today*, 16 November 1993.
63 P. Junor, *Margaret Thatcher*, p 49.
64 *Today*, 26 November 1993.
65 Interview with authors.
66 *Daily Mail*, 10 October 1961.
67 *Sunday Telegraph*, 24 November 1974; *Sun*, 8 February 1982.
68 *Sun*, 8 February 1982.
69 P. Junor, *Margaret Thatcher*, p 49.
70 *Ibid*.
71 Interview with authors.
72 *Punch*, 14 March 1984.
73 Murray, *Margaret Thatcher*, p 63.
74 Interview with Carol Thatcher, 16 November 1993.
75 Farr, *Five at Ten*, p 194.
76 Interview with authors.
77 P. Junor, *Margaret Thatcher*, p 64.

78 Interview with authors.
79 Interview with authors.
80 Jeremy Paxman, *Friends in High Places* (London: Michael Joseph, 1990), p 167.
81 Michael Cockerell, *Dear Bill* (profile of William Deedes), BBC2, 9 January 1994.
82 *The Downing Street Years*, BBC1, 20 October 1993.
83 Interview with researcher for authors.
84 *Harpers and Queen*, April 1991.
85 Murray, *Margaret Thatcher*, p 59.
86 *Daily Telegraph*, 24 November 1994.
87 P. Junor, *Margaret Thatcher*, p 64.
88 Interview with researcher for authors.
89 Murray, *Margaret Thatcher*, p 60.
90 Interview with researcher for authors.
91 Interview with researcher for authors.
92 *Tatler*, April 1991.
93 Interview with *The Times*, 5 October 1970.
94 Interview with researcher for authors.
95 Interview with researcher for authors.
96 *Old Harrovian*, 20 March 1971.
97 *Sunday Times*, 12 February 1984.
98 Interview with researcher for authors.
99 *Daily Express*, 28 October 1969.
100 Letter to authors.
101 Interview with *Woman's Own*, 2 February 1980.
102 Interview with researcher for authors.

Chapter Two

1 Mark Thatcher to harassed shopkeeper. Quoted in Farr, *Five at Ten*, p 205.
2 *The Times*, 5 October 1970.
3 Interview with authors.
4 Interview with authors.
5 *Woman's Own*, 2 February 1980.
6 *Ibid*.
7 *Daily Express*, 13 February 1975.
8 *Ibid*, 21 February 1975.
9 Interview with authors.
10 Interview with authors.

11 *Daily Express*, 25 July 1975.
12 Murray, *Margaret Thatcher*, p 63.
13 *Ibid*, p 64.
14 *London Evening News*, 30 April 1975.
15 *Daily Express*, 18 May 1977.
16 *Sunday Telegraph*, 19 July 1981.
17 Interview with authors.
18 Interview with *Hong Kong Tatler*, December 1991.
19 Interview with authors.
20 P. Junor, *Margaret Thatcher*, p 114.
21 *Accountants Weekly*, 18 June 1979.
22 *Ibid*.
23 *Daily Express*, 24 March 1975.
24 Interview with authors.
25 *Daily Mail*, 17 June 1977.
26 *Guardian*, 14 February 1980; *Daily Express*, 15 February 1980.
27 *Daily Mail*, 15 July 1988.
28 *Nationwide*, BBC1, 28 February 1980.
29 *Daily Mail*, 15 July 1988.
30 *Woman's Own*, 2 February 1980.
31 Interview with authors.
32 *Sunday Mirror*, 16 February 1975; *Daily Express*, 25 July 1975.
33 *The Times*, 18 October 1994.
34 *Woman's Own*, 2 February 1980.
35 *Tatler*, December 1994.
36 Interview with authors.
37 *Woman's Own*, 3 May 1986.
38 *Daily Express*, 13 October 1978.
39 *Daily Mail*, 15 October 1978.
40 *News of the World*, 15 February 1987.
41 London *Evening Standard*, 23 April 1979.
42 *London Evening News*, 24 April 1979.
43 *Ibid*.
44 *Woman's Own*, 2 February 1980.
45 *Ibid*.
46 Ronald Millar, *A View from the Wings* (London: Weidenfeld & Nicolson, 1993), pp 267–9; Farr, *Five at Ten*, p 200.
47 *Woman's Own*, 2 February 1980.
48 *Ibid*.

49 *Ibid*.
50 Accounts of Monteagle Marketing Ltd, 1979–80.
51 *Washington Post*, 2 July 1979.
52 Accounts of Monteagle Marketing Ltd, 1979–80.
53 *Woman's Own*, 2 February 1980.
54 *Washington Post*, 16 February 1987.
55 *Sunday Times*, 4 March 1984.
56 *Ibid*.
57 *Woman's Own*, 2 February 1980.
58 *Daily Mail*, 14 February 1980.

Chapter Three

1 *London Evening News*, 7 June 1979.
 2 *Daily Mail*, 18 September 1979.
 3 *Woman's Own*, 2 February 1980.
 4 *Daily Telegraph*, 1 October 1979.
 5 Interview with authors.
 6 *Daily Mail*, 13 February 1980.
 7 London *Evening Standard*, 13 February 1980.
 8 Interview with authors.
 9 *Daily Telegraph*, 13 February 1980.
10 *Daily Mail*, 13 February 1980.
11 *London Evening News*, 13 February 1980.
12 *Daily Mail*, 13 February 1980.
13 London *Evening Standard*, 13 February 1980.
14 *Sunday Times*, 17 February 1980.
15 *Daily Telegraph* and *The Times*, 29 February 1980.
16 *Daily Mail*, 13 February 1980.
17 *Daily Express*, 14 February 1980.
18 Press Association, 18 February 1980.
19 *Sun*, 6 March 1981.
20 *Daily Mail*, 14 February 1980.
21 *Daily Express* and *Daily Telegraph*, 15 February 1980.
22 *Daily Telegraph*, 16 February 1980.
23 *Daily Mail*, 16 February 1980.
24 *News of the World*, 17 February 1980.
25 *Western Mail*, 29 February 1980.
26 *Daily Express*, 14 February 1980.
27 *Daily Mail*, 16 February 1980.
28 *Daily Telegraph*, 13 February 1980.

29 *Ibid*, 29 February 1980.
30 *Nationwide*, BBC1, 28 February 1980.
31 *Ibid*.
32 *Daily Mail*, 29 February 1980.
33 *Sun*, 6 March 1981.
34 Interview with authors.
35 *Daily Mail*, 22 April 1980.
36 *Ibid*, 16 June 1980.
37 Interview with authors.
38 *Daily Express*, 29 May 1980.
39 Interview with authors.
40 Interview with authors.
41 *Daily Mail*, 28 April 1980.
42 *Sunday Telegraph*, 2 August 1981.
43 *Daily Mail*, 22 April 1980.
44 *Daily Express*, 12 August 1980.
45 Interview with authors.
46 New Zealand Press Association, 25 September 1980.
47 *Sydney Morning Herald*, 1 October 1980.
48 *Daily Express*, 16 February 1981.
49 Peter Taylor, *Smoke Ring – Tobacco, Money and Multi-National Politics* (London: Sphere, 1984), p 145.
50 *Daily Mail*, 6 August 1981.
51 *Woman's Own*, 2 February 1980.
52 *Sunday Telegraph*, 19 July 1981.
53 *The Times*, 14 May 1981.
54 *New York Times*, 12 October 1980.
55 London *Evening Standard*, 29 June 1981.
56 *Daily Mail*, 1 July 1981.
57 *Daily Express*, 6 October 1981.
58 *Sunday Express*, 9 August 1981; *Sunday Telegraph*, 19 July 1981.
59 *Daily Express*, 11 March 1981.
60 *Sunday Express*, 22 August 1982; *Options* magazine, November 1982.
61 *Daily Express*, 11 January 1982.
62 *Daily Telegraph*, 8 March 1982.
63 *The Times*, 16 January 1982.
64 Article by Carol Thatcher, 15 January 1982.
65 P. Junor, *Margaret Thatcher*, p 156.
66 *The Times*, 13 January 1982.
67 *Ibid*.

68 *Ibid*, 15 January 1982.
69 *Daily Express*, 13 January 1982.
70 Interview with Carol Thatcher, 17 November 1993.
71 *Daily Telegraph*, 14 January 1982.
72 *Daily Mail*, 14 January 1982.
73 *Ibid*.
74 P. Junor, *Margaret Thatcher*, p 157.
75 *The Times*, 15 January 1982.
76 *Daily Telegraph*, 8 March 1982.
77 Press Association, 15 January 1982.
78 *Daily Express*, 15 January 1982.
79 *The Times*, 16 January 1982.
80 *Ibid*.
81 *Daily Mail*, 16 January 1982.
82 *The Times*, 16 January 1982.
83 Press Association, 15 January 1982.
84 *Daily Telegraph*, 16 January 1982.
85 *Daily Express*, 15 January 1982.
86 Carol Thatcher, interview with *Sunday Express*, 22 August 1982.
87 *Daily Mail*, 16 January 1982.
88 *Daily Telegraph*, 18 February 1982.
89 *News of the World*, 24 January 1982.
90 *Daily Telegraph*, 25 January 1982.
91 *News of the World*, 24 January 1982.
92 *Daily Mail*, 26 January 1982.
93 Interview with authors.
94 Interview with authors; *Observer*, 5 February 1984.
95 *Daily Express*, 5 March 1982.
96 *Honey* magazine, April 1982.
97 *Private Eye*, 10 February 1984.
98 Donald C. Bauder, *Captain Money and the Golden Girl – A $200 Million Fantasy of Love, Power and Greed* (San Diego: Harvest and HBJ Books, 1986), p 122.
99 *Ibid*.
100 *Daily Express*, 5 November 1982.
101 *Ibid*, 28 March 1988.

Chapter Four

1 *Weekend World*, LWT, 15 January 1984.

2 Interview with authors.
3 House of Commons, *Hansard*, 15 March 1984.
4 *Economist* Special Report, 11 August 1979.
5 *Ibid.*
6 *Observer* archives.
7 *Business In Oman, World In Action*, Granada TV, 23 July 1984.
8 *Ibid*
9 Export Intelligence Service Notice, No. 404.
10 *Observer*, 26 February 1984.
11 House of Commons, *Hansard*, 13 February 1984.
12 *The Times*, 20 April 1981.
13 *Ibid*, 21 April 1981.
14 *Observer*, 22 January 1984.
15 *Ibid.*
16 Thatcher, *The Downing Street Years*, p 163.
17 *Sunday Times*, 31 May 1981.
18 Interview with authors.
19 *The Times*, 25 April 1981.
20 Trade department minister, in interview with authors.
21 *Observer*, 15 January 1984.
22 Thatcher, *The Downing Street Years*, p 163.
23 *Panorama*, BBC1, 9 April 1984.
24 *Business In Oman, World In Action*, Granada TV, 23 July 1984.
25 *Observer* archives.
26 Letter to the *Observer*, 18 January 1984.
27 *Weekend World*, LWT, 15 January 1984.
28 *Financial Times*, 17 March 1982.
29 *Daily Mail*, 9 March 1984.
30 *Ibid.*
31 *Observer*, 5 February 1984.
32 *8 Days* magazine, 18 August 1979.
33 *Reading Evening Post*, 22 March 1979.
34 *Daily Express*, 18 October 1994.
35 Letter from Richard Helms, president of Safeer International Consulting Group, to Orin Atkins, chairman and CEO of Ashland Oil Inc.
36 *Observer*, 5 February 1984.
37 *World In Action*, Granada TV, 23 July 1984.
38 Interview with authors.
39 *Observer*, 5 February 1984; 'How Mrs Thatcher Swung

University Contract', special report, *The Times*, 18 November 1981.

40 *Sunday People*, 1 April 1984.
41 *Sunday Times*, 4 March 1984.
42 *Observer*, 18 March 1984.
43 Letter to the authors, 11 February 1994.
44 Thomson, *Margaret Thatcher*, p 115.
45 *Ibid.*
46 Tom Bower, *Tiny Rowland – A Rebel Tycoon* (London: Heinemann, 1993), p 447.
47 Alan Clark, *Diaries* (London: Weidenfeld & Nicolson, 1993), p 70.
48 Thomson, *Margaret Thatcher*, p 115.
49 *Panorama*, BBC1, 9 April 1984.
50 House of Commons, *Hansard*, 5 April 1984, col 122.
51 *Panorama*, BBC1, 9 April 1984.
52 Letter from Margaret Thatcher to Peter Shore, 11 April 1984.
53 House of Commons, *Hansard*, 17 January 1984, col 159.
54 *Ibid*, 18 January 1984, col 242.
55 *Ibid*, col 243.
56 *Ibid*, 24 January 1984, col 326.
57 *Ibid*, 2 February 1984, col 268.
58 *Sunday Times*, 12 February 1984.
59 *Mail on Sunday*, 1 April 1984.
60 *Harpers and Queen*, April 1991.
61 *Sunday Times*, 26 January 1992.
62 *Event* magazine, 16 October 1983.
63 *Daily Mirror*, 30 January 1986.
64 *Mail on Sunday*, 1 April 1984.

Chapter Five

1 *Woman's Own*, 31 October 1987.
2 *Mail on Sunday*, 1 April 1984.
3 *Sunday Telegraph*, 8 June 1980.
4 *Mail on Sunday*, 1 April 1984.
5 Interview with authors; *Mail on Sunday*, 16 November 1986.
6 *Daily Express*, 26 March 1984.

7 *Mail on Sunday*, 1 April 1984.
8 Correction in *New York Times*, 28 March 1984.
9 *Mail on Sunday*, 1 April 1984.
10 *Daily Mirror*, 5 January 1984.
11 *Ibid*, 13 March 1984.
12 *Mail on Sunday*, 25 March 1984.
13 *Ibid*, 1 April 1984.
14 *Daily Mail*, 12 September 1983.
15 Interview with authors.
16 *Ibid*.
17 *Ibid*.
18 *People Weekly* magazine, 12 March 1984.
19 *News of the World*, 13 May 1984.
20 *Harpers and Queen*, April 1991.
21 *News of the World*, 13 May 1984.
22 *Daily Mail*, 9 January 1984.
23 *News of the World*, 13 May 1984.
24 *Daily Mail*, 20 February 1984.
25 *News of the World*, 13 May 1984.
26 *Daily Mail*, 14 May 1984.
27 *Sun*, 22 July 1984.
28 *Ibid*.
29 *Sunday Times*, 26 January 1992.
30 *Mail on Sunday*, 1 April 1984.
31 *Daily Mail*, 11 January 1984.
32 *Daily Express*, 30 March 1989.
33 *Ibid*.
34 *New York Times*, 27 April 1986.
35 *The Times*, 13 February 1989.
36 *Vanity Fair*, June 1991.
37 *Dallas Morning News*, 11 August 1984.
38 Twentieth Anniversary of Harvard and Radcliffe Alumni Report, 1991. Quoted in *Dallas Morning News*, 11 August 1984.
39 *Harpers and Queen*, April 1991.
40 *Tatler*, April 1991.
41 *Hong Kong Tatler*, December 1991.
42 *Dallas Morning News*, 20 April 1994.
43 *Dallas Times Herald*, 14 November 1986.
44 *Daily Star*, 11 April 1985.
45 Interview with *Ultra* magazine, Dallas, March 1990.
46 *Sun*, 11 April 1985.

47 *Daily Star*, 11 April 1985.
48 *Daily Express* and *Sun*, 7 March 1988.
49 *Daily Telegraph*, 13 November 1986.
50 *Ibid*, 14 November 1986.
51 *Daily Telegraph*, 14 November 1986.
52 *The Times*, 14 November 1986.
53 *Daily Mail*, 14 November 1986.
54 *Daily Express*, 3 October 1994.
55 *Daily Mail*, 12 February 1987.
56 *Mail on Sunday*, 15 February 1987.
57 Interview with authors.
58 *Sunday People*, 8 February 1987.
59 House of Commons, *Hansard*, 9 March 1987, col 31.
60 *Sun*, 14 February 1987.
61 *Daily Mirror*, 14 February 1987.
62 *The Times*, 16 February 1987.
63 *Daily Mail*, 16 February 1987.
64 *Daily Express*, 16 February 1987.
65 *Daily Star*, 24 February 1987.
66 *Today*, 29 March 1994.
67 *Ibid*.
68 *Ibid*.
69 *Ultra*, March 1990.
70 *Daily Star*, 12 February 1987.
71 *Today*, 29 March 1994.
72 London *Evening Standard*, 3 March 1989.
73 *Daily Express*, 30 March 1989.
74 *Daily Mail*, 4 May 1989.
75 *Ultra*, March 1990.
76 *Sun*, 9 June 1994.
77 *Daily Express*, 12 and 13 October 1994.
78 *Sunday Express*, 30 October 1994.
79 *Ibid*.
80 *Hong Kong Tatler*, December 1991.
81 *Daily Express*, 13 October 1994.
82 *Sun*, 9 June 1994.
83 *Financial Times*, 31 October 1994.
84 *Tatler*, April 1991.
85 *Sunday Times*, 26 January 1992.
86 *Observer*, 22 November 1987.
87 Deposition of David Wallace, Laughlin v Wallace, 14 April 1994, p 46.

88 *Ibid*, p 49.
89 *Ibid*, p 66.
90 *Observer*, 22 November 1987.
91 *Guardian*, 4 December 1987.
92 *Ibid*, 21 November 1987.
93 *Observer*, 22 November 1987.
94 Ogden, *Maggie*, p 79.
95 *Daily Express*, 19 October 1987.
96 *Ibid*.
97 London *Evening Standard*, 15 October 1987.
98 *Dallas Morning Herald*, 3 November 1987.
99 *Ibid*.
100 Thatcher, *The Downing Street Years*, p 700.
101 *Dallas Morning Herald*, 11 April 1989.
102 *Financial Times*, 31 October 1994.
103 *Ibid*.
104 Wallace deposition, p 26.
105 *Financial Times*, 31 October 1994.
106 *Dallas Morning News*, 17 December 1992.
107 US Internal Revenue Service Counter-Claim, 23 December 1992.
108 Wallace deposition, p 64.
109 *Independent*, 17 October 1994.
110 *Financial Times*, 31 October 1994.
111 *Vanity Fair*, June 1991.
112 *Sun*, 3 January 1990.

Chapter Six

1 *Mail on Sunday*, 16 April, 1995.
2 London *Evening Standard*, 28 September 1981.
3 *Today*, 9 April 1988.
4 *The Times*, 21 February 1980.
5 *Daily Mail*, 9 March 1982.
6 John Junor, *Memoirs – Listening for a Midnight Tram* (London: Chapman, 1990), p 259.
7 *Woman's Own*, 7 April 1984.
8 *Sunday Express*, 23 January 1983.
9 *Daily Telegraph*, 29 March 1982.
10 *Daily Mail*, 8 April 1982.
11 Interview with authors.

12 Interview with close and long-standing friend of Mark
   Thatcher; *Daily Star*, 10 December 1988.
13 Letter from William (now Lord) Whitelaw, then home
   secretary, to Douglas Hoyle, Labour MP for Warrington.
   Quoted in *Sunday People*, 19 September 1982.
14 *Daily Mirror*, 7 October 1982.
15 House of Commons, *Hansard*, 18 October 1982, col 8.
16 *Daily Mirror*, 5 October 1982.
17 House of Commons, *Hansard*, 18 and 19 October 1982,
   cols 8 and 90.
18 *Daily Mail*, 31 January 1993.
19 ANS news agency copy, 26 May 1983.
20 *Ibid*, 7 June 1983.
21 *Today*, 9 April 1982.
22 *The Times*, 21 June 1984.
23 House of Commons, *Hansard*, 30 January 1984.
24 Interview with authors.
25 *Ibid*.
26 Evidence to 'Exports to Iraq', an enquiry by House of
   Commons Select Committee on Trade and Industry, 5
   February 1992, p 338; DTI report into the affairs of Astra
   Holdings plc.
27 Interview with authors.
28 *Ibid*.
29 *Ibid*.
30 *Ibid*.
31 Frank Greve, *Philadelphia Inquirer*, 25 April 1987.
32 Interview with authors.
33 *Mail on Sunday*, 29 January 1984.
34 Interview with authors.
35 *Ibid*.
36 *GQ* magazine, February 1993.
37 *Philadelphia Inquirer* and *Miami Herald*, 10 November 1991.
38 *Sunday Times*, 9 October 1994.
39 *Financial Times*, 8 June 1991.
40 Union Bank of Switzerland, Phillips & Drew analysts
   report, UK Equities, May 1992.
41 *Ibid*.
42 *GQ*, February 1993.
43 *The Middle East*, April 1985.
44 *Guardian*, 23 November 1991.

45 *Sunday Times*, 12 February 1984.
46 *GQ*, November 1992.
47 *Ibid*.
48 *Ibid*.
49 Register of Members Interests, 13 January 1992, HMSO 170.
50 *Business Age* magazine, June 1994.
51 *GQ*, November 1992.
52 *Daily Mail*, 12 December 1990.
53 *Daily Telegraph*, 26 September 1994.
54 *The First Thatcherite, Dispatches,* Box Productions for Channel 4, 25 November 1992; *New York* magazine, 1 February 1993.
55 *The First Thatcherite*, Channel 4, 25 November 1992.
56 *GQ*, November 1992.
57 *New Yorker*, June 1986.
58 *Guardian*, 13 May 1992.
59 *GQ*, November 1992.
60 *Business Age*, June 1994.
61 *GQ*, November 1992.
62 *Ibid*.
63 *Sunday Times*, 9 October 1994.
64 London *Evening Standard*, 20 March 1987.
65 *Daily Mail*, 25 May 1990.
66 *Mail on Sunday*, 13 October 1987.
67 *Daily Mail*, 17 December 1990.
68 *Jane's Defence Weekly* magazine, 10 June 1989.
69 *Tatler*, August 1992.
70 *Financial Times*, 26 November 1991.
71 Union Bank of Switzerland, Phillips & Drew Analysts Report, UK Equities, May 1992.
72 *GQ*, February 1993.
73 Thatcher, *The Downing Street Years*, p 626.
74 *Sunday Times*, 9 October 1994.
75 *The First Thatcherite*, Channel 4, 25 November 1992.
76 *Ibid*.
77 *Ibid*.
78 *Ibid*.
79 *Ibid*.
80 *Today*, 10 October 1994.
81 *Financial Times*, 31 October 1994.
82 *Observer*, 19 March 1989.

83 Interview with authors.
84 *Independent*, 11 October 1994.
85 Interview with authors.
86 *Ibid.*
87 *Ibid.*
88 *Tracking Down Maggie*, Lafayette Productions for *True Lives*, Channel 4, 19 May 1994.

Chapter Seven

1 *Sunday Times*, 21 April 1991.
2 *Hong Kong Tatler*, December 1991.
3 *Hong Kong Standard*, 14 August 1981.
4 London *Evening Standard*, 23 September 1982.
5 Company accounts of Ulferts Services, 1981–82.
6 Press statement by Monteagle Marketing Ltd, 24 March 1984.
7 *Ming Pao Weekly*, 10 December 1983.
8 *Hong Kong Standard*, 16 March 1984.
9 *Ibid.*
10 *Ibid.*
11 *Ibid.*
12 *Ibid.*
13 Press statement by Monteagle Marketing Ltd, 24 March 1984.
14 *Insight* magazine, Hong Kong, December 1982.
15 Interview with Ho-Pak Hong.
16 *Hong Kong Standard*, 18 March 1984.
17 *Observer*, 29 January 1984.
18 Interview with authors.
19 *South China Morning Post*, 25 November 1980–14 June 1981.
20 *Ibid*, 4 January 1986–7 July 1986.
21 *Ming Pao Weekly*, 10 December 1983.
22 *Sunday Times*, 12 February 1984.
23 *Ming Pao Weekly*, 10 December 1983.
24 *Mail on Sunday*, 4 December 1983.
25 Gower Report. Quoted in the *Observer*, 11 March 1984.
26 *Observer*, 11 March 1984.
27 Press statement by Monteagle Marketing Ltd, 24 March 1984.

28 Interview with authors.
29 *South China Morning Post*, 31 May 1994.
30 *Eastern Express*, 13 December 1994.
31 *South China Morning Post*, 6 August 1994.
32 *Sunday Times*, 12 February 1984.
33 *New Statesman*, 16 February 1984; *Daily Mirror*, 17 February 1984.
34 *Ming Pao Weekly*, 10 December 1983.
35 *South China Morning Post*, 26 November 1983.
36 *Ming Pao Weekly*, 10 December 1983.
37 *Hong Kong Tatler*, December 1991.
38 *Guardian*, 23 November 1991.
39 Interview with authors.
40 *Vanity Fair*, June 1991.
41 House of Commons, *Hansard*, 5 May 1993, col 145.
42 *New Straits Times*, Malaysia, 28 September 1988.
43 *Jane's Defence Weekly*, 25 March 1989.
44 *New Straits Times*, Malaysia, 2 September 1990.
45 *Guardian*, 16 February 1994.
46 *Sunday Times*, 25 February 1994.
47 *Ibid*, 6 March 1994.
48 *Guardian*, 3 March 1994.
49 *Sunday Times*, 6 March 1994.
50 *Ibid*, 25 February 1994.
51 *The Times*, 12 May 1992.
52 Interview with authors.
53 Letter to authors, 9 May 1994.
54 Memorandum of Conviction from West London Magistrates Court, 24 June 1989; *News of the World*, 30 July 1989.
55 Official record of Sri Lankan parliament, 18 June 1993.
56 Interview with authors.
57 *Daily Mirror*, 16 December 1982.
58 *Newslanka*, 18 September 1993.
59 *Silverarrow*, September 1993.

Chapter Eight

1 Thatcher, *The Downing Street Years*, p 525.
2 *Ibid*, p 526.
3 *Ibid*, p 524.

4 *Independent*, 9 June 1993.
5 *Ibid*.
6 *Today*, 28 March 1994.
7 *Mail on Sunday*, 14 August 1994.
8 Today, 15 August 1994.
9 *Guardian*, 12 February 1994.
10 *Today*, 30 March 1994.
11 *Ibid*.
12 Legal petition by John J. Laughlin lodged in Harris County Court, Texas, Laughlin *v* David G. Wallace, 28 January 1994, p 5.
13 *Ibid*.
14 *Today*, 28 March 1994.
15 *Houston Chronicle*, 25 June 1994.
16 Laughlin petition, p 22.
17 *Ibid*, p 7.
18 *Ibid*, p 10.
19 *Houston Chronicle*, 25 June 1994.
20 *Ibid*.
21 *Today*, 15 August 1994.
22 *Ibid*.
23 *Ibid*.
24 *Ibid*, 10 October 1994.
25 *Ibid*, 15 August 1994.
26 Clark, *Diaries*, p 187.
27 Interview with authors.
28 *Daily Mail*, 15 November 1989.
29 *Today*, 16 November 1989.
30 *Observer*, 15 December 1991.
31 *Today*, 28 March 1994.
32 *Ibid*, 27 October 1990.

Chapter Nine

1 Epigraph to Thomson, *Margaret Thatcher*.
2 Kenneth Baker, *The Turbulent Years* (London: Faber and Faber, 1993), p 153.
3 *The Downing Street Years*, BBC1, October 1993.
4 *Independent*, 24 November 1990.
5 The 'Taffy Mafia' was generally considered to be Michael Heseltine, who stood against Margaret Thatcher,

Geoffrey (now Lord) Howe, whose resignation speech inspired Heseltine's candidature, and Tristan Garel-Jones, the former Foreign Office minister, who hosted a party at his house between the first and second ballots to discuss what should happen next in the Tory leadership challenge.

6 *Sunday Times*, 1 September 1991.
7 *Ibid*, 16 December 1990.
8 *Ibid.*
9 *Guardian*, 2 October 1993.
10 *Vanity Fair*, June 1991.
11 *Guardian*, 26 April 1991.
12 *Selling Thatcher, World In Action*, Granada TV, 11 November 1991.
13 *The Times*, 13 March 1991.
14 London *Evening Standard*, 24 September 1991.
15 *Vanity Fair*, June 1991.
16 *Dallas Morning News*, 12 March 1991.
17 *Vanity Fair*, June 1991.
18 *Daily Mail*, 17 June 1991.
19 *Sunday Telegraph*, 23 June 1991.
20 *Observer*, 11 August 1991.
21 *Independent*, 3 September 1991.
22 *Hong Kong Standard*, 13 September 1991.
23 *Ibid*, 18 March 1991.
24 *Mail on Sunday*, 6 September 1992.
25 *Ibid.*
26 *Ibid.*
27 *Ibid.*
28 *Independent on Sunday*, 22 December 1992.
29 *Financial Times*, 29 June 1991.
30 *Ibid.*
31 *Sunday Times*, 11 April 1993.
32 *Ibid*, 19 July 1992.
33 *The Fag Lady, World In Action*, Granada TV, 11 July 1994.
34 *Ibid.*
35 *Ibid.*
36 London *Evening Standard*, 11 November 1992.
37 *The Times*, 20 July 1992.
38 ASH-UK press briefing, autumn 1992.
39 *Selling Thatcher, World In Action*, Granada TV, 11 November 1991.

40 *Vanity Fair*, June 1991.
41 Clark, *Diaries*, pp 384–5.
42 *Ibid*, p 386.
43 *Vanity Fair*, June 1991.
44 Roy Greenslade, *Maxwell's Fall* (London: Simon & Schuster, 1992), p 358.
45 *Selling Thatcher*, *World In Action*, Granada TV, 11 November 1991.
46 *Vanity Fair*, June 1991.
47 *Sunday Times*, 26 January 1992.
48 *The Times*, 18 February 1994.
49 Rachel Ehrenfeld, *Evil Money* (New York: SPI International, 1994), p 159.
50 *Sunday Times*, 13 November 1994.
51 Peter Truell and Larry Gurwin, *BCCI – The Inside Story of the World's Most Corrupt Financial Empire* (London: Bloomsbury, 1992), p 87.
52 *Guardian*, 3 May 1994.
53 *Vanity Fair*, June 1991.
54 *New Yorker*, 6 September 1993.
55 *Ibid*.
56 *Ibid*.
57 Interview with authors.
58 *Today*, 6 June 1992.
59 *Vanity Fair*, June 1991.
60 *Ibid*.
61 *Sunday Times*, 21 April 1991.
62 *Observer*, 25 June 1991. Confirmed by former officials of Lady Thatcher's private office.
63 *Sunday Times*, 21 April 1991.
64 *Vanity Fair*, June 1991.
65 *Channel 4 News*, 28 June 1991.
66 Press release by Charities Aid Foundation, 24 November 1991.
67 *Sunday Telegraph*, 24 November 1991.
68 *Sunday Mirror*, 4 October 1992.
69 *Ibid*.
70 *Guardian*, 22 November 1991.
71 *Business Age*, September 1993.
72 *Ibid*.
73 Deposition by David G. Wallace, in Laughlin *v* Wallace, 14 April 1994, p 13.

74 *Guardian*, 5 February 1993.
75 *Independent on Sunday*, 22 November 1992.
76 London *Evening Standard*, 21 November 1994.
77 *Mail on Sunday*, 13 November 1994.
78 *Daily Mirror*, 10 November 1987.
79 *Institutional Investor*, international edition, September 1991.
80 *Ibid*.
81 *Today*, 27 February 1992.
82 *Ibid*.
83 *Daily Express*, 27 August 1992.
84 *Mail on Sunday*, 27 December 1992.

Chapter Ten

1 *A Week In Politics*, Brook Productions for Channel 4, 23 March 1984.
2 Thomson, *Margaret Thatcher*, p 116.
3 Farr, *Five at Ten*, p 205.
4 *Tatler*, December 1994.
5 Interview with authors.
6 *Harpers and Queen*, April 1991.
7 *Ultra*, March 1990.
8 Former employee, in interview with authors.
9 *The Times*, 16 January 1982.
10 Thomson, *Margaret Thatcher*, p 118.
11 *Sunday Times*, 21 April 1991.
12 Letter to the authors, 16 March 1993.
13 Ogden, *Maggie*, p 80.
14 London *Evening Standard*, 31 August 1988.
15 Carol Thatcher, interview with *Today*, 15 November 1993.
16 *Observer*, 26 February 1984.
17 House of Commons, *Hansard*, 25 February 1952, col 701.
18 *Daily Telegraph*, 24 March 1986.
19 *Mail on Sunday*, 23 March 1986.
20 House of Commons, *Hansard*, 25 March 1986, col 781.
21 *Questions of Procedure*, p 2. *Guidelines for Conduct of Ministers, Cabinet Office*, First published in 1992.
22 *A Week In Politics*, Brook Productions for Channel 4, 23 March 1984.

23 *Ibid.*
24 *The First Thatcherite, Dispatches*, Channel 4, 25 November 1992.
25 Interview with *Woman's Own*, 2 February 1980.
26 *Sunday Times*, 12 February 1984.
27 *Mail on Sunday*, 2 January 1993.

Bibliography

Baker, Kenneth, *The Turbulent Years* (London: Faber and Faber, 1993)

Bauder, Donald C., *Captain Money and the Golden Girl – A $200 Million Fantasy of Love, Power and Greed* (San Diego: Harvest and HBJ Books, 1986)

Bower, Tom, *Tiny Rowland – A Rebel Tycoon* (London: Heinemann, 1993)

Clark, Alan, *Diaries*, (London: Weidenfeld & Nicolson, 1993)

Ehrenfeld, Rachel, *Evil Money* (New York: SPI International, 1994)

Farr, Diana, *Five at Ten* (London: André Deutsch, 1985)

Gardiner, George, *Margaret Thatcher – From Childhood to Leadership* (London: William Kimber, 1975)

Greenslade, Roy, *Maxwell's Downfall* (London: Simon & Schuster, 1992)

Junor, John, *Memoirs – Listening for a Midnight Tram* (London: Chapman, 1990)

Junor, Penny, *Margaret Thatcher – Wife, Mother, Politician* (London: Sidgwick & Jackson, 1983)

Millar, Ronald, *A View from the Wings – West End, West Coast, Westminster* (London: Weidenfeld & Nicolson, 1993)

Murray, Patricia, *Margaret Thatcher*, (London: W. H. Allen, 1980)

Ogden, Christopher, *Maggie – An Intimate Portrait of a Woman in Power* (New York: Simon & Schuster, 1990)

Paxman, Jeremy, *Friends in High Places – Who Runs Britain?* (London: Michael Joseph, 1990)

Ranelagh, John, *Thatcher's People – An Insider's Account of the Politics, the Power and the Personalities* (London: HarperCollins, 1991)

Taylor, Peter, *Smoke Ring – Tobacco, Money and Multi-National Politics* (London: Sphere, 1984)

Thatcher, Margaret, *The Downing Street Years* (London: HarperCollins, 1993)

Thomson, Andrew, *Margaret Thatcher – The Woman Within* (London: W. H. Allen, 1989)

Truell, Peter, and Gurwin, Larry, *BCCI – The Inside Story of the World's Most Corrupt Financial Empire* (London: Bloomsbury, 1992)

Wapshott, Nicholas, and Brock, George, *Margaret Thatcher* (London: Macdonald, 1983)

Young, Hugo, *One of Us* (London: Macmillan, 1989)

Young, Hugo, and Sloman, Anne, *The Thatcher Phenomenon* (London: BBC Publications, 1986)

Index